THE

PUBLICATIONS

OF THE

SURTEES SOCIETY

VOL. 206

THE

PUBLICATIONS

OF THE

SURTEES SOCIETY

ESTABLISHED IN THE YEAR
M.DCCC.XXXIV

VOL. CCVI

At a MEETING of the SURTEES SOCIETY, held on 9 December 1999, it was ORDERED—
'That the Diary of Thomas Giordani Wright: Newcastle Doctor, edited by Dr Alastair Johnson, should be printed as a volume of the Society's publications'

THE DIARY OF THOMAS GIORDANI WRIGHT NEWCASTLE DOCTOR 1826–1829

EDITED WITH AN INTRODUCTION
BY
ALASTAIR JOHNSON

THE SURTEES SOCIETY

THE BOYDELL PRESS

First published 2001

A Surtees Society Publication
published by The Boydell Press
an imprint of Boydell & Brewer Ltd
PO Box 9, Woodbridge, Suffolk IP12 3DF, UK
and of Boydell & Brewer Inc,
PO Box 41026, Rochester, NY 14604-4126, USA
website: http://www.boydell.co.uk

ISBN 0 85444 045 3

ISSN 0307-5362

A catalogue record for this book is available
from the British Library

Details of other Surtees Society volumes are available
from Boydell & Brewer Limited

This publication is printed on acid-free paper

Printed in Great Britain

CONTENTS

Appendix

ACKNOWLEDGEMENTS

The importance of Thomas G. Wright's *Diary* as an historical document of particular interest to the Tyneside region was first recognised by the members of the Nanaimo Historical Society, Nanaimo, British Columbia, Canada, who carried out a painstaking initial study of the original manuscript. I wish to express my personal thanks to them for their donation of the manuscript to the City of Newcastle upon Tyne which made it possible for me to transcribe it for publication. In this work I have been particularly encouraged by the support of Anne Royle, a member of the Nanaimo Society, who has been closely involved with studies of the *Diary* since its discovery and who shares my appreciation of, and affection for, its young author.

I am indebted to the members of staff of the Tyne and Wear Archives Service. My own interest was first captured by the accurate and informative description of the *Diary* in their document catalogue, and the work of transcription could not have been done without their help. The Tyne and Wear Archives Service also furnished much of the local material used in annotation.

Other sources of information I found particularly useful include: the Local Studies Section of the Newcastle Central Library; North Tyneside Library; Stockton-on-Tees Library; Darlington Library; the Northumberland Record Office; the West Yorkshire Archive Service and Wakefield Library and the libraries of Newcastle University, Edinburgh University, the Newcastle Literary and Philosophical Society and of the Royal College of Surgeons of England. I am grateful to the staff members of all of these organisations for their help. I also thank Mr John Goodchild for help in finding information in Wakefield, Dr Janet Birkett, of the Theatre Museum, London, for providing the material used in the notes concerned with the nineteenth-century London theatre, and Jane Morson for telling me about the family background of Dr W. S. Morson.

Many individuals have given valuable advice and encouragement. I am particularly grateful to Drs Maureen Callcott, Alec Campbell, and David Gardner-Medwin, who kindly read early draughts of the transcript and made numerous useful suggestions for its improvement, and to Mrs Joan Foster for many helpful comments.

I am pleased that Thomas G. Wright's *Diary* is being published by The Surtees Society and thank the officers of the Society for their help. I am particularly indebted to Mr A. J. Piper, former Honorary Secretary, who guided the preparation of this volume in its early stages, and to Professor R. H. Britnell, who has overseen the final editing and preparation for publication.

A final warm word of thanks to my wife, Margaret, for tolerating both me and Thomas Giordani Wright, and for contributing in so many ways throughout the project.

ABBREVIATIONS

ARLP   Annual Report of the Literary and Philosophical
        Society of Newcastle upon Tyne
BEN   J. Grundy, G. McCombie, P. Ryder, H. Welfare,
        H. and N. Pevsner, *Northumberland*, The Build-
        ings of England (London, 1992)
BED   N. Pevsner, *Durham*, The Buildings of England
        (Harmondsworth, 1983)
BSE   J. Gifford, C. McWilliam, and D. Walker,
        Edinburgh,   The   Buildings   of   Scotland
        (Harmondsworth, 1984)
DNB   Leslie Stephen and Sidney Lee (eds) *The Diction-
        ary of National Biography*, 2nd edn, 22 vols
        (London, 1908-9)
Hume   W. E. Hume, *The Infirmary Newcastle upon Tyne
        1751-1951*, (Newcastle upon Tyne, 1951)
Lit. and Phil.   The Literary and Philosophical Society of New-
        castle upon Tyne
Mackenzie 1825   Eneas Mackenzie, *History of Northumberland*
        (Newcastle upon Tyne, 1825)
Mackenzie 1827   Eneas Mackenzie, *A Descriptive and Historical
        Account of the Town and County of Newcastle upon
        Tyne* (Newcastle upon Tyne, 1827)
Middlebrook   S. Middlebrook, *Newcastle upon Tyne: Its
        Growth and Achievement* (Newcastle upon Tyne,
        1950)
MN   David Gardner-Medwin, Anne Hargreaves and
        Elizabeth Lazenby (eds), *Medicine in Northumbria*
        (Newcastle upon Tyne, 1993)
NRPB   Theatre Royal Play Bills Collection, Central Lib-
        rary, Newcastle upon Tyne
NYB   T. and J. Hodgson, *Northumberland Year Book*
        (Newcastle upon Tyne, 1830)

PW	W. Parson and W. White, *History, Directory and Gazetteer of Newcastle, Durham and Northumberland*, 2 vols (Newcastle upon Tyne,1827-8)
Sykes	John Sykes, *Local Records* (Newcastle upon Tyne, 1831), vol. 2.
TGW	Thomas Giordani Wright
Watson	Robert Spence Watson, *The History of the Literary and Philosophical Society of Newcastle upon Tyne 1793-1891* (London, 1897)
Wilson	Wilson Collection, Local Studies Section, Central Library, Newcastle upon Tyne

INTRODUCTION

DIARY OF A DOCTOR

A funeral service in Wakefield Cathedral in 1898 commemorated the death at the age of ninety years of Dr Thomas Giordani Wright. He was a familiar and well-loved figure in Wakefield, where he had lived for more than sixty years, working as a medical practitioner and leading an active life in the community. As a young apprentice, just beginning his long medical career, he kept a diary to record his experiences. Remarkably, much of his unique manuscript, *Diary of a Doctor*, has survived, and now has become available for us to read, more than 170 years after he wrote the last page.[1]

Between leaving school at the age of fifteen and starting his diary, Thomas had spent almost a year as apprentice to a doctor in Darlington and already had served more than two years of his five-year apprenticeship in Newcastle, where he lived in the house of his master, Mr James McIntyre, Surgeon. Thomas began his diary soon after he had returned from a session of medical studies in Edinburgh. He had now reached a stage in his career when he was given new responsibilities. Entitled to refer to himself as 'Assistant to Mr McIntyre', he regarded himself as superior to the other apprentices in the practice. Unfortunately, this higher status was not always adequately recognised by his master, a cause of much chagrin to Thomas.

His responsibilities certainly seem quite onerous. Thomas was

---

1 The original MS of *Diary of a Doctor* is now kept by the Tyne and Wear Archives Service, Blandford Square, Newcastle upon Tyne, NE1 4JA (document reference Tyne and Wear Archives Service DX47/1/1–9.). Publications concerning the *Diary* include a selection of extracts: Alastair Johnson (ed.), *Diary of a Doctor: Surgeon's Assistant in Newcastle upon Tyne, 1826–1829*, (Newcastle, 1998), and an article: Alastair Johnson, 'The Diary of Thomas Giordani Wright: Apprentice Doctor in Newcastle upon Tyne', *Medical History*, 43 (1999), pp. 468–84.

in charge of the patients from six collieries and 'the inferior practice of the house'. He was often on his own when he went out to
handle cases resulting from the frequent, sometimes horrendous,
mining accidents and to treat patients suffering from all sorts of
diseases. This was in an era long before the introduction of medical techniques we now take for granted, such as the use of anaesthetics, antiseptics, and X-rays. In his diary, Thomas regularly
recorded the number of patients he had seen: a total of 2896,
between August 1826 and May 1829. His self-confidence, as well
as his work-load, increased as his apprenticeship years went by
and he became widely liked and respected by those in his care.

The *Diary* describes the scene in Newcastle in the late 1820s
through the eyes of someone living at that time. If suddenly
transported back to that period, no doubt we would be horrified
by the medical ignorance, and overwhelmed by the lack of
modern facilities. But to Thomas Wright things were better than
they had been, and his writing conveys a sense of optimism and
hope of continued improvement. He saw himself as a warrior
against disease, and had confidence and pride in the weapons
that medicine provided. He was keen to be up-to-date in his profession, avidly reading the available medical literature and enthu-
siastically discussing the theory and practice of treatment with
other doctors. He was ready to experiment on patients with vari-
ations in medication, attempting to match cause and effect, and
keeping notes on the outcome of treatments in many cases. Rarely
depressed, Thomas took the most daunting cases in his stride,
usually looking forward to having a meal or, at least, some tea
and cake afterwards. Many of his patients did get better, and he
justifiably took some credit for that – although we now might
think it was probably in spite of, rather than because of, the treatments. Certainly, the *Diary* gives the impression that, whatever
the limitations of medicine at that time, Thomas Wright had the
ability to help his patients with the comfort, reassurance and support expected from a good doctor.

Thomas Wright's *Diary* is interesting from many different
points of view. Much of it is concerned with doctoring, as experienced by an intelligent young trainee in a busy practice, and
many cases are described in detail. There are descriptions of the
actual treatments used and information about day-to-day matters, such as transport and practice organisation, as well as tales
of the coal-miner patients and their families. But life was not all

work, and Thomas had many other interests. He played the flute, and composed music for it, enjoyed singing, dancing, playing cards, and going to the races. He took great pride in becoming a member of the Literary and Philosophical Society and wrote his own accounts, sometimes not too flattering, of some of its meetings. Although his involvement with young ladies was kept within the strict conventions of the age, at least as far as his diary reveals, he does discreetly mention many of the girls that catch his fancy. Most of all, the *Diary* gives some idea of what it felt like to be a young man, full of optimism at the outset of his career, living in a rapidly developing industrial town with all sorts of new opportunities opening up.

BIOGRAPHICAL NOTE ON T. G. WRIGHT[2]

Thomas Giordani Wright was born in 1808 in Stockton-on-Tees, where his family had been established for many years. His father, Thomas Wright (1763–1829), a musician and inventor, had followed his own father Robert Wright (d. 1797) as organist in Stockton church, and was well-respected as a music teacher in the area. He married Elizabeth Foxton, who has been described as a 'lady of some literary attainment', in 1794.[3]

Thomas Giordani had his first lessons at home and started to attend classes in Stockton with the local curate, Mr Cundell, when he was 7 years old. This continued until 1818, when his father resigned his position in Stockton and moved his family to the village of Haughton-le-Skerne, near Darlington. Shortly afterwards Thomas began to attend an academy in Darlington established by the Society of Friends. Although he was successful in this school and received a sound education, as the only non-Quaker pupil there at the time Thomas's school-life was not without difficulty.

In 1823, the year he left school, Thomas was indentured to Mr Allison, a medical practitioner in Darlington. Unhappy with the arrangements there, he stayed for less than one year before joining Mr McIntyre in Newcastle, where he remained from March

2 Except where other sources are indicated, the information in this section is from the *Diary* itself.
3 See Eric Blom (ed.), *Grove's Dictionary of Music and Musicians*, 5th edition, 9 vols (London, 1954), IX, p. 372.

1824 until shortly after he had completed his apprenticeship in March 1829. During his apprenticeship with McIntyre, Thomas was allowed to attend one session of a medical course, and he opted to do this in Edinburgh, where he lived from October 1825 to April 1826. In Edinburgh his teachers included many of the top medical personalities of the day. His studies in Edinburgh did not lead to any formal qualifications. At that time, many budding doctors like Thomas took courses at Scottish medical schools without the intention of taking examinations.[4]

After leaving Newcastle in 1829, Thomas enrolled as a student at London University, which had opened the previous year. He became a Licentiate of Apothecaries Hall in 1830 and Member of the Royal College of Surgeons in 1831. As a student, he was elected president of the University Medical Society. Having completed his courses in London in 1831, Thomas then qualified in the same year for the MD degree at the University of Leyden.[5] After some years in practice, he became a Licentiate of the Royal College of Physicians of London (1841) and a Member (1859).

Thomas settled in Wakefield in 1833 when he was appointed consulting physician to the West Riding Asylum, a position he held for 65 years. He built a prosperous private medical practice in Wakefield, and held many prestigious honorary appointments.[6] In 1835 he married Elizabeth Hubbard whom he met in 1830 while on holiday at Redcar during a University vacation. Elizabeth's father was a wool-stapler from Leeds, and Chairman of the North Midland Railway. Thomas and Elizabeth had 13 chil-

---

4 The Edinburgh medical courses and the training of apprentices are discussed in detail in L. Rosner, *Medical Education in the Age of Improvement. Edinburgh Students and Apprentices, 1760–1826* (Edinburgh, 1990).

5 A list of successful candidates for the Diploma of Membership, MRCS, recorded by the Court of Examiners of the RCS (London) in the Examinations Book, 7/1/1831, includes Thomas Giordain (*sic*) Wright, Stockton-on-Tees. The regulations for the MD degree at Leyden are described by R. W. Innes Smith, *English Speaking Students of Medicine at the University of Leyden* (Edinburgh and London, 1932).Wright's MD thesis, which was defended on 11/6/1831, was published with the title *Disceptatio Medica Inauguralis de Scrofulosi* (Leyden, 1831): a copy, presented by Wright to Newcastle Infirmary Medical Library, is held by the Library of the University of Newcastle.

6 For further details of TGW's career and his place in the society of Wakefield, see Hilary Marland, *Medicine and Society in Wakefield and Huddersfield 1780–1870* (Cambridge, 1987).

dren, but only 6 of them – three girls and three boys – outlived their parents. Elizabeth died in 1890, aged 76.[7]

Not surprisingly to anyone who has read the *Diary*, Thomas Giordani Wright's life was active to the end. As well as attending to his medical duties and interests, he became a founder member of the British Association in 1831, and for most of his working life was an active President of the Wakefield Mechanics Institute. According to his obituary in the British Medical Journal,[8] he 'gave up much time to scientific pursuits, especially astronomy and physical science, taking a special interest in the development of the electric telegraph'. On retiring from his medical practice, he 'was presented with a testimonial, amounting to 900 guineas, by a large circle of friends'.

Thomas Wright died in his ninety-first year. His funeral in Wakefield Cathedral on May 30, 1898, described in detail in the local Wakefield papers, '. . . as attended by nearly all the medical men in the city and suburbs, by many of the principal residents, and by representatives of several public bodies'.[9]

BACKGROUND TO THE DIARY

Early nineteenth century Newcastle[10]

Newcastle, the main centre of population, business, and commerce of the Tyneside region, grew in size and importance with increasing industrialisation after about 1760. At the time Thomas G. Wright lived there in the late 1820s the population exceeded

---

7 From the obituary of TGW in the *Wakefield Express*, 28 May, 1898.

8 *The British Medical Journal* (1898), p. 1493.

9 The description of the funeral fills several columns in the *Wakefield Free Press and West Riding Advertiser*, 4 June 1898, and in the *Wakefield Express*, 4 June 1898.

10 Unless otherwise stated, information in this and the following sections has been taken from MacKenzie 1825, MacKenzie 1827 and PW, I (the local trade directory), which are all roughly contemporary with the *Diary* and give a detailed picture of Newcastle and the surrounding region at that period. For the history of Newcastle see, for example, Middlebrook, particularly chapters 15 and 16. A more recent account of the nineteenth century economic and social development of the region is given in N. McCord, *North East England: An Economic and Social History* (London, 1979). For a detailed account of the architectural development of Newcastle and other towns in the region, see *BEN*, pp. 408 ff.

40,000 and was steadily growing. The town, which had already begun to extend beyond the medieval town walls in the eighteenth century, was in the early stages of a phase of rapid development of better-class housing and business premises, the start of the changes that would transform the appearance and style of Newcastle in the 1830s.

Newgate Street, where Mr McIntyre had his house and surgery when Thomas first joined him, was described as 'a broad and commodious street . . one of the best streets in the town'.[11] Eldon Square, to which the practice moved in 1827, was newly-built in the most fashionable part of the town, providing very superior accommodation for the doctor's business.[12]

Most ordinary people were less fortunate in their housing, and lived in crowded, unsanitary conditions with few public amenities. Water was supplied by about 20 public stand-pipes or 'pants', supplemented by wells, rain-water butts, and river water. Most residential streets and alleys were without drains or sewers. Earth closets were used, and refuse often thrown into the streets. There was some gas lighting after 1818, but mostly people depended on candles and oil-lamps for light in their homes and public places. Pollution in industrial areas at this time was notorious; on Tyneside it came from coal mining and the many associated industries, particularly glass production, chemicals, soap and paper making, as well as from domestic coal fires. The River Tyne was badly polluted and the air, at times, was thick with corrosive smog.[13] Thomas Wright does not dwell on this aspect of life in Newcastle in his diary, but does make the odd reference to 'this smoky town', and contrasts the green country near Backworth with the 'dingy smoky brown fields' of his usual rides around Newcastle.

---

11 This description of Newgate Street is from MacKenzie 1827, p. 172.
12 The building of Eldon Square is described in detail in L. Wilkes and G. Dodds, *Tyneside Classical: the Newcastle of Dobson, Grainger and Clayton* (Newcastle, 1964). The building at No. 1 continued to be a doctor's residence long after McIntyre's death in 1837, at least until the 1890s, and still exists in the section of Eldon Square that survived redevelopment in the 1960s.
13 The chemical industry and the pollution it produced is described in W. A. Campbell, *The Old Tyneside Chemical Trade* (Newcastle, 1961), chapter 16. MacKenzie, commenting on Newcastle Infirmary, wrote that 'during the east winds in the spring months, it is considerably annoyed by immense clouds of smoke brought from the town and the glass houses': see MacKenzie 1827, p. 509.

Social life

Apart from private parties and get-togethers, the main social events recorded in the *Diary* are visits to the theatre, balls and concerts. Membership of the Literary and Philosophical Society provided Thomas with opportunities for socialising and going to lectures and meetings, as well as supplying most of his reading matter.

The Theatre Royal[14] in Mosley Street, Newcastle, opened in 1788 and survived until 1836, when it was demolished to be replaced by the new (and still thriving) Theatre Royal in Grey Street. The Mosley Street theatre had seating for 1,350 (800 gallery, 200 in pit and 350 boxes), yielding about £112 a night from a full house. The Theatre Royal was normally open four months in the winter, and also at times during the rest of the year, such as assizes and race weeks. The customary double-bill began at 7 pm: the main play was followed by an interlude with songs, then came an afterpiece, usually a light comedy or farce, to end the evening by 11 o'clock or shortly after. As a concession, well-used by Thomas, half-price admission was usually allowed at 9 pm. This made it possible to see at least the second play on the bill, and often an act or two of the first play as well. The social importance of the theatre – a place to see people and be seen, especially on 'fashionable nights' – is very evident in the *Diary*.

The Assembly Rooms building was opened in 1776, and provided an elegant venue for social occasions. The Rooms included a saloon, card-room, coffee room, news room, and library as well as a ballroom. Subscription balls held there were open to the public as advertised in the local press.

The Philharmonic Society began in Newcastle in November 1826, and ran a series of monthly concerts in the Concert-room in the Bigg Market. There were 100 ordinary members who paid four shillings each per month and were allowed three tickets of admission, and 36 honorary members, or performers, who got two tickets. The band consisted mostly of amateurs, who performed gratis. Evening musical concerts were also often held in the Turk's Head Long Room, usually with an orchestra and singers.

---

14 For details of the history of the theatre in Newcastle, see H. Oswald, *The Theatre Royal in Newcastle upon Tyne* (Newcastle, 1936).

The Literary and Philosophical Society,[15] founded in 1793 to promote interest in literary and scientific subjects, moved in 1825 to its own fine, new building that it still occupies, where Thomas happily spent a lot of his leisure time. The 'Lit & Phil' was a centre for much of the intellectual life of Newcastle, with an excellent library and museum as well as meeting rooms. The Society held monthly meetings, with papers being given on a variety of subjects, regarded as 'matters of real importance'. Often these concerned technical matters of interest to local industry, particularly coal-mining. From 1803, the Society also sponsored the New Institution to provide courses of lectures on Natural and Experimental Philosophy. William Turner was appointed as lecturer, a position he held for more than 30 years, giving courses of 12 to 32 lectures every year.

Local newspapers and magazines

The three most important local papers, all weeklies, were the *Newcastle Courant*, *Newcastle Chronicle*, and the *Tyne Mercury*. The *Courant*, 'long considered an organ of the Tories in the district', was first published in 1711. The *Chronicle*, 'a cool, moderate advocate of the Whig party', began in 1764. The *Tyne Mercury*, first published in 1802, was 'not distinguished by any particular set of principles but advocates the cause of reform'.[16] These papers were similar in their appearance and news coverage, usually having four closely printed broad-sheet pages, with local, national and international news, editorials and many classified advertisements.

The *Newcastle Magazine* was edited by William A. Mitchell, who also edited the *Tyne Mercury*. It was published in monthly volumes, starting in 1820, and contained articles on a very wide range of topics as well as features such as gossip columns, mathematical puzzles, theatrical and book reviews, and often a report 'by a Surgeon' on health in Newcastle. Other magazines were available, including the *London Magazine* and the *Edinburgh Magazine* (Blackwoods).

---

15 Information about the Lit. and Phil. is from Robert Spence Watson, *The History of the Literary and Philosophical Society of Newcastle upon Tyne 1793–1891* (London, 1897).

16 The comments on the political affiliations of the newspapers are from Mackenzie 1827, pp. 727–9.

Transport and communications

By the late 1820s travel between the main English towns had been much improved by the road-building systems developed by McAdam, Telford and others. On the main roads between many towns, fast commercial coaches were able to make an average speed of up to 12 mph. The regular coach service from Newcastle to Edinburgh took about 16 hours and to London about 38 hours. Much slower, carrier services operated regularly to most towns in the area, and there was a land-carriage network by van to all parts of the country. Local roads were less developed. The best of them were the turnpikes, such as the Shields Road, connecting Newcastle and North Shields, but the minor roads were little more than bridle tracks.

Transport for hire was available on the Shields Road: in 1827 there were 28 gigs and 10 coaches offering an hourly service between Newcastle quayside and North Shields, but an omnibus service was introduced only after 1832. The river was also used with 'upwards of 40 Steam Boats' on the River Tyne between Newcastle and Shields, charging 6 pence for an adult and 3 pence for a child. There were also a few hackney carriages in Newcastle.[17] For most journeys however, residents of Newcastle were mainly dependent on their own private carriages or horses, if wealthy enough, otherwise on their own legs (or 'Shank's Nag', as Thomas puts it).

The Post Office in Newcastle was open most of the day for sending local mail, and two deliveries by carrier were made daily. Charges depended on the destination: for example, five pence for 15 to 20 miles and six pence for 20 to 30 miles; there was a special rate for a letter to London of one shilling. Normally, the recipient was responsible for paying the postal charge. However, it was possible to avoid paying for a letter if one could persuade an MP to 'frank it', write the address himself in his own hand-writing, and send it with his own mail, which went free of charge. Thomas several times mentions sending letters 'to be franked' by Sir John Lowther, MP, one of his father's employers.

Mining villages

The villages where Thomas's miner patients lived have long been incorporated into the Newcastle conurbation, but in the 1820s

---

17 Middlebrook, p. 226.

they were still separate communities and to Thomas his rounds were 'rides in the country'. However, these villages were hardly idyllic, being dominated by the coal mines and other industries, with most of the working population living in the rows of houses built near the mines and owned by the mining companies.

Although much of the more easily accessible coal had been worked out, coal mining was still the most important industry in the region with a workforce of about 8,500 working underground, and about 3,500 on the surface.[18] Wallsend was the largest colliery in the area[19] but there were many other mines, large and small. The usual practice was for a mine to be operated by an entrepreneur, who held a lease from the land owner, which meant that conditions of employment were not uniform throughout the coal field. It appears, from comments made by Thomas Wright in his diary, that engagement of a doctor for a particular colliery was dependent on arrangements made with that colliery's owner.

In the mines, the contract system of employment was still in operation, with men being bound to their employer for a year after being hired. Digging the coal and moving it, mainly by manpower, was arduous and dangerous work in restricted space lit only by the feeble light from safety lamps. As shown by incidents in the *Diary*, there were many possible causes of accidents, including gas explosions, falls of rock, and encounters with rol-

---

18 In the coalfield north and south of the Tyne, there were 41 working collieries in 1828–9. The capital invested in the Tyne mines was estimated as about £1.5 million and they supplied almost all of the 2 million tons of coal taken to London by sea: John Buddle, 'Evidence to the Select Committee on the Coal Trade', in *The Evidence Taken before the Select Committee of the House of Lords, Appointed to Take into Consideration the State of the Coal Trade in the United Kingdom* (London, 1829), p. 29; see also McCord, *North East England* (note 10 above), pp. 36–42.

19 Wallsend colliery's first shaft, to what became known as the High Main seam at a depth of 666 feet, was completed in 1781. In the following two decades, six more shafts were sunk in the area around Wallsend to mine the highly profitable, good quality, coal from this thick seam. By the 1820s, however, much of the High Main seam was exhausted, and the new Bensham seam, 204 feet lower down, was opened in 1821 using some of the old shafts. The coal available here was of poorer quality, and more difficult and dangerous to mine because of the presence of large quantities of explosive gas. See William Richardson, *History of the Parish of Wallsend* (Newcastle, 1923).

leys – the low, wheeled waggons used down the mine to carry corves, the wicker baskets of coal.[20]

Although the conditions under which miners worked might now seem insupportable, it has to be borne in mind that in some respects miners were better off than many other workers at that time.[21] Their wages were above average, at least in times of economic prosperity, and there were some fringe benefits with the families of injured miners being helped.[22] Also, many of the pitmen either had themselves originally been land-workers, or came from country stock, and often were able to grow vegetables and to keep poultry and a pig to help feed their families.

Medicine in the early nineteenth century[23]

By the early part of the nineteenth century, the effects of industrialisation on public health were being felt increasingly in growing towns like Newcastle. Overcrowding, dirt and environmental pollution, together with poor or contaminated food, aggravated the causes of ill-health that had existed from earliest times. Every-

---

20 Steam power was available, but was used at this time mainly for pumping water. Horses were used mainly near the main shaft and on the surface. Information about the mining procedures and conditions of work are given in MacKenzie 1825, pp. 145–150. See also Frank Atkinson, *The Great Northern Coalfield 1700–1900* (London, 1968).

21 See e.g. McCord, *North East England* (note 10 above), pp. 38 ff.

22 According to Buddle (note 18 above) the men on a 12-month contract earned between 14 and 40 shillings a week. They were paid two shillings and sixpence a day if there was no employment for them, otherwise they were on piece work. Families were provided with a house and fuel for threepence a week. Buddle illustrated what he referred to as 'the extent of humanity' of the employers by pointing out that the consequences of accidents were mitigated because 'cripples were given employment if possible' such as 'boys work e.g., trapping and furnace keeping'. Also 'widows homes and fuel continued' and a 'remaining young child, of 6, 7, or 8 years, was given employment at advanced wages'.

23 The material in this and the following section is based mainly on the following works: W. E. Bynum, *Science and the Practice of Medicine in the Nineteenth Century* (Cambridge,1994), Anne Digby, *Making a Medical Living* (Cambridge, 1994), Christopher Lawrence, *Medicine in the Making of Modern Britain, 1700–1920* (London, 1994), Irvine Loudon, *Medical Care and the Medical Practitioner* (London, 1986), Dorothy Porter and Roy Porter, *Patient's Progress; Doctors and Doctoring in Eighteenth-Century England* (Cambridge, 1989), and Roy Porter, *The Greatest Benefit to Mankind* (London, 1997).

one lived under a constant threat of pain and grief, caused by disease or accidental injury. Common serious ailments included whooping cough, measles, consumption, rheumatism, heart disease and fevers – not clearly differentiated at that time but typhoid, typhus and scarlet fevers were all prevalent. Death in childhood was common. The average life expectancy was not more than about 40 years. Growing scientific knowledge and better training of medical practitioners, together with changes in theories of disease and in attitudes to illness, were to lead to dramatic advances later in the century. But in the 1820s, therapeutic medicine was essentially the same as in earlier times and any marked improvement in treatments was still very much in the future.

Towards the end of the eighteenth century, operative surgery had become more adventurous and successful, with techniques increasingly being based on anatomical and physiological knowledge. However, without anaesthesia, surgery was extremely restricted as well as being highly dangerous in the absence of even a basic knowledge of the causes of wound infection. For medical cases, apart from vaccination against smallpox (first used in Newcastle in 1799), a doctor had few specific remedies to hand. Although many different drugs were readily available, they were used mainly for symptomatic treatments, with little or no understanding of how they produced their effects. Unfortunately, some of the drugs in common use, particularly those containing mercury, arsenic or antimony, were extremely toxic, and no doubt added to the patients' problems.

Some treatments from the earliest days of medicine were still popular. In general, these attempted to 'purify' the body, or bring it 'into balance', by purging, vomiting and bleeding – often using all three procedures together. Although the efficacy of such treatments was beginning to be questioned, they remained popular until much later in the century. A doctor's skill was often perceived as knowing which purgative or emetic to use – the battery included a considerable range, herbal and mineral – and how it should be administered. A doctor also had some choice in how to remove a patient's blood – cutting a vein, leeching, or cupping – and was expected to know exactly when it was appropriate to let blood and how much should be taken. Another ancient treatment, known as blistering, was certainly painful and damaging: one of Mr McIntyre's horses, not to speak of his patients, was lamed by application of a blister!

A serious problem, encountered increasingly by the growing medical profession, was that of obtaining subjects for study by post-mortem dissection. Public opinion generally was strongly opposed to dissection, which was associated with the punishment of murderers and the murky dealings of the resurrectionists.[24]

Medical practitioners

Traditionally in orthodox medicine there were three main categories of practitioner: physicians (who treated internal diseases), surgeons (who treated external disorders) and apothecaries (who dispensed the prescriptions written by physicians and were sellers of drugs). By the early nineteenth century, this traditional division had largely broken down. Some physicians and surgeons, usually those with a university degree or other qualifications recognised by the Royal College of Physicians or the Royal College of Surgeons, continued to specialise and charged fees that only the wealthy could afford. However, there were many practitioners at the lower end of the market who were prepared to treat both medical and surgical cases, and often practised midwifery and supplied drugs as well. They were, in effect, acting as what would now be known as 'general practitioners', although this term was not widely used at the time. Some of them had studied at medical schools, usually in London, Edinburgh, or Paris, although often they had no recognised qualification but had learned their trade by following an apprenticeship of some kind. Their broader practice enabled them to charge fees lower than those demanded by the specialists, and they filled a growing need in society. Members of the expanding middle class might not be able to afford an old-style specialist physician or surgeon, but many were increasingly willing to pay the lower charges demanded for the services of a practitioner who had, at least, some training and experience, rather than rely on a friend or neighbour, or on one of the many dubious irregular purveyors of medicine. As competition between the different types of medical practitioner became ever more unmanageable and acrimonious, there was a growing realisation of the need for some new regula-

---

24 For a detailed account and discussion of the problems associated with dissection in the nineteenth century, see Ruth Richardson, *Death, Dissection and the Destitute* (London, 1988).

tion of the medical profession. This led, eventually, to the Apothecary Act of 1815.[25]

The Apothecary Act still regulated the practice of medicine in England at the time when Thomas Wright served his apprenticeship and qualified as a doctor. Under the Act, anyone wishing to practise medicine was required to be licensed by the Society of Apothecaries, unless they had another qualification recognised by the Royal Colleges. To obtain a Licence, it was necessary to follow an apprenticeship, to take specified courses and to pass an examination.[26] The Licence of the Society of Apothecaries was the minimum qualification for a medical practitioner but, although further qualifications were not essential, in a highly competitive business the better qualified doctor might expect to have an advantage in attracting clients, and therefore it was not unusual for aspiring doctors to follow a path similar to that taken by Thomas Wright, who followed his apprenticeship by obtaining, not only the Licence from the Society of Apothecaries, but also a Diploma from the Royal College of Surgeons and a Doctor of Medicine degree, by examination.

Medical services in Newcastle

The Infirmary[27] at Forth Bank, established in 1752, was enlarged and improved in 1802. In the late 1820s it had a yearly average of about 800 in-patients and 700 out-patients. It was run as a charity and was paid for by subscribers, who could recommend patients for admission. Interestingly, the Town Council made a significant financial contribution to the Infirmary, which allowed the Mayor or any two Aldermen to issue a letter of application for admittance to a Newcastle resident. The paid staff included a resident House Surgeon, a Secretary, Chaplain and Matron, as well as nurses and servants. Treatment was given by local practitioners, appointed as Honorary Physicians or Surgeons, who gave their services free but, obviously, could benefit in their private practices from the prestige of a hospital appointment. It was

---

25 For a full discussion of the Apothecaries Act of 1815 and its consequences, see Loudon, *Medical Care* (note 23 above), particularly chapters 7 and 8.

26 Details of the courses for the Licence are described in C. R. B. Barret, *The History of the Society of Apothecaries of London* (London, 1905).

27 Information about the Infirmary is from MacKenzie 1827, pp. 501–13 and Hume, pp. 91–102.

normal for apprentice doctors to spend some time in the Infirmary as part of their training, walking the wards and observing
operations.

The House of Recovery, or Fever Hospital, was opened in 1804
in Bath Lane, just outside the old city walls. This took 'febrile
diseased patients' who had to provide their own medical attendants. The Dispensary, in Low Friar Street, established in 1777 to
help any sick person not able to gain admittance to the Infirmary,
provided an out-patient service as well as treatment at the
patient's home.[28]

There were also institutions for special needs, such as the
Infirmary for Diseases of the Eye, opened in 1822, a Lunatic
Asylum with accommodation for 80 inmates, built in 1776, and a
Lying-in Hospital, built in 1826, which was an 'asylum for poor
married pregnant women, admitted on production of a letter
from a subscriber and a certificate of marriage'.[29]

Established doctors and the institutions, were in competition
with many unqualified practitioners and quacks offering their
services. And, of course, self-medication was universal, most
people treating themselves, at least for a time before calling in
professional help. Thomas Wright was warned by his mother to
be careful to check, before making his diagnosis, what quack
'remedies' his patients had been taking. Medicines for home use
were readily available from pharmacists – there were 32 chemists
and druggists in Newcastle and Gateshead – as well as from other
outlets.[30] 'Remedies' were widely advertised in the local newspapers. For example, the week Thomas started his diary, typical
advertisements in the Newcastle Courant were for Wessel's Jesuit
Drops – 'Cure for Strangury, Gleets, Weakness of the Kidnies or
Bladder. Bottles 2/9, 10/-, 22/-' – and for Solomon's Drops for
treating '... Scrofula, Cutinaceous Erruptions, Bilious Complaints & Chronic Rheumatism, not to speak of diseases more
immediately connected with an Infected System. . .'.[31]

---

28 A contemporary description of the Newcastle Dispensary is given in MacKenzie 1827, pp. 513–16. For a recent account of the foundation and the work done
   by the House of Recovery and the Dispensary, see Fred Miller, 'Dr John Clark
   1744–1805: The Forgotten Physician', in MN, chapter 7.

29 MacKenzie 1827, pp. 517–20.

30 For an account of the Chemists and Druggists in Newcastle, see W. A.
   Campbell, 'Pharmacy in Old Newcastle', in MN, chapter 18.

31 Newcastle Courant, 30 September 1826.

Mr McIntyre and his medical practice

At the time Thomas Wright was an apprentice, there were 10 physicians and 43 surgeons listed in the Newcastle trade directory.[32] Apart from a few of the more prominent and successful practitioners,[33] little is known about the qualifications or the actual work of these doctors and an interesting aspect of the *Diary* is the insight it gives into the business of one of the surgeons, Mr James McIntyre. A Licentiate of the Faculty of Physicians and Surgeons of Glasgow since 1814, McIntyre became MRCS in 1830,[34] that is, after he was already well-established in his Newcastle practice. Shortly afterwards, in 1831, he was elected to the Honorary position of Surgeon to Newcastle Infirmary, and his name appears in a brief tribute to the staff at the Infirmary: 'Among the surgeons, the names of Ingham, Baird, McIntyre and Henry Heath are still recalled for what they contributed to their art, and for their skill in its practice.'[35] He was still in practice in Newcastle when he died in Cecil St, London, after a short illness, on 8 May 1837.[36]

In 1826 McIntyre had an assistant and four apprentices working in his practice in Newcastle. The assistant, John Gibson,[37] had studied medicine in London, but his qualifications are not known. Thomas Wright, although still officially an apprentice, had taken courses in Edinburgh and was experienced enough to be treated as assistant. One of the other apprentices, William

---

32 PW, I, pp. 122 and 125.
33 Some of the successful Newcastle doctors have been described by Dennis Embleton (1810–1900), who was an apprentice doctor in Newcastle at about the same time as TGW: see D. Embleton, 'Biographical Notices of Members of the Philosophical & Medical Society of Newcastle 100 years Ago', in *Proceedings of the Northumberland and Durham Medical Society*, Session 1890–1, pp. 178–210, and Hume, pp. 99–102. John Snow (1813–58), later famous for his work on the epidemiology of cholera and for the early use of anaesthetics, was an apprentice in Newcastle in 1827: see Anthony Ashcroft, 'John Snow – Victorian Physician', in *MN*, chapter 16.
34 See Examinations Book, Royal College of Surgeons (London), 4/6/1830.
35 See Hume, p. 43
36 See *Newcastle Courant*, 19 May 1837.
37 John Gibson was a son of Mr Taylor Gibson, a well-established chemist and druggist in Newcastle. He was senior to TGW, having returned to the practice after studying medicine in London, shortly after TGW became apprentice in 1824. He is often mentioned in the *Diary*. For details of Taylor Gibson's business, see Campbell, 'Pharmacy in Old Newcastle' (note 30 above).

King, had joined the practice at about the same time as Thomas, and was about to begin his studies in Edinburgh. The two junior apprentices, Greenwood and Spearman, turned out to be unsatisfactory recruits to the medical profession and were eventually dismissed.

The main surgery or 'shop' was in Newcastle, and there was another at Backworth, about seven miles away, which was run mainly by another Assistant (Mr Cochrane). Some of the Newcastle patients lived in the town, but most of Thomas's work was with miners whose homes were near the mines at Benwell, Heaton, Walker, Wallsend and Felling. The Backworth branch, where Thomas worked for a time in 1828, looked after cases from five nearby collieries.

Thomas refers to Mr McIntyre having 'an extensive colliery business', and, although he does not describe the financial arrangements in any detail, he lists the numbers of his patients in two categories: 'colliery and private' and 'sick': he mentions that the term 'sick' refers to patients subscribing to the practice. Accounts were sent out annually – writing these was a disagreeable task that took up a lot of Thomas's time over Christmas and New Year. There is no information in the *Diary* about the amounts patients were charged for medical services. Probably, McIntyre's charges were in line with those of similar Newcastle practitioners.[38]

---

38 For a detailed general survey of the remuneration of doctors, see Digby, *Making a Medical Living* (note 23 above). Legally, only physicians could charge for medical attendance while surgeon-apothecaries like McIntyre could only charge for medication. Embleton, 'Biographical Notices' (note 33 above), indicated a method of overcoming the legal problems used by his master, Thomas Leighton: 'The bills were made up by us in detail thus: daily, a mixture, a box of pills, three draughts, a liniment, &c., with the charges opposite; and at the bottom was written "To attendance," a blank being left for the patient or his friends, executors, administrators, or assigns, to fill up at their discretion. This blank was filled up variously; but we were now and then told that Mr So and So had put down the same sum as the total of the charge for the medicines, and this was considered the right thing for a well-to-do person to underwrite.' Another Newcastle doctor, in a paper delivered to the Medical Society of Newcastle in 1824, complained that many doctors were obliged to derive most of their income from the sale of medicines, with a consequent loss of dignity and a tendency to over-prescribe and over-charge. He proposed that there should be fees for visits and suggested that there should be a meeting of the town's practitioners to decide the level of fees: see T. M. Greenhow, 'Hints Towards the Adoption of an Improved Principle of Remunerating the Surgeon

Inevitably, mining accidents yielded a high proportion of McIntyre's cases. However, many cases of illness were also treated, including private patients as well as those of miners and their families. The practice also supplied medicines, made up in the surgery. Thomas Wright occasionally mentions patients coming to the surgery in Newcastle for medicines or treatment, but usually he visited and treated them in their homes. In a practice spread over a good part of North Tyneside, this meant long journeys on horseback, a form of transport not without its problems: criticism of the mounts provided by Mr McIntyre is a recurrent theme in the *Diary*.

In those days, hospitals had little to offer in the way of special treatment and their patients were always under serious risk of cross-infection. Certainly it is evident from the *Diary* that Mr McIntyre did not normally refer his patients to any of the medical institutions. It is mentioned that one patient was sent to the Infirmary with a bone in her throat, and one miner was admitted after an accident – he subsequently died. Apart from this, the only other case where an institution is mentioned is when a family, who used to be patients, had been smitten with fever and ended up in the Fever Hospital. However, Mr Church, the House Surgeon at the Infirmary, was sometimes consulted and visited a patient with the other doctors from the practice.

Although designated 'Surgeon', Mr McIntyre was clearly functioning as a general practitioner which was not unusual at that time. His actual surgical work involved mainly the treatment of wounds and bone fractures, although tooth-drawing, removal of a tumour near the eye, and trepanning for concussion are also mentioned. Serious cuts were usually sutured and bandaged. The expectation was that simple fractures, treated skilfully, would heal well. However, it was accepted that a compound fracture of an arm or leg, was likely to become infected, and often could lead to loss of the limb or even, in the worst cases, to death. Although none of the patients mentioned in the *Diary* suffered either of these fates, Thomas Wright's account reveals some of the misery, suffering and disability that a compound fracture could bring. It is interesting that many of his cases apparently did heal fairly quickly, suggesting that the standard of hygiene often was

Apothecary or General Practitioner in Medicine', *Literary and Philosophical Society of Newcastle upon Tyne, Tracts*, vol. 66, no. 3.

adequate, and possibly reflecting the fact that in most cases the injuries were treated in the patient's home, rather than in hospital, thus avoiding cross-infection. Fractures of the skull caused great problems: there was no effective way of treating, or even detecting them. Trepanning was tried in a few cases, with the object of 'removing pressure', but otherwise, apart from the usual bleeding and purging, little was attempted. Medical cases included most of the ailments known to be common at that time, with a variety of medication being used in treatment, together with, inevitably, bleeding and purging.

It is apparent from the *Diary* that the McIntyre practice prospered during the time Thomas Wright was there: more collieries became subscribers, the business moved to fine, new premises in Eldon Square, and McIntyre was joined by a qualified partner. Thomas clearly felt that he had contributed significantly to the success of the practice and, indeed, towards the end of the *Diary* he began to think that he could make a better job of running it than Mr McIntyre. However, it is known that in later years Thomas recognised that, professionally, he owed much to Mr McIntyre and that his apprenticeship was the foundation for his further qualifications, and ultimately his own successful and lucrative medical career.

THE MANUSCRIPT

The manuscript of *Diary of a Doctor* was found in a house in Nanaimo, British Colombia, Canada. How it came to be there is not known for certain, but probably it had been in the possession of a grandson of Thomas G. Wright called Arthur Leighton who at one time occupied the house. In 1985, the manuscript was bequeathed to the Nanaimo Historical Society whose members, appreciating its significance as a unique record relevant to the Tyneside region, in 1990 generously sent the original work 'home' as a gift to the City of Newcastle.

The *Diary* was written in booklets, made by Thomas himself, each of which he referred to as a volume. There were originally twelve of his volumes altogether, and nine of them were found in Nanaimo. The fate of the other three volumes is not known. The page size is the same in each of the known volumes (about 14 x 18 cm) but the number of written pages varies, with an average of about 90 written sides in a volume. The length of an entry varies from a few lines to several pages. The *Diary* covers the period from 1 October 1826 to 30 April 1829, with a gap between the end of August 1828 and early March 1829, corresponding to the three missing volumes. The first volume includes a short 'Preface', written by Thomas in 1834 and dedicated to Eliza, his future wife. At the end of the final volume, there are brief notes made by Thomas about his activities after he left Newcastle, between May 1829 and April 1831.

All of the existing manuscript is well-preserved; the handwriting can be read quite easily, and there are remarkably few alterations or illegible words. Although one of his reasons for keeping a diary was to practise his style of writing, Thomas could express himself clearly from the outset, even though at busy times he was obviously in a hurry to get the day's entry written. The *Diary* is not personal and private: sometimes Thomas mentions it being read by others – 'my family and friends' – and often refers to himself as 'editor', just as if it were a magazine.

As well as writing about daily events, from time to time Thomas wrote into his diary more considered and mannered essays that he called 'Magaziniana', on a variety of subjects including 'About a Flute', 'Beauty', 'On Mottos', 'Rides in the Country'. Interestingly, he also used the 'Magaziniana' pieces to write his autobiography. This covers the years from his birth in 1808 to the start of the *Diary*, and includes fascinating information about his family, his school days in Darlington, his early apprenticeship years and studies in Edinburgh.

EDITING THE DIARY

Much of the charm of Thomas G. Wright's manuscript lies in its appearance and style. I have therefore tried to edit it lightly in the hope that the printed version will preserve at least some of the flavour of the original. The transcription has been made directly from the original manuscript, and includes all of the material in the nine existing volumes of the *Diary*, with the exception of eleven of the essay (Magaziniana) sections: the titles of these omitted sections are given in the Appendix and their original position in the *Diary* is indicated in the main text. The order of some of the material has been changed as follows.

1. The autobiographical essays (Magaziniana Nos 1–2, 4–6, 8–10, 12–20), which appear in Volumes 3 to 5 of the manuscript, have

been collected into a section entitled 'My Autobiography'; this section is placed in the present edition before the dated diary text. For each chapter of 'My Autobiography', the date of its manuscript entry is given, and the original position in the manuscript is indicated at the appropriate place in the transcript. The contents list for the present volume includes the summaries of the chapter contents as they are written in the diary manuscript.

2. A 'Preface', written by Wright some years after the *Diary* was concluded and which is pasted into Volume 1 of the manuscript, is included here before 'My Autobiography'.

3. An essay, entitled 'Rides in the Country', which describes some of the localities where the diary events take place, is here placed immediately after 'My Autobiography' instead of in its original position in Volume 6 where it formed Magaziniana Nos. 22, 23 and 25.

Apart from these omissions and rearrangements, the main changes and additions due to editing are as follows.

1. Underlined text, extensively used in the manuscript, has been changed to non-underlined italicised text.

2. Editorial insertions are italicised and in square brackets; round brackets are those of the author.

3. The pages in the transcript are numbered for convenience (the original manuscript pages are not numbered); the page breaks of the manuscript are not indicated in the transcript.

4. Minor alterations have been made to the punctuation, but mostly it has been left as in the original, even when it seemed somewhat inadequate.

5. Spelling has been left unchanged where this is obviously archaic: ancle, shew, favor, neighbor, etc. A few other words, apparently spelt incorrectly, have been changed without comment.

6. Abbreviations have been expanded only where it was felt that the meaning was not clear.

7. Days of the week have been inserted throughout: these are included in the original manuscript only from Volume 5 onwards.

8. Lists of numbers of patients, given almost weekly in the manuscript, have been omitted from the text and collected as Table 1 in the Appendix. The original positions of the patient number lists are indicated in the main text.

9. Some cross-references are given in the text mainly to allow the progress of particular patients to be tracked: the date given [*day/month/year*] is that of the immediately previous diary entry for the patient.

10. Footnotes that were included in the original manuscript by the author of the *Diary*, are indicated: [*TGW footnote*]; footnotes not so indicated have been added by the Editor.
11. Where additional information is available about a named individual, it is given in a footnote usually at the first mention of the name.

PREFACE

To Eliza

A word or two before you begin the perusal of this often talked
of diary, my love! You will find it a very different sort of work
from the Note Book you have been so much pleased with. This is
by far less interesting. It is ill-written, ill-composed, and in many
instances mis-spelled: but remember, dearest, it is my first
attempt at scribbling, and that the rude pages you have now
before you contain the effusions of a pen at eighteen whose writ-
ings you are very well satisfied with at six and twenty. If I had
not practiced in my Diary, my Note Book would never have been
worthy of your smiles: be merciful, therefore in your criticisms. I
know, love, I need say little on that score as you are already
predisposed to be sufficiently partial, but really on looking over
a few pages of this first number, it does seem so full of arrant
nonsense that all your partiality will be requisite to make you
think it worth reading. There will certainly be a little improvement in the future numbers, but a little is all I dare promise. I had
not, when I scribbled their illegible pages, the inspiring emotions
which now animate my pen, and give it a fluency (however little
merit it has else) that it never before possessed.

In the Diary you will find much that was not intended for publication beyond my immediate friends; and much that would not
have been inserted in a book that was solely for lady's perusal.
My Diary, however, at the time, was my Case-Book professionally as well as non-professionally; and in its details there is, of
course, much that is unintelligible to you. All that you can skip
over; as you proceed you will come at many passages that will
be more interesting.

In order that you may understand the *dramatis personae* of the
narrative, I must premise, that at the time the Diary opens Mr
McIntyre's establishment consisted of the following persons. McI
himself then residing in Newgate Street Newcastle: a low-bred

Scotchman Mr Cochrane who yet remains his assistant in the Backworth district, and who had just gone to reside at a house Mr McI had taken for him near Backworth; he attended the practice connected with five collieries in his neighborhood: next myself, living with Mr McI and having charge of six collieries around NCastle and the inferior practice of the house; Mr King an ill-educated lad who was indentured to Mr McI about the same time I was, and who was about to take his turn of a winter's session at Edinburgh, – a simple but good-natured fool: and two junior apprentices who were both reprobates and whose fate was at length equal to their deserts; – one after being turned away three times was finally dismissed with a conviction of theft added to all his other misdemeanours, and the other after being indulged beyond measure, and only threatened when he should have been punished became so debauched that he attempted to poison himself in a drunken fit, and was twice turned away – the last time peremptorily so.

With these rebellious spirits as my subs, and a reserved proud and selfish Scotchman as my Governor (though he has done much to make up for what I then thought unjust treatment, since I left him) my Eliza may now contemplate me, six weeks after my return to Mr McI from Edinburgh and assuming my place as his *Assistant*, entering upon the details of the 'Diary of a Doctor'. May 13 1834[1]

---

1 This Preface is written on sheets of paper pasted into Volume 1 before the title page. Eliza of the dedication is Elizabeth Hubbard, afterwards wife of TGW (see Introduction).

MY AUTOGIOBRAPHY

'Men should know why
They write, and for what end, but note or text
I never know the word which will come next.
So on I ramble, now and then narrating,
Now pondering . . .'

Don Juan[2]

Chapter 1 [*Magaziniana 1, 5/4/27*]

'The wight whose tale these artless lines unfold
Was' – born as soon and briefly doth appear –
'His birth no oracle or seer foretold;
No prodigy appeared in earth or air;
Nor might that night the strange event declare'

Beattie

'And yet poor Edwin was no vulgar boy
In truth he was a strange & wayward wight'

Beattie[3]

[*The above lines are written on paper pasted over earlier (illegible) text.*]

On the 8th of February 1808 as you have before been informed (*Vide* that day Vol 2) my lungs first felt the oxygenating influence of the atmospheric fluid; my eyes received the beams of the solar luminary; I began to exercise my intuitive powers in producing that pathetic exclamation of grief, vulgarly termed a squall, or as others would say '*a roar*'; & I first inhaled the balmy freshness of the morning – no by the way it was evening – air; *in one word I did begin to live.* This event was got over, as all genteel events of the kind *should be* got over – quietly. There was no ringing of bells, – except the bed room bell; no roaring of cannon, not a roar but mine own; no shouts of the populace, I had all the noise to

---

2 This quotation from Lord Byron's poem *Don Juan*, Canto 9, verse 42, is written at the beginning of each volume of the *Diary* MS.

3 From *The Minstral, or, The Progress of Genius*, Book 1, verses 22, 30, by James Beattie (1735–1803).

make myself; no one would have recognised in the little dumpling then tumbled into the world, ('tis not the first time I have
been compared to a *dumpling*[4] tho' the truth is, that, as to corpu-
lence I am more like a pancake, if you will have palatable
similes,) – the present grave, silent &c &c author of this article. It
is a very true remark that 'one half of the world does not know
how the other half exists'. Here is an accident – the most important that has ever occurred during *my* life, – which, while it happened, millions were unconscious of. Neither the sun nor moon
stood still, no earthquakes happened, and even history has taken
no notice of the event; yes, perhaps it was recorded in the *'papers
of the day'*, but as my retentive faculties were then but partially
developed, I cannot *precisely* recollect the circumstance. This work
therefore will rescue from oblivion, what is worthy of a more
honored fate. What my feelings were upon this subject, at the
time I am considering, I cannot exactly say for reasons above
mentioned.

How delightful must be an infants sensations for the first few
years of its existence! – everything novel and hence every thing
pleasing, for novelty is generally pleasing, *says logic*, – [*section
scribbled over with pencil*]{no more *logic* if you please, Mr Author,
besides your assertion is not true with the greatest pleasure I
avow, that I perfectly *agree* with you, Ma'am, and sometime we
will discuss that point; but to our subject} – *says logic* – he finds
everyone around him smiling and happy; and also that *he* is the
cause of their joy, can he be otherwise than delighted? if he cries
for anything, – but they say I did not cry much, – right or wrong
everybody runs to get it – it is indeed the sole aim of all around
him to humour his fancies and promote his pleasure. Hence I say
that in regard to mere sensuous enjoyment the first two years of
a man's life are decidedly the happiest. I have somewhere seen
rather a different opinion put forth, however *n'importe*.

I shall never get through tho' at this *lengthy* rate, but I promise
to be more concise in future, – *if I can*, – only this is so important
a part of my memoir, that a little indulgence *must* be granted.
Here then I shall adjourn my discourse *sine die*.

---

4 [*TGW footnote*] A Gentleman one day asked my little niece which she loved
most – 'Uncle or the apple dumpling'.

Chapter 2 [*Magaziniana 2, 20/4/27*]
Authors are addicted in general to laying before the public, – for the benefit and terror no doubt of future adventurers in the mazes of scribbling, the difficulties they have had to surmount, and the obstacles they have overcome in preparing the rich feast they offer to their readers; so that I may be allowed to state to *mine*, that few but autobiographers can have an idea of the perplexities in writing ones own life. Anecdotes and events there are in abundance, but then to select such as may amuse the reader, to relate them well, to dress them up in proper colors, and to introduce them in an appropriate and fashionable way – aye, – there's the rub. Now, having these *almost insuperable* stumbling blocks to *leap* over, you must, courteous reader, take *my tyroism* into consideration in passing sentence upon these my memoirs.

We left *me* just scrambled into existence, and getting my supper for the first time amongst the inhabitants of this *middle* world. It will be necessary here to take a hop, step, & jump over a few years till I entered that hot house for young understandings – a school. I may just mention one anecdote, to shew that my memory was sufficiently developed to be of use to me, in my *fourth* year.

I had, like many folks, a mighty deal of inquisitiveness; (Mem: to examine my skull the first phrenological opportunity for the size of the bump denoting that organ) and a *piano-forte* excited my wonder & admiration from the effect of its mechanism. I had got a bad habit when 'Papa' was out, of opening the lid of his *piano*, and, while sounding the notes, poking my hand thro' the side ledge *'to feel where the sound came from'*. A brush for removing dust from the surface of the keys also lay in this compartment, with which I was always desirous of preventing dirt from accumulating. *Papa* however suspected my favorite haunt, and soon contrived to detect me *'in the act'*. A pair of spectacles were said to be missing; and this set me on the alert to find them for Mamma. Pursuing as usual my *philosophical researches* one day as to the cause of sound – I discovered in the aforementioned compartment, not the nice ivory brush but the lost spectacles! I immediately ran with joyful exclamations to Papa – 'I have found the spectacles!' 'Where were they?' – 'in the side of the piano-forte!' – This as Farmer Broadcast says, 'was a *puzzler*'. I however promised to leave off my *Explorations* and so the matter ended.

At this time I was very little, for I also *recollect* that, on a story from 'Rhymes for the Nursery' being read to me about 'a little boy' 'no higher than the table', – I very sagaciously went to the table to measure myself – to see if the poetry 'could mean me'. I was just able to reach the table with my nose and 'the table' was a low one.

How I was taught my alphabet I know not; nor whether I was a very apt or a very stupid scholar. *I of course* am decidedly of the opinion (and surely, gentle reader, you will allow my judgement to be correct,) that the former was the case. I could, however, spell pretty fluently words of three or four syllables in Lindley Murray's spelling book[5] at 6 yrs old. My lessons were marked, as I said them, by my dear sister: G, GG, or – (which signified *bad*) I shall like to preserve this copy as the Gs are the almost universal mark! In spelling one day I came at '*Pennsylvania*' and was told 'it was the name of a country'; and then wondered (and for a long time retained the association) what *connection* there was that could induce people to 'call a country after a *pencil*', without it was that pencils came from thence!!

At 7 years of age I went to school, to Mr Cundell[6] the *then* curate and present vicar of Stockton. The first morning was one of fear & trembling. As may be expected I attended to everything around – but my book, and I well remember feeling *in idea* all the horrors of flagellation, on hearing Mr Cundell tell one of the boys 'he would punish him if he did not behave better'! Such was my awe of scholastic punishment. My next chapter will see me entered upon a new era as

> . . . . the schoolboy
> With shining morning face and satchel on his back
> Running like a hare so willingly to school.[7]

---

5 The spelling book referred to is probably *English Grammar: Adapted to Different Classes of Learners* by Lindley Murray (1745–1826). First published in 1795 (York), this textbook went through nearly fifty editions, and was very widely used in schools during the early part of the nineteenth century.

6 TGW also writes this sometimes as 'Cundill', however Cundell appears to be correct and has been used here, throughout.

7 Based on Jaques' speech in Shakespeare's *As You Like It*, Act 2, Scene 7: 'Then the whining schoolboy, with his satchel/ And shining morning face, creeping like snail/ Unwillingly to school . . .'; see also note 83 below.

Chapter 3 [*Magaziniana 4, 14/5/27*]

> 'Prithee tell us something of thy self
> The secrets of thy private life unfold'
>
> Address to Belzoni's mummy[8]

I do not mean to insinuate that I am a mummy, gentle reader, – by no means. I hope you will give me credit for my due share of flesh & blood, whatever I may be in regard to sense. Not that I in the least despise, but rather admire and venerate that sage-looking relict of mortality and specimen of *im*mortality. I intend one day to become one of the fraternity myself. I have no notion of being devoured by reptiles when I & my body quarrel, and feel inclined to follow the example of the late professionally patriotic gentleman who bequeathed his *corpus* to be useful to others; only I shall make a further proviso, *viz.* that I shall be injected and properly prepared; so as to cut a figure among the rest of my companions on a lecture room table, or in an anatomical museum. I can indeed contemplate with perfect satisfaction the idea of being stuck in a glass case– the terror of young ladies and little boys – the admiration and study of professors – and being at any rate, able then to contribute to the good of society whatever advantages I may have been to it during life. But this is sadly too long a digression my chapter is *not* on Patriotism.

To proceed – the life of a schoolboy, tho' as full of cares, vexations, & disappointments which affect him in equal degree, that of mature age is in general very little noticed by even an observer of human life. As however we are neither considering at present 'Education' nor 'Moral Economy' my life at this period will be found scarcely interesting to the general reader. What is at all so will be related as connected perhaps with other incidents. Suffice it to say that I remained with Mr Cundell till I was ten years of age when some infamous business caused my F & M to resolve to leave Stockton.[9] During the time I was with him I learnt in the

---

8 The source of this quotation has not been identified, but it probably refers to one of the acquisitions of Giovanni Battista Belzoni (1778–1823), who became famous as an explorer and archaeologist after an expedition to Egypt in 1819, where he was employed to collect for the British Museum.

9 The 'infamous business' is not further explained in the *Diary*, but there is a hint in an article commemorating the death of TGW: '. . . Dr Wright's mother was also an accomplished lady and the author of various works. Amongst them was one entitled *A marvellous pleasant love story*. References are supposed

usual school way (for Mr Cundell tho' a very worthy man, was *not* a clever teacher) Latin Grammar; was able to get scrambled through a few chapters of Caesar and could manage to do a few questions in Practice. I wrote, (and still retain the fault,) a very *'poor hand'* and knew a little of Geography. My master was pleased when I left him to give me a very high encomiums in a letter to my parents though heaven knows I was while under his care 'an idle scoundrel'. This was not *altogether my* fault however. The only time I was ever flogged was by Mr Cundell and then as he himself afterward acknowledged rather unjustly I had been flying my kite along with some schoolfellows between dinner and two oclock, and time slipped over our hands so pleasantly and the kite having got fast in a tree detained us so long that *three* struck when we were in the midst of our amusements; and to our great dismay never supposing that we were beyond school time. I flew off to Mr Cundell's instantly but my companions thought as they had trespassed, half an hour would make the offence no greater. They were right for as it turned out it made the offence less. When I entered the schoolroom my master was in the heat of anger and all remonstrance from me was vain. He went out and thro' the window I trembling saw him cut an apple-tree [ash *crossed out and replaced with* apple tree *in pencil*] switch (many a time did we wish that tree at Jericho) which when he came in he laid over my back with a vengeance. When the stick and his rage were alike worn out he let me sit down; and presently in came my fellow truants. They were more fortunate. I was the victim who had been immolated to his wrath and the sacrifice was sufficiency. Mr C too was about tired of thrashing and so dismissed my companions with a frown and a few angry words – a very light and evanescent punishment to a schoolboy.

to be made to certain local personages of the time and these being of influence and not relishing the allusions, Mr Wright [*i.e., TGW's father*] lost his post of organist': see *Darlington and Stockton Times*, 11/6/1898, p. 7. However, with reference to the resignation TGW's father, the *Durham Chronicle* reported 'The interest of the legacy left by G. Sutton, Esq, in 1817, as an addition to the stipend of the organist was, by his directions, to accumulate for 20 years. This long restriction of payment of interest to the organist appears to have been caused by unintentional offence given by Mr Wright, who, after gratuitously bestowing considerable time and labour in improving the organ, had ventured to ask Mr Sutton and the authorities for the small sums he had disbursed on its account.' See Thomas Richmond, *Local Records of Stockton and Neighbourhood* (StocktononTees, 1868), p. 154.

When 9 years old my kind Father indulged me with a ticket to Mr Richd Dalton's course of lectures on Nat: Philosophy.[10] Never was I so delighted as on lecture nights. Mr D too having had introduction was a visitor at *'our* house' and took a great deal of notice of me. I was indeed a most attentive auditor and then got a ground work in and liking to Philosophical studies which have increased almost daily with me. I was taken to one of a course of lectures on the same subject by Mr D nearly 5 years before this time, and I even have a perfect recollection of the experiments though I could not understand the subject. First impressions may be partly a cause but certainly I have never heard a lecturer I liked so well or whose apparatus or experiments I thought so much of or from whom I gained as much knowledge as this Mr Dalton. I have lately supposed Mr Dalton of Manchester to be my identical friend; but I find his name is *John* while the above mentioned lecturer is *Richard*. The latter is residing now at York and has resigned his lectureship and apparatus to his son.

This leaving Stockton was a great era in my life and therefore justly forms a conclusion to this chapter. My F & M left it I believe on the 18th of March 1818. I then was of course 10 years of age.

Chapter 4 [*Magaziniana 5 , 27/5/27*]

> 'I do not believe that an individual ever existed whose life written by himself with candour and simplicity would not be interesting and in some points even instructive'
>
> Hogg preface to '209 days'[11]

I am resolved now to write nothing without a motto. Mottos are the fashion; and it is a *good* fashion, in as much as they serve the purpose of an introduction, which I have before alluded to as an important part of every work. My readers will perhaps be kind enough to insert (mentally) the above passage from Hogg (*Jefferson* Hogg) prior to all the *mottoless* chapters of this my life.

---

10 The lecturer was probably Richard Dalton of York, who published *Syllabus of a Course of Nine Lectures on Mechanics, Hydrostatics, Hydraulics and Optics* (York, 1816).

11 Thomas Jefferson Hogg (1792–1862) published *Two Hundred and Nine Days: or, The Journal of a Traveller on the Continent* (London, 1827) after a tour of Germany and Italy (1827). Hogg, friend and biographer of Shelley, was the eldest son of John Hogg who lived in Norton House, Stockton-on-Tees, and was possibly known to TGW's family: see *DNB*, IX, p. 998.

And lest they should think me *Irishlike* in *now* making such a request I will insert a note to this effect at the places alluded to.[12]

To resume our subject – During the time my F & M were in the bustle of removal from Stockton I of course was free from the trammels of a school. F had promised to go for a fortnight to Swillington, there to continue his instructions to Mr Charles Lowther, (a son of the present Sir John Lowther & long a pupil of my Father)[13] and thinking it would benefit my Mother's health, which was then quite broken up by our Stockton troubles, it was determined that my Mother & I should accompany him as far as Swillington, taking up our abode at the village while F joined us every night. This was the first *long* journey I had ever been; and with it I was highly delighted. Leeds & Wakefield are each 6 miles from Swillington and both places we visited for a day while other days were spent by my Mother & me [I *deleted, and* me *inserted in pencil*] in wandering about the beautiful scenery on the banks of the 'Aire & Calder navigation'.[14] I was delighted with seeing thus the whole processes in a paper mill, a pottery and several locks on the canal. Lady E. Lowther was so kind as give me what she called 'a keepsake'. It was a little turned rosewood box and on opening it I found it full of silver 'to buy something at the pottery with' Lady E. said. I think it contained 16/- but I set more value on the box than its contents. The former I have

---

12 These references have been omitted from this transcript.
13 John Lowther (1759–1844) was the younger son of the Rev. Sir William Lowther of Swillington. His elder brother, William, was the first Earl of Lonsdale. John Lowther, on whom a Baronetcy of the UK was conferred in 1824, first became an MP in 1780 and, at the time TGW was writing, was Member for Cumberland, a seat he held until his retirement in 1831. He married Lady Elizabeth Fane, daughter of the ninth Earl of Westmoreland, in 1790. They had six children, but only three of them, two sons and one daughter, survived to adulthood. The second son, Charles Hugh Lowther (1803–1894), the pupil of TGW's father, is referred to as a playmate of TGW in the latter's obituary (*Wakefield Express,* 28/5/1828). Charles became blind after an illness when he was six months old. In spite of this disability, he received an excellent education and, in later life, he played a prominent part in the development of education for the blind: see H. Owen, *The Lowther Family* (Chichester, 1990).
14 The Aire Calder Navigation, one of the oldest canal systems in England, was started early in the eighteenth century. It made the rivers Calder and Aire navigable, thus linking Wakefield and Leeds to the River Ouse and giving access to the River Humber and Hull. It was an important water-way by the time TGW saw it in 1818. See Charles Hadfield, *The Canals of Yorkshire and North East England,* 2 vols (Newton Abbot, 1972–3).

yet. We returned north again on my birthday passing thro' Leeds, Rippon &c to Thirsk. And here I remained with my Grandfather till my F & M had got comfortably settled at our new residence – *Haughton-le-Skerne*. The very next week I was sent to resume school duties.

The Quaker academy at Darlington (but a mile & half from Haughton) was celebrated in classical tuition, and Mr Sams was named to my F & M before we left Stockton as the superintendent of this academy. Accordingly as soon as I returned from Thirsk Mr Sams was sought out – found – and in a day or two I was duly installed a pupil of Mr Sams' 'Classical & commercial academy'. A few days after I went to the school Mr Sams' head pupil left him, and I then became the leader of the first class which was not very large consisting of myself – *solus*. Nor was there a boy in school who could form either a second or third class to me! Mr Sams was an excellent French scholar, but I knew nothing of French; and the *Caesar* he used to hear me read my lessons from was interlined with an English translation in pencil! To complete my disappointment we found that Mr Sams had been dismissed from 'the Quaker academy' 6 months before and was now in an establishment of his own. Mr Smith had undertaken his previous charge where I expected I had all along been. Luckily the period was now approaching when Mr Sams gave his summer vacation and at the vacation I was no longer his pupil – the following autumn saw me in possession of a desk at Mr Smith's 'the real Quaker academy'.[15]

By this time I had forgot the little I knew when with Mr Cundell but unfortunately for me my testimonials could not alter their expressions; I was therefore rated too high. This though I believe

---

15 The teaching career of Joseph Sams is briefly described in Henry Spencer, *Men that are Gone* (Darlington, 1862). Sams went to live in Darlington about 1812 and became first master of a school established by the Society of Friends in Paradise Row. He resigned his post, probably in 1817, and opened his own 'Classical and Commercial Seminary', which survived until 1824. Presumably the school in Paradise Row was the 'real Quaker academy' described by TGW. 'Mr Smith' is probably H. F. Smith, who is said by William Robson of Sunderland to have 'removed to Darlington in 1817 to start a school': see *W. Robson, 1817–18 His Journal*. (A typed and bound transcript of this diary is in the possession of the Society of Friends, Darlington.) Robson also mentions attending the examination of 'cousin H. F. Smiths' scholar's in 1818, and being 'much gratified . . . particularly with their Latin performance'.

not generally a misfortune to the few who are so estimated, was such to me; and it is a circumstance which has on several occasions proved detrimental to me, though it also has had its good effects. In this instance however it was my lot to be kept back for almost a year by the supposition of my knowing more by one half than I really understood.

I was now at home among a completely new set of companions. My Stockton associates were, most of them, forgotten. I was at no loss for play fellows however for our neighbours next door Major and Mrs Malcolm had 6 children the three eldest boys somewhat of my own age; and the rector's family the Le Mesuriers[16] consisted of 12, the elder ones quite grown up, and the others of all ages down to the baby in the cradle. With these youngsters I passed many a happy hour, for I was only a day boarder at Mr Smith's and generally got home about $\frac{1}{2}$ past five PM after going away at $\frac{1}{2}$ past 6 AM.

About this time I fell – in – love. Could I do otherwise? That only is wanting to complete my romance. But as I intend to devote two or three chap solely to this subject I shall say no more now.[17]

As this going to Mr Smith's forms another era in my life it shall commence another chapter. A more positive reason is that my paper & patience are exhausted; and as without both these requisites I cannot *proceed*, nothing is logically proved to be left for my choice but – to conclude – I dare say my reader, being similarly affected, will readily unite with me in my decision.

Chapter 5 [*Magaziniana 6, 9/6/27*]

> – Each lighter care,
> Each trivial disappointment and misfortune,
> Are by the schoolboy full as keenly felt,
> And cause as bitter grief, – as in maturer age
> We feel from ever freak of adverse fortune.
>   'The Passions' an *unwritten* poem

Reading about fevers this morning has reminded me of one incident which I had previously forgotten *viz.* my having a severe

---

16 TGW commented further on the Le Mesurier family on seeing a newspaper report of the death of James Le Mesurier: see Volume 1, 14/11/26.

17 [*TGW footnote*] Vide vol: 8 and 12 [*This is probably a reference to Magazinianas entitled 'Confessions'. The first of these, no. 1, was apparently in the missing Volume 8. No 2 (chapters 1 and 2) is in Volume 12 of the MS.*]

attack of Typhus fever two years before we left Stockton. I caught the infection at Mr Cundell's and was released from school duties for quarter of a year in consequence. My sister, following my good example, was laid up in the next room; but her attack coming to a crisis in one third of the time which mine did, – 7 days while I did not 'get the turn' for 21, she was almost well before I was able to leave my bed.

I could not then stand without support, and it was long before I regained my usual strength. This was the first serious illness I had; and it, at one period, threatened to stop my further proceedings in the way of adventure. The old proverb says 'nought never in danger'; however that may be applicable I know not, but certainly with the assistance of my good friend Mr Alcock I got scrambled out of reach of old *Charon's* clutches on this occasion.

Shortly after this I was again laid on the shelf by another disease which did not use me in the lightest manner. I took the measles in the midst of F & M's troubles at Stockton, but got well again in much less time than on the former occasion.

And now to *begin* where we last *finished*. – Fancy me trudging, gentle reader, a mile and a half every morning *winter* and summer, *at half past six* to school, and *re*trudging this same ground again in the evening; which I did for about twelve months, and till I knew every stick and stone on the road.

I one day calculated, on my way home, the number of miles I then walked in a year and made it out about a thousand! In summer however my pedestrian labours were often lightened by my playfellows the Mesuriers; who, to get me quicker home to join them in fishing leaping archery &c, would come upon their poneys, or bring the donkey cart to meet me on leaving school at 5 oclock. Harry and James were then at home for the holidays, and unfortunately the Winchester & Charter House vacations did not correspond in time with ours.

My troubles on first going to Mr Smiths however were rather more vexatious than usual with a schoolboy, but still they have been of infinite service to me, by accustoming me to the ways of the world on a small scale. I was admitted to this Quaker's academy founded by the Friends expressly for their sect, as a great favor; only one had been allowed to enter besides myself. To increase the favors I was buffeted & kicked about with the most opprobrious epithets, and, in short, became the butt of the whole school. And why? merely because I was not a Quaker. The old birds of this sect are very much given to starch and outward simplicity of appearance; but I assure ye I found the young ones internally very unfledged sort of cubs. They fully exemplified to me the truth of a passage from the same author as my motto

>'How are we kicked
>And buffeted on this same stage of life
>As football 'mong the clownish rustics!'

Some may ask why I did not thrash them into awe, and in return for cracked jokes give cracked skulls. I answer that I have not a large organ (i.e. bump) of combativeness, and do not relish *fighting* unless *words* be the weapons and an argument the field of battle. Besides their religious tenets were such that by my using *compulsion* to the pupils my most probable fate would be *expulsion* by the master, a thing I was not at all desirous of just then.

Mr Corrie (now a classical master at Mill Hill academy near London) was at that time head classical teacher at Mr Smiths, and under his care I was principally placed.[18] As I had read part of Caesar I was put into his first class at once, who were employed on Horace, Caesar & Virgil alternately. The real extent of my knowledge of the principles of the Latin language at this time was comparatively – nothing. I knew the Eton rules 'tis true and could parse a little, but I could not *understand* what I read; I was not grounded in the *Elements*. Nevertheless Mr Corrie, though a very clever teacher and a good classical scholar, kept me fagging on at the bottom of this class, (and without disgrace be it spoken) without my ever being able to say a single lesson *properly*. I dare say he attributed all my stupidity to laziness and inattention. So much for my introductory recommendations giving too high ideas of my attainments. Not but these testimonials might be well merited when they were bestowed, but recollect I had then been nine months unoccupied by studies; for during three of these I was with Sams I learnt nothing but some Geography, from his great map of the Saxon Heptarchy; a smattering of Astronomy from his immense picture of the moon. I daubed a few maps and wrote some '*specimens*'. So that by the time we were speaking of I had forgot at least one quarter of all the Latin I ever knew before that.

---

18 A note written on a small piece of paper inserted between the MS pages at this point reads: 'Mr Corrie – afterward an Usher at Harrow and subsequently a surgeon where I found him in general practice (in 1830) in that village'.

Mr Corrie left Darlington. A Mr Rogerson who was then dying (he did leave this world shortly after) of consumption succeeded him. He left, and this first class was *pro tempore* committed to the care of Mr Wm Cowan the professor in a college or class room, which, as a separate establishment was added to the school that year, but still my improvement in classical lore continued on the same slow ratio. In 1819 Mr Jas. Cowan brother to the *professor* (as he was by courtesy styled) was engaged as head classical tutor in the school and from this moment I date the commencement of my improvement and of the distinction with which I was finally honored in that establishment. The particulars of this will begin another chapter.

Chapter 6 [*Magaziniana 8, 20/7/27*]

> '*Jam liber, et bicolor positis membrana capillis*
> *Inque manus chartae, nodosaque venit arundo*'
> 'At length to study see the youth proceed,
> Charged with his book, his parchment, & his reed'
> Persius *Satire 32*

When Mr J. Cowan, at the time I am speaking of, assumed the reins of government over the classical department in the establishment of which I was a far from exalted member, I soon found opportunity of placing myself, with his assistance, in a surer road to advancement than the one I then trod. He was possessed of those talents particularly requisite for a *teacher* in an eminent degree; hence, though by no means so profound a scholar as his brother the *professor*, he had the *knack* of communicating instruction much more rapidly and unconsciously to his pupils. By diligently studying the temper & dispositions of those under his care he was enabled to adopt that course of rewards or punishments which was calculated to make the most impression on the individual to whom it was addressed.

The first act of Mr J. C.'s tutorship was to revise and remodel his classes; but still I was retained in the first class, Mr C. then yielding, I *imagine*, to the prevalent feeling that it was not from *inability*, but from *inertia* that I did not get forward. At my request however he at length allowed me to descend to the second class, and also he set me to work to recommence my study of the Latin language upon new grounds. I had learnt at Mr Cundell's and till then retained the rules of the Eton Grammar. Mr J. Cowan, however took Adam's accidence[19] as his text book – and to it I applied myself, committing to memory (as was always my masters plan) everything essential from the *article* onwards. To this task I gladly gave my attention, as I now was determined to shew all parties concerned the injustice of the former charges against me. In proof of this I may relate one circumstance which gave me a little trouble in the enacting. On leaving school one afternoon I referred myself to Mr Smith, (Mr Cowan not being in the way) for the task I was to prepare against the following morning. Mr S, who took little part in the minutia of the business merely superintending the whole establishment, was at a loss and enquired what I was then learning. I replied that I had just finished getting by heart the rules of Syntax in Adams Grammar by six at a time. 'Well then, suppose thou revise the whole and say them in the morning.' I no doubt thought this a difficult business, but after sitting up till midnight and a studious application next morning I accomplished the undertaking and came up to the desk to repeat my overnights performances. Mr J C who said he had quite forgot to set me my lesson was astonished when I offered to repeat all the 62 rules! Mr Smith coming up the business was soon explained.

The class I entered were reading Caesar & subsequently Virgil & Sallust, but Mr Cowans chief aim was to ground us firmly in the principles of the language and hence we were daily drilled in the accidence. I enjoyed this exceedingly and to use Mr Cs expression had many a hard fought contest with a youth[20] till then indisputably head of the class, for the enviable situation of – first. There was a young lady[21] too who often participated in our struggles. The old first class, reduced by my secession to only two, had now disappeared and I was once again in *'the first class'*, which consisted of six or seven boys, and this young lady who soon, however left us.

---

19 Alexander Adam (1741–1809) published the first edition of his *Principles of Latin and English Grammar*, in 1772 (London). The book referred to by TGW was possibly the fourth edition (London and Edinburgh, 1793).

20 [*TGW footnote*] Mr Isaac Pease since dead. [*Isaac Pease, who died in September 1825, apparently from consumption, was the son of Edward Pease (1767–1858), a successful industrialist and entrepreneur and one of the group of businessmen responsible for the inauguration of the Stockton and Darlington Railway, the world's first public railway: see Sir Alfred E. Pease (ed.)* The Diaries of Edward Pease : The Father of English Railways *(London, 1907)*.]

21 [*TGW footnote*] Miss Eliz Pease his cousin.

A public school has been very justly called a kingdom in mini-ature, for we have only to consider the Head of the Establishment as the ruling power, King or Emperor; the Tutors – Princes and the great officers of state; the most distinguished of the boys as statesmen and courtiers and we shall find as many cabals, and as much of plots & counterplots, party spirit & perfidy as ever entered the precincts of a throne though less harmful to society.

From some cause or complication of causes or rather perhaps from no cause at all, Mr Cowan experienced much the same reception in the school (making allowance for the difference of our stations) that I had been greeted with, and from sympathy, and perhaps his having known a little of me while at Stockton, where he had a school previous to coming to Darlington, Mr C & I became more intimate than fell to a lot of his other pupils; hence both partook of the general opprobrium which was unceasingly lavished on our devoted heads by those who should have been examples of an opposite line of conduct *viz* the elder boys in the school. These educated at home in the old school of quaker man-ners were certainly the most narrow minded & bigoted creatures I ever had intercourse with. These *few* – these *mali, parvi, atque pravi*, in a while left; the others who had been *led by the nose* (to use a homely phrase) began to see the injustice and absurdity of *their* conduct.

Mr Smith who no doubt connived at the practices I have men-tioned found it his interest (rather I believe than that a sense of duty prompted him) as the fame of Mr C's tuition brought increasing numbers to his board, to treat his Assistant with more marked respect, and in short the tables were completely turned, and Mr Cowan looked up to as the very life and soul of the estab-lishment. Mr C one day gave the pupils a very severe lecture on their past conduct which, being followed by apologies from the various classes, and as many pardons, all went swimmingly for some years.

I am afraid I enlarge too much for the reader's patience on these school details but I assure him *I* felt the occurrences they relate to be very important matters, and were I not to be as brief as possible for my own sake – would fill up much more time than I can patiently devote to them.

The next chapter will I hope finish these relations after which I shall be able to come at *data* whereon to found my story which will save much unnecessary paper.

Chapter 7 [*Magaziniana 9, 25/7/27*]

> 'The spirit of that competition burns
> With all varieties of ill by turns,
> Each vainly magnifies his own success,
> Resents his fellow's, wishes it were less
> Exults in his miscarriage – if he fail;
> Deems his reward too great if he prevail'
>
> Cowper's Tirocinium[22]

In this manner did the business of the school proceed (as is also described in the latter part of our last chapter), during my stay as a *day-border* at Mr Smiths.

Meantime my F & M who had kindly considered the walk from Haughton to Darlington too great a distance for me in the winter, removed to lodgings in Darlington; but Father having taken an engagement at Kirkleatham in Cleveland the following spring, he was induced to settle me as a boarder in Mr Smith's house on removing to the former place. My mother was extremely out of health and other causes also contributed towards an agreement being made with Mr Smith for my being absent a quarter of a year beyond the usual school holidays. During this time a gentleman who had sometime before taken a *penchant* towards my sister had the address to persuade all parties concerned to join in his schemes; and, having gone to church one morning committed no less than matrimony. 'The happy couple' set off on a tour through Wales and the south of England to London a few hours after, and from that day (Sept 12 – 1820) I saw no more of *Mr & Mrs Green* for several years.[23]

After spending a few weeks with my Mother at Middleton I rejoined my schoolfellows the beginning of October. I had not been altogether idle during the summer having availed myself of my sister's knowledge of the French language to improve myself by her instructions.

School affairs went tolerably well for some months until I was thrown back by an attack of *scarlet fever*, which confined a dozen of my companions at the same time under the disguising title of *sore throat*. I was then with my class diligently learning Greek

---

22 From *Tirocinium; or, A Review of Schools*, lines 474–9, by William Cowper (1731–1800).

23 See chapters 10 and 11 for an account of TGW's visit to his sister in London in May 1823.

grammar, and the surgeon prohibited my studying at all till I was well again. I was laid up about 3 weeks and during this time the class had got so much ahead of me that I despaired of regaining my station. Mr Cowan was not pleased at the medical attendant interfering with my lessons, though I *was* laid up, for he had no idea of even ill health itself being a bar to study; and vented his displeasure upon me. With a commendable zeal no doubt for my interest he '*kept me in*' during play hours for some time, but still the class got on as rapidly as I did. Mr C then tried a different plan – he refused to speak to me or to have concern with any of my tasks till I was enabled to take my station in the class. This worked miracles: after about 3 weeks or a month's unhappiness which affected me more even than all the previous ill usage of my schoolfellows, – worn out in both mind and body (having my breakfast and supper untouched day after day) I *did* stand up once more with my compeers; and a hearty shake of my master's hand made up for all my miseries.

So well were we grounded in Greek that we learnt nothing but the Grammar for the space of twelve months – after which we could have repeated every rule and observation worth remembering from beginning to end of Dunbar's grammar[24] without missing a word.

In the year 1822 this establishment was at the height of its glory and popularity. The classes had been arranged so as to constitute two school rooms. The writing English & arithmetic with the junior classes were taught in one, while all the higher branches were conducted in the lower room where Mr Cowan alone presided. Every hour or half hour had its proper study, and a bell announced the time for change. As soon as the bell rang all was bustle for a minute or two, but each knew his business and the place of rendezvous for his class so that as quickly all was again silent. Strangers indeed very justly admired the extreme regularity and discipline which prevailed throughout.

Each class under Mr Cowan had its *dux* who superintended their studies in Mr C's absence especially during the two hours in the evening which were regularly devoted to learning lessons for the ensuing day, and when only one of the ushers attended

---

24 George Dunbar (1774–1851), Professor of Greek at the University of Edinburgh, published several Greek textbooks. TGW possibly is referring to *Exercises on the Syntax*, 3rd edition (Edinburgh, 1822).

merely to see that attention and order were observed. I then arrived at the pinnacle of greatness, being installed *Dux of the 1ˢᵗ Class!* (which was designated by Cowan his own *10ᵗʰ Cohort*) and in virtue of my office had in charge all the other *Duces* and *par consequence* their classes! My station was an envied one, as may be supposed, *ergo* not a very pleasant one in performance. Every eye was on the watch to lay hold of some *faux pas* which might hurl me from my honored seat.

Attempts were not wanting to do this, but in several instances they fell with the compliment of a task on the contriver's head. On one fatal night however the mention of a certain young lady's name among my class fellows was a charm too great for my resolution to withstand. I exchanged a few sentences as regarding the said lady and resumed my studies. This inadventure was joyfully reported by one of my class the next morning, and I of course pleaded '*guilty*'. I was discharged from office and another *dux* had been appointed, when Mr Cowan allowed me a chance of restoration by leaving it to the votes of the class. The point was carried in my favor – I having the good will of all (the new *dux* included) except the plaintiff and another. The class consisted of eight I think. I was therefore reinstated in *ducal* authority, but my next offence would have carried condemnation 'without benefit of clergy' or appeal of any kind. This next offence however I never committed.[25]

This 10ᵗʰ Cohort[26] of ours enjoyed many privileges over the rest of the school and hence was a distinguished regiment. If Mr Cowan was absent we were under the authority of no other tutor; our lessons were left to our own discretion; each of the class having

---

25 The girls in the school, and TGW's relationships with some of them, are mentioned in an obituary of TGW: 'Besides Dr Wright and another boy who were not "Friends", it was permitted to three young ladies to attend the school for the advantage of higher education in Latin and other subjects. They were "sweet-girls" graduates among the Quakers, and Dr Wright openly confessed during a lecture at the Wakefield Mechanics Institute on February 21ˢᵗ 1837, that he fell in love with one of the girls, when he was nearly eleven years of age, and began to compose verses and valentines, a dreadful violation of Quaker propriety, and not at all the kind of higher education intended for the young ladies. Indeed he indignantly heard from one of the young ladies that her papa had got hold of one of the valentines sent by post and had ignominiously put it in the fire': see *Wakefield Express*, 4/5/1898, p. 5.

26 [*TGW footnote*] Caesars' own peculiar body guard & favorite troups were the 10ᵗʰ Cohort.

pledged his honor as to his good behaviour, and a more diligent class (if their leader may I hope be excused saying it) – never studied in a public school. Each of us had a Greek grammar class of his own, – the most stupid lads having the most able masters, – and Mr Cowan examined these altogether every week. We along with two or three other classes met every evening for an hour to practise an expeditious method of addition, over which I had the honor to preside *absolute*; no master or tutor being present!

At this time *we* (i.e. Class 1st) could read Virgil, Sallust &c at *the opening of the book*, as also the Greek Testament & the easier French works. We were construing Livy, Horace, Homer, Anacreon, and *L'Histoire D'Angleterre* nor were the rudiments of these languages neglected, a portion of the grammars, usually a third, being repeated every Saturday along with half the Syntax rules. We were well acquainted with Ancient Geography and History, which we were taught upon an improved system; and had a good general knowledge of Modern Geography & Astronomy with the use of the Globes. I and another youth, the only geometrical class, were working *equations* and demonstrating the elements of Euclid.

This could not last however with Mr Smith's character & temper. He grew jealous of Mr Cowan's popularity; and to lessen it treated him in a more haughty way. The breach became more violent and after a series of disputes Mr Cowan was discharged. Two other tutors who had shared in Mr Cowan's ill treatment gave in their resignations. These were Mr Gillan and Mr Hudson the two junior classical ushers. About 20 of the boys signed a testimonial of friendship which was presented along with a snuff-box to Mr Cowan and after an affecting farewell address Mr C's reign and along with it my honors were over.

Chapter 8 [*Magaziniana 10, 3/8/27*]

> 'Mercy on us! what a collection of circumstances you have crowded together!
> A moment's patience ma'am'
>
> *The Liar*[27]

In attempting what I could not accomplish in the last chapter, – the finishing of my school adventures, – I hurried my relations,

---

27 The quotation is probably from *The Liar*, a comedy by Theophilus Cibber (1703– ?).

and cut short my sentences so much, that I find I shall have still to devote another part to the same subject, in making up omissions, and concluding as I purposed to do in the former volume.

In the dispute which terminated with Mr Cowans leaving Mr Smith, I was a party considerably interested; for one of the *piques* which the latter laid hold upon was my being in the post Mr Cowan had assigned me. Mr Smith no doubt wished a quaker boy to hold it: and one day at dinner when some rather high words took place between the two, said that in his opinion a nephew of his was as fit for the office as me. At this the boys could not suppress a *titter*, as the lad alluded to was *technically* denominated among his playfellows – 'the ass'.

Smith had then a marked spite against me which considerably increased on the testimonial of our attachment before mentioned being given to Cowan, for it soon reached the former's ears which were long enough on these occasions. There were now – I am speaking of the time after Cowan's departure two violent party factions in the school. Smith had fabricated a lot of stories concerning his late usher, which were told to the class boys; and they, siding most completely with him, busied themselves in making proselytes to their cause in the school.

They succeeded so far as to get the assertion of the four or six of the twenty who had signed the *round-robin*, that they 'were sorry for having done so'. One of these *students* immediately wrote to Sunderland to say that certain of his late pupils 'begged to *detract* (!) their names' from Mr Cowan's paper. Mr C came over to Darlington with this in his pocket, and insisted upon an explanation of *it* and the charges which he now found were being circulated against him. This Mr Smith at first refused, but when it was insisted on by the Quakers and friends of both parties, he was obliged to allow a meeting between Mr C and the class-boys (not a duel gentle reader – the Quakers do not deal with powder and bullets – but a Quaker meeting – for peaceable motives). Mr Cowan in the presence of mutual friends to their satisfaction (as they expressed by a public testimonial) completely refuted the charge against him.

All this was kept a great secret from the school boys. I and my party of perhaps eight or nine staunch *cavaliers*, firmly attached to the ex-government, were most pointedly made the marks for Smith's displeasure; and he did not scruple on one or two occasions to make some vile and unfounded accusations against me.

One day – and for a charge I was innocent of as the child unborn, and the only one I believe in the school who *was* innocent of calling a unanimously unpopular tutor by a nick-name, (I had suspected I should be blamed as the origin, and had consequently never used the term,) then I say (with [*illegible name*])

> – 'he struck me
> Gods! while I tell it do I live?'

I was shortly to leave the school and therefore bore all with resignation. Master Fry an enemy of Cowan who was a leader in the above practice, was by some unaccountable accident overlooked! though he was called up to answer for the same at the time I was included!

During my F & M's residence at Kirkleatham I passed my six weeks vacation at Midsummer most delightfully. Among the visitors at Redcar (only 3 miles off) were numbers of my Father's friends and with *lots* of companions the time passed most agreeably.

My F, in being at Darlington on business asked me shortly before I was to leave school if I had thought of any profession with preference, and I then told him I had had a liking for the church, but it had never been subject to serious consideration. My Father named the surgical profession, recommending it to my notice, but at the same time most kindly leaving me to have a fair choice and chance in what I thought would be most to my taste and benefit. This *'surgeon'* was a new idea to me; the trade of potions and pill boxes had never entered my head, – it embraced chemistry, mechanics and all branches of philosophy which I was extremely partial to. After due consideration (my F was to see me soon again to know my decision) – surgeon – surgeon thought I – I *will* be a surgeon! My liking for the church had only originated in *vanity* – I prided myself on my reading well – and thought a pulpit was an excellent *forum*.

Mr Smith used to encourage in his pupils a taste for science, – his chief merit as a master, – and afforded us every opportunity for such improvement by allowing a well assorted library of his own to circulate amongst us; and by taking us to hear all the scientific lecturers who taught in Darlington. In this way I attended Mr Jackson on Natural Philosophy – Mr Longstaff on Astronomy M – [*name omitted*] on Elocution and Mr Woods excellent discourses on History connected with Architecture.

Thus with the very liberal education my kind parents had bestowed upon me, and the excellent precepts inculcated at home, I was, when I left Mr Smith on Thursday the 27 March 1823, (though I had learnt little after Mr Cowan left the autumn previous) fit to enter on almost any profession, and was also bound to do my friends and my teacher credit in that profession. A surgeon was now fixed to be my destination but how far I have realized their anticipation is not for me to say.

I took leave of the Quaker's academy and its high walls with no heavy heart, and, after both drinking tea and breakfasting next morning with my kind friends Mr Bowes family, I rode with my Father to Kirkleatham. I now clapped my wings joyfully as freed from bondage but I was not long destined to enjoy my newly acquired liberty.

Chapter 9 [*Magaziniana 12, 10/8/27*]

> 'O, you Tom, Dick, Jack, Will,
> Who hold the balance or who gild the pill'
> Prologue to *The Apprentice*[28]

After staying at home a few days I went to spend a week with my friends the Miss Brays at Sunderland previous to returning to Darlington to business. It was originally intended that on leaving school I should have paid a visit to London for the first time and there sojourned till my Father & Mother who were going there in the summer returned with me; but a report having reached the north of a little business being expected in the way of an increase to my sister's family, my journey was delayed till we should all proceed together. This arrangement, though it by no means met with my unqualified approbation, I was of course to submit to and according had a trial month of physic before I saw the great metropolis.

> 'A man in many a country town we know
> Professing openly with Death to wrestle
> Entering the field against the grimly foe
> Armed with a mortar and a pestle,' &c

used to be a favorite recitation with me and of such a man I have now to speak.

---

28 The quotation is probably from *The Apprentice*, a farce in two acts by Arthur Murphy (1727–1805).

Mr Allison[29] (for so was he yclept [*i.e. called*]) enjoyed the first surgical practice in the neighborhood and at one time the reputation of great skill which in his younger days he perhaps deserved. He was *of the old school* however and that was not favorable to a modern apprentice. Being an old friend of my Fathers and much in want of a pupil matters were soon adjusted between them which only waited for my concurrence to be put into execution. Large promises were entered into on one side which were trusted to on the other and my Father having kindly laid the whole negotiation before me I went on a month's trial previous to going to London and if on my return matters still kept favorable I was then to be – bound.

During this trial month Mr Allison certainly did take some pains to instruct me in the elements of *my profession* (for such I may now call it) but I found already that *all* his promises were not to be depended on. He had another youth whom he represented as only a kind of errand boy & who being taken without any *fee* would be quite on a different foot with myself with whom he demanded £100. This lad I now found was a regular indentured apprentice though not residing in the house and hence to make the matter short I had to be *under him*. This was indeed a descent to my pride. To think of *me – I – myself* – but lately *strutting* sole chief and head of my companions in a large establishment of the sons of *gentlemen* and now to be set under a scrub of a fellow who to being the son of an upholster bacon and egg seller joined far worse qualities those of excessive ignorance impudence and low assumption of gentility he could only *ape* at. This was to me pride shall have a fall. I had on thus leaving in some measure parental authority and *surveillance* determined to make light of any difficulties or disagreeables I had to encounter and to take no notice of *trifles*; this rule perhaps the sequel may prove I followed too scrupulously. The situation was a new one to me, and I thought all others in the same case were equally well off, and besides, as my Father & Mother had chosen the situation, I thought it *my* duty to give it a fair trial, at any rate.

The arrangements in the house were pretty comfortable; and, as I sat in the evenings always with Mrs Allison, and both she and Mr A took some notice of me, and I had flattering attention

29 William Allison, Surgeon, 1762–1832.

from my other friends in Darlington, it was only in the shop that my troubles were at all felt. As I have an old pocket book with the occurrences mentioned on their proper dates, and have continued the plan up to the first formation of my Diary, I shall now be enabled to make extracts from them so as to be independent of memory and to note circumstances *in proprio ordine*.
At this time I find –

> '1823   Arrived at Mr Allisons – April 15
> 20 Dressed a wounded finger first time
> 24 Made up my first medicine for Mrs Fry, Dinsdale
> May 3 Inoculated my first patient'

There was an arrangement which my F & M considered as a great advantage made on my going to Darlington – *viz* that I should every alternate Saturday evening be permitted to go to Croft (whither my parents were coming to reside) and that I should return on the Sunday afternoon in time for Bewicke (my fellow apprentice) to get to church, to evening prayers which were held at D then instead of afternoon service. On the Sunday I was not at Croft, Bewicke was out in the morning while I had liberty in the evening.

Mr Allison too was the attendant of the Darlington Dispensary[30] which I had to attend every alternate week for an hour morning and afternoon. This was an advantage in practice for making up medicine and had I staid long enough might have been so in a medical point of view. Mr Allison lost it however the year after I left him.
Accordingly I find among my memoranda

> 'April 29 Father & Mother came to Croft
> May 3 Went to Croft this evening'

I did not begin to attend the Dispensary however till after I was bound. On the 14 I left Darlington preparatory to setting out on my journey to London but as these events will form another Chapter we will here leave them.

Chapter 10 [*Magaziniana 13, 16/8/27*]

> 'First I came to London town
> On a visit – on a visit

---

30 A detailed account of the work of the Dispensary in nearby Stockton-on-Tees in the early nineteenth century is given by R. P. Hastings, *The Local Historian*, 10 (1972–3), pp. 221–7.

> When first I came to London town
> In heavy rain and thunder'

                                                            Song

Though I cannot vouch for the 'thunder', the other part of this verse is as we shall see strictly true; but I have not room now for prefaces to every chapter, so must take up the thread of my discourse with out any preliminary remarks.

On the 14 of May (1823) I left Mr Allison for the purpose of proceeding on my intended excursion to the South; and, after staying a short time at Croft to get all ready, on the 20th left that place on my Fathers poney for Thirsk, where I was to join him the following day, at the Highflyer Coach.[31] My Mother was to have made one of our party but from indisposition she was compelled to remain behind.

After staying all night with my friends in Thirsk, under whose care I left the poney, I got safely seated to my infinite joy (the very memory of it indeed is quite elating) beside the guard of the coach, – my old friend John Mather; whom I knew more of after from travelling a good deal from Newcastle to Croft &c.

We staid that night at York, and at eight am next day once more were in rapid motion toward the metropolis which we then contemplated 200 miles distant and to be arrived at the very next day! In going down 'Coney Street' the wheel of the coach came in contact with that of a woman's fruit cart; and turned the latter so violently around that the horse was obliged to seek shelter by poking his nose through two or three panes of a haberdasher's shop window.

The usual stoppages of changing horses and dinner being past we found ourselves at nine oclock in the evening at the village of Coultersworth (I think it is called) where supper was provided. My Father, some ladies and myself the only passengers except one preferring tea we got some while an elderly Spanish gentleman who had an inside berth to London requested me to ask for 'du beurre et du fromage' for his repast. As I was the only one who understood French and I could manage to make myself intelligible to him (who could speak very little English) I paid

---

31 'The Highflyer', a mail coach, with four inside seats, departed from the Turf Hotel, Collingwood Street, Newcastle, for London every day at 5 a.m. It passed through Durham, Rushyford, Northallerton, Thirsk, York, Biggleswade, Hertford and arrived at the White Horse, Fetter Lane, London at 7 the next evening: see PW, I, p. 133.

his bills and got him what he wanted to his great gratitude and satisfaction. This passenger left us in Fleet Market and I saw no more of him. We now prepared for the raw night. I could not travel inside but my Father kept his snug berth of course.

I shall never forget the beauty of the scene on driving off from that inn. The moon was full and though a cloudy sky served to hide much of the otherwise brilliant canopy of stars and occasionally to obscure for a minute the full orb before us, – it contributed greatly to the loveliness of the landscape. The milestone told us we were 103 miles from Shoreditch Church. About 3 AM the air was very cold and frosty as the damp rose in mists from the rain which I omitted mentioning fell in heavy showers the day before.

We were an hour too soon at Biggleswade where we were to breakfast. The cloth was just laid but scarcely all up it being $\frac{1}{2}$ past 4. The guard allowed us more than the usual 20 minutes as he could well afford to do and after much difficulty and not a few peals at the bell we got a good breakfast and started within 40 miles of our *port*. Every stage shewed a change in the garb and manners of the peasants which I had observed all the way from York but now the more numerous country houses, villages and villas and then one continued line of shops and houses showed us to be in the environs of London.

How great a difference in this respect from Edinburgh! where a traveller is no sooner free from the splendid streets and a half mile of suburbs than he meets with the thatched roofs and pigsties with the most rustic looking inhabitants.

We soon were on the rattle of the pavement and the guard very obligingly pointed out to me each street and building as we passed it. After going past & through *Bishopgate St, Threadneedle St, The Bank of England, Fleet Market* and *Holborn* we drew up in the yard of the *White Horse Fetter Lane*!

Every one 'who has e'er been in London that overgrown place' knows and speaks of the quick fingered ledgerdemain of the London porters about a coach office. I knew this and stood sentinel over the luggage while my Father 'called a coach.'

'Go call a coach', and let a coach be called, and let him who calls the coach, call 'coach' – 'coach'!

While the coach was being called however or rather perhaps in handing the trunks into the coach we had a trifling specimen of the *handiness* of these gentry above spoken of – our umbrella cover was not forthcoming! The loss however was fortunately not worth mentioning except to make us look sharply out. The hackney man was told to drive to Calthorpe Place – he did not know where it was!! I had however studied the map of that part of London before I went and told him if he went to Mecklenburgh Square I could direct him! Here was an extraordinary undertaking! a youth who had never seen this great and intricate labyrinth till half and hour before, presuming and necessarily obliged to do so, to guide through its mazes one of its own regular attendants and who professed to know every corner about the city. When we got into Grays Inn Lane I was all at home and directed our chaperone quite straight to our destination where we surprized the good folks, as Mr Green[32] had placed a porter at the Bank to inform him of the arrival of the coach, but this man had been too late in taking his station, as we got in an hour before the stated time. My sister's surprise therefore was that we had found the way without Mr Green having met us at the Inn door. I spied the number on the door, which was at the same moment opened, and in five minutes we were all sitting at a second breakfast in No 7 *Calthorpe Place!*[33]

Chapter 11 [*Magaziniana 14, 28/8/27*]

'Bout Lunnun Ive heard aye sick wonderful spokes
'At the streets were a' covered wi' guineas
The houses sae fine an sick grandees the folks
To them huz i' the North were but ninnies!'
                        Song 'Canny Newcassel'[34]

---

32 Mr Green was the husband of TGW's sister.
33 The cab driver's lack of knowledge of the whereabouts of Calthorpe Place may be excusable because it was a very new development when TGW visited in 1823. No. 7, Calthorpe Place, the residence of TGW's sister (Mrs Green), was one of the first group of sixteen houses (now nos. 262–292 Grays Inn Road) built on the land of the Calthorpe Estate between 1820 and 1823. This was the first venture into house building by Thomas Cubitt (1788–1855), who became one of the most famous building developers of his time, see Hermione Hobhouse, *Thomas Cubitt Master Builder*, 2nd edition (Didcot, 1995), chapter 2.
34 The song *Canny Newcassel* was written by Thomas Thompson (1773–1816). It has been printed in several collections, including *A Beuk o' Newcassel Songs* collected by Joseph Crawhall (Newcastle upon Tyne, 1888, reprinted Newcastle upon Tyne, 1965). The dialect words of this printed version differ slightly from those in the *Diary*.

London that great emporium of arts & artifice, of talent and ignorance, of wealth and poverty; the stage on which all that is great and good flourishes and where also the most refined vice is conspicuous; – which in short gives birth to the greatest extremes of our nature with every fractional grade between each; – London – was now for a few weeks to be my *locataire*.

I shall very naturally be expected to give some account of the sensation a first sight of the metropolis inspired me with. A few words however will suffice for this end. I was neither surprized nor disappointed with its general appearance. I had to be sure before then seen several of the second rate towns as Newcastle, York, Leeds & Wakefield so that though I did not, like the pitman in my motto, expect the streets to be paved with gold I had a tolerably correct prospect of London 'in my mind's eye', prior to visiting it. The shortest way (for brevity here is a necessary quality) to describe all the 'sights' I beheld will be to copy from my old note book and make a few observations as we go on. Double columns too will perhaps facilitate this arrangement by leaving less paper unoccupied.[35]

1823 May 24 Sat 'Goulding's Music shop'.[36] Here my Father had occasion to be very frequently and I liked to accompany him.

'Covent Garden theatre' *Clari* had just been produced in which I had the pleasure to hear Miss M. Tree. The size and magnificence of both Winter Theatres,[37] I own astonished me. Tonight the other performances were *The Sleep walker* with Yates powers and *The Duel or my two nephews* in which Farren played.[38]

---

35 In the MS the remainder of this chapter is written in double columns.

36 Probably, George Goulding, music-seller, 6, James Street, Bloomsbury Square: see P. Barfoot and J. Wilkes, *The Universal British Directory*, 2nd edition (London, 1793).

37 The Winter Theatres, so-called because they were the only ones in London legally entitled to remain open during the winter months, were Covent Garden and Drury Lane. At the time of TGW's visit, the Covent Garden theatre was the building of 1808, which was replaced in 1856 by the present building. Drury Lane Theatre, the fourth building on the site, was built in 1812.

38 *Clari, or the Maid of Milan*, was a musical drama with a text that has been variously credited to John Howard Payne and James Robinson Planche. The music was by Henry R. Bishop. *Clari* introduced the famous song 'Home Sweet Home'. On 24/5/1823 it was receiving its eighth performance. Miss Maria Tree (1801–1862) was Clari. *The Sleepwalker* was a one-act play, author unknown, featuring Frederick Yates as Somno, the Sleepwalker. *The Duel, or my Two Nephews* was a farce by Richard Brinsley Peake, receiving its fourteenth

25 Sunday. Being Trinity we took the opportunity of hearing High Mass at the Catholic chapel in Moorfields[39] and attended evening service at the beautiful chapel of the Foundling hospital[40] which was very near Calthorpe Place.

26 Lounged about Holborn &c looking at the streets shops &c and concluded the evening at Drury Lane. We went in at half price and such a crush! The house was crammed – Kean & Young both engaged at one house the only season they had then been together.

Othello, Deaf as a Post in which I saw Liston as also in his favorite part Lubin Log in *Love Law & Physic*.[41]

27 Gerard St to call upon some friends – Gouldings, Bazaar &c

28 This was rehearsal day for the annual meeting of the charity schools and Father and I went to hear the performances. The effect of 10,000 children joining in sacred chorus was very striking.

29 Mother joined our party having come up just a week after F & me. Being the only holiday at the Bank of England (in which Mr Green is engaged) during our stay Mr G took advantage of it for an excursion with me to Richmond Twickenham &c. It was a delightful day. We went to Kew by coach walked to Richmond, boated it to Twickenham saw Popes villa[42] – dined at Richmond and came home in the evening by a steamer to Blackfriars bridge.

30 Gouldings – I was almost knocked up with walking about and took a rest today.

31 Whitechapel – Drury Lane *Lord of the Manor* with Braham,

---

performance on 24/5/1823. The principle player was William Farren the younger (1786–1861), taking the part of Sir Pryer Oldencourt.

39 St Mary's Chapel in Moorfields, consecrated 1820, was the metropolitan Roman Catholic chapel of London: see Thomas Allen, *The History and Antiquities of London*, 4 vols (London, 1828), III, pp. 415–17.

40 The Foundling Hospital in Lambs-Conduit Fields was established in 1739 by Thomas Coram to care for 'exposed and deserted' infants.

41 In the performance on 26/5/1823 at Drury Lane, the celebrated tragedian, Edmund Kean (1789–1833), played Othello, with Charles Mayne Young (1777–1856) as Iago. The popular comedian John Liston (1776–1846) appeared as Tristram Sappy in *Deaf as a Post* by John Poole, and as Lubin Log in *Love, Law and Physic* by James Kenney, which was being presented for 'positively the last time', according to the play bill.

42 Alexander Pope (1688–1744) moved to a villa near the River Thames at Twickenham in 1719: see Simon Jenkins, *The Companion Guide to Outer London* (London, 1981), pp.127 ff.

Misses Stephens, Cubitts, &c *Swiss Villagers* ballet and the then new farce of *Simpson & Co.*[43]
June 1 Sunday New Pancras ch[44] & Foundling.
2 An excursion to Greenwich the Park &c I was highly delighted with this trip.
3 Soho Sq: Lady Darlington[45] Cleveland House
4 Prestons – Watlens Grosvenor Sq to Lady E Lowthers.[46] These were calls of Fathers of his pupils and he was so good as to take me along with him.
5 'Stodarts' 'Smarts' all Music shops
6 At home
7 Bank of England Covent Garden – *Venice Preserved. Three weeks after marriage* & *The forty thieves.*[47]
8 Sunday St Stephens Walbrook. St Sepulchres. Bow Church. Christi Hospital. A pretty fair mornings work. We heard part of the service at each and saw the Christi hospital boys sit down to dinner.[48]

43 In the performance on 31/5/1823 at Drury Lane of the comic opera *Lord of the Manor* by John Burgoyne, with music by William Jackson, the cast included John Braham (?1777–1856) as Truemore, Miss Stephens as Annette and Miss Cubitts as Sophia. *The Swiss Villagers,* which was receiving its twentieth performance, was billed as a 'New Pastoral Ballet' by Mr Noble. *Simpson & Co* was a comedy by John Poole with a cast that included Mr Terry – probably Daniel Terry (1789–1829) – and Harriet Smithson (1800–54).
44 St Pancras Church, described as 'queen of early nineteenth century churches', was built at a cost of £70,000, beginning in 1816: see John Summerson, *Georgian London*, 3rd edition (London, 1978), pp. 216–19.
45 Elizabeth, second wife of William Harry Vane, third Earl of Darlington, created first Duke of Cleveland in 1833. TGW mentions visiting Raby Castle, Co. Durham, seat of the Earl of Darlington, see Volume 5, 24/9/1827.
46 For Lowthers see note 13 above.
47 On 7/6/1823 at Covent Garden, Charles Kemble and William Charles Macready played in Thomas Otway's *Venice Preserv'd* (spelt as *Preserved* on the playbill). Kemble (1775–1854), who played the part of Jaffier, was the younger brother of the actor and manager, John Philip Kemble, and of the famous actress, Sarah Siddons. Macready (1793–1873), one of the greatest tragic actors of the period, appeared as Pierre. *Three Weeks After Marriage* was a popular comedy of the day, written by Arthur Murphy. First performed in 1764, it was receiving its first performance when TGW saw it, with Richard Jones (1779–1851) in the part of Sir Charles Racket. *The Forty Thieves*, by an unknown author, was billed as a 'melo-Dramatick Romance'.
48 Christ's Hospital was founded by Edward VI in 1552 for the maintenance and education of poor orphans. On certain Sundays the public were admitted into the dining hall '. . .to witness the ceremony. After supper an anthem is sung,

9 British Museum. I would have liked to spend as many days as I did hours in this interesting building.

10 Making a call in Piccadilly

11 St Pauls with all its curiosities but we did not make curiosities of ourselves by going into the lantern. Guildhall and its beautiful paintings. *Vauxhall* This is indeed enchanted ground. Never shall I forget these gardens.

12 Stodarts – Butchers

13 City

14 Prestons – Davis' Amphitheatre. Tom & Jerry with Crib & Spring spurring Horsemanship. Tightrope by M Longuemare and the Blood Red Knight. This is the only minor theatre I visited.[49]

15 Sunday St Pauls Covent Garden

16 House of Commons, House of Lords.[50]

17 With great regret I took leave of my friends and London in the Highflyer at 8 am and after travelling all night arrived at York next day (18 *inserted*) by 11. From thence we posted to Thirsk and two days after (20 *inserted*) regained our home at Croft.[51]

Though I had not seen all the Lions of London having omitted

---

and the boys then pass in rotation in couples before the president . . . to whom they make their bow and retire. The sight of so many children, where there is so much order preserved, some with bread baskets, others with knife baskets, table cloths &c, can surely be termed an interesting sight.' Allen, *History and Antiquities of London* (note 39 above), III, p. 556.

49 Davis's Amphitheatre was the name under which Astley's Theatre in Lambeth was operating in 1823. Astley's, which opened in 1770 and finally closed in 1893, underwent many name changes. William Davis, an equestrian performer and Manager of the New Olympic Circus in Liverpool, in 1803 entered into partnership with John Astley and leased the amphitheatre. Davis carried on after Astley's death in 1821 until 1830. The Amphitheatre was famous for its equestrian shows. *Tom and Jerry, or Life in London* was a popular burletta, adapted by William Thomas Moncrieff from Pierce Egan's book, *Life in London*. Cribb and Spring appear on the play bills as 'The Retired Champion, Cribb and his Pupil, The Present Champion, Spring, who will exhibit a Scientific Display of the Modern Art of Attack & Defence'. M. Longuemare made frequent appearances at the Amphitheatre, giving 'elegant performances' on the tightrope.

50 [*TGW footnote*] Unfortunately I heard no brilliant speeches in either house. The London Bridge question excited a few words from Mr Canning, Alderman Wood and some others and in the upper house the Lord Chancellor, Lord Londonderry &c uttered some unintelligible observations (ie to me below the bar they were inaudible).

51 The dates 18 and 20 are written in pencil above the text.

visits to the Tower, Exeter Change, Somerset Ho. &c &c we had viewed all that could reasonably be wished for in so short a time. My F & M had been here before but neither knew much of the streets or had seen many of the curiosities generally looked after by strangers. I had however cause to be very grateful for the indulgent attention which was paid to my enjoyment and gratification and returned home highly delighted with my visit and determined to shew that the kindness had been felt and should be deserved.

The second day after my arrival at Croft I returned to Mr Allison. What then took place I shall reserve for another chapter which shall be shortly produced to make up for the brevity of this.

Chapter 12 [*Magaziniana 15, 3/9/27*]

> 'Twas just before I took my first wife'
> 'Thou *taken a wife*! Ar't married?'
> 'I once was, my lord, but to no woman'
> 'What *wife* then?'
> 'A parchment wife, my lord, the lawyer acted parson'
> 'Oh ho! thou wert indentured then!'
> 'Even so, Sir' [52]

On Saturday June 28 I drank tea at Mr Bowes previous to which I had gone through the very important ceremony above alluded to – I was bound – engaged to be under the sway and in the service of a master for five whole years. My feelings on the occasion I shall not attempt to describe but those who have been in the same predicament can easily conceive them – I felt – *very queer*. Mr Bowes who knew Mr Allisons disposition better than my Father used a written and minutely drawn up form of indenture instead of the usual printed one; to endeavour to tie my master by the letter to make me comfortable should he ever be disposed to do otherwise. I read them over and these momentous papers (for there were two copies) were signed by Mr A my Father, and myself.

After I was bound however matters took a rather different aspect between my master and myself. At the end of six months, I found I was decidedly considered under-apprentice, – I had to

---

52 Unidentified source. There are several occasions in the *Diary* where apprenticeship is referred to as 'taking a wife'.

saddle, and unsaddle & feed the horse, to sweep the shop, light the fire every morning and to clean the mortars scales &c (in which my fellow shopman ought to have shared the drudgery) all by myself. The work about the horse was particularly *infra dignitate* and highly improper, for the stable was situated at the bottom of a long field and through the garden, and a man only came night and morning to look after the mare in the way of cleaning her &c. To add to all this Mr A once or twice ordered me out of the parlour and I found I was now considered an intruder there. The shop-fire was to be put out at 8 PM and we two youths were to bear the servant company in the kitchen!

I however rather remonstrated with Mr A than make any complaints to my friends, but I found this was useless and about that time my F & M began to question me very closely as to the real state of affairs. Mr Bowes, in whose family I frequently spent very pleasant evenings and where I had a general invitation, being a near neighbour of Mr Allison, had seen a little into the manner of my treatment and had spoken to my Father about it. After a good deal of deliberation it was resolved it seems that a remonstrance should be made to Mr Allison upon the subject for one afternoon I received a message from my Father, who was at Mr Bowes that day, that he wished to see Mr A and myself down there. To make a long story short as possible – after a long discussion during which Mr Allison refused to alleviate my situation at all, thinking no doubt that he had me safe, Mr Bowes took advantage of some legal informalities and by threats of a prosecution in King's bench for defrauding the stamp office obliged Mr A to quit his hold of the indentures. Mr A in his parsimoniousness, – for he was an Elwes[53] the second, had made my Father pay for the stamp of the indenture and by act of parliament that alone renders the indenture void, it being the masters duty to pay that expense. Allison again thinking he might have this to pay for had given in the fee as £98 instead of £100 to avoid the higher duty by which he rendered himself liable to the prosecution above spoken of. After deducting a fair premium for the eight months I had been with Allison, he at last consented to refund my fee and I was once more a free man.

This business kept the scandal mongers of Darlington in full

---

53 John Elwes was a famous eighteenth century miser. He is also mentioned by Charles Dickens in *Our Mutual Friend*, chapter 5.

talk for one winter; and a more gossiping place perhaps does not exist. Numerous stories were in circulation on both sides [of] the house which afforded me a high degree of amusement. One was that Mr A (this no doubt originated from himself) actually turned me off; but certain it is that he relinquished his hold of my indentures though no force but that of words was used of course – as if his very entrails had been appended to them. So much however for Mr Allison. I certainly learnt more of the rudiments of the profession with him than I would where necessity compels the tyros into active service as soon as possible; but after I was bound my masters wish for my improvement, if his *spanking* my books & c on the floor! when he caught me in the egregious crime of studying my profession can be received as proofs, was very doubtfully displayed. I saw nothing of practice of medicine but had a good drilling in compounding physic. My pocket book gives me these memor:

July	14	Began to attend the Dispensary
	29	Bled for the first time at the Dispen:
Sept	14	Mr & Mrs Allison dined at Croft and –
	17 (!)	Mr Allison ordered me out of the parlour because I 'could not read when he was talking', and bid me sit in the kitchen in future'
1824		
Feb	3	Left Mr Allison !!!'

Chapter 13 [*Magaziniana 16 in an appendix to Volume 5*][54]

A member of the Asculapian line
Lived in Newcastle upon Tyne
No man could better &c &c'

NCastle Apothecary [55]

---

54 This and the following autobiographical *Magaziniana* appear in the MS as an appendix to Volume 5. The reason for this is explained in the following note, which appears at the beginning of this Chapter: 'NB The purpose of this addition is explained in the remarks dated September 28. An index of all the biographical chapters will be given after the memoir is completed.' The remarks referred to are to the effect that, since there might be some delay before TGW could find time to begin a new diary volume, he would use his leisure time to concentrate on completing his autobiography (see Volume 5, 28/9/27). In fact he started the new Volume 6 on 11/10/27.
55 *The Newcastle Apothecary* is a poem by George Colman (1762–1836).

Upon my leaving Mr Allison another situation was of course to be looked out for me. My parents then again kindly referred it to me whether I liked to continue in the surgical profession, which, however, I had then acquired such a taste for, as would by no means allow me to think of abandoning it.

My Mother was greatly surprized on my arriving at home with my Father the night of our remonstrance with Allison; and altogether perhaps did not very cordially give her consent to what had taken place. After the first feelings of chagrin were over, however, she and my Father agreed that the best school should be enquired after, and that there, if possible, I should be fixed.

Enquiry was instituted among my Fathers friends, who kindly interested themselves in my behalf; and all agreed that Newcastle was of all others the place best calculated, on account of its surgical advantages, among the Collieries, and in the Infirmary, for initiating a young surgeon in the practice of his art.

The Infirmary surgeons were at first appealed to – Mess[rs] Moore, Baird and Smiles[56] – Leighton[57] was considered as of too old a school. None of the former however had vacancies at that precise time; and Mr Paget[58] was next applied to. He wanted an apprentice exceedingly, and laid out the domestic comforts of his establishment to the Miss Crawfords, (who obligingly undertook this office in consequence of our intimacy with Mrs Bowes) in the most enticing colors, and so as greatly to influence my Mother in his favor. Accidentally Mr McIntyre was heard of, and the advantages of his extensive colliery practice, and professional arrangements highly extolled. He was called upon. He had just taken a young man but if my friends wished it would take me in a week or two.

Mr Bowes, my Father & I came over to Newcastle for the purpose of *seeing* these two gentlemen, and deciding the matter. Of course neither knew the other had been applied to, or were acquainted with even my name. We called first upon Mr McIn-

---

56 The Infirmary doctors are mentioned again in Volume 5, 7/8/27, see also Volume 5, note 11.

57 Thomas Leighton (1762–1846) was a surgeon in Newcastle. For an account of the experiences of a pupil of Leighton, see D. Embleton, 'Biographical Notices of Members of the Philosophical & Medical Society of Newcastle 100 Years Ago', in *Proceedings of the Northumberland and Durham Medical Society*, Session 1890–91, pp. 178–210.

58 Probably John Stevenson Paget, 1 Saville Row, Newcastle; see PW, I, p. 125.

tyre, and were so sensible of the superiority of his situation that without further trouble it was agreed that I should be bound to him that afternoon. The choice rested thus; *Mr Paget* promised comforts in the house; and introduction into all the society he visited – the first circles in Newcastle. I was, in consequence of being 8 months with a surgeon, to be placed in a higher rank than one he had just taken, who was a complete tyro. *Mr McIntyre's* plans were that I should be on a footing of equality with a youth who had been with him about six weeks; that in rotation I should enjoy the privileges usual in his surgery *viz.* that of going to attend lectures one session during my term with him, and after that of becoming *bona fide* his assistant in the full practice of his ten collieries, (one has since been added); with, of course, the frequent benefit of his observations and instruction. As my aim was *professional* improvement I was very glad to find my F & Mr Bowes so readily coincide with me in thinking it best to relinquish the *rather* superior advantages of Mr Pagets domestic & social arrangements, for Mr McIntyre's extensive and rare opportunities. To Mr. McI then I was indentured as *'House Pupil'*; and the fee of £150 changed owners.

I found his establishment, for, – after being at home for ten days to *make ready*, I immediately joined my regiment, and took my station, – very comfortable, but as regarded those of the young men whom I then saw nothing very intellectual. *Mr Hobson*, had been too gay, and was paying the forfeit of irregularity with his life; he was the senior apprentice in the surgery, though one was then in London attending his stated course of lectures. *Mr Cochrane*, a Scotch ill-educated surgeon, had just been engaged as assistant to reside about 8 miles off (Backworth), and attended to the four collieries in that neighborhood. And lastly Mr King, – son of a Hexham draper, whose parents being very parsimonious had miserably neglected his school education, and who by placing him with a surgeon consulted not his inclination and certainly not his advantage. He was to be my compeer! Such indeed are the private portraits of two thirds of the surgical profession of the present day!

Chapter 14 [*Magaziniana 17, in appendix to Vol. 5*]

'Well, well, the world must turn upon its axis,
And all mankind turn with it heads or tails;

> And live and die, – make love, and pay our taxes,
> And, as the veering wind shifts, – shift our sails'
> Don Juan [*Byron, Canto I verse IV*]

This last change of my destiny was certainly a sudden and unlooked for one; but new prospects and new views had opened out, and these were to be made the most of. All has eventually been greatly to my advantage; and, for events that at one time seemed untoward, I have now reason to be highly thankful.

Not long after my settling in Mr McIntyres establishment an event occurred which, though deplorable and melancholy in itself, tended in no slight degree to advance my interests in the surgery. Mr Hobson whom I have mentioned as being in a weak state of health – *died*. This youth had fastened upon me with great friendship from my first going, and having no friends near that looked after him (he was from Maidstone) I was a good deal with him during his last three weeks illness and he expired as I was supporting him. This was the first instance of death I had seen, and the scene affected me much.

Poor Hobson's removal, however, threw me a great deal more forward than I should otherwise have been; I had to fill his place. After this Mr McIntyre, though King and I were *nominally* upon equal footing, paid me such attentions as in a very agreeable manner shewed me he considered me, as he ought to do, somewhat superior to my companion.

For dates and memoranda we shall again refer to note book

1824

March	19	Bound to Mr McIntyre
April	6	Arrived at Newcastle to join him
May	7	Mr Hobson died
	18	My first journey on horseback to Benwell to dress a patient who had been severely burnt
Aug	26	First visit with Mr McI to dress a severe compd fracture
Sept	10	Was present at post mortem examination. Never *flinched* or felt *sick*
Oct	6 – 8	Newcastle Musical Festival. I attended the evening concert, and heard 'the Messiah' in the

church. Was highly delighted with the performance.[59]

Nov   8   Mother staid a week at Ncastle

1825

Jan   30   Father came & staid two days

March 29   F & M staid a fortnight at NC

May   18   Called upon Sir RS Hawks![60]

June   2   Called upon and was introduced to Mr Turner Sec:
            Lit: & Phil: Soc:[61]

Aug   Was weighed at the beginning of this month in
            shoes &c 9st 2lbs

Sept   11   Went to Croft where after staying two days I
            proceeded on a visit to my friends at Thirsk. This
            being Yorksh: festival week I formed one of a
            party to that City on the most engaging day the
            15th. I was 'highly delighted' with the perform-
            ances at Newcastle last year where 120 musicians
            were engaged. I do not know how I shall find
            terms to express the rapture I felt on listening to
            the exertions of the *600* employed at York. We
            returned to Thirsk the same night, and I
            remained there till the 20th, when I returned to
            NC in the prospect of leaving that place again in
            a few weeks on a longer absence and very much
            gratified with my present holiday.

I omitted mentioning that about four months after I became
one of Mr McI's establishment, the member who had been absent
in London joined us, and formed a worthy and agreeable addition to our number.[62] Mr John Gibson (a son of Mr Gibson,

---

59 This was advertised as 'Grand Music Festival 1824, Friday Morning 8 October
    at St Nicholas Church, Handel's Sacred Oratorio The Messiah'. The conductor
    was Sir George Smart. For a poster advertising the performance, see Wilson 48.

60 Sir Robert Shafto Hawks was a wealthy industrialist, one of the owners of
    Messrs Hawks, Crawshay and Company, iron manufacturers.

61 The Reverend William Turner (1763–1859) was Minister of the Unitarian con-
    gregation in Hanover Square Chapel, Newcastle from 1783. He was the
    founder of the Literary and Philosophical Society and of many other institu-
    tions in Newcastle. He was appointed Lecturer to the New Institution in 1802.
    See Introduction, also Stephen Harbottle, *The Reverend William Turner: Dissent
    and Reform in Georgian Newcastle upon Tyne* (Leeds, 1997).

62 [*TGW footnote*] Two more have since come W Greenwood & T Hunter.

Wholesale Druggist in Ncastle[63]) was this senior apprentice, or as he was now to be styled *assistant*. He was of a rather intellectual standing, and had paid very diligent attention to his professional pursuits. Though the *dignity* usually kept up among the senior grades of *us* pupils would not allow him to be very intimate with a junior *in general*, he cultivated my friendship closely; and I found him on the whole a very pleasant companion, and one to whose attention and observation on medical subjects I gladly acknowledge myself indebted.

Cochrane I never was on social terms with, nor was Gibson to a greater extent than civility required. He left NCastle to reside in the house and establishment Mr McI had formed at Backworth a few weeks after Mr Gibson joined us, and all remained very comfortable until I went to Edinburgh.

The time was now arrived when Mr Hobson, had he lived, would have taken his term of attending at the Medical Schools of London or Edinburgh. Mr McI proposed the same advantage to me and my Father & Mother approving his offer was accepted.[64]

Edinburgh was advised by Mr McI and other professional friends as the best *elementary* school. Edinburgh therefore was fixed on. My arrival there and the occurrences of the session will form the subject of next chapter.

Chapter 15 [*Magaziniana 18, in an appendix to Diary Vol. 5*]

'Modern Athens' !

After a long and tedious day of travelling[65] by Morpeth, Cold-stream, Flodden, Black shiel &c I arrived about midnight at the Black-bull Hotel Leith walk in this far-famed Scottish metropolis. All the beds at this inn were engaged so I, for the first time my own *governor* in this great city, and at this dread hour had to seek out for other accommodation. Luckily a 'third year student' had been my companion in the coach, and, along with two young military officers, we were soon seated by a good fire at McKays – 17 Princes Street. The *'cadie'* had the affrontery to charge me 1/6 for carrying my portmanteau and a trunk that short distance to

63 See Introduction, note 37.
64 A few lines are crossed out here; the original is not legible.
65 The 'Wellington' coach from Newcastle to Edinburgh via Coldstream was scheduled to leave at 6 am and arrive at 10 pm: see PW, I, p. 133.

which imposition I was obliged to submit. After a light supper and a good glass of *negus* our party all retired in fit humour for a sound sleep.

Next morning, having made up for coach meal deficiencies by an enormous breakfast, Mr Duff (the student) and I walked out to see a little of the new town and to proceed to the College. I had previously studied the ground plan and plates in 'Starks picture of Edinburgh'[66] so as to have a tolerable knowledge of the bearings and appearance of the principal streets and buildings and I was delighted to find myself quite at home – among old acquaintances as it were, whilst traversing the noble causeways of this 'gude town'.

After glancing at the college I went to seek out an old school fellow, son of a leading quaker family in Edinburgh, and who had described their residence to me when at school. I soon found him out and in this family met with such kindness, – such real and hospitable friendship, as I never before experienced, and I shall never cease most gratefully to hold in remembrance. Mrs Cruickshank (the lady's name) immediately interested herself about my getting comfortable lodgings and sought among her friends and thro' personal applications the whole of that day and the next to procure such for me. I dined at Meadowside (their residence) that day, and drank tea the next. As it is impossible for me to express in appropriate language my sense of Mr & Mrs C's (and indeed the whole family) attentions to me during my visit, I will let the subject rest; merely stating that under a dangerous illness their attentions were those of the kindest parents, and in every way such as could be most gratifying to my feelings. In these sentiments imperfectly as they are stated my parents, who were in Edinburgh during part of my stay there, will, I am sure, perfectly concur.

Mrs C not being able to procure apartments that she liked for me amongst those she knew, or which were recommended, I set out on Thursday morning to hunt out for myself, and soon found some which I liked extremely well. As my F & M were intending to join me about Christmas I engaged lodgings rather more expensive than would have been warrantable had I sought for a

---

66 *The Picture of Edinburgh* by John Stark, a guide book containing a description of the city and its environs, was first published in 1806 with several later editions. TGW may have used the 4th edition (Edinburgh and London, 1825).

domicile merely for myself. The rooms I took were on a first floor, a large handsomely furnished sitting room, with a closet bed adjoining, and a small bedroom, with a large four-post bed in it. The situation was a handsome new street within sight and two minutes walk of the College. I closed accounts at the Hotel put my luggage and *myself* into a hackney coach, and in a short time was comfortable settled in No 30 Lothian Street.[67]

My agreeable sensations on sitting down to tea after having unpacked and appropriated my wardrobe &c; and, after three days incessant anxiety and uncertainty, to be now in my own house (as it were) and for the first time in my life completely and independently my own master, (for a few weeks at least,) can only be imagined by those similarly situated.

I had attended lectures the previous day; but the 'general fast' which commenced on this day, put a stop to all further business till the following Tuesday.[68]

I now had leisure for consideration as to what lectures to attend. Mr McIntyre had given me letters of introduction to Mr Lizars and Mr Liston as lecturers whom I should probably attend but of course these were only to be delivered conditionally. Mr McI was so good as to give me also a private introduction to Dr Campbell, one of the surgeons to the Infirmary. My F had other introductions offered for me, but, with the exception of one, I took only the above, – business was to be my exclusive object. Mr Lizars letter I never delivered as I did not attend his class; the rest I found all conducive to my advantage either social or professional.[69]

---

67 Lothian Street is within a few minutes walk from the University. Coincidentally, Charles Darwin and his brother Erasmus, who arrived in Edinburgh to study medicine in late October 1825, lodged at 11 Lothian Street, renting 2 bedrooms and a sitting room from a Mrs Mackay for 26 shillings a week: see Adrian Desmond and James Moore, *Darwin* (London, 1992), p. 22. The side of Lothian Street that included no. 30 has now been demolished for road extensions.

68 It has not been possible to obtain any information about this 'general fast' which, according to the *Diary*, ran from Friday, 4/11/1825 through Monday, 7/11/1825.

69 For a description of the organisation of the medical teaching in Edinburgh University and in the extra-mural schools see Lisa Rosner, *Medical Education in the Age of Improvement: Edinburgh Students and Apprentices 1760–1826* (Edinburgh, 1991); Isobel Rae, *Knox the Anatomist* (Edinburgh and London, 1964); J. A. Shepherd, *Simpson and Syme of Edinburgh* (Edinburgh and London,

On the morning of my first calling at Mrs Cruickshanks I accidentally met Dr Knox (partner and successor to the eminent Dr Barclay).[70] Dr K was on a visit to his patient & friend my old schoolfellow Edward. A few days afterwards I again had the opportunity of conversing with Dr Knox and subsequently I attended his lectures and dissecting room. This was the origin of a friendship of a most agreeable nature which on the Doctor's part was especially manifested during my severe illness before spoken of. He was so good as visit me *four* or *five* times a day during the most critical period and his after attention during the time my F & M were with me were sources of happiness to us all. I am happy to add that I have, since I left Edinburgh, received flattering proofs of being still in his remembrance.

Chapter 16 [*Magaziniana 19, in an appendix to Vol. 51*]

'Then forward they March
This the principal arch
The first time they had been at College

Lapsus Linguae[71]

You may imagine, gentle reader, my picture when, as *large as life*, I stalked out of the library with my matriculation ticket in my hand wh[ich] cons[ti]tuted me '*Civis Bibliotheca Academiae Edinensis*' – Member of the University of Edinburgh!!
But my dates will convey the most brief and concise idea of my proceedings.

1969). Biographical information on many of the teachers mentioned by TGW can be found in John D. Comrie, *History of Scottish Medicine*, 2nd edition (London, 1932).

70 Dr Robert Knox, at the time TGW met him, was 35 years old and an eminent anatomist, having studied in Edinburgh, London and Paris. He had served as a Medical Officer in the Army before returning in 1820 to Edinburgh, where he carried out and published highly respected anatomical studies. In 1825, Knox was appointed as successor to Dr John Barclay in the successful extramural school of anatomy that Barclay had established in 1804. Robert Knox was famed for his lectures, which were presented without notes: see Rae, *Knox the Anatomist*, and Shepherd, *Simpson and Syme* (both cited in note 69 above), and Andrew S. Currie, 'Robert Knox, Anatomist, Scientist and Martyr', in Zachary Cope (ed.), *Sidelights on the History of Medicine* (London, 1957), chapter 19. For later comments on Knox by TGW see Volume 11, 24/3/29 and Addenda.

71 *The New Lapsus Linguae, or, the College Tatler*, was a student publication in Edinburgh University in the 1820s.

Oct 31, 1825 Left Newcastle at 5 AM and arrived in the Scottish metropolis at 11 PM.

Nov	1	At McKays Hotel 16 Princes St.
	2	Heard lectures from Drs Hope & Barclay[72] and Mr Liston. Matriculated
	3	Got into lodgings 30 Lothian Street
	4	Called upon Dr Campbell
Nov	5	Breakfasted with Dr C. and was intr: to Mr Smith son of Dr Smith of Newcastle, and then a student. This youth is since dead in London. Drank tea at Mrs Gillans – the family of a quondam tutor of mine at Mr Smith's.
	6	Went thro' the wards of the Royal Infirmary – St Peter's Chapel[73]
	7	Called at Mrs Cruickshanks. Took a drive with Mr Edwd to see the aquaduct of the Glasgow canal at Slateford about 4 miles from Edin:
	8	Lectures recommenced. Attended today Drs Hope & Monro, Mr Lizars, Liston & Thompson. Called upon and took a ticket of Dr Hope.
	9	Heard Dr Knox & Mr Liston
	10	Attended Dr Knox & Mr Liston
	14	Took tickets from Drs Knox & Thompson and Mr Liston.

My teachers were therefore fixed upon and I continued regularly to attend Dr Hope Professor of Chemistry, Dr Knox's lectures on Anatomy &c and his dissecting rooms; Mr Liston's lectures on Surgery; and Dr Thompson on Practice of Physic. Dr Knox was so good as to invite me to attend his evening class (in addition to the morning) if I had the leisure, which polite offer I frequently availed myself of.

The following was the routine of my studies as fixed by a paper I still have, and to which I scrupulously adhered so long as I was

---

72 Barclay (see note 70 above) retired after giving only one lecture in the 1825–6 session, and died in 1826; it would appear that TGW attended this last lecture by Barclay.

73 The Royal Infirmary of Edinburgh first opened in 1741. The original building was demolished in 1879.

by myself, and afterwards as much as attention to my F & M would allow. Rise at $\frac{1}{4}$ bef: 8; Study Chemistry $8\frac{1}{2}$ Walk till 9; Breakfast till $\frac{1}{2}$ p: 9; Dr Hopes $\frac{1}{4}$ bef 10; Dr Knox 11; Dissecting room 12 to 2; Mr Liston 2; Dine $\frac{1}{2}$ p: 3; Write lectures till 5; Classics study &c 6; Surgery, Anatomy & Physic alternately till $\frac{1}{4}$ to 7; if I did not attend Dr Knox evening class at 6; Dr Thompson till 8 (from 7); Drink tea and copy Dr T's lecture after which Flute or other recreation till I chose to go to bed generally about 11.

The hour for classics &c was Monday Latin; Tuesday Greek; Wednesday Euclid; Thursday French; Friday Algebra. Saturday unlimited as regards rules; the lecturers some having holiday on that day others not. With regard to taking notes – I adopted a plan which required a good deal of labour, but which I found by far the most advantageous *viz*: that of mostly taking heads of subjects &c into a little *thumb book* in the lecture room, and afterwards writing out at home as much of the lecture as I thought important and could recollect. These being bound up now form useful references.

But to continue extracts from '*mem:*'

Nov	15	Began dissection. A Head. Called upon Mr Campbell Pitt the other introduction I mentioned.
	19	Dined at Mrs Cruickshanks
	21	Breakfasted with Mr Campbell
Dec	14	Mother arrived in Edinburgh
	24	Went to the Theatre[74] to see Mr Matthews in his Trip to America and Jonathan in E. I was highly gratified with Mr M.[75]

---

74 The theatre in Shakespeare Square, Edinburgh, was first opened in 1769, and had undergone several reconstructions and name changes before becoming the Theatre Royal after a visit by George IV in 1822. In 1825, it was under the management of W. H. Murray, brother-in-law of Henry Siddon, who acquired the first patent in 1809. It survived until 1830. See James C. Dibdin, *The Annals of the Edinburgh Stage* (Edinburgh, 1888), pp. 151 ff.

75 A visit of the popular actor Charles Mathews (not Matthews as written by TGW) was an important event for the Edinburgh theatre in December 1825: see Dibdin, *Annals* (note 74 above), p. 315. Mathews, a brilliant mimic, was known particularly for his one-man shows, called 'At Homes', with which he toured the provinces for many years, starting about 1815: see Jim Davis, *John Liston, Comedian* (London, 1985), pp. 29ff. The performance seen by TGW was advertised as ' . . . a celebrated entertainment called *A Trip to America*, after

26   Father joined us
28   Theatre trip to Paris & Bashful Man.[76] I had never seen Mr Matthews before and Mother & I being both partial to the drama caused us frequently to visit at $\frac{1}{2}$ play (i.e. after my lectures were over for the day) this delightful and unjustly appreciated little Theatre.
31   Spent the evening at Mrs Cruickshanks to meet Dr Knox, Dr Green & Mr Burn

1826
Jan   1   Dined with Dr Knox. Mr Lizars invited to meet me; but was professionally prevented joining us. Dr Howison came to tea. All lecturers!
       3   Recommenced lectures after a 10 days vacation
Jan   7   Supped with Mr Liston. 6 more of his class formed the party
Jan   14   Skating at Duddingston loch.[77] This was perhaps the most imposing scene I ever witnessed. 10000 people were present upon an average the whole day; hundreds of the beauty and fashion of Edinburgh in gay attire, the skating club, the curling clubs, and three bands of military music were present. I had got a pair of new skates and enjoyed the exercise the first I had the opportunity of taking for four years and of which I am particularly fond, – extremely. Here I caught the cold which, with over exertion and other causes, brought on the dangerous illness I had.
       15   St Pauls Chapel, York Place.[78]
       17   Taken ill and was laid up by a bilious attack, which was followed by *Enteritis*. Typhoid fever accompanying my complaint my strength was reduced till I was not able to stand unsupported and Dr Knox has since confessed he at one time despaired of my life being saved. Through his care and my

which the new Farce called *Jonathan in England. . .*': see *Edinburgh Evening Courant*, 26/12/1825, p. 3.
76 Presumably sketches by Mathews (note 75 above).
77 Duddingston Loch is in Holyrood Park, Edinburgh.
78 Now called St Paul and St George Church, built 1816–18: see *BSE*, p. 280.

Mother & Fathers excellent nursing I recovered so far as to be lifted into a chaise on Feb 11, and taken to *Lasswade* about 6 miles from Edinburgh. Here I stayed four days the balmy air being so beneficial to me that on the Monday we left I was able to walk two miles!

Feb 20   Resumed attendance at classes

24   Attended one of a set of concerts to wh[ich] F & M were subscribers with Father

Mar 1   Theatre Paul Pry – 'Twas I, Cramond Brig.[79]

4   Leith Pier

5   St Johns (Bp Sandford Chapel)[80]

9   Holyrood Ho: Chapel & curiosities

11   Took a trip with F & M to Glasgow after morning lecture (Saturday). Got to the Black Bull in time for $\frac{1}{2}$ play at the Theatre and saw H Johnstone in Rob: Roy and Rugantino

12   To Episcopal Chapel[81] , called upon Mr W Cowan[82] once a tutor or rather professor at Darlington; now a master in the high school here.

Chapter 17 Conclusion [*Magaziniana 20, in appendix to Vol. 5*]
Last scenes of all – which *close* this *queer* eventful history[83] – Chapter after chapter presents itself and still the memoir is unfinished; however *by my pen I swear* a conclusion shall and must now be made; though this chapter should be a long one it is to be the last. To continue then in Glasgow.

---

79 Of these plays, all frequently performed in Edinburgh in the 1820s, the best known is *Paul Pry*, a comedy by John Poole. This was one of the greatest hits of the age, first performed on 13/9/1825 at the Haymarket Theatre, London, with John Liston in the title rôle: see Davis, *John Liston* (note 75 above), pp. 56 ff. The first Edinburgh production was on 21/11/1825, with William Murray as Paul Pry, and it was performed 28 times that season: Dibdin, *Annals* (note 74 above), p. 313.

80 St Johns chapel, in Princes Street, was built 1815–18, the cost being raised by Bishop Sandford: see *BSE*, p. 277.

81 St Johns (note 80 above).

82 See chapter 8.

83 This is based on the end of Jaques' speech in Shakespeare's *As You Like It*, Act 2, Scene 7: 'Last scene of all,/ That ends this strange, eventful history. . .' (cf. the quotation at the end of chapter 2 above).

Mar	13	Breakfasted with Mr Cowan. Inspected a spinning & weaving mill. The Hunterian museum & the Cathedral. Returned to Edinburgh.
	18	Newhaven[84]
	21	Theatre. C Kemble (Criticisms on these performances are more than time and space will allow) Bold Stroke for a Wife, 'Twas I, King Charles 2nd or Merry Monarch.[85]
	23	Went to see the Royal Exhibition of Paintings at the New Building called the 'School of Arts' on the Mound.[86]
	27	Called with Father at Mr Withams; a family from Durham where he once taught the young ladies.
	28	Father left Edinburgh.
	29	Theatre. Jane Shore. Catherine & Petruchio & Cramond Brig. C Kemble, Vandenhoff and Mrs H Siddons played in the first.[87]
	31	Professional Society Concert.
Apr	6	Caledonian Theatre $\frac{1}{2}$ price.[88]
	9	Berryblow & St Georges churches.[89]
	13	Spent an exceedingly pleasant evening at a ball at Dr Campbells.
	19	Arthurs seat. Salisbury [Chaise]
	21	Drank tea at Mrs Cruickshanks.
	22	Walked by Roslin to Lasswade &c

84 Newhaven: a village near Edinburgh. Its harbour dates from the sixteenth century: see *BSE*, p. 602.
85 The plays mentioned by TGW were amongst those performed that season by the famous actor Charles Kemble (note 47 above). Kemble's visit to Edinburgh, 'for 12 nights only', began on 20/3/1826: see *Edinburgh Evening Courant*, 20/3/1825, p. 3.
86 Probably the Royal Society of Arts, originally built 1822–26: see *BSE*, p. 309.
87 Mrs Sarah Siddons is mentioned in note 47 above.
88 The Caledonian Theatre, Edinburgh, was first erected for equestrian performances and, after being fitted out by Stephen Kemble as a theatre, it was converted to a place of worship. In 1822, it began to be used as a minor theatre 'for the performance of such pieces as are not protected by the patent of the regular theatre': John Stark, *Picture of Edinburgh*, 4th edition (Edinburgh, 1825), p. 269.
89 Probably St George Episcopal Church, York Place, Edinburgh: see *BSE*, p. 277.

23   Dined with Dr Knox met Dr Bogie and Miss Clarke (a very pretty lassie) Dr Knox, Dr Thompson and Mr Liston had now finished after lecturing twice a day for ten days past; Dr Hope was to conclude in a day or two.

25   University museum

Apr   26   Made farewell calls upon all my friends, and, on the

27   following morning left Edinburgh with my Mother at 5 AM. The day was very unfavorable and a heavy fall of snow at night made our journey anything but pleasant. We came by Berwick &c. I cannot travel inside and my Mother wished to be by my side so we encountered all the brunt of the storm.

28   After staying all night at Newcastle (the Turf Hotel) I called at Mr McIntyre.

Mr McI had seen me twice while in Edinburgh and finding my health a good deal broken up by application and illness, had taken an assistant for six months and very obligingly given me leave to *rusticate*, and as he said 'grow fat upon Yorkshire puddings', during the summer, and till *Bewicke* (who by a strange coincidence was again in my way being engaged (tho very unfit for the office to fill my place,) had left him. We then proceeded to Seaton[90] where I soon recruited strength, though it was rather an early season for the seaside.

My sister and her family had long talked about coming into the north; and at last fixed upon paying us a visit this summer. In consequence we left Seaton on the 27 May to return to our *home* at Croft. On the 29th June I went down to Stockton to await the coming in of the vessel having on board my sister, and her accompaniment of children, nurses and luggage. After staying there three days, a vessel hove in sight, bound for the Tees; I went down with a steam boat to tow her up; but lo! it was the wrong vessel. We waited at the Tees mouth till it was supposed no other vessels could come in that tide, and I returned to Stockton and to Croft. Next morning my sister arrived the ship having

90 Probably Seaton Carew, Co. Durham.

come into the bay (upon comparing accounts, we found) not above a quarter of an hour after we left the river mouth the day before! They were all safe, however, so I for one sang 'alls well'.

The days passed pleasantly and quickly during my stay with our visitors at Croft. Mr McIntyre had written to say I need be in no hurry about rejoining him, he would write when he wanted me; so I had nothing to do but to enjoy myself and 'make myself agreeable'.

During this happy time the following 'mem:' occur:

July	2	Mrs Green and family arrived at Croft
	18	Called and spent the afternoon at Dr Sherwoods – Snow Hall[91]
	20	Went with sister to Thirsk
	23	Spent the day at Mr Fowles, Ottington
	25	At Carlton – fishing
	26	Returned from Thirsk
Aug	10	Drank tea at Mr Bowes to meet Col: Gilmore[92] from Newcastle
	12	Accompanied Father to Rokeby
	16	Received a summons to Ncastle

Mr Green had made a tour by Edinburgh Glasgow &c, and I was to join him at the lakes in Cumberland the 17 of this month, whence we both were to return to Croft about the 22nd, but as Mr McIntyre had been so obliging in allowing me a long holiday, I determined immediately to obey his summons, though he still did not fix a day for my return to business. Bewicke was to leave him on the Thursday, and therefore, taking that day to make preparations, on *Friday the 18* I returned to Newcastle. On the 28 Mr Green followed me to Newcastle and spent two days there to see 'the Lions' [*i.e., to see the sights*] and to allow me the pleasure of seeing him. Little else of importance took place during the following month, and on October 1st I began this Diary!

For what took place after this period my 'Diary' will afford in some instances but too minute a record; and now, therefore,

---

91 Snow Hall is near the River Tees, about 7 miles west of Darlington. TGW mentions another visit there in 1827: see Volume 5, 24/9/1827.

92 Colonel Gillmore (always mis-spelt Gilmore by TGW) was Barrack Master at Fenham Barracks, Newcastle, and lived at Elswick Cottage: see PW, I, p. 35.

gentle reader, I have completed my task. Though numerous omissions have been made, and the whole has been very hastily compiled, I am sure my friends will excuse its imperfections, which may be easily corrected and amended. Here then I take my leave with my best and most engaging bow. Such as they are you have before you a brief sketch of the juvenile reminiscences and if not exactly the last dying speech, at any rate the birth, parentage, and education of

T: G: WRIGHT CBAE
MLPSN, ASC, PSPNI
EFLGS, PPPF, &c, &c[93]

---

93 The last three lines, which appear to have been printed using a rubber stamp, are on piece of paper, pasted onto the MS page and scribbled over in pencil. MLPSN is Member of the Literary and Philosophical Society of Newcastle, the significance of the other 'qualifications' is not known, but see TGW's comment in Volume 5, 1/8/1827 and 3/8/1827.

RIDES IN THE COUNTRY

[*The three chapters of this essay are Magazinianas nos. 22, 23 and 25 in Volume 6, 4/1/28, 25/4/28 and 25/5/28, respectively.*]

Chapter 1

> Next morning early – rose,
> And to the patient's house he goes
> Upon his pad,
> Who a vile trick of stumbling had,
> It was indeed a very sorry hack;
> But that's of course,
> For what's expected of a horse,
> With an apothecary on his back!'

Colman[1]

The whimsicalities in character manners and appearances to be met with in the medical profession have always appeared to me as a wide field in which extensive funds of amusement might be culled; and one which has hitherto been little trodden. To the observer of men & manners such a scope would be invaluable; for who gains so keen an insight into private character as the medical attendant? Or what professions are more likely to meet with oddities in all grades of life. A class of amusive light works of this kind would supply a desideratum in the profession by forming a library in which the professional student might wile a tedious hour without altogether neglecting his peculiar subjects of study.

Mr Wadd's Mems Maxims & Memoirs and a work (The Gold headed cane) reviewed in this Jan^r Ed^n. of the Medico-Chirurgical Journal are the only volumes I am acquainted with of this caste. When speaking of the above subject I was once told that a work entitled 'the Medical Sketch book' was in print; but had its merits been great, fame would have spoken more extensively of its pub-

---

1 From *The Newcastle Apothecary*, George Colman (1762–1836): see 'My Autobiography', note 55.

lication.[2] The title is exactly suited to the kind of compilation I wish to see got up by some able hand.

In my own humble way I shall attempt a description of one or two of my rides among patients, embodying perhaps in one ride what occurred at different periods during my rounds among the pitmen.

The picture of a 'doctor' on horseback is generally held up as companion for that of a tailor; and Mr Colman has in the passage quoted contributed largely to the prevalence of this idea. Now though there be many & glaring exceptions to the rule I must acknowledge that professional men in general are far from bearing in their figure an impression that the saddle is their element, nor are they more likely to be mistaken for centaurs. The supposition runs that medical men feed their steeds with their own physic and hence the meagre limbs and lean sides of the horse always form prominent features in the portrait. I *have* seen a country surgeon whose mounting and departure on a night journey would afford an excellent subject for the pen & pencil of a Cruickshank a Hood or a Smith,[3] but alas! I am none of these and should only spoil the canvass.

'Twas one morn when the wind from the northward blew keenly' that I received orders to mount horse and away to see my usual round of patients on that well-known, hard-beaten, straightforward picturesque road – the road to Shields &c from the goodly town of Newcastle upon Tyne. Of course like

>'Obedient Gamen
>Answered Amen
>And did
>And I was bid'

The weather though cloudy and dull was not positively rainy and

---

2 Two of the books referred to are *Mems. Maxims and Memoirs* (London, in 1827) by William Wadd (1776–1829), and *The Gold-Headed Cane* by William Mac-Michael, MD, first published in London in 1827. The latter is an anecdotal account of some of the experiences of celebrated physicians, written as an autobiography of the gold-headed cane, a symbol of office, which was handed down to successive holders of the office of the President of the Royal Society of Physicians, starting in the seventeenth century. The 'Medical Sketch book' has not been identified.
3 George Cruikshank (1792–1878) was a well-known English illustrator and caricaturist. Hood and Smith have not been identified.

following the example of Dr Syntax in search of the Picturesque[4] I was disposed to sentimentalize on all I met with.

After riding down street, past St Nicholas[5] remarkable pile and descending Dean Street my attention was excited by the delightful harmony of human voices issuing from that classic building lately made a conspicuous ornament of the Moot Hall and yclept [*i.e. called*] the Fish Market. The fine forms & pleasant countenances in all aspects of 'the human face divine' with the polite language, refined accent, delicate phraseonomy and pleasing address here introduced make this part of 'our gude town' 'highly deserving a visit from the admirer of nature', a subject supremely picturesque & sentimental and rivalled only by the proud majesty of Billingsgate!

The Quayside of any commercial town is a field more calculated to excite pleasurable sensation in the mind of the traveller or the mechanichian than the sentimentalist. The surgeon & physician however may frequently view the bales in the process of being unshipped which contain quantities of physic under importation sufficient to kill or cure (as chance may direct their use or abuse) whole nations – carrying renewed life and destruction under the same cover, the produce perhaps of some tree. To trace the fate of a particular piece of gum, wood or bark from its first being plucked from its parent plant in some foreign clime to its destination as chance may direct it to the elegant draught of some fair delicate damsel or the homely bolus of the less dainty patient. A similar reflection with regard to a more agreeable viand often occupies my thoughts as I pass in review the piles of chests containing oranges to serve the community from the prince to the beggar.

Paper & patience being exhausted though materials may become more abundant as we advance, I shall conduct the reader forward on our ride the first opportunity.

Chapter 2

Sit mihi fas spectata loqui   Virgil
What I have seen permit me to relate

---

4 Probably a reference to *Doctor Syntax's Three Tours: in Search of the Picturesque, of Consolation and of a Wife*, by William Combe (1741–1823), first published about 1823 in London and often reprinted.
5 St Nicholas Church, now the Cathedral of Newcastle upon Tyne.

To resume my journey along the quayside where I was moraliz-
ing on the tar barrels and sweeties there deposited in the wholesale abundance. I will not further notice them barely to mention
one comfort in *riding* along the quay in contradistinction to *walking* thereon, *viz* the comfort of being relieved from the incessant
and rude importunities of those Mercurys of the district the
Shields gigmen, who should you be in the latter predicament
annoy you at every step with 'Going down to Shields sir!' 'Going
down sir?' – 'I'll go with you directly sir?' 'I've two passengers
&c' 'fresh horse sir!' &c &c.

On turning up to the left from the west end of the Quay I pass
the end of Sandgate, the old entrance to the town and the worse
than St Giles of Newcastle. I have passed the place occasionally
during the night and the scene was beyond any thing Pierce
Egan[6] ever depicted in the Black Houses or All Max East.

Passing the Keelmen's Hospital[7] and the Royal Jubilee school[8]
we come upon the veritable Shields road which barring and
excepting a preterparticularly considerable thick eight-inch
covering of mud in winter, and an impenetrable cloud of *stour*
[*i.e. dust*] in Summer, is a very delightful piece of turnpike. Here
then we go a jog trot to Ouseburn a sort of outskirt Village where
your every faculty is put in instant requisition. After crossing the
bridge your nose is assailed by a combination of all the odours
that can render smell disagreeable, and till your taste shares the
sensation. A steam mill and iron foundry vapour on the one hand
and lime kilns on the other, with a tripe shop in the van and a
general receptacle for manure at the rear, all lend their aid toward
this delectable perfume. Nor do your ears enjoy a greater repose;

---

6 Pierce Egan (1772–1849), a successful sports writer, in the 1820s wrote and
  published in instalments *Life in London* which depicted scenes of high and
  low life, illustrated with drawings by George Cruikshank (see note 3 above),
  engraved in hand-coloured aquatint. The work became very popular and successful, with many imitators, and was adapted for the stage as *Tom & Jerry;
  or, Life in London*.
7 The Keelmen's Hospital, overlooking the suburb of Sandgate, was erected in
  1701 at their own expense by the keelmen, who operated the keels, i.e., the
  lighters used to transport coal down the River Tyne to ships at the river
  mouth.
8 The Royal Jubilee School, dedicated to the education of poor children, was
  opened in 1810 to commemorate the fiftieth year of the reign of King George
  III.

the combined powers of a dozen or two of hammers upon the melodious tones of a steam engine boilers from three forges *in close contiguity* afford a delicious & harmonious treat while the unchapelled, crowded burial ground,[9] backed and shaded by a well-controlled pit heap rising like a mountain in the distance and flanked by a high row of houses with not the most seemly habiliments hanging from the anything-but glazed windows, present a picture equally agreeable to the eye.

Ten to one but your horse takes fright at one or other of these phenomena and then you are kept floundering so much longer in the complication of misfortunes.

Some troubles one may escape from but this is one which must be endured. One may shut his eyes but at the peril of running over some unlucky passenger or being himself capsized. The ear and the nose one cannot guard.

> The eye it cannot chuse but see
> We cannot bid the ear be still
> Our bodies feel where'er they be
> Against or with our will
>
> Wordsworth[10]

Escaping however up the bank as speedily as fate will permit I pass the turnpike gate where one is sure on paying his three half-pence to receive a smile from the damsel who attends. On arriving at this point I enter my colliery district by coming to Heaton domain. It extends from this point about 2 miles north – $1\frac{1}{2}$ east and half a mile south; and upon it are two pits in full work and three at present unemployed.

The pitmens' houses are generally built in long rows of two houses in breadth each containing one room a garret and a pantry. The overmen and those who have large families or who are favorites may obtain two rooms, perhaps three, as some of the houses are so built for the purpose. These are furnished

---

9 [*TGW footnote*] This burial ground has since been railed in and enlarged though still presenting as little green sward as before. The steam mill was burnt down a week since. [*The burial ground referred to here is probably the Ballast Hills burial ground. After being used for more than 100 years by dissenters and poor of all denominations, it was closed when these needs were met by a new cemetery at Westgate Hill, opened in 1829. Some of the grave headstones now form part of a public pathway at the Ballast Hills site.*]

10 The quotation is from William Wordsworth, Expostulation and Reply, verse 5, lines 16–20. Published in *Lyrical Ballads*, 1798.

according to the disposition or means of the occupier but one thing is uniformly good – the fire.

Coals, lodgings and flannel dresses are supplied by the Colliery owners and the additional wages amount from 15/- to 20/- a week per man.[11]

In many instances large masses of high built houses are rented by the colliery and separate rooms portioned out to each family. Every householder is provided with a small garden and generally keeps a pig or two, fat bacon being a favourite dish.

With these premises I shall proceed to visit a few patients. About 200 yards from Byker Gate I came to Johnson's houses a mass belonging to Heaton where I have to dress a boy who has long been under care with an abscess in his knee. On entering the door not without many qualms and sundry hints from the nose to the stomach, one would suppose a family of negroes and copper colored indians were mingled. Those of the batch who had just returned from the pit were of the former color while the rest having the *'thick scraped off'* presented the latter appearance. The lady-mother was Mrs McClarty *out-clartied*. Obadiah Lapstone[12] descants on the Glories of Dirt but here he would have seen it in the quintessence of perfection and refinement. Dinner is on the table. The frying pan unsullied by dish-clout for the last six months stands on the fire sending forth the savory fumes of a few fat slices of bacon. A dish of half-boiled potatoes is under the bars and a half dozen of broken plates, dirty spoons and one-pronged forks strewed about the chairs and table, if the furniture be worthy of that title. A mess of cabbage leaves and hot water with some bread in it serves the bairnes for broth and washing their fingers in. The salves &c are brought out for my use without at all disarranging the dinner set out, the steaming poultices laid on one of the plates; – but I dare not finish the picture; suffice it I completed my operations as quickly as possible and from this amalgamation of salve, soup, salt butter, plaster, pancakes & poultices I made a bolt and mounting my horse rode off to call as I hoped on some more delicately inclined *mater familias*.

---

11 [*TGW footnote*] The coal trade is now so bad that 20/- per fortnight is often all a man can make being only allowed to work 3 or 4 days a week.
12 Obadiah Lapstone was a nom-de-plume of W. A. Mitchell writing in the *Newcastle Magazine*, of which he was editor.

Chapter 3[13]

It is by no means to be inferred from the specimen of Colliery cleanliness I have endeavoured to describe that such scenes are the usual spectacles of my morning rides, – Heaven forfend! There is here the same variety we find in every other station of life though of course the diversities more strongly marked, pride and fashion having little controul.

In some houses, and those not a few, order and cleanliness are seen in as high a degree of perfection as dirty confusion was in the opposite case.

The clean neat mahogany bedstead, patchwork quilt & shining inlaid chest of drawers immediately fronting the door, eight-day clock in one corner and glass fronted cupboard, stored with 'the wedding china' &c tastefully displayed in the opposite one; a *mahogany polished* table covered with a bit of green cloth and sur-mounted by the *betterma* [*i.e., best*] teaboard and looking glass each rivals in the honor of reflection; chairs which you seem afraid should slip from under you, – so glassy their surface; 'the wife' – a picture of neatness with half a score of brats around her and the gudeman at the chimney corner smoking his pipe after his ablutions on coming from work; – all are features which, con-sidering the poverty of the inmates, makes the better sort of pitman have a just claim to the noted distinction of English peas-antry *comfort & contentment*, though upon the whole of an inferior caste.

It is at such places as these last that I make a pleasure of gratify-ing the good folks by occasionally partaking of their homely meals. This is by them considered as great a compliment as an invitation would by some. Nor is this surprizing when we con-sider the estimation the name of 'Doctor' confers upon its owner – should his manners be such as command their respect and win their friendship. Their solace and hope in sickness, their advisor in misfortune and the benefactor of their families, the colliery Doctor is in his peculiar district respected, beloved, almost revered. He is prayed for at the bedside of his patient; he is treated in social company, and by a word or a look he commands the services and attention often of some hundreds of men. As

---

13 [*The motto of Chapter 2 is repeated here with the footnote:*] I have not time at present to recollect a new motto so make use of the same as last Chap.

soon as he is in sight some hands are ready to hold the bridle, others prepare the basin warm water, soap and clean dimity towels while an old table with the salves, plasters is set in order for his reception.

Every sentence uttered by the surgeon is noted in the memory of all present and canvassed and discussed in his absence; a jest or a kind word instantly makes the patient forget his trouble and serves him for comfort during the next twenty-four hours.

Constantly liable to accidents even the little 'trapper'[14] if he gets a cut will let nobody touch it, till 'his own doctor' comes. Every little child knows him and is taught to regard him as a kind friend and benefactor.

Pursuing my way from Johnson's Houses and leaving Heaton Hall[15] on the left we pass Cattericks Buildings and Hunters Houses, and make a call at Byker Hill a long row of houses the principal depot of Heaton Colliery, and our 'sick'. Here on some occasions I pay my visits by houserow being well known in every one.

The names of the pitmen are provincial and peculiar; Jobling, Pratt, Joice, Ramsey, Blackburn, Hall, Penley, Widdrington, Manley, Shelaw, Curtiss, Bowes, Gilderoy, Cairnton, Proctor, Owen, Boggon &c are amongst the most frequent.

In the pronunciation they are odd in the extreme. If one ask for *Urwin, Hindmarsh, Turnbull* – no one will be able to give information; but Orran, Hyeners or Trummell will instantly find the wished for person. In the appellation of their residences and local designations the pitmen are equally whimsical. The following may be cited as instances. 'Smasher's Row' (*Smasher* – a two penny fruit tartlet) 'Mouldewart Row' (A Mole) 'Shiney Row' (of this very common name I cannot make out the origin) 'Twice-baked-bread Row' alias 'Bridge Row'; 'Bog Row'; 'Peggy Bakers Pit'; 'Tommy Maris pit'; 'Windy Neuk'; or they have 'East Row' 'West Row' 'Low Row' 'Paradise Row' (!) &c. The Long Row at Wallsend contains a mass of about 90 houses under one long uneven roof and several other rows are nearly equal in length.[16]

---

14 A 'trapper', usually a boy, often less than ten years old, was employed in a coal mine to open and shut a trap door as required.

15 [*TGW footnote*] The residence of Sir MW Ridley Bart MP.

16 The early twentieth century equivalents of many of these old place names are given in William Richardson, *History of the Parish of Wallsend* (Newcastle, 1923), p. 508

Leaving Byker Hill and arriving at the 2 mile stone we come at Smasher's Row which may be set down as the commencement of *Walker Colliery*. This concern is as large (but not so respectable) as Heaton having 3 pits at present working. It includes Biggs Main, Battle Hill and other masses of Houses.

Wallsend (the Roman Wall ends here) contains more workmen and a greater extent of territory than any of the rest of *our* collieries and yet little business is carried on in the doctoring way there. The work is very bad just now at this concern and men are employed to do all the work by way of bettering their wages the horses having been sold about a month since.

Turning my horses head about at the Church Pit Wallsend, – my utmost limit and a little beyond the fourth mile stone – I continue my route through Biggs Main – past the Red & White Halls, Benton farm, Heaton High Pit – Jesmond Bridge – Lambert's Leap and Sandyford stone. I return into Newcastle at the opposite end to that by which I left it *viz.* the Barras Bridge, having seen in my tour on a moderate calculation about a score of patients and with my brain full of prescriptions ready for delivery into the day book. I trot down street and delivering my nag to the groom rest my weary limbs after the fatigues of the morning's *'Ride in the Country'*.

V O L U M E 1 (October 1, 1826 to November 30, 1826)

October 1 *[Sunday]*
The first questions which I ask *myself*, and which 'merit mention,' as Dr. Monro[1] says, are what is the use of this? or is it any use? or will it be any use? 2nd will I be able (pooh! that is Irish,) – shall I be able to continue my resolution of keeping a diary? Now the best answer 'self' can give to 'me' upon this occasion is, 'Time will try'. – 'The best resolves may fail'. And why 'October 1st' is a necessary tho' unimportant question. Fancy might be a ready, but not a sufficient answer. The first of this month being the commencement of the medical year; the why & the wherefore of which I cannot at present enter into, (*Quere*. Can it be from this months being [*illegible word*], the most lucrative of the twelve to the profession?) I see no reason why Phoebus or Diana or Julius Caesar or any other of these godships or demigodships who have been pleased to quarter old Saturn should have more influence with me (*reverenter dicitur*) in this respect than that overruling of all overruling arguments, and deathblow to all learned authority – Custom.[2] Next – what is to be the plan of this said diary. Is it to be professional, historical or common place? It is to be all; to contain remarks professional & remarks nonprofessional; comic & sentimental; spiritual & temporal; military & civil; it is to receive observations on the wind & on the weather; observations literary; scientific, & philosophical; it is to contain superscriptions, subscriptions, inscriptions & prescriptions; prognoses diagnoses and all the rest of the family of noses; remarks pathological, physiological, osteological and all the

1 Possibly Professor Alexander Munro ('Tertius'), who held the Chair of Anatomy in Edinburgh University when TGW was a student there in 1826.
2 [*TGW footnote*] . . .Usus/ Quem penes arbitrium est et jus et norma loquendi (Horace) [*Ars Poetica, 70:* . . . *Usage shall will it, in whose hands is the arbitrament, the right and rule of speech*].

other compounds of logical; in short it will [*be*] as varied in its pages as its authors life & thoughts, dull or lively as his humour prompts, and leave existence for a day, or swell that day 'thro leaves *unnumbered*' as leisure or inclination permits; or finally in all probability be brought to a premature end.

So much by way of preface, now for a few introductory facts relating to this said first of October & following days.

Several new arrangements have or are about to take place at this juncture. *Imprimis,* I have got a new steed to ride my daily rounds on, – a little frisky, fiery fine-legged, fly away, foreign Flanders 5-yr old filly, – which so far, (I have gone two journeys on her) I like exceedingly. She seems unaccustomed to the country, which is rather a startling one to most horses at first. Mr Cochrane is to ride her as soon as the grey highland mare, at present out at grass, returns; i.e. *if he can.* This little mare was the first '*beast*' I fell off, as yesterday I unfortunately lost my balance in looking at her feet, while only walking, and was '*spilt*'. No detriment to my equestrian skill tho: be it known to all whom it concerneth.

The rest of the important 'arrangements' are of the 2nd class I think *viz* the 'about to take place' ones, of which more hereafter & *in prolixo ordine.*

As to professional news; I have two or three severe accidents under my care just now; they are (according to form) as follows; *Ritson, Benwell High Cross* A severe cut upon the front of the tibia, extending more or less from the patella downward. A little above the ancle the bone was laid quite bare for about $\frac{1}{2}$ inches. A great deal of coal dust & dirt were fixed into the wound, which I have removed by poultices; and the wounds are now dressed with Mag: Resin: Flav: He got his accident by a stone falling upon him on the 20th of Sept'.

Grantson, Elswick New Row An accident in every respect like the above but not quite so severe. It happened Sept': 28th. The lad is applying Poultices, still.

Gascoigne, Heaton High Pit The Index of the right hand was hanging by the skin off by the second phalanx. The middle finger is quite off by the third phalanx. The index of the left hand is split down in the end, and the integument of that middle finger totally detached & torn. I have endeavoured to unite the right index by the first intention, after removing the bone *in spicula.* Poultices are applying & yesterday I opened out the plaster, but I am afraid it will come off. He got his accident last Wednesday the 27th.

Thornton, Wallsend Shiney Row A terrible comp[d] fractured leg. He has had it nearly a month, and it is now healing, but the sinuses and abscesses are very numerous. As Mr McI is oftener down that way, he attends principally to this case tho' I often dress the patient. I was there with Mr McI this morning.

There are numerous other cases of minor importance, but which may perhaps require to be mentioned hereafter.

Apropos I have just met with a few lines which, as being applicable, I will insert in the blank page as a motto.[3]

This is Sunday, or I should never have been able to have written this long rigmarole for a *commencement*. I must now however leave off for tonight.

October 2 *[Monday]*

Now for it – my first *war-day* – what of October second? Being the first Monday after Michaelmas, it is the day on which 'wor new Mayor' is chosen, or as it is called 'Mayor choosing Monday'; when little bairns, (and many up-grown bairns), get dressed up as 'the Mayor', and go about begging halfpence. I have been *gammoned* out of twopence (luckily all the change I had) by two *mayorified* pitmen. For the benefit of the antiquarians of the next century, and others who may in after ages peruse this erudite composition, I may as well mention that on this day Archibald Reed Esq was elected to the right worshipful dignity of Mayor of Newcastle.

Been round by Benwell, Elswick and Felling. Patients doing well. Ol: Croton given great relief in a case which has every appearance of Worms, tho' none yet evacuated. It may yet be Dyspepsia tho'.

Mem: To insert among the 'Christian names of Men' (or names of Christian men) in my Dictionary 'Jonas Rosenbohm' of the worshipful company of Pawnbrokers – I should not like to sit in Mr Rosin – what's his name's – chair, by the bye![4]

---

3 The motto referred to is the quotation from Byron's *Don Juan* reproduced here at the beginning of the section 'My Autobiography'.

4 It is not apparent what is meant by this remark. George Rosenbohm, Pawn-broker, 21 Church Street, Gateshead is listed in the trade directory: see PW, I, p. 121.

Called out to an accident at 6 PM Johnsons houses. Nothing very severe, a cut on the ancle. A long chat with Brown the cutler[5] finished the day.

October 3 *[Tuesday]*

I called yesterday upon, & left my proposal to the Phil: Institution[6] to be signed by Col[n] Gilmore, and intended this morning to have called again for it, but was prevented doing so till afternoon by having to go down to Wallsend & Backworth. Neither the Col: or Mrs G: were in; I got the paper however & delivered it to the librarian to give to Mr Turner.[7]

I dined with Cochrane at 'Backworth Establishment' as he is pleased to call it, 'Backworth Allotment' other folks say. Mr McI desired me to call upon him on business; I staid a hour or two, and in coming home called at Elswick Cottage. I never was at Backworth before – it is a very pleasant situation in summer, what it may be in winter I know not; but I should think rather bleak.[8]

Saw my Wallsend patients. One poor man under Mr McI's care evidently dying. Hiccough came on last night. Disease Chronic Hepatitis. Another patient died this morning. A child of the disease which has been very prevalent this autumn among infants teething, and to which I scarcely know what name to apply, but of which I shall tomorrow give a detail. Other patients going on pretty well.

October 4 *[Wednesday]*

As I promised yesterday to describe a disease very prevalent just now, I may as well begin this morning.

This Disease (as I have before said) *I* have chiefly met with in children teething, and from 2 to 16 months old. The symptoms are Diarrhoea (tho' sometimes in the first instance Constipation),

---

5 Probably John Brown, surgical instrument and truss maker and working cutler, 51 Dean Street, Newcastle: see PW, I, p. 108.

6 The 'Phil Institution' referred to was almost certainly the Literary and Philosophical Society of Newcastle upon Tyne. The name 'Institution' may have been used at the time although, strictly, this would apply to The New Institution, formed in 1802 under the patronage of the Lit. & Phil.: see Introduction.

7 For comment on Turner see 'My Autobiography', note 61.

8 The Backworth surgery is mentioned in the Preface. TGW later spent some time there and described it in more detail: see Volume 7, 28/7/28 to end.

evacuations of a green unnatural color, often mixed with blood; great listlessness; more or less cough & sickness; as the disease advances, the breathing becomes hurried; the head affected, apparently hydrocephalic, the eyes glazed & insensible; partial Hemiplegia; and the patient dies sometimes comatose at others apparently of suffocation. The pulse throughout is quick & feverish, and the mouth sore. The appetite disappears, but great thirst annoys the little sufferer. In two cases Hydrocephalus seemed the principal & idiopathic part of the affection, had it not been for obstinate diarrhoea which prevailed. The recitation of a few cases will better explain the treatment which I have found in every case but 3 out of about 20 patients very successful.

Case 1 *Scott Hunter's Houses*
Aetat: 3 yrs. This child had been under Mr McIntyre's care for a short time before I returned to him, and had taken some astringent medicine, & had its gums lanced.[9] The Diarrhoea however still continued obstinate, and when I saw it, it had lain for some days in a con stant sleepy state, never raising its head off the pillow except when obliged to do so. Evacuations of a feeted, chopped green, nature, eyes evidently deadened, fontenelle not quite close, head swelling and all the symptoms (except costiveness) of Hydrocephalus. *I* indeed thought, & told the parents so, that the child was moribund however to try the utmost ordered it the following mixture.

> ℞   Julip Salin Syr Papaver aa ℥ vj
>   Sulph Quinine gr vj Pulv Rhei gr xij
>   Hyd' Submur gr vj
>   ft Mist Capt cochl j min: bis tervi die

In a day or two the purging abated. The stools became natural, the appetite increased, the child became more lively, and by the continuance of the above medicine was well in the course of a fortnight. The head is still preternaturally large, I fancy.

---

9 Through the ages there has been a persistent belief that the natural process of teething in babies could be a cause of disease. Lancing of the gums, to facilitate tooth eruption, was introduced into medical practice as early as the sixteenth century, and came to be advocated for every childhood disease. Gum lancing was questioned in the 1850s, but continued at least until the 1880s. The belief in a relationship between teething and illness continued to be firmly held by many medical practitioners until at least 1918, and still persists, at least as a folk myth. See Ann Dally in *The Lancet*, 348 (1996), pp. 1710–11.

Usher Byker Old Engine
Aetat 8 months. Obstinate diarrhoea which neither Creta nor opium could control. Eyes glazed & afterwards blind. Comatose. Evacuations unnatural & chopped. The child died on the fourth day of the disease. I could not prevail for an examination of the body.

Smart Croft Stairs
Aetat 16 months. This little girl was affected in the usual way but by the use of the following powder she grew better and apparently got well.

> ℞   Pulv Rhei Magnes Calcin aa gr xxiv
>   Pulv Sacchar c Cal gr xviij ft Pulv vj
>   Capt j bis dei

In a about a week however the disease returned, and in a few days carried off the patient, with partial blindness & hemiplegia of the left side.

I have given these two unfavourable cases as they shew the disease in its most aggravated form. In the rest the above description of powders, (in that form or dissolved in a little Julep Salin & Syr. Papaver was used). If the Diarrhoea was severe a little Creta instead of Magnesia; or in the end a little Sulph. Quinine was added. I am exceedingly sorry not to have had an opportunity of a post mortem examination of any of my Patients defunct.

As I intend to keep a *numerical* list of the new patients taken thro' the year, I here put down the number I have already seen since I returned (Aug 18) and shall at the end of each week continue the list.
[Patient numbers]

Been down at Brown's with a pattern for him to make a revolving apparatus for shewing the connection between Galvanism & Magnetism.[10]

Out at Benwell, Elswick, Heaton &c all going on as it ought to be. Gascoignes finger end coming off. [1/10/26]

Sat an hour with Travis in the evening. Drank tea with J. Gibson last night. I forgot to mention.

---

10 There is insufficient information to be sure what this apparatus was, but it sounds like a simple electric motor. There was much interest in electromagnetism following the investigations of Oersted, published in 1820. Faraday announced the discovery of what was, in effect, the first electric motor in 1821.

October 5 [*Thursday*]
Went down to the Quayside with a young German physician, to
a gig. He was to meet Mr McIntyre at Wallsend, and go down a
coal pit. He afterwards dined with us. A pleasant young man
from Austria, had travelled round by London, Oxford, Liverpool,
Dublin, Belfast, Glasgow & Edinburgh.

I put on trowsers, thinking I should have to go nowhere on
horseback, but was obliged to change costume for an accident at
Battle Hill. A man got his foot hurt, nothing serious.

An idea occurred to me at Walker, on my journey, which I
intended to put down, but what it was I have completely forgot –
Mem: Dr Knox told me, 'it is said *a new idea* is an occurrence of
once in a century'. I cannot think that is true, tho' it may be as
far as concerns me.

Mr McI came home in a coat never made for him, and hat
shewing symptoms of his or its having been on a low shelf. I
wonder if he has been thrown from my mare, which he was
riding.

We have had beautifully fine weather this last week though
very frosty at nights. A white rime was on the fields this morning
I am told.

Wonder at not receiving my flute solos & spurs they will surely
come tomorrow, – carrier day. Dreamt last night about [*a few
indecipherable characters of what appears to be a shorthand are written
here – presumably a name*]. 'Tis said 'dreams never come true if
told before breakfast'; I doubt mine never come true at all! Met
Mr Hall on the quay – shook hands *en passant*.

October 6 [*Friday*]
My mare lame as a pikestaff (*Quere* what is the derivation of that
comparison? A pikestaff being itself inanimate, & being only used
by those who are already lame, or who intend lameness to their
neighbours) this morning. I however rode to Elswick, Benwell &
c. A grand tea drinking given to all the old wives & young
women of Elswick, for assisting and in fact principally putting
out a fire which endangered the new Pit. I was half an hour too
soon, but was often invited to go in.

Met Col^n Gilmore twice on Benwell road. Mem: to ask Mr McI
for the loan of Phil: Inst: Catalogue for him.

Sat an hour with J Gibson. Under went the operation of having
my superfluous hair amputated by Mr Parsons, and was sent for

by Jeavis. Introduced to and played a few duets with Sang. No parcel from Croft.[11]

Been highly amused with reading Washington Irving's 'Salma-gundi'.[12] Mem: to mention to Father an excellent satire on modern imitative music – Tourist's memoranda capital ('past 10 oclock').

October 7 [Saturday]

Called out this morning to a man burnt at Elswick. Not very severe. Mare goes quite well again, or nearly so.

A cast of a tumour sent home this morning for which the mould was made last Saturday. The dimensions are Extreme length ft 2 3 in D° Breadth ft 1 10 in & greatest circumference ft 4 4 in. It is situated on a woman's right shoulder & back, and is supposed to weigh about 2 stones.

2 PM Here I am *Major domo* for the second time since I returned from Scotland. Mr McIntyre has been called away to Harrogate with a patient[13] and left *me* in charge of his patients. Mr McI told me to send W^m [*William King*] to Heaton H Pit. I offered him the mare, but he dare not ride, poor man!!

By the bye a large abscess formed in Gascoigne's hand [4/10/ 26], which Mr McI opened yesterday.

Called down at 4 PM to a lad at Walker, who was 'bleeding to deead'. He had got a cut on the head about a week ago, in which, I presume, some branch of the temporal artery had been partially cut thro; and which had ulcerated the coats, and so caused the accident. The boy (about 12 years old) was very weak & excess-ively pale when I got down to him, but the haemorrhage was stopped. I probed the wound, but as no bleeding returned, I judged it better to apply a compress and bandage than to search for the open vessel. Got a cup of tea with patient's mother Mrs Shields; I drank tea with Mrs Jennant, Benwell, yesterday too.

On calling upon a patient at Johnson's Houses I encountered a large cheese and a spirit bottle set out upon the table. The dame

---

11 TGW's parents then lived at Croft Cottage, Croft, Co. Durham.

12 *Salmagundi, or, the Whim Whams and Opinions of Launcelot Langstaff Esq and Others*, by Washington Irving (1783–1859), a popular and prolific American author, was first published in 1808. It was a collection of humorous articles and essays, originally written for various newspapers by Washington Irving, his brother William, and J. K. Pauling: see M. Drabble (ed.), *Oxford Companion to English Literature* (Oxford, 1985), p. 497.

13 [*TGW footnote*] Mr Carr (Shields) *vide* Nov 30.

having been 'brought to bed' on Thursday. A capital cheese it was.

Made a call upon Mrs Scott Castle Street. Mr McIntyre had tried Acid Nitros c Opio in Mist. Camph. (vide Ed: Journ: July 1826) without effect in stopping a violent cholera. She was complaining of excruciating pain in the head when I saw her in the morning, and vomited all her medicine (mistr. Creta c Opio & Pil Opii c Hydr. et Ipecac). I gave her one of her pills, and after it T^r Opii gutt xxx in a small quantity of water, which remained upon her stomach and gave her ease in ten minutes. Mr McI came in whilst I was yet there in the morning, and ordered me to see her this evening. When I called she was a great better. 'Believes if I had not seen her she would have died', 'wonders Mr McI never gave her those drops', as this is the second time I have relieved her in the same way; the Mist Creta &c being in too great a quantity to be retained on the stomach. Mrs S. both received & dismissed me with many a blessing. People talk of the vexations of a surgeons life, this is one example of the contrary.

Called upon Mr Church[14] to request him to go with me to Wallsend tomorrow. I wished to persuade him to take the gig, (the real reason was I had no clean breeches to put on, & I make a rule never to ride in my dress black trowsers) but he will not, and wishes to have my mare, fearing he says that 'the black horse, being a foreigner, may have learned some foreign manners'. Mr McIntyre wrote to me from Chester le Street where he stays all night.

[Patient numbers]

October 8 [Sunday]

Called upon Dr McWhirter & Dr Smith. Mr Church & I went down to Wallsend to see Bowden's Dau^{tr} (Chlorosis). I had some time ago given her some Drops (T^r Cinchon:– Mur Ferr:) which she said did her more good than all the medicines Mr McI had ordered her, but when they were done, she became she thought worse last Friday, and as I was afraid of an unfavourable change I requested Mr C[15] to accompany me upon the strength of the

---

14 Mr James Church held the position of House Surgeon at the Newcastle Infirmary from 1817 to 1837: see Hume, p. 145.

15 Probably James Church: see note 14 above.

maxim 'two heads are better than one be they calf's heads'. Mr C is inclined to try Sulpht: Quinine in Infus: Rosae.

Got a good cup of tea & spiced loaf at Mrs Thornton's, Wallsend. N.B. These country 'cups of tea' (seldom exceeding three or four) do not prevent me from enjoying my quantum when I get home again. Saw my Walker patient [*Shields, 7/11/26*] running about, but still very pale.

Viewed the body of a poor wretch who had fallen down the pit early this morning, supposed while intoxicated as he was known to be a great drunkard. He lay for some time unowned. His skull was quite broken to pieces & his brains protruding. His legs fractured in two or three places &c &c. An inquest is to be held upon him tomorrow at 1 PM.

Opened another abscess in Gascoigne's hand [*7/10/26*].

As it came on raining whilst I was at Gascoigne's I borrowed a great coat of him, of the latest Bond Street cut; I *don't* think. However it was very serviceable in saving my best black coat from the wet.

Mr Crawford sat half an hour.

October 9 [*Monday*]

Been at Heaton H Pit, Walker, & Felling. My patient [*Gaer, 2/10/26*] with Tape Worm (as I supposed) to whom I gave Ol: Croton, & who has since passed a multitude of what she calls long pieces of skin, says, I have given her a new lease of life, for she has got better 'not daily but hourly' since she came under my care. She *subscribes to* & had been previously treated by '*Mr Wood Surgeon, Bonesetter & Druggist*' Gateshead.[16] She is quite well by the use of some tonic aperient powders, and requests her bill, which she declares she will pay cheerfully!!

Been down to Brown's[17] about a pair of new straight tooth forceps. Met Davidson (of Leightons[18] formerly who is uncommonly civil & polite. Finished Salmagundi – capital.

October 10 [*Tuesday*]

Sent for to Sunnyside; from whence I went by Fawdon, Kenton to Wallsend, & home, having completely tired the little bay mare.

---

16 Probably Wood, Surgeon, 24 High Street, Gateshead: see PW, I, 95.
17 See note 5 above.
18 For comment on Leighton see 'My Autobiography', note 57.

After snatching my dinner, I took the black horse to Benwell & c &c brought him home quite lame from what cause I know not. Received a letter from Mr McIntyre and answered it by tonight's post. Intended to write home but J Gibson came up for me to go down to tea with him, where I sat the evening. Called to see Mrs Crawford this afternoon who is very poorly. She seems not likely to last out the winter if till then.

Had the *honour* of a *wave* from Miss G in the window & met Miss I G in the street.[19] Have not seen them since I don't when before. Here is the third carrier day and no news from Croft I *must* write tomorrow night. Have no time for *thoughts* just now but must be content with noting *facts* till Mr McI comes home.

October 11 *[Wednesday]*
Mr Crawford has been here this morning to say that his mother died at 2 AM. Called upon Mr Watson for Mr McI. Met Mr Turner & Mrs Charnley both shook hands. Mrs C desired to be remembered to my F & M.

A beautiful morning so I took a ride to Felling & then to Byker Gate. Rather for pleasure and to keep my mare in exercise than to see patients as none required it particularly. As I invited Mr McI if he had leisure to call at Croft he may bring me some news so I will give the chance of tonight for hearing.

Got Travis to initiate me a little into the art and mystery of *quadrilling*. Nearly, almost, not quite learned the first three figures of the first set. Mr McI not returned.

October 12 *[Thursday]*
A long but expedite journey down to Wallsend, Battle Hill, Heaton H P &c and after dinner to Sunnyside, where I sat an hour over a glass of wine with Mr Robson. My patient there (most fortunately for my credit, as first impressions are deep) *better considerably*.

8 PM thanks to the gods propitious[20] Mr McIntyre has returned; I am heartily sick of being both master and assistant; alias of

---

19 Probably Miss Gibson (Fanny) and Miss Isabel Gibson, sisters of John Gibson: see Introduction, note 37.

20 [*TGW footnote*] '. . .of Poetry tho' patron God/ Apollo patronises Physic' Coleman [*unidentified, possibly George Colman*]

doing both his work and my own. I am more completely tired tonight than I have ever been since I came to Newcastle.[21]

Had a long consultation & numerous *pros and cons* with myself after dinner as to whether I should go to Sunnyside, as it was raining hard; – however I determined that duty to my patients & my master should overcome all other considerations; so I e'en went, and I am now glad I did, notwithstanding the rain, as I was very politely received by Mr & Mrs Robson (my patient better mind) tho' I thought *Mrs* R did not seem over-cordial my first visit. *Mr* R was not in then.

Mr McI has said not a word about Croft &c, however I will give the chance of tomorrow's carrier. If no parcel I *will* write. Mem: to write to London & Thirsk first leisure day. Mrs Coser called to see me.

October 13 [Friday]
My spurs & music come at last, and, as I expected, a concomitant caution from Father as to the moderate use of the former. I however pride myself rather on my careful, and yet quick riding without distressing my steed; and I fancy (indeed am sure) I have improved my new mare in her paces not a little, trotting especially; tho' I doubt she never will trot so well as I at first expected.

Tried over Drouet's solos 'Rule Brittania' & 'Gramachree'.[22] The former too hard, the latter I think I can manage with a little practice.

Been out only at Benwell &c today. Mr McI went to Sunnyside, but brought the black horse home lame. He wishes to return him, as having been warranted. I don't care how soon, for I am not pleased with the idea of having him to ride, he is so lazy & awkward. My mare has therefore had a jaunt to Wallsend this afternoon.

---

21 [*TGW footnote*] My reader will perceive I have got a most illegible and author-like method of daubing my finger over a miss-written letter or word to save time in scratching out. It must be put down to 'haste' therefore.
22 Louis Drouet (1792–1873), flautist, teacher, conductor and composer, composed 150 works, said to be admirably written for the flute: see Stanley Sadie (ed.), *The New Grove Dictionary of Music and Musicians* (London, 1980), p. 638. *Rule Britannia*, still well known of course, was written for a masque, *Alfred*, by the Scottish poet James Thompson (1700–48) in collaboration with a friend, David Mallet; *Gramachree* was a very popular Irish air, published in many arrangements.

Obliged to appeal to headquarters about Mr Wm King & his *delicate* trick of cleaning the surgery windows by *spitting* upon them and rubbing, or rather daubing it over with a piece of tow. Mr McI has so far taken no notice to W^m; perhaps he may let it pass as the youth is going to Edinbro' soon.

I have been today, for the first time put upon the list as an 'efficient' man to serve in his majesty's forces; *viz* in the Militia list, but 'exempt' as an apprentice.

October 14 [Saturday]

I was highly amused this morning on going out into the country about 10½ oclock, (the first *Saturday* morning I have been out at that time) to observe the crowds of pitmen, their wives, & bairns coming 'to the toon', all in their 'Sunday cleais'. *Here* was a Jerry Sneak[23] looking man with 'the bit bairn' in his arms, while his wife of more tummified dimensions luggs a large empty basket, destined to contain the ' few necessaries' for the ensuing week. *There* a group of lads with their hands in their breeches pockets going merely 'for pleesurin' or to buy a new hat or 'pair o' shoon' or get a new 'pick-shaft' &c. And others to 'have a pint with some friends'; which probably ended in Gallons. Two or three times I met large long carts with two horses tandem, completely laden with women & their baskets. On the Shields road there was a stream like that toward a race course on the cup day, or to Duddingston loch[24] when frozen. My accostations from the parties were numerous; and the hat and hand were constantly meeting before me as I rode down.

'Here's a fine day, doctor!' (The native English address on meeting any one). 'Hoo are ye, doctor?' 'Ye're in a hurry today doctor, is ought matter?' 'I say doctor, I wish ye'd give a caaal and leuk at the wife, she no'but badly the day, puir body. She feels [*illegible word*] somehow, and does na reest weel at neights, but maybies ye'll see her as ye gang by' (Very well I'll see how she is but how's the lad now) 'Oh! thank ye sir, he gotten nicely soon, his appetite's coming round and he thinking o' trying wark

---

23 A 'Jerry Sneak' is a stereotypical hen-pecked husband, from the character in the play *Mayor of Garrat or The Humours of the Army* by Samuel Foot.

24 TGW describes skating on Duddingston Loch, Edinburgh, together with most of the population of the city, in January 1826: see 'My Autobiography', chapter 16.

o' Monday, if ye hae nae objection like.' 'Holloa, doctor, ye need
no caall at wor house, the wife's no in and aw's goan to try if aw
can git as far as to toon, ye see, with this leg o' mine; it feels quite
strong now, ye said ye'd order me a bottle to rub it with, if aw
caall, I suppose t'lads in't shop can gie me't' (Oh yes, mind you
don't get drunk now or else you'll be breaking the other leg and
you'll have that job to pay for yourself you know) (How's your
wife) 'She just her *ordinary*, thank ye sir, whiles better & whiles
worse.'

The foregoing is a small specimen of the conversation carried
out on these occasions; 'in these cases' Dr Barclay[25] would have
said.

A man [*Snaith*] came in tonight with his hand curiously cut.
He was 'nearly in for it' or in other words 'had got strabismus'
(double sight) *alias* was almost drunk. He had been chopping
wood, and, as he said, 'had made a *little* mistake' by hitting his
finger with a sharp axe instead of the log. The blow had severed
the Metacarpal bone of the index (of the left hand) close to its
articulation with the first phalanx, and a kind of comp^d fracture &
dislocation was the consequence. The Extensor tendon of that
finger was divided, and the finger hung quite loose. The wound
was only about 2 inches long. I reduced the fracture &c, and
having brought the wound close applied strips of plaster, compress, splint along the inside of the hand, bandage and sling.

By the bye, Gascoigne's finger is going to stay on after all
[7/10/26]. Three abscesses have been opened in that hand. The
granulations will, I hope, unite and fill up the chasm made by
sloughing &c. I am already beginning to put it, as well as the
finger of the other hand into the most *fashionable* shape, as last
brought down from London.

I have somehow a kind of a sort of a species of a bit of a small
idea of going down to Shields tomorrow. J Gibson seems particularly anxious to go with me, if I go!!, *to take care of me*, I guess.

A child died at Heaton H Pit this morning it had taken a large
quantity of Aperient Medicine but without any effect. Mr McI did
not see it, but ordered it something last night from the report of
its Grandmother; I saw it and ordered some aperient powders in
the morning all however failed. I have spoken to Mr McI wishing

---

25 For comment on Barclay see 'My Autobiography', notes 70 and 72.

an examination. He says he will very likely go out with me in the morning for that purpose.

October 15 *[Sunday]*
Went out this morning to Heaton High Pit in the full expectation of *sectio cadaveris* but the mother obstinately refused to allow it. Mr McI took W^m *[King]* in the gig and all was prepared.

I went out with the intention of asking Mr McI's leave to continue my ride to Shields but as I did not get done amongst patients till 5 o'clock, it was then too late; besides being rather unfit for *visiting* in another way.

My mare is getting a very bad habit of running away before I get mounted, which she did today and after a deal of difficulty (notwithstanding I was just laid across her, like a calf on a butcher's horse, *length ways*), got me off. The shock completely deprived me of breath for a few moments however I luckily came off in the end with a bruised finger, and a dirty great coat, which I got brushed at a patient's house close by. I have had leeches on my finger, and am writing this with it (the forefinger of my right hand) bandaged up.

J Gibson was down at Shields today. I *must* go if I can next Sunday. I intended to have written some remarks on the *fortnight's* existence of this diary but must leave it till some other opportunity, as my hand is rather awkward for writing. I forgot to give a list of new patients yesterday, however here it is to last night.
[Patient numbers]

October 16 *[Monday]*
I was called out of my bed about 7 AM by Mr McI, who had taken a *whim wham* to go to Sunnyside thus early. No sooner had I got my breakfast, preparatory to going to Benwell &c, than a call came for me to go down to Brown, Wallsend. He was very ill from not having had his bowels open since Friday. He had his leg hurt some time ago, but was getting well of it, when he was attacked on Saturday with a pain in the side & bowels. Mr McI bled him, and his blood presented the most beautiful specimen of 'cupped'ness[26] that I ever met with. I took down the forcing

---

26 See Bloodletting, in Medical Glossary.

syringe, and used it twice during the two hours I staid by him. I had not then relieved his bowels of their load, tho' a slight evacuation had in great part removed the pain.

Mr McI has seen him and bled him again this afternoon and they are to send in at six o' clock to say how he is. He had taken when I saw him this morning Mist. Purg: (c $\frac{1}{2}$ ij Ol Ricini et Antimon tart gr iij) and Infus Senna c Sulpht Magnes $\frac{1}{2}$ vj , *ten* compound Colocynth Pills, besides some purging medicine he took on Friday.

By the bye, with all due deference I beg to question the propriety of Mr McI bleeding so frequently. The man was bled twice about a fortnight ago. Mr McI will say perhaps ' the blood was cupped and buffy, a sure indication of venesection requiring to be repeated'. Not always, my good master; the circulation will be restored to its tone when the bowels are put regular again, depend upon it. Another reason, may be you wish to weaken the patient, and thereby causing laxity of the intestinal fibre, in part remove the obstruction. Tho' some physicians say so, I doubt it will have much effect and the prejudice this will be to the after strength of the patient will more than counterbalance the present advantage. *I* am not very fond of bleeding with a foul stomach. First put all right there then if disflammation is going on in the system *to the lancet*. Mr Liston's lancets do not see daylight often for months together, and yet (in his extensive practice) he says, 'no one is more ready to use them *when requisite* and that *freely* too'. I say the foregoing however with all the diffidence of a young practitioner, and one too who may recant the opinions of today, by the experience or the study of tomorrow; but my intention in this place is to put down on paper 'thoughts as they rise'.

Somehow or other three or four of our patients are in a bad way just now. Bowdens Dau[tr], Wallsend (Chlorosis) [8/10/26] seems dying hourly. A child of Blackburn's, Byker Hill, is very bad of a Dysentery of which I cured him about a fortnight ago, but which has relapsed and seems affecting his head, in the way I have lately described and which for want of a better name I may call 'Atrophia Lactatorum'. Brown is very bad. And a child at Heaton H Pit was attacked yesterday with the above infantile complaint.

Tho' I am a 'Newcastle Apothecary'[27] and 'fight with death',

---

27 A poem with this title is quoted in 'My Autobiography', chapter 13.

'still we're' *not* 'sworn friends to one another', and I will endeavour to cheat him of some of his intended victims yet, if I possibly can; always reserving this comfort on the expiry of a patient, 'I have done all in *my* power for him'.

6PM. They have come in from Brown. He has had no passage. Been in the warm bath; 7 minutes only. Could not bear the syringe to be used after I left. It seems he took a shillings worth of castor oil too yesterday. And some pills with Ol: Croton in each today – If not eased before morning Mr McI has ordered Enema Tabaci. And some Powders with Hyd^r Submur gr x Pulv Scammon gr x Pulv Gambogia gr ij [th] M Capt j 4ta qq hora. Also Reptr Pil: Croton: Also Mist Purgant [*illegible abbreviation*] Subcarb Ammon: [th] (*An effervescence* takes place Mr McI!) Capt ℥ j 2nd qq hora.

My forefinger is rather better today, but still painful. I am going to poultice it tonight.

October 17 – October 18 [*Tuesday – Wednesday*]
I said in my first chapter that this diary would leave existence for a day occasionally, and here is the first specimen. The truth is John Gibson got me down last night to coffee, and a glass of wine with Tyler and I therefore had no time for notes.

*Mirabile dictu pro*digious – I have not been across a horse today, nor seen a single out of town patient, Mr McI having been away all day upon my mare. I consequently have worn breeches and *gaiters* all today.

I called to enquire after the Miss Crawfords this morning (not having seen or heard anything of them since Mrs C's death) and was surprised to find Mrs Bowes there. Mr Bowes & John called upon me this evening.

Brown has had copious evacuations and is greatly relieved, but is still taking Ol: Croton and Mixt: Purgant [*16/10/26*].

By the bye – in consequence of an argument I had yesterday with J Gibson on bleeding in Constipation, I am inclined to revoke *my* opinions in favour of bleeding, *if carried to Syncope*, but not without. We had a long disputation too about Mr McI's splints[28] in fractures of the thigh.

---

28 Mr McIntyre's leg splint was apparently well-known in the medical profession at the time. James MacIntyre published a tract entitled *Description of a Splint, Invented for the Treatment of Fractured Limbs* (1825): Royal College of Surgeons

October 19 *[Thursday]*

I was, for the first time since I became assistant, called out of my
bed to an accident. The people sent off in a great hurry, thinking
the lad (at Biggs Main) was nearly killed, but on mature & deliberate consideration, which took place before I got down he was
adjudged to be mistaken, and very little worse; accordingly put
to bed, the doors closed, and all made quiet, so that when I got
to the house, I had the family (patient & all) to waken from their
beds & a sound sleep. I met the usual consolation upon such
occasions,(after a cold ride for nothing at 5 in the morning, and
the lad just a bit cut on the leg which he said he could 'haeve
dressed weel aneugh hissel) – 'Oh! aw's sure its weel its nae
warse, its a marcy he wasna killed outright', together with a *twentieth* edition of a full & particular account of his miraculous
escape &c &c.

William's mother been here today & her son fixed to go to
Edinburgh on Monday, or at any rate leave here then. I have got
a letter written to Dr Knox for him, to take with him along with
the D^{rs}'s book.

Got a cup of tea with Urwin Benwell H Cross.

Rode the black horse twice today. He is *dead lame*, & Mr McI
has had my mare away all night. I wish to goodness he would
get another.

October 20 *[Friday]*

Been down at Heaton & Walker met with J Gibson at Heaton Pit.

Blakeburn's child Byker Hill dead. *[Blackburn? 16/10/26]*
'Wished much to have seen *me* yesterday, instead of Mr McI'
'They think Mr McI did not pay any attention to it, but *I* seemed
to understand it so well (having warned the parents of the danger
long since, tho' it after that got well, but has since taken a relapse)
and they were so well satisfied with what I had done for it that

---

(England) Library, Tract No. 675/4. The McIntyre splint is mentioned in articles in *The Lancet* (1837–8), I, pp. 81–6 and 111–15, and its use was described
in detail by TGW in an article written on 12/4/1838 and published in *The
Lancet* (1837–8), II, pp. 202–3. TGW's obituary in the *British Medical Journal*
(1898), p. 1493, comments that TGW had in his possession one of the original
splints. A modified 'M'Intyre splint' was exhibited at the Great Exhibition of
1862: see the diagram in Robert Mallet (ed.), *The Practical Mechanics' Journal:
Record of the Exhibition* (London, 1862), p. 560.

tho' they thought there was no chance for it, they would have liked to have seen me'.

Widdington's child is better with the powders I ordered it. As D^r JG was going past when I was there I got him to look at her. He agrees with me that there is danger of the head. A Blister too (as I had before told the friends) is ordered to the right side of the head. The child is much more lively and complaints less a good deal than when I last saw her.

Mr McI has *walked* out to Byker this afternoon, to see a new patient who sent in for him or 'Mr Wright'. I lent him my umbrella which he has brought home broken in two whalebones. I am to get it mended at his expense.

I was weighed yesterday at Mr Scott's, and was in full uniform 9 st - 9$\frac{1}{2}$ lb.

J Gibson & Mr McI have had a long *tête a tête* tonight over a cup of tea & some shrimps.

October 21 [Saturday]
Called out of bed this morning about 6$\frac{1}{2}$ oclock to a man [*Reavely*] that had got his 'theegh beane broeken' at Biggs Main. Mr McI mounted the bay mare & I had to hobble down on old lamelegs. *Greenwood* closed the procession on foot. The femur was obliquely fractured close to the condyles. It was quickly reduced, and the patient doing well.

I have been out this evening at Benwell, & am thinking (7$\frac{1}{2}$ PM) of going down to Gibson's to hear the result of the consultation last night.

Mr McI took a tumour off a persons eyelid this afternoon in the surgery. She shouted most tremendously and tossed her head so that it was with difficulty that the tumour was got off and then only by cutting away a piece of the conjunctiva. [*later insertion*] Nov 4 Quite well.

[*Patient numbers*] NB. Eight children vaccinated rather increased the list of private patients this week.

October 22 [Sunday]
A nasty drear rain. John Gibson came up for me last night (I had called and he was not in about 8 PM) about 9 oclock and I went down with him. Mr McI had been explaining his theories with regard to gout, cholera &c to him. Mr McI however could not carry his point with him, (*he* says) tho' he acknowledges his

speculations are ingenious. They parted very amicably however. I have been this morning out at Sunnyside to Mr Robson's hand. [12/10/26] Neither Mr or Mrs R were in, having gone to church.

Got written to my Sister. One good job done I must have my Aunt written to and then I will surely be done with epistles for one week. Mr Bowes promised to leave word on Friday when he was to leave. It is strange that he has never sent any message.

October 23 [Monday]
Not been out of town today and nothing particular occurred. I went with Jos Watson thro' all parts of Lit: & Phil: Society, and had the pleasure of seeing my name on the proposal list. John Gibson sent for me to ask where [illegible word(s)] was. Ben Gibson[29] and Bowes Wilson came in when I was there.

October 24 [Tuesday]
Two accidents today. One in the morning. The messenger said a lad [Ramshaw] had got his leg cut at the 2 mile stone.[30] As Mr McI was going down that road, he saw him; and it proves to be a compound fracture of the leg!! Shortly after they came in from a lad [Cowan] that had got burnt at Benwell, and I was obliged to ride 'Black Jack' as Windchip calls him.

I met Mr Crawford today who tells me Mr Bowes left on Sunday morning! I must therefore write to Thirsk & home tomorrow.

October 25 [Wednesday]
Heard from home this morning. Father coming on Friday, so that I need not write till he comes. Out at Benwell & Sunnyside on the lame horse which came down (all but on to his knees) three or four times. Met Col^n Gilmore – desires his best comp^{ts} to Father, and will be happy to see him, if he has the leisure to call.

Brown nearly got that Galvo-Magnetic *whirligig* made; but I doubt it will not do after all not being true enough set and the magnet not strong enough.[31]

I somehow or other have got all my patients well too quickly, or the weather is healthier, or not having been down the Shields

---

29 Benjamin Gibson was a brother of John Gibson: see Introduction, note 37.
30 A milestone on the turnpike road between Newcastle and North Shields.
31 See note 5 above.

road this week, or from some cause or other I have got very little
to do just now. The fair begins soon when we will surely get
another *rideable* steed for me to get out on, as Mr McI rides the
bay mare altogether.

October 26 [Thursday]

'Richard is himself again'[32] I have once more got down the Shields
road in top boots & spurs & mounted upon little bay, a regular
round amongst my patients. Some of them told me they thought
that certainly 'summit had happened me 'at I had not been down
sae lang'. I set off at 2 PM and got a cup (3 cups) of tea with Mrs
Thornton Wallsend; Got home to dinner(!) about $1\frac{1}{2}$ past 6 and
have just recollected that I forgot to get my tea (10 PM) however
I suppose I must relinquish the idea of it tonight.

Got my machine finished – Brown says he made it answer – I
cannot.[33]

October 27 [Friday]

This day will be an eventful era in the annals of many a family.
When sitting expecting my Father every minute an express came
to say that the 'Benwell Pit had fired',[34] and *he* had scarcely got
his message delivered, before he was followed by another man
on the same errand. Luckily Mr McI was in, and 'to horse and
away ' was the immediate order. Just as I was mounting, the
postman brought me a letter which I made shift to read as my
horse was cantering to the place of rendezvous.

The first person I saw was a lad with his thigh broke & which
I left, while getting washed, to attend to a man severely burnt all
over at Paradise Row. *He* I hope will recover. Just as we were
leaving him, the cart brought home one of the remaining two,
who were till then missing dreadfully burnt, and tho' he was

32 'Conscience avaunt, Richard's himself again' is from the revised version of
   Shakespeare's *Richard III*, by Colley Cibber (1671–1757), where it occurs in act
   5, scene 3.
33 See note 5 above.
34 The disaster at Benwell is described in Sykes, p. 199: 'An accident took place
   in the high part of Benwell Colliery near Newcastle, by which two young men,
   named Joseph Whitfield and William Peel, were killed instantly. Several men
   were injured. There were upwards of 100 men and boys in the mine at the
   time. The cause assigned for this explosion was, that Peel went with a candle
   into a part of the mine where he and the rest had been cautioned not to go.'

properly dressed I doubt he will not survive long. The lad we first saw was then dressed. His right thigh was fractured, and that leg very much cut, his right clavicle started from its articulation at its sternal end. About 5 of the front teeth in the upper jaw completely knocked out; three of those in the lower jaw broken quite inwards, the lips cut, & the face all scratched & cut with the coals he had fallen (or rather been shot) amongst. The leg was dressed; the fracture reduced, then the dislocation of the clavicle, and lastly the teeth put right. The extremities were at first very cold, but by warm bricks &c a more general warmth pervaded when we left him. Greenwood, from not returning, has, I suppose, (6 PM) been left to look to the burnt men. Several accounts have been in; the last just now says the man so dreadfully burnt is living yet.

My father dined with us, and is just gone to call upon Mrs Charnley. This accident has prevented William from getting home today as intended.

10 PM Just bad my father good bye at the Turf Hotel; rec. a letter from Dr Knox by a Mr Dick.

They have been in to say that that man at Benwell is dead.

October 28 [*Saturday*]
Too busy to write anything.

October 29 [*Sunday*]
Got a new mare yesterday in exchange for the black horse, and Mr McI rode her this morning to Benwell (with me on the little mare) to dress the men hurt at the 'misfortune' on Friday. The burnt man [*Brabant?*] is doing as well as expected; and the lad with the fracture [*Hepplewhite?*] equally so.
[*Patient numbers*]

October 30 [*Monday*]
Walked to Benwell this morning, patients doing pretty well. Another man [*Gordon*] got burnt tonight at Benwell with some gunpowder. An accident at Wallsend too this morning. Plenty doing now surely.

October 31 [*Tuesday*]
Rode out to Benwell. Men all doing well.

November 1 *[Wednesday]*
Got a cold which requires nursing. Rode to Benwell – same report as yesterday.

A month of the Diary has now expired, and one purpose of its existence is answered, *viz*, that of affording a retrospective scetch of my common routine of practice in my present situation.

In the hurry of business, combined with my prescribed studies just now, the latter days of the month have been very briefly filled up; and, in consequence, I have determined to avail myself of my proviso in the introduction of – not quite giving it up altogether, – but just putting in a word now and then; not allowing it to come to a premature termination, but retarding that termination, (as limited by the size of the volume) by greater brevity of annotation.

I have fallen into a systematic method of arrangement in subjects for study &c, which keep me, along with business, employed till after tea, and that time is generally taken up with other more important or interesting subjects. I will therefore in future confine myself to medical cases, lists of patients each week, and an occasional desultory remark when leisure allows it. The weather has now set in for a change. The unnaturally fine weather we have had for this month past, has given way to rain, frost, & other symptoms of approaching cold weather & winter. It had its usual effects upon my constitution, *viz.*, chopped lips and a rather violent cold. I take Sudorifus & aperient medicine tonight and hope to be better tomorrow.

November 2 *[Thursday]*
My cold today is a good deal better. Mr McI I think saw I was not well, and went with the young men himself to Benwell this morning.

I have therefore been nowhere today, except to get myself a chain-fastener for a cloak; and a curious hunt I have *[had]* after it. First at a drapers, who sent me to his neighbour; he had none; so I called at a clothiers, & furriers, who directed me to a Hardwaremans, who recommended me to a silversmiths, who happened to have what I wanted.

I must have some more Nitr Potassae &c tonight and a couple of Pil Rheice. My cold is not gone yet.

As I intended to give a months *total* of patients, since I returned

to Mr McI, on Saturday I may as well give it here, and it will not interfere with this months list.
[Patient numbers]

November 3 *[Friday]*

I have had a long round this morning, to Byker Old Engine, Walker, Wallsend, Biggs Main, Heaton H Pit &c and saw about 30 patients; amongst them a number of children in Dysenteries & the 'Atrophia' before spoken of [6/10/26]. I have got a bad headache tonight from some cause or other – my cold almost well.

November 4 *[Saturday]*

No sooner had I come in from Benwell (dressing that burnt man) [*Brabant, 29/10/26*] than I was called out to a lad at Elswick, who has got very much bruised between two corves. Nothing would remain on his stomach then.

Hirudrius xij Abdomini Appl:

℞   Ol Ricini ℥ iv T^r Opii ℥ j Sum coch j 2nd qq hora

They are to send in this evening to say how he is.

Brabant (Benwell) is rather better today than yesterday – discharge considerable, pulse quiet, is taking Mist: Cinchon c T^r Opi: i Zingiber & Carb: Ammon: Has not been moved (in a bed) since 12 PM on the 2nd Inst. Mr McI ordered him to continue the mixture of bark and not to take his opening medicine till tomorrow.

I have in making out accounts today come at two most visible instances of Mr Bewicke's[35] *greatness* while here. First to a patient is put 'Making an incision in the Arm and extracting portion of wood' which *being interpreted* means (W^m [*King*] says) cutting out a little splinter from the thumb which he B had broken in. Secondly – two or three journeys are charged to a patient with the *momentous* items of 'applying bandage to the leg' – a thing which never found its way into Mr McI's day book before I will venture to assert.
[Patient numbers]
Gascoignes hands (Heaton H Pit) have all healed; the finger end

---

35 Bewicke was an apprentice to Mr Allison, Surgeon, in Darlington when TGW was indentured there in 1823. Later, Bewicke became a temporary assistant of Mr McIntyre while TGW was a student in Edinburgh. See 'My Autobiography', chapters 12 and 17.

has staid on, and tho' not a very seemly one now it will improve I hope. [14/10/26]

Snaith whose hand was cut by an axe (*vide* Oct 14) has had an abscess opened in his hand, but it is now, I expect, doing well. The wound is healing after a great deal of discharge.

Ritsons leg (Benwell) is not yet quite healed in consequence of walking a great deal about upon it. [1/10/26]

November 5 [*Sunday*]

They sent in last night to say the lad at Elswick was much the same [4/11/26]. An injection had been given, but with no effect, and nothing would remain on his stomach. The leeches had bled well. I ordered the warm bath, and 'I would see him in the morning'. The father was in first thing this morning to say he was no better, his bowels swelled, and very painful, but he had taken a drink of coffee and some biscuit without vomiting. I went up to consult Mr McI, and he gave his opinion as follows, (I had previously ordered a blister & some Croton oil pills to be got ready). 'You had better give him some leeches & a blister afterward' 'He has had a dozen leeches, sir, and a blister is preparing' 'They must use injections'. 'He has had some, sir, but without effect'. 'Give him some Croton oil pills then, you know you *must* get his bowels open; and some purging mixture'. 'The pills are ready, I believe, sir'. Accordingly I went out to see him but on the road met a messenger to say he was *dead*. Most probably a rupture of some of the viscera caused death. I have since been down at Wallsend, Heaton &c most patients doing well. Brabant (Benwell) [4/11/26] is a great deal better this morning.

November 7 [*Tuesday*]

An accident yesterday morning at Wallsend at 11 AM; Mr McI was at Benwell, and said he would be home soon, and as expected he would be going down that road. I waited till 1 for him. The other mare was getting shod so I had nothing to ride either, if I had wished to go sooner. Mr McI said nothing about going till near two when he told me to 'get a gig down' (giving me a half crown) to my not small chagrin; as there were then two horses in the stable. He said however that he should want one, and the other was not to go out at all yesterday, having had a hard day's work the day before. I had made myself sure of Mr McI's going, and catching the 'blowing up' for not going sooner;

and was accordingly obliged to prepare myself for the storm as I went down. Luckily however the folks were *wiser*, and had been applying the leeches sent down by messenger, fomenting &c very contentedly till 'the doctor comes'. The man's ancle was a good deal bruised. In going down I met the Heaton horse keeper to say there was an accident. 'First come, first served' tho' I was going past the back door. He said he 'would make Mackintyre come then' *Mackintyre* had not come however when I saw the boy on my return. His leg was also severely bruised. I could get no gig back so walked home.

I had just got myself seated to a mutton chop &c, and had not begun my dinner when the sound of a horses feet coming again down the yard met my unwilling ear – '*an accident at Benwell*'! Mr McI's mare was then going to meet him, and I sent him word while I finished my dinner. I was just going to mount the *restricted* mare, when word came (I was tired of waiting made me prepare for going) that (agreeable news on a frosty night 7 PM!) William [*King*] was to walk out to see him. The man was only slightly cut on the leg.

There were two boys burnt by setting fire to some gunpowder last night also at Benwell. One, fortunately for us, sent in for *Hosegood*,[36] and the father of the other, knowing, I suppose, that stimulants were the best applications, at first sent for no surgeon, but – laid a horsewhip over his son's back by way of a warm application!! *He* is not much worse.

I was out at Benwell this morning by 8 oclock!! and a precious cold ride it was. A hard frost during the night and a bleak frosty wind this morning. Patients all doing well. I told my burnt patient [*Brabant ? 5/11/26*] 'I could afford to laugh at him now'; as he was making faces over swallowing a couple of aloes pills. He laughed too himself.

I was to 'ride the taller mare' this morning for the first time. Mr McI has taken quite a fancy for my little one; he has always ridden this three or four days. I do not like this other one; she has no *life* in her and requires the spurs to be used pretty freely. She goes well in the gig tho' and trots fast when put to it.

---

36 Probably George Hosegood, surgeon, Tyne Bridge End, Newcastle: see PW, I, p. 45.

November 8 *[Wednesday]*
Only out at Benwell. Patients doing well. I called at the Society's rooms last night, – paid Mr Turner my guinea & half, and was, as I hear this morning, duly elected MNL&PS.[37]

What was my astonishment when strolling in the library this morning, to be accosted by one of a party of ladies – *Miss Meek!* She had come over from Sunderland with some friends (for the morning) with whom she is on a visit.

November 12 *[Sunday]*
What with the Society and other matters, – oh! aye, parcels, letters &c (I had almost forgot, and was beginning to wonder what I had been doing these four days) I have made a hop, skip, & jump from 8 to 12.

I received a large box on Friday which my Mother calls a complete schoolboy dispatch; one corner filled up with 'Miss Skelly's apples'; another with walnuts; and two or three more *corners made* to fill up by a large circular pasty into a square or rather parallelogramatic box; two round bottles &c &c &c. One corner was filled up however by some mental food, *viz.* a bundle of letters; among them six close written *folio* pages from my Mother!! Oh! that I could compose such an epistle! The one deficiency in my cerebral development I lament most is that of *composition*, a ready flow of ideas (which constitutes *real wit*) 'presence of mind' 'rummul gumption' which some may please to Anglify 'common sense'. It is no use however filling up this page or two by pursuing this, to me, unpleasant turn of thought, so to professional remarks which I vowed should chiefly fill up the rest of this book.

Patients at Benwell doing *pretty* well i.e. burnt man [*Brabant, 7/ 11/27*] very well, fracture but badly, *ergo* I take the mean. The lad with the fracture [*Hepplewhite, 29/10/26*] will not keep still, and has had the thigh once set over again. Yesterday it appeared to be displaced again, and I have sent out another splint, which will *probably* hold it better. Mr McI or I will have to apply it this morning. This case is a good illustration of Mr Liston's assertion that ' in fractures above the half of the thigh, (this is one) a long splint reaching from the axilla to the heel is better than Mr McI's; in

---

37 Member of the Lit. and Phil.: see Introduction.

fractures below the half, Mr McI's is the best splint he has seen.'
Mr McI's splint has no purchase over the body & hips which by
getting out of line displaces the fracture.[38]

A number of children just now are affected with a kind of
water- [*illegible word*] eruption but the spots are smaller. J Gibson
has met (as well as myself) with a number of cases. The disease
dies away in about 10 days naturally. A dose of opening medicine
being all sufficient.

Synochus is making its appearance. A family of three, father &
mother & daughter were admitted into the fever Hospital on
Friday. The father had been a patient of ours. Another patient
has since come on the books. It appears true Synocha and *uninfec*-
tious in the commencement but ends in *infectious* Typhus.

A slight cough remained for some days after *I* had got rid of
cold, but it too has yielded and now the only symptom not *perfectly* in accordance with healthy function is about two drachmas
p. diem surplus of nasal discharge.

I quite forgot yesterday to get Parsons to work at my hair. I
must get it done tomorrow.

Amongst 'other things new' (a general question with some folks
and almost the only one thing they utter – 'have you anything
new?') I have got a *new* upper garment in the form of a Cloak; –
'Toga' my Mother calls it. I was afraid of some new and *peculiar*
fashions being introduced in it, as it was made under my
Mother's superintendence. Tho' I do not in the least doubt, but
rather can bear witness to Mrs Wright's taste in female attire; yet
a gentleman's winter costume in town can be so badly judged by
a person in the country, that I must say I was rather afraid of it.
I confess however I was *'agreeably disappointed'* (for that is actually
an English phraze) on receiving this said cloak which is *bona fide*
a genteel thing. – I must write home tomorrow to make all right,
and patch up the business the best way I can. I have got one
sharp retort from my Mother already.

I have got the New Monthly the Newcastle & part of the
London Magazines read thro' for this month; as I generally go,
at least have gone so far, about an hour a day to the rooms of the
Lit & Phil Soc. I was last night making diligent search thro' the
Philosoph: Transact: London & Trans: Soc: Arts Lond: for data

---

38 See note 28 above.

respecting the praemium which ought to have been awarded to Father for his coal machine. I was successful but I cannot say all about it here so *verbum sat*.[39]

[*Patient numbers*]

Two or three more accidents these four days. One man severely bruised at Wallsend. I bled him &c but have not seen him since Mr McI having [*gone*] down that way himself yesterday.

November 14 [*Tuesday*]

Burnt man at Benwell very poorly yesterday, but better this morning. [*Brabant? 7/11/26*] Mr McI & I went out this morning and put a fresh splint on the lad with the fractured thigh. [*Hepplewhite,12/11/26*] It too is doing better.

A ludicrous scene occurred this morning. I followed Mr McI down and as the morning was fine, did not (after his example) put on my 'upper Benjamin'.[40] By the time I got to the High Cross however, a shower came on and I was glad to borrow a coat or jacket such as I could get of a man there. I left it & my horse at Benwell Stables, when I met Mr McI, and we walked down to Paradise Row where the man lives. It was raining hard when we got back to the Stables, and Mr McI asked Ritchie (a very stout man and horsekeeper) for the loan of his great coat. Ritchie produced it. It hung about Mr McI like 'Will Waddles' skin in Colman's story.[41] He asked at first for a *straw rope* to put about it to *complete his dress* but finally got a *strap* buckled round him. When I put on the one I had brought down, which was the counterpart of the one Mr McI had on, and had been in the owners possession (he said) about 20 years, we formed a most ridiculous set out to ride to Newcastle, and set to work to laugh at one another. The rain going off by the time we got back to the High Cross again, we 'doffed' our outer costumes and left them there.

I got a letter of about 7 large folio pages to my Mother sent off last night; enclosing one to my Aunt, and another to my Grandfather also! My mind is, in consequence, exceeding relieved. 'I reckon'; and I must now consider about writing again to London.

---

39 TGW returns to the subject of the coal machine later in the *Diary*, when he gives a talk about it to the Lit. & Phil.: see Volume 6, 11/10/27.

40 A type of overcoat.

41 The story is probably one by George Colman (1762–1836), but it has not been identified.

One is never done writing letters, I declare. But I do not feel so averse to the system as I did once, luckily for myself.

Called at Colⁿ Gilmore's with a catalogue of the Lit: & Phil: Soc: for him to look at. I had asked Mr McI (the owner)'s leave to do so. The Colⁿ not in, left my card.

Evening I have been down at Wallsend, Byker &c since dinner. Heavy rain when I set off, but soon cleared up, and now seems set in for frost.

A man got his leg broke last night by a horse falling on the waggon way. I tried to get to the farm at Wallsend where he resides (tonight), but had to cross a burn, which my mare would not come near. I tried for some time, but as it was growing dark, I was obliged to give up the attempt.

In a Newcastle Chronicle I accidentally laid my hands on last night, I found in the *obituary* the death of 'John James' Le Mesurier, on the 20 June at *Panama* South America.[42] My old playmate at Haughton – *Jimmy* Le Mesurier! This is the second of that unfortunate orphan family, who has died so far from his friends within this year. *Harry* Le Mesurier was with Wm Bewick at Genoa. This cannot surely be *Johnny*, as the paper states him to be 'the third son of the late Thos Le Mesurier'. Jimmy was the third. He died of the yellow fever.

A patient [*Gardner*] who has been about a week under Lands[43] is *considerably* better today, indeed almost well again. I at first considered his complaint as Dyspepsia, and accordingly kept him low (he had some fever) gave him purges &c with a little tonic medicine after them. He got no better; and gave me a long history of his being often affected with this complaint, and lying 7 weeks under *Mr Tullock's* care,[44] when his complaints ended in nervous fever &c &c. I, having read a little while ago a paper in the Medico chirurgical review (I think it was) on *Gastralgia* conjectured it might very probably be a case of that disease, and *reversed* my plan of treatment. I ordered him a mutton chop and a glass of brandy and water daily, along with some more powerful *tonic*

42 See 'My Autobiography', Chapter 4. The death of John James LeMesurier is recorded in the *Newcastle Weekly Chronicle*, Saturday, 11/11/1826.
43 Lands was probably another local doctor but he has not been identified.
44 Probably Benjamin Tullock, surgeon, New Bridge Street, Newcastle: see PW, I, p. 87.

powders. This has been followed by the best effects, he has been better ever since he took the powders on Sunday, and says he is now better than before I took him through Lands. His wife says 'he cracks sair o' them last poothers he got'.[45] He is the more pleased as he expected another 'seven weeks bout'.

This among many very pleasant visits I pay, and very gratifying to a young practitioner. The people were at first wanting (naturally) to see Mr McI, but now say they do not care to see him at all, I have done the gudeman so much good. I must however in candour state that I *do* now and then meet with an *unpleasant* visit, but they are not frequent, and I avail myself of the general custom among *authors* to say nothing about them; and look only at the white side of the shield. But I must go to the library a bit.

November 17 *[Friday]*
Patients doing well at Benwell. Burnt man *[Brabant? 14/11/26]* complains severely when dressed.

Three accidents happened yesterday and one today. Nothing serious. One man a cut just on the internal condyle of the humerus. I have met with two or three cases of Whooping cough at last. One child *[Marne]* has had it near a month. I should like to bring it round – *well*. Another case of Synochus *[Miller]* has come under *my* care at Heaton. The girl, who has come in twice for his medicine, has, by the bye, pertinaciously affirmed that 'Mr McIntyre himself seed him'. *I* must have got very sage-looking certainly, for Mr McI has not been within half a mile of the place; and the girl was in at both my visits. But this is not by any means the first time I have been called 'Mr McIntyre'. I was down at Byker Old Engine, Heaton, Walker, & Battle Hill this morning, and Benwell this afternoon; and at Benwell & Heaton New Pit yesterday. Mr McI went to Shields yesterday afternoon, and just got home to dinner today.

A gentleman from South Shields a Mr Richardson called about his son being apprentice here. I wish we had another then W^m *[William King]* would surely get away.
[Patient numbers]

---

45 Tyneside dialect: can be roughly translated as, 'he talks well of those last powders he got'.

November 19 [*Saturday*]

Scarcely had I got in from Benwell this morning, when a man came in from 'Ritchie' the horsekeeper, to wish him to be seen. [14/11/26] They had not seen me when I was out tho' I had ridden close past the door. He spoke to me of being unwell on Friday, with a cold. He subscribes to Mr Mark[46] and had sent in to him yesterday to come out to see him. He has not been there, so the messenger who came in for me, was to leave word that *he need not* come. Mr McI was away. As it was a *new* patient and from Mr Mark, I tho' sore against inclination was obliged to go out after dinner. He has got a slight inflammation on the chest from cold. I bled him &c. He says 'he'll have nea mair to do with Mark' he only wishes he'd applied 'to Mr McI or me, for its a' the same thing, sooner'

I have had a more than usually amusing specimen of the effect of my quondam colleague and present junior *William's* [*King*] schoolboy-way (and great self importance withall) of 'going about things'. He had gone down to an accident at Forth banks during Mr McI & my absence yesterday morning. The man [*Asle-bruff*] was bruised about the shoulders & legs. The wife of the patient came up in the afternoon to request I or Mr McI would see him. Before going away she repeated her injunction 'now ye'll mind and come yeerself, sir, if ye please and dinna send the *'little boy* doon this time'. Some more slurs were cast upon poor Will's *dignity* during my visit yesterday, tho' he was with me. Today I saw the man and dressed his knee &c as they had not understood directions properly. 'Aye now ye see', says the man to his wife 'when one comes that understands these like things how different they do it, but that bit lad as come yesterday did nought but –' I did not exactly catch the word but I think it was '*gowk* about him' 'Out Owt! Man' replied a neighbour, 'why he was only a bit bairn, ye knaw, what can you expect'. This is one among many examples of the effect of William's literally 'gowking' manner of behaviour, and of which I have frequently tho' vainly admonished him; but he thinks I merely do it from ill nature, and does not believe a word of all this.

One bore out of the way for six months at least. William set off for Edinburgh via Hexham & Carlisle yesterday. This journey has

46 Probably Mr Ed. R. Mark, Surgeon, 4 Angas Court, Bigg Market, Newcastle: see PW, I, p. 56.

been I understand (partly from experience) his incessant talk for this last twelvemonths.

November 22 *[Wednesday]*
I have scarcely had time for breathing these three days. I was a long and tedious ride on Monday. I went down the Shields road by Byker Old Engine, &c, seeing as usual all my patients on the way down, and when I had got to Heaton, about ½ thro' my round, I had to go back to Byker to a man upon whom a stone had fallen. The man was not got off home when I had word, as I was just passing the Colliery office when the messenger arrived *there* to send off express to Newcastle. I therefore determined upon finishing my round as quickly as possible, and seeing this man on my way back. I rode very hard to accomplish it, but, after I had visited this said new patient, I was obliged to cut across the country to Heaton High Pit to see an overman's wife there, one of our subscribers. The man at Byker *[Yule]* was a good deal bruised but is doing very well. I was at Benwell yesterday, patients doing very well.

About seven oclock PM Thornton's brother of Wallsend (vide Oct 1) *[8/10/26]* came in to say that he had broken his leg again. Mr McI was rather engaged so he sent me down to see if *[it]* was really broken, (which he could scarcely believe) and with orders 'if it was broken not to attempt to reduce it but lay it on a splint', and he would be down in the morning and set it. Thornton had just got to walk a little on his crutches, and had last night tripped in going across the floor, fallen, and fractured the bone about three inches above the old break. Yesterday was precisely the thirteenth hebdomad from his former accident. I thought of reducing it if possible to gain some credit with Mr McI, but found I wanted proper assistance, and was obliged to leave the limb as it was. I laid it extended upon a splint and left him quite easy. I really feel for that man very much, as he & I used often to have a joke together on his getting well. Such a clean well behaved respectable family they are too.

Glorious Apollo! Mercury[47]! Aesculapius! and all the other pat-

---

47 [*TGW footnote*] Mercury god of thieves, kidnappers and *trepanners*; hence including *a part* of the medical profession. [*A detailed account of the significance of mythical lore in medicine is given in Hermione de Almeida,* Romantic Medicine and John Keats *(Oxford, 1991).*]

rons of Physic, only hear and hearing understand!! Thornton's father has just come in for some medicine for his son and reports Mr McI has done nothing at the leg – 'saying that it is very well set'!!!!!!!!!!!!!!!!

I could make exclamations (but nonsense) notes of admiration, I mean, all over the page. My first fracture and of the leg too. 'Mr McI merely raised the heel a little'. I did not like to say so before, lest I should not have accomplished it properly, but I *did attempt* to reduce the fracture last night, but did not get it done *to my own satisfaction* – the leg did not appear to me to be straight *enough*. I had told the people therefore that 'it was not *quite* as it ought to be but I required more assistance for that' and that 'Mr McI would see it in the morning' &c &c. But still, I must damp my joy a little yet awhile. Mr McI has not got home yet. I will say no more till he comes about that subject.

I have got finished at last a Diagram of the Eye from Dr. Knox's papers on that organ in all the publications I could lay hold of them in, as Edinburgh Philosoph. Trans; Edin. Wernerian Soc: Trans:, Edinborough [*sic*] Journal of Medical Sciences; Notes of his lectures &c &c and which has occupied my leisure time this day or two.[48] As I have a case or two in point just now I am studying Travers on Diseases of the Eye[49] too. Theory & Practice should always go hand in hand.

Got my 'Members ticket' for Lectures on Practical Mechanics (not Belles Lettres as at first intended) to begin next Monday at the Lit: & Philosoph: Institution.[50]

I got home from Wallsend last night about $\frac{1}{2}$ past ten PM, and had just got into a sound sleep, when Mr McIntyre called both Greenwood and me up – just about 12 oclock. We went down stairs, and Mr McI gave G. a prescription to make up and called me into his room, – he was writing, – I stood, after a while 'take a chair' says my master – I sat down – at last he told me what he wanted – I was to take the medicines with me (giving me another

---

48 The importance of the work of Robert Knox on the eye is discussed in Isobel Rae, *Knox the Anatomist* (Edinburgh and London, 1964), pp. 30 ff.

49 A treatise by Benjamin Travers, Senior Surgeon to St Thomas's Hospital, London, titled *A Synopsis of the Diseases of the Eye and their Treatment* (London, 1820), was one of the earliest works in English to deal with this subject systematically: see, e.g., A. Castiglioni, *A History of Medicine* (New York, 1941).

50 For comment on the Lit & Phil lectures, see Introduction.

prescription) to Ridley Place, to a lady with whom he had just been, (and where he staid greatest part of the previous night,) and to sit there till I found the medicines had taken effect in giving relief to the patient. I accordingly popped on a clean cravat &c, and my cloak, and went up to Mrs Atkinson's. I had always inferred that 'Miss Aveling' & 'Miss Jane Aveling', whose names I had seen in the day book, and the elder of whom was the present patient, were Mrs Atkinson's (with whom they reside) nieces – ergo *young ladies*. Alack and alas! They are two *elderly ladies* and (as I now guess) *sisters* of the aforesaid Mrs Atkinson.[51] My patient was soon relieved, and, after sitting about an hour & half, I got home just as the watchmen were calling 'past two oclock'. I did not wake till after eight when Mr McI came to my room to enquire after Miss A. I have only seen one out of door patient today and have not been at all on horseback.

Mr McI came home but said not a word about the leg [*Thornton, 22/11/26*], tho' he would hardly believe me when I told him last night that it was broken, and questioned me minutely as to the situation, nature &c of the fracture. But though he *says* nothing, I hope he will *think*; and, as I have passed the Rubicon (almost unconsciously) set me out to plenty of fractures now. This lesson will make me *not quite* so diffident, and to have more reliance on my own opinion. I have said plenty on this subject though, so I will now treat myself with a glass of my sister's good homemade, as I am by my self, to drink success to the fractured leg! [*the last five words are emphasised by being written in very large letters*]

November 24 [*Friday*]

I have had pretty long rounds these last two days. Benwell & Elswick, then to Byker, Heaton & Heaton H Pit &c &c. I have had a strange throbbing pain in my head this morning, but it has in a great measure gone off after a good dinner. Patients at Benwell &c doing well. The young man who was burnt importunes me *if possible* not to let Mr McI come anymore to dress him (Mr McI saw him a day or two back) but always to come myself.

I must write home tonight about my intended new pair of 'inexpressibles',[52] for Scarlett has none of the shag cord my

51 TGW later changed his opinion of Miss Aveling, see Volume 4, 20/6/27.
52 Inexpressibles: often used as a euphemism for trousers.

Mother wants me to wear. One of my Mother's reasons is 'Does not Sir M W Ridley wear them?' That kind of argument always reminds me of an anecdote I heard some time ago. A Mrs W– wished her son to swallow (by way of making his breakfast slip down more readily, and partly because '*it was good for the inside*', I suppose) every morning a wineglassful of sweet or salad oil!! Among other persuasions used to the unwilling patient was this, that Lady D–s & Mrs C–r gave their daughters the same. Some time afterward I happened to hear that the Miss C's used to take in a morning a wineglassful not of sweet oil, – but – Capillaire!! [53] which Mrs W's informant had mistaken for *oil*. So much for a wrong precedent; and I fear it may turn out after all that it is Sir MWR's *servants* who wear this shag, as it is rather *groo*mish stuff.

The Patient whom I took or rather took himself out of Mr Mark's (surgeon) hands and came under my care last Sunday is about well.

November 27 [*Monday*]
Not been down the Shields road these four days. Patients at Benwell doing well; the left arm of the burnt man [*Brabant 17/11/ 26*] skinning very rapidly the other parts healing fast.

I was yesterday out at Benwell in one of the most bitter snow storms I ever encountered except one as I was coming outside the coach from Edinburgh.[54] Mr McI said 'you will have the young man at Benwell to see sometime this morning you know', so, as the day did not look at all likely to improve, I set off directly, thinking the sooner I got my visit paid the better. I armed myself well against the cold, but the North wind upon exposed road, with thick, heavy snow was bitter to face. The storm was a good deal abated as I came back.

This morning was a beautifully clear frost. As the mare was not sharped,[55] and the roads very slippery, I agreed with Mr McI that it would be safer *walking* to Benwell, and a delightful walk I had. The sun was powerful, shining in a cloudless sky, and the air 32° if not lower. I called at G Field Place as I went up the Hill on my way out of town.

---

53 Capillaire: a syrup flavoured with orange flower water.
54 A description of the journey from Edinburgh is given in 'My Autobiography', chapter 17.
55 Sharped: sharp-shod, i.e., with spikes in the horseshoes to prevent slipping.

I have just come from hearing Mr Turner's first lecture on Practical Mechanics,[56] – his course for the season. It is really painful to hear him lecture, especially when he gets out of his written path. His assistant, or the man who performs his experiments is the most regularly sheepish looking fool, the most complete spooney I ever saw. On the whole I was greatly disappointed; and have the self assurance to think that if I had time to prepare I could commence a course *almost* as well *myself*!!
[Patient numbers]

November 28 *[Tuesday]*
I have been out at Benwell this morning and such a ride or rather slide. My mare not sharped, and the roads with a mild thaw after the hard frost of yesterday and last night, are very slippery. I rode with my feet out of the stirrups almost all of the way, and my steed slid all ways but *downwards*. She *did* come down upon 'the side which follows all other sides' once or twice in going downhill – I ought to go down to Heaton, Carville &c after dinner, but I dare not ride the mare without sharping, and Mr McI's hackney has disappeared for these last two days. He came home without her on Sunday but has said not a word as to what he made of her.

Apropos of that word Carville or Caraville. For a long time I could not make out the meaning of this *Carveal* as the Pitmen termed it; and *calf-like*, I thought it had something to do with *veal*. In the newspaper one day I saw it spelled *Carville*. It is the name of a seat close to one of the Wallsend Pits, and from which part of Wallsend receives its name, tho' *Wallsend*, properly so called, is a village apart from Carville, and more like a *Yorkshire* village than any in the neighbourhood; being a farming hamlet, with two or three gentlemans seats in or near it. Still this *Car*-ville puzzled me; at last I saw upon a cart Mr – *Cara*ville which explains the meaning at once *Cara villa*, dear villa![57]

56 The function of lectures at the Lit. and Phil is described in the Introduction: see also note 6 above.

57 TGW's speculation about the origin of the place name Carville although ingenious is unfortunately incorrect. The village of Carville took its name from a seventeenth century mansion, originally known as Cosen's House, which passed in the eighteenth century to Robert Carr, who renamed it Carville: see, for example, S. Middlebrook, *Pictures of Tyneside* (Newcastle, 1969).

When on the subject I may mention that close by Wallsend village is a railroad[58] upon scaffolding over a burn. This bridge which looks very slender, but seems to have stood for ages, presents a short cut to some pitmen's houses on the other side; accordingly it has been the custom for Mr McI and his assistants to go this way for years. The bridge, in the middle overtops some high trees in a garden below, and is I should guess about 40 or 50 feet. This mare that I now ride crosses it very steadily, but I would not attempt doing so in the night. The bridge is not very broad but has, or once had a rail all along the side. Two carriages could not pass, I dare say, upon it, – it is of no great length however. A cart road goes under it, but I should not have much ambition to leap down even upon a cart of hay.

7 PM The bigger mare has cast up again. Mr McI had given her to a young man in Pilgrim Street on Sunday night to bring home, and the chap had taken her to a public house down below. Mr McI ordered the gig just now, and was amazed at hearing the gig mare was not to be found. Search was commenced immediately and the lost beast was soon found.

A thought just struck me that I would condense the next month into the remaining part of this volume; but as I have many observations to make after finishing the Diary, and as three days yet remain of this month, I will not cramp what I may have to say for want of room.

Mr McI is going to take me in the gig as far as Wallsend; 'and then', he says 'I can come back in another gig'. It is now four oclock and is getting dark before we set off. I shall most likely have to walk back after all, as I have patients on the road to see.

I got a box sent off home this morning containing amongst other things a *notary* sketch of a paper to be read at the Society on my Father's coal machine some meeting soon.[59]

November 29 [*Wednesday*]

After 'a real to do' Mr McI & I got down as far as Byker last night in the gig; the road was very slippery, and I was in full expecta-

---

58 The word 'railroad' was used for a waggonway used to transport coal from a colliery to the River Tyne. A comprehensive account of the waggonways on Tyneside is given in C. R. Warn, *Waggonways and Early Railways of Northumberland* (Newcastle, 1976).

59 TGW describes the presentation of his paper in Volume 6, 4–14/11/27.

tion of the mare coming down with gig and all her precious burthen. Mr McI left me at Catterick's buildings and said he would meet me at Byker Hill '*shortly*'; I meantime seeing the patients about there. After waiting an hour at Byker Hill Mr McI came, but it was only to tell me I need not go farther. He was going down to Shields, and I was to meet him at Wallsend this morning at twelve oclock. Last night was North Shields ball, to which I suppose Mr McI would be going by the portmanteau which went into the gig box. I got home to tea about 7 o'clock, and went down by appointment to John Gibson's and sat the evening.

As I had the boy at Benwell to dress and to be down at Wallsend at 12, I was out early this morning, performing my West ride before breakfast. I rode down the Shields road with Tyler (at Mr Moores[60]) and was at the place of meeting an hour & half before Mr McI, though I was half an hour behind time, not expecting *him* to be very punctual. I was to see certain patients, he would see others and both were to be home as fast as possible. We subsequently met on the way home and rode into town together at full speed, splashing the dirt about in regular *style*. I came home in a pair of *literal mudboots* i.e. a case of mud over my topboots.

There was a beautiful eclipse of the sun this morning which I had a fine view of on my journey. The cloudiness of the atmosphere prevented the want of smoked glass or any such dense medium.

My horse and I had a complete skaiting of it to Benwell again this morning. The snow having melted left only a hard stratum of smooth *ice* below, making the roads if anything worse than yesterday. I durst not ride down the bank to the Benwell stables, but led my mare sliding down. It seems like a frost tonight, if so the horses must be sharped tomorrow or there will be no such thing as riding at all.

Mr Crawford just calted to say that Mr Bowes is here with Dick. Mr C. wishes me to call in the morning upon Mr B.

After being on horseback the greatest part of the time from 8 AM to 4 PM I am *preterparticularly* tired tonight, and will go to

---

60 William Moore, surgeon, 11 Bigg Market, Newcastle: see PW, I, p. 125. Moore was also a surgeon at the Infirmary, see Hume, p. 143. Tyler was probably his assistant or apprentice.

bed soon. Mr McI has a party of the Carrs &c to dinner. [*see 30/ 11/26*] They drove up in his gig from Shields this morning, and he rode young Carr's horse.

November 30 [*Thursday*]
I have so far (4 PM) not been on horseback today and hope I shall not have to go now. Mr McI has been down the Shields road himself, and he told me 'if the boy at Benwell *required* dressing today to send Greenwood' as he wishes me to sit beside Mr Carr till his return. I accordingly did so. Mr Carr is an elderly *hypochondriac* gentleman a patient of ours, a great colliery owner and 'monied man'. He was first a pitman or something nearly as low about the collieries, and from not being worth 50 pence became by lucky speculations, master of £30,000. He is not now quite so prosperous however, as many of the concerns he holds shares in are not doing well just now. He has been staying all night, and will most likely stay tonight here. His son & daughter were both up from Shields too and dined with Mr McI yesterday as aforesaid. While I was sitting beside him in the drawing room this morning, I had the pleasure of seeing Mr McI's said-to-be-intended bride (and *I* think with more, *tho' still little*, reason) in the person of Mr Carr's daughter[61] Mrs Hutchison. She is a young widow with great fortune. Her husband died after having been married a few months, so she is still young and *I* think very *pretty*, from the little I saw of her. Mr McI had not then gone off and came into the room just after the ladies. As I was not exactly trimmed for receiving callers especially *ladies* (my coat being rather the worse for its numerous contacts with the bedclothes of my patients and consequent brushings) I was withdrawing, but Mr McI said 'you need not go' – and then pausing said 'well, you can come back'– I slipped on a pair of sleevelets and my betterma [*i.e., best*] black coat, and was ready to make my appearance, when the old gentleman went out with the ladies (another lady was with Mrs H) and Mr McI set off on horseback. When Mr Carr came back I sat beside him till about $3\frac{1}{2}$ PM. As Mr C is not very talkative, Mr McI very politely brought me in Dec^{br} number of Blackwood – the latest Edin^{br}: Review, the last no. of the Lancet &c to read.

---

61 [*TGW footnote*] I am not so sure of that opinion being just after two or three days reflection but I only profess to note down thoughts not fixed opinions.

When Mr McI came home and took his post beside Mr Carr, I came away; but previously Mr McI asked me if I 'had had dinner', if not no doubt I should have been invited to dine with him. Mr Carr, Major Johnson & (I think) Mrs Hutchinson & the other lady are at dinner just now. The housekeeper had unfortunately made ready our dinner at two o'clock – otherwise I should most likely have seen more of this rich widow.

I have positively so far not been outside the front door today. I want to go to the Society or up to Travis or somewhere this evening.

[Patient numbers]

Here are two months expired and five or six pages wanting to complete this volume. I think in the first place it will be important to notice the state in which the patients mentioned in my remarks are, at least those not previously mentioned *well*. The date in which the *case* is mentioned had better be prefixed

Oct 1	*Ritson*	well long since [4/11/26]
	Grantson	D° D° D°
	Gascoigne	*His* finger is well some time ago, but the end is rather unseemly he is applying caustic to the edges of the gap in one or two places to inflame and thus attempt to heal it. [4/11/26]
	Thornton	has had his leg broke since again (*vide* Nov 22). I saw him yesterday his last *simple* fracture is doing very well.
	Scott	this child continues well. The disease I since find is a *species* of *Marasmus*.
Oct 7	*Mrs Scott*	has been well and bad again various times since then. I am a great favorite there since the above.
	Shields	Walker – soon got well.
9	*Gaer*	Tape Worm. Keeps well
14	*Snaith*	Cut forefinger. Well but lost the use of that finger. [4/11/26]
16	*Brown*	Wallsend – Well and got to work.
20	*Widdington*	child – Keeps wonderfully well.
21	*Reavely*	Biggs Main – doing very well.

24	Ramshaw	(fracture) nearly well.
	Cowan	burnt – was well in a week.
27	Brabant	burnt – is doing well, – the burns are skinning rapidly, but it will still be a tedious case. [27/11/26]
	Hepplewhite	fractures – almost able to move about. [14/11/26]

[*Note apparently added later*] *Hepplewhite*'s thigh is far from being as straight as I could wish, but it is his own fault. He could not be made to keep still when the bones were uniting, and it will be difficult if not impossible to make them any better now – the fracture was so high up that the splint would have little effect in keeping it steady. Mr McIntyre though hit upon an ingenious expedient to keep the bones as straight as might be notwithstanding the boy's restlessness. He bent the splint very much, and so suspended (as it were) the thigh from the knee.

30	Gordon	burnt, soon cured.
Nov 2	Wright	cold – Keeps quite well.
7		All three patients well long ago.
14	Gardner	Gastralgia 'Keeps better' he says 'than he has been for many months'
17	Marn's child	Whooping cough; is well of the cough but has now got chicken pox.
	Miller	Synochus – doing very well. Able to sit up.
19	Ritchie Hunter	as stout & hearty as ever again.
	Aslebruff	bruised nearly well – rather stiff.
22	Yule	Heaton – well and at work.
	Miss Aveling	Have not seen her since – suppose she is about well.

Having wound up all matters *necessary* to complete this Diary for so long as it lasts, it now only remains for me to make a few *observations*.

This work has been, what I intended, a good exercise for me in English composition; and hence a useful employment of a few leisure hours. My language, I doubt will be found in many places very *bad*, but my remarks have been made in so hurried a manner (I intended it to be spontaneous composition) as to give no time for thought as to elegance in that point, or regard to style. By the bye speaking of style, as Paul Pry[62] says ('by the bye talking of doing – how do you do?') 'Style is – style' 'Linkum Fidelius' hath it[63], and is a matter of pure *taste*, but tho' I like the style of one or two prose writers in Blackwood and the New Monthly, the *style I* prefer even to that of the 'Great Unknown' is

Washington Irving's!

I observe that a material part – (often, as regards the success of his work) – of an author's business is omitted in this volume – a dedication. I will therefore place in the last page what ought to have been in the first, and, as I like a dedication that every one *may* apply to him or herself.

To The Reader who is most gratified by an attentive perusal of this Diary it is most respectfully Dedicated by The Author.[64]

---

62 Paul Pry was a very inquisitive character in the play of the same name. TGW saw this play in Edinburgh in 1825: see 'My Autobiography', chapter 16 and note 79.

63 'Linkum Fidelius' may be an erroneous reading; the reference is obscure.

64 [*TGW footnote*] Himself probably the *only* person to whom the dedication is applicable.

V O L U M E 2 (December 1, 1826 to February 28, 1827)

December 1 to 11 *[Friday – Monday]*

It is a *custom* pretty general, I believe, amongst *Authors* to await the reception of a first volume by the public before *publishing* a second. In this instance *I* have conformed a second time to custom. A continuation of the *'Diary'* has been called for already, and a continuation is commenced accordingly.

As the first volume of a work *ought* to be read *before* the second (though it is the practice of some to read a novel as they would a Hebrew book – backward), no further introduction is here wanting than to state; that the plan which is approved shall be strictly maintained; and, with the most profound thanks for the liberal encouragement so far given, the Author hopes that each succeeding day may be more deserving of a continuance.

I had determined, in the event of this miscellany being abandoned, to try my *composive* powers at a more connected matter, and had actually begun to arrange my ideas on two subjects. One – 'a tale' in which I intended to attempt descriptions of scenery, situations, characters &c *from life* which had particularly struck my fancy.[1] My other project, a work of (as I purposed) more *research*, but perhaps less difficulty, than the tale, was no less than 'An essay on Female Beauty'.[2] Not a collection of flowery paragraphs, flattering parentheses, witty remarks, or trite sayings but a Metaphysical, Physiognomical, Phrenological, Philosophical dissertation on the subject, (a weighty concern truly, methinks) attempting in some degree to account for that Cestus-like spell which Beauty possesses over the sterner sex. These ideas or as my Mother calls them *'fractional parts of ideas'*

---

1 TGW later did write a tale in his diary, 'The Fisherman's Grave': the surviving parts of this are in *Magaziniana* nos. 26, 28–30, written 16/6/28 to 29/7/28. It was presumably completed in the volumes that are now missing.

2 TGW wrote an essay 'On Beauty' as *Magaziniana* no. 11, 5/8/27.

must however for the present be laid aside, as one work is quite enough to carry forward at once – for me at least.

But *to business*. Since the termination of last month several accidents happened. I was called up on the first & twice on the second of this month. A lad got his leg cut, a man his foot bruised, and another man burnt. Three men got bruised at Elswick &c & c. All doing well.

[*Patient numbers*]

No fractures except two of the fibula. One of which Mr McI told me *in triumph*, 'a surgeon in London had had under his care and had not discovered'!! A ship captain.

Thornton last time I saw him was going on well. His leg laid very straight. [*1, 30/11/26*]

Brabant is doing well [*1, 30/11/26*]. His arms shoulder and breast, – *all* his burns in fact, – are cicatrized with the exception of a little fungus here & there. This is rapidly yielding to Hydrargyrus. The new skin is very tender though yet.

I have been very much put out of my element by my mare taking ill of a severe cold; and my consequently not getting so much among my patients, I have had to walk myself, or send my junior Greenwood to dress Brabant every day, and have only got twice down the Shields Road these ten days. I went with Mr McI in the gig. Mr McI's horse was knocked up too, so we had to get a hack for the vehicle even. We were in both instances behind times and in a great hurry to the great annoyance, and astonishment of our Byker Hill patients. Our last visit of the kind was Sunday se'enight, and unless a call at the door from Mr McI in passing, these Byker Hill folk (Byker Hill being the *focus* of Heaton Colliery & a great *depôt* of our '*sick*'[3]) had never been seen from then to the following Saturday. On Saturday three or four of them (i.e. the patients friends) came in almost together. I stood over the fire, with my *coat-laps* toward it, the wives sat around, while the husbands were talking at the door. The women began to attack Mr McI's *bustling* attentions pretty sharply, while I defended him as well as I could, poor man! They 'sure'd Mr McI needn't be in sich a hurry in coming to see them, or to think he did them a favour by coming to see them himself, for they did

---

3 'Sick' patients are subscribers to the practice: see Introduction.

na want to see him'. They liked me to go a deal better; and 'as long as Mr McI had sich nice foremen as the last three or four, *he* might keep away as lang as he liked; without it was a case of particular necessity, like; then he ought undoubtedly to knaw better, but still even then some people put as much confidence in Mr Gibson, when he was there, as himself'.

The general opinion of *Mr Bewuk* [*Bewicke*] seems to average that he was a nice free young man, but they did na think he was sae skilful. These folk on Saturday too told me that if I got as good a word every where as I did at Byker Hill, and about there, *I would do* (as Mrs Wilkinson said also of my sticking plaster.) My Benwell patient's mother told me the other day too, that if all my patients 'made sae mich wark about me coming to see them mysel as her son did' she 'did na knaw how I would get through them all'.

So much for my *getting in* among my patients. All this is very pleasant to me. I called at Col^n Gilmore's last Wednesday. The Col^n honored me by a call the Saturday previous – I was not in. An engagement for my Father to teach there when he comes to Sunderland to reside which he has fixed to do shortly.

Got home my new shag breeches – very comfortable winter wear – never mind *stylishness* they are genteel & warm.

I have regularly attended lectures at the Institution. They inform greatly but still the experiments are bungled thro'.[4] Mr. Turner has just got through a brief revision of the mechanical powers as described in last years course.

I have learned too the first set of Quadrilles ready for dancing any day. I am quite pleased at having made up a little in that accomplishment, which I was certainly backward in. I must go to the lecture tonight though, and finish any other remarks tomorrow or when I can find time.

December 12 [*Tuesday*]
6 PM I have just been down at the rooms reading the New Monthly; Gent: Monthly &c Magazines after dinner, and a previous journey round by Heaton, Byker, Heaton High Pit &c. A long list of 'sick' patients. I went into six houses in succession at Byker

---

4 [*TGW footnote*] The experimenter before mentioned is a mathematical instr: maker, I understand.

Hill. At Byker Town I have a patient [*Marley*] whose sympton though by no means urgent rather puzzle me. I think there is some affection of the Heart or disease of the Ventricular Valves or Aorta. I will try auscultation if I have opportunity. Mr Church having been so polite as to return a stethoscope Mr McI had given him (he has now got several more) to me for my use.[5] I have got a new patient with Chlorosis today too.

I received yesterday a most delightful packet of letters from my Mother & Sister. I wrote to London on Sunday week to know the cause of so long a silence. I got a *note* & parcel to Croft in the packet yesterday with the promise of a *letter* soon. Some beautiful lines by Mr. Stewart (which by the bye I must copy) and a stanza from some poetry of Cowpers which are *surgically poetic* and the idea pretty,

> 'For *friendship*, like a sever'd bone
> Improves and joins a stronger tone
> When aptly reunited'

It is in some early poems of Cowper in the Gent: Magazine.[6]

My Mother gives me a very useful *caution* as to the probability (in *some* cases) of drowsiness in children's ailments being taken as a symptom, which has been produced by the Cordials, Elixirs or other quack medicines given to the patient by the parents before the calling of a surgeon. A minute enquiry is therefore requisite as to what *has* been previously given.[7]

---

5 The stethoscope, which later became a symbol of progressive medicine, was a relatively new medical instrument at this time. It came into general use by about 1825, a few years after R. T. H. Laennec published a monograph describing its application to diagnosis of lung and heart diseases. See, for example, W. E. Bynum, *Science and the Practice of Medicine in the Nineteenth Century* (Cambridge, 1994), pp. 37 ff.

6 The reference is to the *Gentleman's Magazine* (October 1826), pp. 336–7, where the lines are quoted in a review of *Poems, the Early Productions of William Cowper: Now First Published from the Originals in the Possession of James Croft* (London, 1825). In this review, it is stated that the lines are from a poem on the theme of a lovers' quarrel, probably composed when the poet was in his twenties. It was addressed, under the name of Delia, to his cousin Theodora Cowper. The full quotation begins: 'Happy! When we but seek t'endure/ A little pain, then find a cure/ By double joy requited'.

7 Many popular and available home treatments, as well as those prescribed by medical practitioners, contained opium. When a doctor was called in, often only as a last resort after home remedies had been used, he was advised to be aware of drugs already taken when making his diagnosis. TGW was later to

December 13 *[Wednesday]*

Out at Benwell and to an accident at Felling. A boy *[Buckam]* got his foot bruised. Mr McI went down to Wallsend & Shields yesterday and did not return till this afternoon. A boy came in this morning with a partial dislocation of the wrist, which I reduced.

I removed all the plasters from my burnt patient at Benwell this morning and put him on a shirt – a thing he had not had on since the accident. *[Brabant 11/12/26]*

John Gibson called and sat an hour. I have got Tyler's MSS music book to copy some trios & duets which I meant to do tonight but lo! when I remember he has got *my* book.

In looking over the 1825 report of the Committee of the Lit: & Phil: Soc:, I see among the new Honorary members 'Dr. Bandinel rector of Haughton le Skerne & Curator of the Bodleian library Oxford'. If the report for 1827 with my name amongst its list of new members should reach him, and, lying on his library table should chance to meet the eye of . . . but hold, I forget that other people are to read this, so *swim* for the rest, or else – that is to say – I mean – that – should chance to meet the eye of the revd Doctor he would be pleased with the number of new members this year, I think, – that is all.[8]

I was weighed today and was in costume as before 10 st 2 lb – with great coat $10\frac{1}{2}$ st. Thus I am 6 lb heavier than I was two months since. I thought the other day I was getting fatter. Before I went to Edinburgh I weighed only 9 st 2 lb.

December 14 *[Thursday]*

My round today at Byker, Heaton & Walker Stables. My patient with affected heart – better; his disease seems to me rather to

campaign against the indiscriminate use of opium preparations: T. G. Wright, *A Letter on Quack Medicines*, delivered to the Wakefield Mechanics Institution, Feb 20th 1843, published as a pamphlet, a copy of which is held by the Wellcome Institute Library, London.

8 This appears to be a reference to one of the girls in TGW's very youthful past, many of whom are described, without mention of their names, in *Magaziniana* no. 47, entitled 'Confessions'. As quoted by TGW, the Annual Report of the Lit. and Phil., 1825, lists Dr Bandinel as a new member. Dr Bandinel was the incumbent of the parish of Haughton-le-Skerne, where TGW spent part of his childhood, see 'My Autobiography', chapter 2. He was also librarian of the Bodleian, Oxford: see PW, I, p. 236.

have been rheumatism (which complaint he has been laboring under some time) slightly attacking that organ. [*Marley 12/12//26*]

A Patient at Byker Hill whose number of *unsystematic* symptoms perplexed me a little on Tuesday is also better. It seems to be a species of Dropsy that affects him. His daughter too presents a severe case of Scarlet fever. [*Hunter*]

My mare not having been out of the stable yesterday, was quite wild this morning, and chose to make a pig, which was walking quietly past, the pretext for breaking away from the woman who was holding it at a door and indulge itself with a half mile gallop on the road towards home again. Luckily a man caught it at Byker Gate where I got it after having walked all the way from Byker Hill for it. As it galloped so far for its own pleasure I determined it should have another gallop for mine accordingly I *tamed* it a little before we got home.

December 15 [*Friday*]

I did not expect to have any ride today as Mr McI sent Greenwood out to Benwell but about six oclock the Heaton Messenger came in – a lad [*Patterson*] had got his head cut at Heaton H Pit. I went out in quick time and a terrible cut it was. A part of the Scalp the size of my whole hand at least was completely detached in a flap, – the cranium denuded of its periosteum for about a third of the wound and the periosteum in some places neatly dissected from both bone & integuments. After a deal of pains & trouble I got the hair cut off, then shaved the head all round the flap and the flap itself clean. I washed the parts well and removed all the hair, dirt &c in the wound. A vessel bled violently, a branch of the occipital artery; so I drew a ligature around it and having brought the surfaces into as close apposition and inserted two sutures I applied adhesive plaster strips, a pledget, compress & bandage. My patient was easy when I left him and inclined to sleep, but roused himself a little to sing out for something to eat! I had given him 25 drops of T^r Opii before dressing. As the whole operation took me an hour & half I was obliged to ride pretty hard to be in time for lecture. I was 20 minutes coming from Heaton H Pit.[9]

Lectures at the Society improve. I wandered about the library

---

9 From Heaton to the Lit. and Phil. building is a distance of about 3 miles.

last night seeking some work to bring away with me but none were in that I wanted. 'Scotts Rokeby'[10] happening to meet my eye and never having had opportunity or time or at least both conjoined to read such literary gems I put it under my arm and have today learned and inwardly digested it. I shall be tempted as Christmas relaxation to take out some more of these sort of books I think.

Benwell patient doing well. [*Brabant, 11/12/26*]

I have had a busy day making out accounts which occupies most of my leisure time just now. A tiresome job it is but as part of my duty I keep working away at it vigorously. I have got most of the longest made out I think.

December 16 [*Saturday*]

Pattersons father was in this morning and says his son has been quite easy through the night but threw the salts this morning. [*15/12/26*] I sent him out some aperient powders and said I would see him tomorrow.

A lad [*Hunter*] fell from Benwell Staith (a great height) this morning upon his head & shoulders at least they are most bruised. Mr McI went out to see him – no bones broke.

I was called this morning to a lad [*Robson*] who works at Elswick but resides in Gallowgate. Three out of a set of five loaded rolleys had passed over his back. He is severely bruised but will not be long on the books I hope.

A child [*Lamb*] in the next yard who has been at death's door with fever produced I think by worms is decidedly better tonight – the parents say they attribute its life entirely to me. Mr McI will not allow its being worms tho' it has passed one whole and since I gave the patient Croton oil several pieces of worms, the friends I think. (I ordered them to keep some against I see them tomorrow). I have prescribed wine and nutritious diet – sago, arrowroot. The boy with the dislocated wrist came in this morning, it has done very well. I have not been on horseback today though I ought to have seen two country patients. One scarlet fever; the other with swelled tongue & face I have not yet seen but the father reported him dangerously ill this morning. I have spoken to Mr McI twice about them but he has given me no orders to see them.

---

10 *Rokeby*, a novel by Sir Walter Scott (1771–1832), was first published in 1812.

December 19 *[Tuesday]*

I have been too lazy to make any progress this last three days. I have been very busy still with the accounts. The patients aforementioned were better when I saw [*them*] the following day. I have not seen them since but I hear tonight that two others of the family where Scarlet fever was have taken it. I must see them tomorrow.

Mr McI & I dressed Patterson [*15/12/26*] on Sunday; his head is partly uniting & partly suppurating. Mr McI will I expect see him tonight.

The boy [*Hunter, 16/12/26*] who fell from Benwell Staith is very much bruised. I bled him today. His fall was 21 feet. He had had concussion of the brain which Mr. McI did not mention to me and said, when I went out on Sunday, if his pulse is quick you had better take a little blood from him. His pulse was 100 & very weak. I did *not* therefore bleed him either then or yesterday. His pulse yesterday 98 still weak. In speaking of him to me Mr McI said I ought to have bled him as the weak pulse was from '*concussion of the brain*'. If he had only told me that there had been concussion I certainly know very well that a weak pulse *indicates* bleeding. Today I did bleed him however. He is doing pretty well after brisk leeching & purging.

I got a letter from Mother this morning with directions for supplying my wants in the Cash & Coat line and have just been down at Scarlets[11] ordering a new black riding coat. No lecture last night nor till the eighth of Jan', Mrs Turner being dangerously ill.

[Patient numbers]

We have had most gloomy wet weather this last week past. By the 'Olympic Courier' (which is published every morning and ought to reach the Earth on the first sunbeam, but which has been delayed for some days by the want of that conveyance, till this morning when it came by one short gleam) I am informed that his godship Phoebus has never been able to get over the affront put upon him by Diana, on the 29th last month, by that goddess confronting him most completely. Phoebus blazed forth his rage for a few days, and has since sunk into sullen ill humour. This preying upon his ardent frame was heightened by the appearance

---

11 George Scarlet, tailor and draper, 31 Collingwood St., Newcastle: see PW, I, p. 75.

of a rival about 10 days since, in the form of a comet, and has thrown the god of light into a violent intermittent fever which has nigh proved a great source of mischief to mortals. Aesculapius has now however pronounced the disease to have 'got the turn', and recommended occasional exercise as beneficial. The 'Courier' further says that on Saturday the fever ran so high, as to cause Delirium which affected the goddesses so much that they were drowned in tears – this I can readily believe for we had incessant rain on earth the whole day.[12]

December 22 *[Friday]*
I dressed my Patient [*Patterson, 19/12/26*] at Heaton H Pit yesterday. His head is healing better than I expected. The boy at Benwell [*Hunter, 16/12/26*] is running about today but very weak. Scarlet fever patients [*Hunter?, 14/12/26*] at Byker Hill doing pretty well – one almost well.

Marley, Byker Town (with Rheumatism of the Heart) was complaining very much yesterday. I ordered him a blister as an experiment. [*15/12/26*]

Received a regular Christmas basket this morning from home. A Yule log, Yule candle, Yule cheese, Yule cake, Yule cordial and many other yule-ish appendages.

I heard an anecdote of William [*King*] this morning which amused me. He had directed a Mixture 'A Tablespoonful of this Mixture to be taken every second'. The astonished patient sent back the direction label when it was discovered that Mr King had *merely* omitted 'hour'.

By the bye talking of seconds reminds me of a second story upon a second similar subject which I believe never before appeared in – (I was going to say 'print') – black & white at any rate. A gentleman was looking over me one day while I was regulating my watch. He being a very able & ingenious mechanichian soon discovered that a tooth of the wheel which turns the second pointer (the *contrate* wheel) was broken and which caused the pointer of course to skip 1/5 of a second each round. Now said Mr. H – very *scientifically* (thinking, like the Irishman, that because the little wheel of the coach ran round faster it was

---

12 This obscure passage seems to be just an elaborate, joking comment on the weather and the supposed effect of the partial solar eclipse, mentioned on 29/11/26.

sure to beat the big one) began to calculate how much ought to be allowed in the regulation for the second pointer *gaining* on the hour pointer!!

J Gibson has just been in speaking about a patient [*Jobling*] at Byker Hill who has got Haemor[*rhois*] in a violent degree. They had called on him in passing today. I let it be known pretty generally among my patients where he was a great favorite, that have not the least objection to their calling in Mr Gibson *in consultation*. So that it has been done once or twice lately. I am invited to dine at Mr Gibson's (Sen[r]) on Christmas day.

December 23 [Saturday]
After making up a packet for Croft I have been down at Parson's &c as the shops will not be open on Monday.

Mr Crawford has been down to ask me to dine there on Monday – being engaged as above I accepted his invitation to sup in Greenfield Place on Frumenty tomorrow evening. I have not seen a patient out of the Surgery today.
[*Patient numbers*]

As the Pits are now laid off till after Xmas we shall have little chance of accidents for a few days. A very slack week this last.

December 27 [Wednesday]
What with visiting, accounts &c I have been closely employed since Saturday. I got the accounts made up so far as posted in Ledger last night, but they are all to add up and enter in a list yet so that I shall have little writing leisure this 10 days yet to come.

I supped in Greenfield Place on Xmas eve and dined at Mr Gibsons on the following day. Both very pleasant meetings. We had a good round game (Loo) on Monday evening at which I just won back my stake. Mr Tyler, a Mr McCuller & myself were the only *visitors*. W[m] Gibson was home from Sedgefield. Miss G[*Gibson?*] is away and has been some time. I was in hopes we should have had a dance but it was not named – there would have been a scarcity of ladies indeed. Misses Bell [*Isabel Gibson?*] & Dorothy [*Gibson?*] only to 5 gentlemen.

Nothing particular among patients. All going on well.
[*Patient numbers*]

1827

January 1 – 4 *[Monday – Thursday]*
Since last Thursday I have been busily engaged every leisure moment – Sunday & all at the accounts but now am singing 'O be joyful' for having got them finished. I must endeavour to make up for lost time by more extended remarks for a few days, but my hand is so completely tired of writing that *it* must have some rest first.

I cannot avoid observing as soon as possible that we have got a new apprentice who took unto himself his first wife[13] the day before yesterday. Master James Gray of Gateshead, a sharp enough looking youth. He is only going to stay with us a short time and is to return to school for a few months then go to Cochrane and his Man Friday John Hunter to come in here.

My hand fairly aches so please gentle (or kind or something) reader excuse my further additions today in pity to so important a member and the brains which guide it. I will promise double amusement tomorrow.

January 8 *[Monday]*
Here is Monday again and no further progress in my *Diary*; but there is too good a reason for this silence, and as it may afford me a *memento* some time hence I will give a right & true account of the business tho' I shall never forget it I dare say. Well then, on Thursday morning finding I had got pretty near through the accounts having sat up till twelve oclock the night before over them – I made myself a promise that if all the accounts were *done* and the books posted up (I had not then made any entries for the new year) by the following night I would treat myself to the Play for the first time this season. The Pilot a new piece was to be the after entertainment so I thought I would only go at half price. Col^n & Mrs Gilmore were going (at least their names were in the box book) so I determined on going to the boxes. J Gibson wanted me to go with him so we agreed to go together to half price. Mrs Clementson from Darlington was staying at Shieldfield and I expected would be there as it was fashionable night an extra inducement to the boxes; And last not least the Miss Gibsons

---

13 TGW refers several times to the act of taking indentures as 'taking a wife', see, for example, 'My Autobiography', chapter 12 and Volume 11, 20/3/29.

were to go to half play, to see the Pilot. When I was down street in the afternoon I found that the arrangement was altered (by desire) the Pilot the first piece and No Song No Supper. I went to J Gibsons and said we might as well go to full play. As I should meet Colⁿ & Mrs Gilmore &c &c I determined upon going to see all; and accordingly to the boxes we went.[14] To begin my disappointment neither the Colⁿ, his lady, nor any one else I knew were there – the snow I suppose having prevented them and to wind up all I found when I got home (or rather to J Gibsons lodgings) that my watch ribbon had given way and *my seals were gone*! I made immediate search at the Theatre & told the Watch-men[15] about to look out for them but no tidings have I yet had of them.

[*Patient numbers*]

January 10 [*Wednesday*]
I never was in a more disagreeable humour (to myself) that I have been in for this last week or since that unlucky Friday. Greenwood has got leave to go home for three days leaving me to do all the business as James [*Gray*] can be of little help. Mr McI too has been putting upon me rather more than I thought consist-ent with my office has found fault too with me for Greenwood's negligence & tho' only three or four words it is more than I like by any means, when I have worked so hard lately for him in the account way, having got them done much sooner than usual. And yet too he comes in –'Have you got them all made out?' 'Where is the list of them?' 'You should have had the ledger posted up' & c &c before the year was up. If he had them to do himself he would find talking and doing are here different matters.

I have almost begun lately to adopt J Gibsons opinion that the more a person does for Mr McI the more they may do. He seems to act upon that plan a good deal thinking, no doubt – 'Yes now

---

14 The play *The Pilot* was advertised as 'The new nautical Drama, 5th time here . . . as acted in London upwards of 200 nights. . . The new scenery painted by Mr Gordon, with entirely new Music, Scenery, Machinery Dresses and Decora-tions'. The part of the Pilot was played by Mr S. W. Butler with Mr Moss as Lieutenant Burnstaple: see NRPB.

15 Newcastle had 26 watchmen on police duty within the city walls, under the direction of a Captain of the Watch, and assisted by 2 night constables. They kept watch between 10 pm and 6 am, going on rounds and calling time every half-hour: see Mackenzie 1827, p. 726.

Wright seems to work very hard and very cheerfully at it too. I think I had better give him plenty to do now that I have got one that will do it without grumbling'. He has even requested me *to carry out* any of the accounts that lay in my rides and I see is planning rounds for me in every direction for that purpose when no patients *require* seeing. But I might continue on with this treasonable train for ever and a day and must try to find some more agreeable subject. *I will keep steady to my duty* and Mr McI will in the end find his mistake in the insubordination and consequent disorder he is creating in the surgery, by lowering my office.

I was going to Wallsend last afternoon in reality only to enquire after Mrs Buddle (because his highness could not go down being out at dinner) but avowedly to see patients where none required or expected it – O yes – one man that Mr McI could not be at the bother to see the day before when he was down. Just as I was setting off an accident at Elswick required my attention and then a message met me at Byker Gate to go to St. Anthonys Pottery to see Mr Sewells Housekeeper [*Mrs Eliot*].[16] From thence I went a new (to me) road and being nearly dark completely lost myself. I managed to get right at last and got to Mrs Buddles. Miss B was just at tea and of course asked me to a cup. Mr Tom Potts, Mr Buddles apprentice was there; but Mrs B being confined to her room Mr B away, and worst of all Miss Burnet staying at Newcastle – 'we three' formed (with a black & white cat the mother of the black one) the only party.[17]

I did not get home till after eight PM. I had intended to have noted many subjects which have taken place this last fortnight – as the snowstorm &c &c, but the unlucky seal–losing business has prevented me even apostrophising the new year and giving

---

16 St Anthony's was then a village near the River Tyne, already heavily industrialised in 1826. Joseph Sewell became owner of Sewell and Donkin, St Anthony's Pottery, in about 1804. It was one of the largest pottery manufacturers on Tyneside, with a flourishing export trade, producing fine table-ware, and being known particularly for its lustreware: see R. C. Bell, *Tyneside Pottery* (London, 1971), p. 104.

17 John Buddle (1773–1843) became Manager of Wallsend Colliery in 1806. One of the foremost mining engineers in the country, he made many innovations in mining and was widely employed as a consultant: see Richard Welford, *Men of Mark 'twixt Tyne and Tweed*, 3 vols (Newcastle, 1895), I, p. 425. John Buddle was unmarried; Mrs Buddle mentioned here and elsewhere in the *Diary* was possibly his mother.

an account of how, where & when I passed the important moment of its entry. I had Tyler & Travis too on New Years night and having brewed a jug of Punch of half a dozen glasses of spirit nutmeg &c &c we fluted & sang away the evening with yule cake & apples to a yule log burning &c tho' Xmas was then past to be sure but to us 'twas all the same.

January 11 *[Thursday]*
I got a letter written home last week which has as folks say 'taken a load off my mind'. I have been a long round by Wallsend &c this morning and came home with Mr McI about 4 PM.

Do not 'courteous reader' from what I said yesterday be after going for to imagine that I *dislike* my master Mr McIntyre. On the contrary, I always have and I hope ever shall have cause highly to respect him. His conduct towards apprentices is in some points reserved and perhaps seems rather haughty to those unaccustomed to his general character but who has not some weak points? and I cannot testify my satisfaction since I have been Mr McI's pupil more strongly than by saying as I have often done that, had I my apprenticeship to begin again with a free choice of masters, Mr McI should *again* be fixed upon by me as Father to my (it would then be) *third wife*'!![18] His *apprentice* though I am not at present in any sense. My indentures specify me as *House-pupil* and he styles me as *Assistant,* either way therefore I escape the (generally to young surgeons) disagreeable appellation *apprentice*!

January 12 [Friday]
Round by St Anthonys, Heaton & D° High Pit &c.

In going along the road, singing, soliloquising &c as usual, I caught myself up beside the High Pit in the middle of something like an original song and lest it should never get more into a finished state than the one in which it first struck me I will pop it down so far as a memorandum. Perhaps I may sometime improve upon the idea by introducing other scenery upon similar occasions exemplifying a round among my colliery patients. The expressions are so far (and I should like when my muse pays me another of her very rare visits to continue the same plan) the

---

18 See note 13 above.

ordinary expressions used by the Pitmen on such occasions. There was a fragment of another verse but it will require alteration.

Song
Air – 'Calder Fair'

Howay now here's the Doctor come for to see wor Nanny
Joe gang an hand the Doctor's horse there's a blithesome mannnie
Now Doctor how d'ye do sur, 'Here's a verra blawy day
Come by the fire an worm yorsel for need it weel ye may

Well how's your Wife? I thenk ye sur we think she's a vast better
She was wanting sair to be out the day but aw thought ye wad not let her
The Powders did a deal o' gude. The bottles dune also
And whether she'll need ony mair why yere the best to know sur.

She's got a nice bit happetite an's thrivin now awain sir
She'll awmost be for in t' town ayen ye come again sir
You must just go on improving now you're doing very well
When next'll ye be here sur, I'm sure I cannot tell

January 13 [*Saturday*]

I received a very comfortable letter from my home yesterday regarding my lost seals. I have heard no tidings of them. I have told every body of my loss and find Mr McI had propagated the same story pretty extensively also. There is no chance of my getting them now however.
[*Patient numbers*]

January 15 [*Monday*]

My old tutor & friend Mr Jas Cowan[19] called on me twice while I was in the country on Thursday. Supposing he would be at Mr Smiles (as Ed^w Smiles called with him) I went up to Travis and found Mr C's chaise waiting at the door. He had only just time to say howdye do and drove off. Mr C was at Croft on Thursday week I find.

I was up at Mr Crawfords on Saturday evening for an hour; amongst other things I had my fortune told; and a very excellent fortune it was.

Miss Bowes has sent some loose leaves – a part of her scrap book with a request through Miss Crawford to me amongst

---

19 James Cowan was a favourite teacher when TGW was at school in Darlington: see 'My Autobiography', chapters 5 and 6.

the rest to contribute. Now if my Muse (whichever of the nine
she be who patronises my headpiece or rather its performances)
would only be kind enough to lend me aid for a short time,
here is a fine opportunity for my distinguishing myself. But I
was never cut out for a poet; my talent lies more in a practical
than a speculative channel. I thought I was going to be wonderfully inspired when four lines came out one after the other
in quick succession.

> How sweet to think ones own light thought
> Should fill so fair a page;
> How sweet to think that what we've wrote
> Should Beauty's eye engage

But 'caetera desunt' and without my rhymes come out pretty
quickly I shall never have the patience to wait long for them.

January 20 *[Saturday]*
[A black ink border surrounds the following paragraph in the MS]
On this day were committed to the Tomb the remains of his late
Royal Highness the Duke of York and Albany Heir Apparent to
the Throne of this Empire, Commander in Chief &c &c as the
reader (in 1927) may learn by consulting the records of the day
all margined with black upon the occasion.[20]

There were notices in abundance of the forms to be observed
on this day but very little regret seems to be shewn. The bells *did*
toll certainly for about 10 minutes in the morning at the firing of
one of the guns from the Castle, and the same was repeated this
afternoon 'midst a salute from the cannon to the great amusement
of a parcel of dirty lads gathered round to catch the burning tow
as it fell, and the great annoyance of the good and peaceable
towns folk who dwelt in the immediate vicinity of the ancient
tower which gives name to 'wor gude toon'.[21]

I have worn a pair of black trowsers all this week to be like
other folk of similar gentility. I always wear a black coat and
having as aforementioned got a new one not long ago in a very

---

20 Frederick Augustus, Duke of York and Albany (1763–1827), the 'Grand Old
   Duke of York', was the second son of George III.
21 The ancient tower referred to was presumably the keep of the Castle. The area
   around the Castle was densely populated from mediaeval times: see
   Middlebrook, p. 32.

decent black. A piece of crape would have been useful in covering a grease spot on my hat but as the gazette does not mention hatbands as necessary for *general* mourning and I had not the honor of being particularly known to his royal highness I must go with my hat as it is.

I have had three cases of Hydrothorax in children lately. Two altogether to myself and one in conjunction with Mr McI. The latter was the most favorable because the disease was attacked sooner. The former were poor people and I was not applied to till too late for medicine to avail. They all died. Hydrothorax seems to have been very prevalent this late changeable weather amongst children.

The Patient [*Marley, 22/12/26*] with affected heart at Byker (vide Dec 14 – 1826) has been seen several times by Mr McI since the last report and still continues better or worse almost daily. The Rheumatism-like symptoms appear to have been the precursor of Angina Pectoris and if as I fear the coronary arteries are ossified I doubt little can be done for him. Mr McI merely ordered him some aperient medicine and has said nothing to me concerning his malady. I must have some conversation with him on the subject. I will try Tartar Emetic Ointment and Lime Water and Antimonical Wine as recommended by Dr McBride.[22] There is an infant with the Submaxillar Glands enormously swelled and to which I am going to apply the Linium Petrolic with T^r Iodine as soon as I get the Tinct^r made.

January 22 *[Monday]*
A bleak raw cold day. I was at Byker & Heaton H Pit.

I really think the portion of my brain allotted to song manufacturing is particularly actively engaged just now. On my road today I was ruminating on the future and thinking how long it would be before I should have anything to break the sameness of my jog-trot daily occupation and of which the anticipation is perhaps greater than the pleasure – anything *to think of in expectancy*, when I set off full gallop with an extempore song – something in the style of those extempore flute concertos &c I amuse myself with occasionally, that is peculiarly original. The air was original too, an original compilation I mean between a gig & a

22 Possibly David McBride (1726–78) who wrote *Practice Of Physick* (Edinburgh, 1772).

German hymn partly made up of 'Carey Owen' 'The Campbells are coming' and a few bars from 'Banks of Banna' or *104 Psalm*). The words began

> Could we live without Hope? ah! no, no, no!
> Could we live without Hope? ah! no, no, no!
> Of joy all the lightness – of pleasure the brightness
> There's no life without Hope! ah! no, no, no!

I however stuck in the midst – my pegasus having from long intimacy with mankind grown like many of *them* very mulish and restive.

F Watkins has brought me a ticket to the Philharmonic Concert on Thursday. I will go if I possibly can. I must write for the last time to Croft this evening. My Father & Mother leave that residence on Wednesday for Sunderland.

January 27 *[Saturday]*

I did write to Croft and also *was* at the concert.

I came home on Thursday night highly in good humour. The concert was *upon the whole* very tolerable – the overtures *rather* out of time. The glees were not worth hearing, but the single songs very good. The concert room, holding about 300, was quite crowded with beauty and fashion. I have had tickets offered and I shall most likely go to the next concert. Mr McI was out when I went to the rooms and did not come in till half an hour after me, which was partly also a good job, tho' I did not expect or intend him to be ignorant of my being out of the way – if going across the street can be called such.

This last two days (by the bye) has made a sad change in my opinion of Mr McI tho' this is no place to express it. I shall always respect him as my present *master*; but I shall never have the esteem for him as a *gentleman* that I had.

Mr *Tom* Gibson gave me a wave and a 'how d'ye do' this morning. He was at the concert with three of the Miss Gs (his nieces) on Thursday. Mr Henzell[23] was sitting with them and tho' I could not get within two rows of their party JG and I joined them coming out. Well – Mr Henzell Surgeon &c &c tho' I have never been introduced to him or spoke before stepped out of his road

23 Probably C. R. Henzell, surgeon, 81, Percy Street, Newcastle: see PW, I, 42.

off the pathway in Dean Street today to tell me it was a sharp
morning or something of that sort.

Mr Hardcastle (another surgeon) & I have also got on speaking
terms by meeting on the roads together.

[*Patient numbers*]

January 28 [*Sunday*]

Wrote to Sunderland to my F & M yesterday on their entering
their new home there.

I went to Mr Turner's chapel this morning. I was at Church too
last Sunday, Mr McI being from home. I was in Mr Gibson's pew
and heard a sermon from the vicar as usual. It was on behalf of
the manufactures.[24] I was feeling in my left hand pocket for a
sixpence when the vicar told us that the churchwardens would
come by houserow on the Tuesday following, which was perhaps
as well for the fate of my sixpence. The worthy clergyman I
thought rather unfairly made the amount of our subscription the
test of our attention to and accordance with his sermon though
he had just before said we were not to give through any motive
but pure *charity*! I was out when they called on Tuesday.

I forgot to say that there were two things to put me in a *very*
good humour for Thursday – *viz*. the concert as before said and
a *Sectio Cadaveris* – an examination after death. Mr McI & I alone
were there. When I was sowing up the parts again, Mr McI said
to some of the friends 'It will soon be just as it was again'. My
thoughts added '*minus* his gall bladder – poor man' ! I have *it*
macerating and expect it will make a fine morbid preparation of
which I will give a description when I have got the dissection
completed. [*3, 11/3/23*]

A great deal of juggling we had to get it snugly pocketed for of
course there were some men in the room.

I was called up last night or rather this morning. 'A man was
taken very ill'. He only lived next yard but so much the worse,
for then one has no time to get ones eyes open before going in to
the patient. Mr McI was out heaven knows where so I had to turn

---

24 A collection 'for the Distressed Manufactures, under the King's Letter' was
announced under the list of collections from churches in the local newspapers:
see *Newcastle Courant*, 16/2/1827, p. 4.

out. A lad got mortal drunk that was all and wanted a good vomit. While it was making up his highness came in.

January 31 *[Wednesday]*
I had to go down to Heaton &c for no other purpose than to call at the Heaton office about some of those everlasting accounts. Upon coming home, there was a severe accident had been wait- ing an hour & half from Elswick – a boy *[Burrell]* had got his arm terribly broke. Greenwood had sent out the amputating case. I went out as quick as possible and found a severe fracture enough with great displacement of the bones – both the Radius and Ulna broken with splintering of their end – great swelling &c. I reduced it and directed that word should be sent in the evening. The messenger then stated that the patient was in great pain. A dozen leeches to be applied the bandages being all taken off & warm fomentations after which the Lotio Sythargyric. Some opening medicine given. I thought Mr McI would be going this morning but he desired me to see my patient. I re-reduced the fracture and applied the splints &c in due form leaving the lad in comparative ease.

A message was twice sent in from St Anthonys yesterday for Mrs Eliott, Mr Sewell's Housekeeper *[10/1/27]* to be seen – she was worse. The case was one of strumous inflammation of the finger & hand. As Mr McI was down that way I concluded that he would see this patient. He had said on going away in the morning he would be home at 3 PM and had asked Mr Church to tea at 6. Upon the second of the above messages coming, about 7, I supposed he must be at St Anthonys which was the cause of his detention. I waited till 11 PM and was just going off to bed when I after a perplexing debate with myself formed the resolu- tion of e'en going myself.

On the road I met a messenger on horseback so that I was glad I *had* set off. The roads were a complete puddle – I had to go thro' several long fields – the night was hazy and the stars of the first magnitude & planets were barely visible – my eyes told me that I was on *terra firma* or something dark colored while my ears intimated that I was crossing some interminable river by the *plodging* of my horse's feet. As there was a man with me and I was going to the respectable housekeeper of a person of *quality*, I was obliged to 'get on' (as someone I know would say) so that on the whole I had a bumping sort of ride there. I bled my

patient &c &c & left her easier. My ride back however was somewhat different. The sky was clearer – the air mild if not almost
warm and I began very unconcernedly to sing most lustily,
frightening all the crows magpies &c for half a mile round. I
began my oratorio with 'This life is all chequered with' &c but
more amongst a numerous collection one more appropriate; –
tho' 'The young *May* moon' – was not beaming there being ne'er
a moon at all nor any 'glow worm's lamp' 'gleaming'

> 'How sweet to rove
> Thro' *Anthon's* grove'

was applicable enough as I was journeying *past* the skirting of
wood in coming from St Anthonys vulgo St Anthon's. I was also
verifying that

> 'The best of ways
> To lengthen our days
> Is to steal a few hours from the night'[25]

I got home just as the Charlies[26] were bawling drawling or calling
(each in his way) 'past two'. Mr McI had got home. I went to bed
and slept soundly till – I woke.
[*Patient numbers*]

February 3 [*Saturday*]
Saw my patient at Elswick [*Burrell, 31/1/27*] yesterday. His arm is
free from pain but still a good deal swelled. Mr McI was at St.
Anthons yesterday. I was called up at $5\frac{1}{2}$ yesterday morning to a
lad [*Urwin*] who had his head cut at Heaton Middle Pit. Nothing
very serious.

I am in wonderment at not having heard a syllable from home
tho' I wrote to Sunderland last Saturday!
[*Patient numbers*]

February 5 [*Monday*]
Rode yesterday down to Wallsend Heaton &c &c. J Gibson who
had been down at S. Shields ball on Friday night, and had wished

---

25 *The Young May Moon* by Thomas Moore (1779–1852) has the lines: 'And the
    best of all ways/ To lengthen our days/ Is to steal a few hours from the night,
    my dear!'
26 See note 15 above.

me very much to go with him then would have gladly persuaded me to ride down to dinner (*he* to enquire after his partner) yesterday. I was half inclined but Mr McI was going to No Shields himself so that settled the matter. I rode with [*him*] as far as Wallsend seeing some patients of his on the road by Willington &c &c.

I was often rather surprized that no message or renewal of former invitations ever came to me from Mrs Heatley or Miss Taylerson by JG [*John Gibson*] and yet *he* was always anxious for me to go down *with him* someday. At length one day when he could not get me persuaded to go by any other argument he tried me by saying that Miss Taylerson had sent several messages of invitation 'wondering I had never gone down to Shields &c' but he could not be bothered to recollect them all. Accordingly I yesterday deemed some apology necessary and desired JG to make one to Miss T (as he gave the former message from her,) at the same time enquiring after Mrs Heatley &c who was ill. JG promised to give it 'if he could think on' and brought me back '*Mrs Heatley's* Compl^ts and that she hoped &c &c' Ah! Jack you're a queer fellow!

I called at a Patients yesterday just in passing and never refusing a good offer got a very good lunch or dinner (which you please) of boiled beef and plum pudding. One of the sons then rode my horse round to meet me while I took a short cut by some fields to a patient at Wallsend Farm with the eldest son a deputy overman. The father is an overman so they are a family of some rank among the pit folk.

I have been an hour at the Society reading the Newcastle Mag: which is very good this month. I have put my name down for the New Monthly this evening.

No news from Sunderland yet. I will write again tomorrow.

February 6 [*Tuesday*]

Mr McI managed to find his own door out yesterday by about 6 oclock PM. He left here on Sunday at 11 without any intimation that he was going to stay all night at Shields tho' I half expected as much.

It is well I altered my determination to write to Sunderland this morning for here is a letter from my Mother, and containing, as a sort of presentiment told me, unwelcome news regarding their lodgings. Worse also, my Father & Mother are both ill from the harass and anxiety of removing in a *snowstorm*. My Mother wishes me to go over and I must try to accomplish it on Thursday or Friday. Mr McI has just asked me if any patients require seeing down the Shields road today, but I will contrive to see all my patients tomorrow so as to be at liberty on Thursday.

February 8 *[Thursday]*
This is always rather an important day in my calendar being the day of the month on which I was born, as a little memorandum which I cut out of an old pocket book once belonging no doubt to my sister then a schoolgirl, sets forth. It is thus '1808 Tuesday Feb 8 – 1 brother born at 12/13 past 5 in the afternoon. Aunt Mary came by the Trafalgar'. How many brothers my dear sister wished for I can't tell, but so runs the minute, a very exact one as to time, we must allow, – as well as number.

While upon antiques, I may as well give copies of two other mem: from the same book – all that now remains 'we regret to add', of so valuable a composition.

'21ˢᵗ – *Little Brother* Christened Mrs Dobson carried him to Church. Aunt & Uncle Foxton[27] and Bell dined with us. Brothers name Thomas Giordani W –' The last part is especially important. '22ᵈ Dined with Uncle Henry and little cousin christened'. Who this was I cannot tell. But had I been fortunate enough to have preserved the whole of the above mentioned vol: it must have proved a valuable family record.

My Birthday was, when I *was little* quite a gala day; tho' now very properly merely the 8 of Feb; remembered perhaps by a letter or two of good wishes.

I can perfectly recollect the occurrence on my fifth year. I had been promised a half guinea to buy good things for my party on condition of saying the multiplication thro' to 12 times 12 before the company came. This I accomplished about 5 PM to my great joy and exultation. I distinctly remember *dancing* with mamma the day I was four years old. The young ladies from Mrs Longstaff's boarding schools used always to be invited on '*Tomma's* birthday'. When I got a year or two older these parties were discontinued and I had on one occasion a party of my own – playfellows. My 10ᵗʰ birthday I left Swillington on the Aire (Yorksh)

---

27 Foxton was the maiden name of TGW's mother.

attended morning service at Leeds old church, passed thro'
Rippon &c in the afternoon, and got to Thirsk in the evening. My
11ᵗʰ birthday we had a party at Haughton le Skerne when I very
well remember sweeping the pool (9/-) at commerce! 12ᵗʰ and
13ᵗʰ most likely at school. Oh, by the bye, both the 12ᵗʰ & 13ᵗʰ
were remembered by a present of a large twelfth cake &c &c
from London. On the 14ᵗʰ birthday I dined at Col McGregors of
Blackwell to meet Father who was teaching there that day. The
15ᵗʰ at school – I believe I drank tea at Mr Bowes. My 16ᵗʰ anniversary at Croft with Father & Mother. 17 at Newcastle at Mr
McIntyre's. 18ᵗʰ In Edinburgh and this the 19ᵗʰ I hope to pass
partly at Newcastle, and in the evening to be with Father and
Mother at Sunderland.

Here is therefore a full & particular account of my life on one
day of the year.[28] In conclusion I must just beg Mrs G –'s[29] pardon
for the liberty of criticism I have taken with her quondam Mem:
book.

February 20 *[Tuesday]*[30]
Here is a gap but it is not my fault I assure you gentle reader. I
took my MS in my pocket by 'particular desire' on the 8ᵗʰ and
only got it returned yesterday. I intended too to have filled up
this volume during the month, which I must still accomplish by
spinning my remarks a little. To make up for this long silence I
will note down what has occurred in it from memory as well as
I can.
Feb 8 *[Thursday]* contᵈ then. I got to Sunderland about 7 PM by
the coach and met my F & M waiting at the end of the street
expecting me. I soon got set down to a comfortable cup of tea, –
very refreshing after a cold ride outside a coach, – and did not
stir out again till 10 oclock when I had some supper and went to
bed at the Bridge Inn.
Feb 9 *[Friday]* Went to see after some new lodgings with F & M

---

28 TGW later wrote his much more detailed autobiography as part of his diary:
see 'My Autobiography'.
29 Mrs Green was TGW's married sister, then living in London.
30 As explained in the continuation of the entry for 20/2/1827, TGW was without
his diary MS for the period 9–19/2/1827, having left it with his parents in
Sunderland.

and called upon Mr J. Cowan. After a good dinner in Villier's Street returned to Newcastle about 7½ PM

Feb 10 [*Saturday*] [*Patient number*]

Feb 12 [*Monday*] Called upon Colⁿ Gilmore to appoint my F's first engagement with Miss G. My patient with the broken arm [*Burrell, 31/1/27*] in on Saturday. Mr McI says it is doing very well.

Feb 14 [*Wednesday*] Being Valentine's day I despatched an Acrostic which has for some weeks laid in my desk to its place of destination. It was only in return for a sonnet dedicated to my flute by the young lady some time ago.

Feb 15 [*Thursday*] Mr McI took himself off saying he was 'going from home a few days' – this afternoon but neither letting me nor anyone else know the where, when, or how long of his journey. I happened to hear the day before that he was going to Edinburgh – then I heard he was gone to near Wooler; and *since* I have been told on good authority he is going to bring one of his sisters from Edinburgh to stay in this neighborhood. Most people agree with me in thinking that 'he is a nice young man' and 'very attentive to his business'.

Feb 16 [*Friday*] I had all along intended going to the Theatre this evening and Mr McI's being from home did not prevent me; as indeed why should it? Whenever I do go the Theatre he is as usual spending the evening somewhere out and therefore I am as liable to be wanted as if he were fifty miles off.

I did go therefore to half play. It was Mrs Mayoress' bespeak 'The School for Prejudice' & 'Luke the Labourer'.[31] I saw the last two acts of the Play which I liked very much. The afterpiece is a melodramatic sort of thing, the plot laid in Yorkshire. Mr Gordon the scene painter has given a pretty view of York in the distance in one scene. Butler played the labourer the hero of the piece; an [*illegible word*] kind of Yorkshireman, *well*. It was a fine piece of acting. I never saw the 'Heir at Law' but I should suppose this 'Luke the Labourer' to be a character similar to Tyke, the celebrated test of *Yorkshire* tragic performance and of Emery's favorite personifications. There was a very full house in all parts and I understand the 8th fashionable night (the preceding one) under

---

31 This was advertised as 'the ninth fashionable evening by desire and under the Patronage of Mrs Mayoress. *The School for Prejudice or, The Lawyer! the Jew!! and the Yorkshireman!!!* was a comedy by Dibdin: see NRPB.

Lady Ravensworth's patronage was a *very* profitable one to the manager.[32]

Feb 17 *[Saturday]*[Patient numbers]

I received a letter from Mrs Cruickshank. It has been a very long expected one but better late than never. I wrote to London last Saturday.

Feb 19 *[Monday]* Father came over to Elswick Cottage to teach Miss Gilmore. I was going out to Benwell and rode so far to shew F the house. After I returned I went down to Lambert's the Engravers[33] to get some alteration made previously to a new impression of Father's Supplement[34] being struck off. On coming up street I called at Taylor Gibson's on Miss Taylerson. She came up to Newcastle to stay for a few days on Saturday and was intending to return yesterday. She was very glad to see me. Scolded me for not going down to Shields &c &c. Mrs Gibson too was very polite, thought I must have been away from home that I was so great a stranger there – hoped I would go often in an evening – they drank tea at seven oclock &c &c.

February 20 *[Tuesday]* (contd)

An accident came yesterday just as I was *going to go* down street with F to the coach. A man [*Cook*] had his collar bone fractured at Johnson's Houses. I went off to the place and set it & reset it & set it again but all would not do; the fool would persist in displacing it as fast as I could put it right; so I bandaged it up and left him to do as he liked with it.

As I came up street, Miss T [*Taylerson* ?], Miss G [*Gibson?*], Miss IG [*Isabel Gibson?*], Mr JG [*John Gibson*] &c were standing in the window and presently after Jack came up to ask me to go down to tea at his lodgings – he expected some 'belles femmes' there. I popped out of my breeches into a pair of trowsers. Donned a clean collar & cravat and marched down to Mr John Gibsons lodgings. Mr Benj: Gibson presently entered followed by Miss

---

32 The performance on 9 February 1827 was '*Faustus* taken from the German Drama *of The Devil and Dr Faustus* with the original Music, composed by Bishop, Horne, and T. Cooke'. There was 'no half price during the run of the piece (in consequence of the expence [*sic*] of Faustus': see NRPB.

33 Mark Lambert, engraver & copper plate printer, 22 St Nicholas' Church Yard, Newcastle: see PW, I, p. 52.

34 The works of TGW's father, Thomas Wright, include *A Musical Primer* and *Supplement*: see also Introduction, note 3.

Taylerson, Miss & Miss Isabel Gibson. We had tea & played a very pleasant game at cards afterwards. I and Fanny (G) lost a rubber & a game.

February 22 *[Thursday]*
J Gibson & I had a long round amongst our patients each seeing the other's the morning before last.

A man that got his collar bone broke [*Cook, 20/2/27*] will not behave himself and tho' Mr Gibson and I set it again several times this morning, there is no getting it kept in its proper place so we e'en left him to his fate.

Just as I was going off to bed last night a messenger came to order the bedroom fires to be lighted as Mr McI would be home very shortly. Accordingly about eleven oclock his worship came and with him a lady *supposed to be* his sister.

I have not yet seen her (5PM), but got a glimpse of the skirt of her pelisse as she was going in the front door. She & her brother are just at dinner, *we* having dined at 2 oclock by ourselves.

There is a concert tonight but I have not yet got a ticket and am uncertain as to whether I shall go as some sort of a row is anticipated in consequence of the conductor having been turned out of the Society.

February 23 *[Friday]*
In making up the lists of new patients for the last two weeks I find that out of the 29 entered last week, no less than 17 were subsequent to Mr McIntyre's leaving home on the Thursday. There have been 15 more booked *this week* previous to Mr McI's return making in all 44 new patients entered in his absence.

I was down at Mr Moore's to see J Gibson last night about going to this concert and found him just considering about the same subject; only tickets were the desiderata. He had slipped out from a dinner party of old aunts &c on occasion of his Father's birthday and was only wishing for tickets & a companion to go either to a subscription ball at the Assembly rooms or to the concert. Mr Kerr, who is lodging in the same house with JG had promised his tickets to some ladies but as he did not take them after waiting till almost 9 oclock we took the liberty of making use of them.

The concert was well attended as to numbers the room being crowded. More ladies were present than at the former one. The two overtures I heard ('Zauberflotte' & 'The Miller & his Men') were very well performed. Zauberflotte was encored. Mr Noakes and a basso (I don't know his name) were the only male voices worth listening to – the females were nothing in particular. I was obliged to stand the whole night, but got near and chatted with a Miss Thompson of Higham Place[35] whom Gibson knew a little. She was with a sister and another young lady also two brothers so as there were two gentlemen to three ladies, JG (I unfortunately never having been *introduced* to them) made the third to set them home and I came away *solus*.

I have been drinking tea with J Gibson tonight and he has been trying hard to persuade me to go with [him] to the So: Shields ball on Tuesday. I feel half inclined never having stirred a foot in the way of a dance this winter. I want to try my hand at a quadrille too. If I go we are to drive down in a gig of Wm Greys (JG's cousin) and get home about 4 or 5 in the morning. I can say to Mr McI that I am wishing to go to a party. The tickets are only 4/- which I think I may afford upon a pinch. I must consider the matter well before morning.

February 24 [Saturday]
Mr McIntyre went to Backworth & Shields yesterday and as I expected was away all night.

There was a call this morning about 2 AM for Mr McI to see a genteel patient [*Miss Aveling, 22/11/26*] who he is always in the habit of attending himself and who was taken very ill. As Mr McI was not at home I of course went and saw the lady. I had just got into a comfortable sleep after coming home at 4 AM when I was again disturbed about $\frac{1}{2}$ past six by a woman [*Mrs Longhead*] who had taken ill on the Quayside. The former patient was considerably relieved before Mr McI came home at noon.

February 26 [Monday]
There have been two accidents this morning. One I was called up to at about 7. A boy [*Turner*] got very much bruised & cut by some rolleys crushing him. The other [*Gaer*] Mr McI will see as he was just setting off on that road – to Felling.

---

35 Higham Place, a terrace of superior houses, was built in 1819–20. These houses, some of which still exist, were the first buildings in Newcastle by entrepreneur and speculative builder Richard Grainger (1797–1861): see Ian Ayris, *A City of Palaces* (Newcastle, 1997), p. 33.

I do not altogether like this Shields plan, but J Gibson has engaged his cousins gig, so I must be forced to go I think.
[*Patient numbers*]

February 28 [*Wednesday*]
Which not being leap year is I suppose the last day of the month and consequently of this volume of the *Diary*.

I had arranged everything for going down to this ball last night and only wanted Mr McI's assent to complete my expedition. I therefore said to him after dinner that 'I was wishing to go out tonight if nothing was wanted' 'Umph you are not going far are you?' 'I have had a seat down to the So[*uth*] Shields ball offered, sir, which is held tonight' 'Umph – why, I am going out myself tonight so that you can't go tonight' 'Very well, sir' and accordingly I withdrew.

JG was vexed at first and said I had prevented him going as he would not go by himself. He had however refused Mr Fryer Jun[r] a seat in the gig in consequence of my agreeing to go and I suppose he *did* go with a gentleman, but as I have not seen JG since, I can't tell who this gentleman was. Mr McI was down at Wallsend in the evening.

I have been a long ride this morning to Felling, Windy Neuck (Nook) and then after coming back over the bridge went to Heaton, Walker, Benton & Forest Hall near Killingworth. In all about 17 or 18 miles.

Just been down at Lamberts the engravers to order 100 copies of Father's supplement, the plates of which he has been altering, to be struck off.[36]

By the bye, I was at church last Sunday and fell in the way of another sermon upon charity from the vicar. There was no collection however.

Blackwood's Magazine has just come in and as I have to write to Mother and the day (of course the vol:) is not concluded I will e'en leave this to tomorrow and set to work with Blackwood.

Mr McI is gone down, to drink tea with Mrs Gibson this evening uninvited to make up for not going twice when he was expected.

I must now look over the patients named in this volume and 'report progress'.

---

36 See notes 33 and 34 above.

Dec 12   Marley, Byker, Angina Pectoris. A great deal better but still far from well. Notable to work. [20/1/27]
13   Buckham, Felling. bruised foot. Well.
Elswick Dislocated Wrist has never appeared since the 16
14   Hunter & family Dropsey & scarlet fever. All well long since. [22/12/26]
15   Patterson's boy – Cut on the Head. That wound to my astonishment as well as the patients united by the first intention and was quite well in about 10 days! [22/12/26]
16   Hunter's boy, Benwell. This lad was dreadfully bruised but got quickly about again.
Robson Gallowgate was soon well.
Lamb's child – next yard – after a severe struggle escaped with life [19/12/26]
19   Phoebus – has been very dull this winter like most of our fashionable folks – the Duke's death perhaps partly a cause.[37]
22   Jobling, Byker Hill. Haemo[rrhois] was quickly well.
1827
Jan 21   Burrell – Elswick fractured arm – was in on Saturday last (Feb 27) when I put him on a strengthening Plaster. His arm has not done so well as I could have wished. The Radius is quite straight but he has been very obstreperous – running about fighting &c which has displaced the Ulna; and the consequence is that he will never have the power of rotation in his wrist so perfectly as before. The arm was quite straight when Mr McI opened it out the week after he had got the accident. [20/2/27]
Mrs Elliot Strumous abscesses in the hand is considerably improved and quite convalescent but this will be a tedious case, the Inflammation at one time extended quite up to the shoulder the arm being three times its natural dimensions. She is applying a Lin^t Ammon^{ed} & tight bandages.
Feb 3   Urwin Heaton Middle Pit well

---

37 This seems to be another reference to the unusual weather: see note 12 above.

20 Cook, Johnson's Houses His collar bone is as well as can be expected from his own awkwardness in managing it. [22/2/27]

Feb 24 Miss Aveling is now nearly well I believe when Mr McI returned he merely ordered a repetition of the medicine I had prescribed, which *I thought* was for him *astonishingly complaisant*
Mrs Longhead, Quayside is considerably better.

26 Turner, Byker Hill was better yesterday
Gaer's boy, Felling – doing very well. I dressed him also yesterday.

My little patient mentioned in the first volume October – Scott's child – has been attacked and brought to death's door in the same manner as before. I have again had the pleasure of bringing it completely round again. It will I doubt prove a sickly one to rear. [*Patient numbers – summary for February*]

V O L U M E 3 (March 1, 1827 to May 31, 1827)

March 1 and 3 *[Thursday – Saturday]*
Vol 3! Many a good periodical has been damned before arriving at Vol 3 yet here I am commencing Vol 3 of this insignificantly important trifle. *I* should have discontinued it long ago, but as my kind readers have taken the matter into their own gracious management, I have, of course, nothing to do but to obey.

In looking over the last volume, I must say I was far from satisfied with it. If one may be allowed to judge of his own works, I should say it is decidedly less interesting, and worse written, than the first number. An amendment must therefore be aimed at in this; for, without it, I shall be apt to doubt the sincerity of any one who shall think it worth looking into. There is one good escape for me however, that, as I only write this to be read by a few, and those my best friends, *criticism* cannot make me a mark for her envenomed shafts; and I may write volumes without dreading one envious critique.

This is Saturday night, & I had fixed Sunday for commencing this; as therefore I am going per agreement to Greenfield Place with my flute this evening, I will leave off scribbling till tomorrow.
[Patient numbers]

March 9 *[Friday]*
Novelty certainly does possess charms of no ordinary kind; I am particularly susceptible of such, and like most *geniuses* exceedingly liable to *Whims*. I have grown partly tired of daily annotation now that it has become more than whim; and unless I take up my pen with a relish I produce nothing but entire nonsense, (my last vol: fully verifies this) I must be excused if I get more slowly on than usual, and just be indulged with a few remarks when anything particular occurs, or according to the Quaker tenets, when the *'spirit moves'* me!

My Mother remarks that I have given fewer *cases* of late, and wishes me also to be more copious in critical remarks, which latter I shall most gladly attend to. In regard to the former I may observe, that nothing of moment has occurred in my medical or surgical practice or it should have been duly noted. Criticisms are so numerous on all hands, and so various that anything I may say in that department will only be like a single flute in a full band, – as little likely to be heard or attended to, – nevertheless and notwithstanding– as I have before said, as it is requested I shall gladly comply to the utmost in my power.

To proceed to occurrences however. I spent Saturday evening in GF [*Greenfield*] Place and saw Mr Bowes. Was also introduced to M. Forster a french lady.

On Tuesday night was held a meeting which had previously caused a great sensation among the members of the L & P Society – the anniversary.[1]

A motion for increasing the subscription was moved by Mr Cookson, who made a very good & amusing speech upon the occasion, demonstrating the necessity (from the bad state of its fund) of his motion being carried. Mr W. A. Mitchell and several *opposition members* had intended vigorously to oppose the motion, and there was great doubt as to which side would prove victorious. A Mr C Raine, a pug-nosed, dirty, insignificant looking chap got up to shew his brilliant powers of elocution, and after first blackballing the building committee then the members for *their* lukewarmness in a very fluent but evidently set speech, advised that the museum should be dissolved, 'the windows should be opened and all the birds set at liberty', the lectureship abolished, three or four of the servants turned off, &c, finally moved an amendment that 'the increase will be detrimental to the interests of the society by causing a diminution of its members'. About 20 hands were held up in favour of this, which was of course negatived. The original motion being carried by a large majority, – I among the rest. If Mitchell, or some person who *could speak*, had taken up the matter, it is supposed there would have been a drawn battle before it was decided, but Mr Raine did the opposition side much harm by his ill timed display. Mr R too moved an amendment to another motion respecting the election of the committee, but it was some time before any one would second

---

1 This was the annual meeting of the Literary and Philosophical Society, see Lit. and Phil. Reports, 1827.

him. When the division on his amendment took place lo!, not a hand but his own was visible 'high in the air' – not even his seconds. Mr Losh V.P.[2] was in the chair owing to the illness of the President.

After the meeting I took part of the alphabet in the calling over of the names in the voters lists, but as I found it would keep me till near one or two in the morning, I got a gentleman to take my sheet and made the best of my way home about eleven.

The subscription is now therefore 2 gns instead of 1½, and each member is allowed to introduce two friends to the museum daily. The consequence is that the museum is now thronged with ladies every morning, and is an agreeable lounge, as well as the amusement of looking over the book where all the visitors names are registered. As my name is down for the New Monthly, and it is time for taking it out, I must conclude for tonight, and resume when the whim next enters my pate.

[*Patient numbers*]

March 11 [*Sunday*]

I did not happen to get hold of my favorite New Monthly the other evening. An old gentleman who sits *spelling* over the pages of some mag: every evening close by the fire, with the most inveterate obstinacy & patience had unfortunately got hold of the one I wanted on Friday, and, as I saw no probability (from the length of time elapsing between each leaf being turned over,) of my getting it by any *reasonable* waiting for, I e'en took up the 'London' which next to the New Monthly I prefer. The London is full as good if not better than usual this month.

The 'Newcastle' too from a glimpse I got at it, just after it came *out*, or rather *in*, seems to be excellent. A paper on Phrenology[3] is I believe by my friend R. Gillan, and the laughable ever amusing views of Life by Obadiah Lapstone are the productions of Mitchell, the editor.

I must think about what journeys I have to go this morning (10 ½ AM). Patients at Wallsend, Byker Old Engine, Heaton H Pit,

2 James Losh (1763–1833) was a prominent barrister and business man in Newcastle, see E. Hughes (ed.), *The Diaries and Correspondence of James Losh*, 2 vols, Surtees Society, 171, 174 (Durham, 1962–3), II.
3 This apparently refers to an article, 'Thoughts on Phrenology' in *The Newcastle Magazine*, XVI(3), p. 96. Like most of the articles in the magazine, it is unsigned.

Benwell, & Felling *ought* to be seen today. As it is impossible to
see them all, *conveniently* at any rate, I must leave it to Mr McI to
judge which are to be left out, and which *he* will attend to.

I wrote a long letter to Mother yesterday, after receiving an
anxious one from her, in consequence of my not writing sooner.

The assizes have been held this last week. I managed to get to
the courts once or twice. I heard [a] good part, – that is the beginning & end, of a trial in which both prisoners were of Benwell
Colliery and in consequence had been patients of ours.[4]

A *thorough-bred rascal Campbell* had led off a young man into a
poaching exploit, on Mr Brandling's estate. They were surprized
by the game keepers, & *Campbell* was seized. *Armstrong*, his companion, to release Campbell, fired at the legs of the keepers and
both got off. Mr Moore & J Gibson attended the keeper who was
severely wounded. Both the poachers were taken after a reward
of £50 had been offered, by *Campbells informing of his companion*,
who had *fired to release him*!! Campbell instead therefore of being
hung or worse, which he richly deserved, was admitted King's
Evidence and pardoned, getting also £50 for his villainy. The
keepers could swear to Campbell, but not to Armstrong. His
employers one and all came forward to give Armstrong an excellent general character, being fond of a gun was his only draw
back. Campbell's evidence only being credited so far as corrobor-
ated by other witnesses, the Jury, after retiring for a long time,
returned a verdict of 'Guilty of firing the gun'. His lordship however hesitating to receive that, the jury retired again, and after
some further consideration returned a verdict of 'Not Guilty', on
the plea of want of evidence I suppose.

Mr & Miss Bowes are coming tomorrow to stay a week at
Newcastle.

Afternoon. I have been at Heaton – Middle and High Pit,
Byker &c Mr McI saying he would *perhaps* see the patients at
Wallsend & St Anthon's. Benwell & Felling may be left till tomor-
row or Tuesday.

There have been two or three accidents lately. A man [*Pratt*]
got his head cut at Byker Hill on the 1st. By taking great pains the
wound was well in three or four days. Another man [*Pyle*] got a

---

4 The Assize Calendar for Newcastle 6 March 1827 lists Thomas Armstrong aged
   25 and Jonathan Campbell aged 23 for unlawfully shooting at Francis
   Charlton. The case was assigned to the court at Gosforth: see Wilson, 508.

cut on the head on Friday at Benwell, who, I hope, will do equally well. In both cases a branch of the occipital artery was divided.

A man [*Boddison*] got a severe cut on his leg at Walker on Friday afternoon. The fibula was quite bared for an inch or two. The Vena saphena divided, which caused great haemorrhage; and, *I think*, a branch of the fibular artery also. I got the bleeding stopped however, and the wound, which was *set in* with coal dirt, dressed. On opening it out this morning I was agreeably sur-prized (my patient turned up his eyes in astonishment,) to find the wound closely united by the first intention! There is great swelling about the ancle yet. Leeches have been ordered *secundum artem*.

A boy [*Davison*] at Benwell old Engine got his shoulders very much bruised, and his collar bone *all but* broke on Wednesday. Mr McI saw him first and I was there on Friday. The collar bone (like that fool's at Johnson's houses, as Mr McI remarked) stands very high but this one is Mr McI's case so mine is not remarkable. The collar bone indeed, without great care to be taken *on the part of the patient*, seldom can be kept in its place to make a *good job*.

A man [*Dodds*] at Wallsend got the upper part of his breast bone driven in a little in by a fall; and a boy [*Gray*] at Heaton had his foot bruised, sums up all that is important.

In being out at Benwell Old Engine the other day, I met with an old patient who I often used to dress when he had a very severe comp^d fractured leg at Benwell High Cross. He was telling me a most laughable anecdote of 'that grand swaggerin' chap & t'Hexham lad' coming out to persuade a man that his arm was broken, and tying it up 'wi their pasteboards & spelks' accord-ingly;[5] whereas on Mr McI's seeing it the following day, it proved to be only a *sprain*!! My informants own *dry* way of telling the story, added to the idea of the *scene*, was as good as a farce.

Mr King often used to tell me of the *many* fractures he and Mr Bewicke had reduced; and which had all done so well!! This and a collar bone are the only two fractures I can hear of their having *attempted* to reduce.

My Mother writing to me last week, gives me what she calls a 'word to the wise' about singeing my wings like a moth fluttering

---

5 The 'grand swaggerin' chap & t'Hexham lad' were probably TGW's fellow apprentices, Bewicke and King, respectively. Spelk, a dialect for wood splinter, here presumably means a wooden splint used to secure the supposed fracture.

around a candle; alluding of course to some wings which Cupid may have lent or given me. This *candle* symbol however does not half suit me. Shade of Hellen!! *A candle!* to compare a ladies eyes, – sparkling like the finest jet, – dazzling like brilliants, or languishing in heavenly blue – to compare these, gentle reader – only think, – to what? to a *candle!* Yea even to a *four mold*,[6] – the princess of candles!! And *me* courteous reader, to compare – to liken me to a *moth* – a sluggish good-for-nothing moth! The only explanation I can give is that my dear Mother must mean that rare and valuable insect *in collections*) the *Death's Head moth* which has a skull painted on its back, – hence is *professional!*

I am, I flatter myself, no inattentive observer of *human physiognomy* especially of *the* most agreeable & interesting kind; but, so far, I have not found a *star* (and I have seen a great many of great splendour) powerful enough to set me in a blaze; or even *'to singe me'*. I hold myself *proof* to everything but a very *comet!!* and that with a preterparticularly considerably long train. Something that will be worth *stand my fire* and *'singeing* ones wings' for.

I made one promise in my last volume [*28/1/27*] which I have so far not performed so here I will redeem my word. It was to give a description of the Gall Bladder which I took from a defunct patient at Walker – (an odd subject to follow the last page aint it?). This said viscus is now in a jar properly strung up. It is immensely thickened and the Cystic duct would no doubt be almost or entirely obliterated. Mr McI said to me on taking it out of the intestines 'I think the duct is quite closed, – I do not see any vestige of it'. No wonder he could see no vestige when he had left that, the most important part – in the body! When I came to examine the specimen minutely at home, I found Mr McI had cut away the neck of the bladder just at the giving off of the duct. [*Patient numbers*]

March 22 [*Thursday*]
I having been put (or rather perhaps having put myself) out of humour this last 10 days on account of some affairs which do not

---

6 Candles were graded, according to the number making up a pound in weight, into sizes known as 'fours', 'sixes', etc. The standard candle, a unit of light-measurement, was 1/6 pound weight.

concern the reader of this, my 'Diary' has suffered a lapse of those ten days which I must now endeavour to make up.

First professionally, for like a traveller after an absence telling his adventures, I must give a straight forward narrative of the events during my absence from my book; – well then professionally. Two men have got burnt, i.e. one at Heaton & one at Benwell scalded by steam (which is all the same as burnt technically speaking). Both are doing well. A messenger came one morning about $\frac{1}{2}$ past 10 to say a man had got *both legs* broken. Mr McI myself and Greenwood went down to Wallsend accordingly. We however only found one leg fractured, an *only* of which the poor man was glad I dare say. He belongs to Jesmond Colliery, one of Sir T Burdons[7] but living at Wallsend is placed under Mr McI's care.

On Wednesday week I went up in the evening to GF [*Greenfield*] Place to meet Mr and Miss Bowes and escorted a party of the Miss Crawfords, Miss Bowes, a Miss Burnet & Mr Crawford to the Museum[8] &c the following morning.

On the Friday evening I went ($\frac{1}{2}$ price) to the Theatre partly to see Miss McIntyre who was going I knew with Mrs & the Miss Gibsons. JG [*John Gibson*] too was to meet me there (at the Theatre) with Mr Henzell. I got into the next box to the Gibson party at first but not within speaking distance. *Mr* McI as I suspected was with them, and looked very huffish on seeing me. Some officers &c going from a box on the other side of them, I went round into it to talk to the Miss Gibsons, which made my sweet master look no pleasanter. The house was very full. The new comedy a School for Grown Children was performed at the desire of the Proprietors. From the last two acts (and I had before read a sketch of the plot). I like the piece exceedingly and the performers exerted themselves with good effect. Giovanni I have seen in London with the powers of Miss Cubitt, Miss Love Harley &c – but still I thought Miss Jerviss very respectable as the Don.[9]

But *gentle reader* you will be impatient to learn what I thought

---

7 Sir T. Burdon was the colliery owner.

8 Presumably the Lit. and Phil. museum: see Introduction.

9 This occasion was the first night for the production of *A School for Grown Children* by T. Morton. The second piece, *Giovanni in London*, was described as 'A broad comic extavaganza': see NRPB.

of this long invisible, this great unknown, this Highland beauty, Miss McIntyre. My expectations may have been raised too high but if they had not they would have been low indeed. My impression that night as to *Beauty* (all I could then judge of) was that she was – *nothing!*

Today however by extreme *condescension* on her *brothers* part (for I have begun to get a better idea of her *sense*) we dined with them or they with us – which you please to call it, a thing that has never happened since Miss McI came before. Miss Mary seemed very desirous of having a little conversation introduced at table – a very great stranger at ours though – and her remarks were chiefly addressed to *me*. As I saw however her lordly brother's brow ready to frown away anything like *sociality* I contented myself with *politely* answering her numerous enquiries about the weather 'had I been in the country?' &c. She then tried Greenwood with a remark or two but with no better success. My sage opinion at present is that Miss Mary McIntyre is a very pleasant agreeable lady – about 30 – no great beauty – has no pretention to it indeed – and were her brother out of the way would be a social sort of a body.

I had intended to go to Mrs Garricks Concert[10] tonight but have reconsidered that as there is nobody *worth hearing* and nobody particularly worth *seeing*, my 3/6 will be better in my purse.

March 24 *[Saturday] [Patient numbers]*

March 27 *[Tuesday]*
Called up this morning by an announcement of two men [*Bell and Patterson*] having got burnt at Heaton. Mr McI & I both went off. One man only was *burnt* however the other having just got his brow scorched a little. His companion's face & hands had rather severely suffered from the effects of the blast. We had a very pleasant ride at 6 AM and got home about 8 oclock.

---

10 Mrs Garrick's concert was advertised in the *Newcastle Chronicle* of Saturday, 10/3/1827: 'Mrs Garrick has the Honour most respectfully to inform the Ladies and Gentlemen of Newcastle and vicinity, that, from the request of many of her musical Friends, she intends giving a Vocal and Instrumental Concert on Thursday March 22, at the Turk's Head Long Room. Vocal performers Mrs Garrick, Mr Noakes, Mr Stimpson, Mr Brown, Master Peele and Mr Jones (from the Theatre Royal). Leader Mr Miller, Flute Mr Richardson. Tickets 3/6 to be had of Mrs Garrick, 21 Northumberland Street . . . .'.

I have lost my little favorite mare and got a black horse to ride instead. Mr McI wanted one beast to run in his gig and as neither of those we had were fit for the purpose a change was indispensable. This black animal is of course bigger than my late poney but not so handsome. He can trot at a tolerable speed however though nothing very remarkable in his paces.

Been studying 'Stewards Philosophy of the Mind'[11] very diligently lately. It requires indeed intense study & complete abstraction to give it the attention it deserves, and I hope I shall be the wiser for reading it.

In one of the month's Magazines, I do not recollect which, there is a very interesting letter from a sea captain who had passed within sight of Maelstrom. The gentleman relates his entering even the dish of the whirlpool which is about $1\frac{1}{2}$ mile circumference and feelingly describes his sensations of despair on first perceiving that his ship was swerving 8 points towards the centre of the vortex and his delight on finding that 'she answered sweetly to the helm'. With a brisk wind he was enabled to steer so close to the gulph as to be near it 20 minutes and within sight an hour & half.[12] Now on seeing a patient [*Widdrington*] the other day who was very ill in Scarlet fever (or rather a spurious kind proceeding from cold and attended with sore throat &c) I fancy my feelings were very similar (but in a less forcible degree) to those of the captain before mentioned. Though not in danger myself I was pilot to my patient who had entered the whirlpool of disease, and was drawing towards its fatal centre. I of course flew to the helm of medicine, and assisted by a fair wind in Nature and a good ship in my young patient, I was happy to find on seeing her the day following that her system 'answered sweetly to the helm'; and we are now safely out of the eddy, and crowding all sail for the Shores of Health.

11 The work referred to was probably Dugald Stewart, *Elements of the Philosophy of the Human Mind*, 3 vols (London, 1792).
12 This incident is mentioned in *The Newcastle Magazine*, XVI, p. 137. In column entitled 'Varieties', under the heading 'The Maelstrom Whirlpool', is a letter 'from a gentleman in Washington to the Hon. A. B. Woodward, judge of middle Florida' that describes the events reported by TGW. The incident is said to have taken place, 'Between two islands ... off the coast of Norway, called the Low-in-staff Islands, between Dronthien and the N. Cape, ... about 69 north'.

Several cases of this species of Scarlatina and one well marked
genuine specimen have been on the books lately.

March 29 [*Thursday*]

> Reader, – I've been scanning these few days
> Byron's much praised – and much reviled 'Don Juan'
> Nay, – do not fix your eyes with wondrous gaze
> For *certis*, – tho' the work is not a new one,
> And partial as I am to poet's lays
> My dixit, I assure you, is a true one,
> I ne'er before could this said poem *light on*
> (Now what the d– shall I rhyme with) – write on.

I believe if I were to read very much poetry, I should be like the
school–boy who even tho' flogged for it could not speak but in
rhyme.[13] With reading Lord Byron's hundreds of lines I am now
constantly making stanzas as in imitation of his verse. But 'write
on' I will *not* for I have some time ago made a vow against *poetis-
ing* any more without my subject required it, i.e. my resolution
was, not to *form any more subjects for rhymes,* but, if necessary,
to find rhymes occasionally for my subject. My former rhymes
however did not please me; if they had done so there are now so
many doggerel *rhyme manufacturers,* and, as I am determined to
be a man or a mouse – '*aut Caesar aut nullus*', I will have nothing
to do with your half & half sort of matters.

I have not got thro' all the cantos yet of this celebrated poem,
but so far I opine that much more cry has been raised against it
than it merited on the score of delicacy, or *morality* if you will. I
have heard a much more *indecent* sermon come out of a pulpit,
and that too from one of the most evangelical & puritanical of
the church of England preachers, – than can be made up from all
the 10 cantos I have read put together!! Don Juan is certainly only
fit for perusal in the closet, or among unmixed (as regards the
ladies) company; but its beauties of description, – its lively
style, & its wit cast a welcome veil over the more objectionable
parts of the scenery.[14]

---

13 [*TGW footnote*] I find the anecdote I allude to is related of Dr Watts who when
a child could not avoid the habit of speaking always in rhyme. His father
threatening to whip him if he did not leave off the practice – the child on his
knees bursting into tears said 'Pray Father, do some pity take,/ And I will
no more verses make'

14 Contemporary attitudes to Byron's *Don Juan* are indicated by its withdrawal
from the library of the Lit. and Phil. in 1820 after a discussion at a monthly

March 31 *[Saturday]*

Mr McI & I had a few words on Thursday morning, but as he has chosen to treat me in such a very *highland fling* sort of way, and has seemed ready to take any opportunity of *affronting* me, ever since I *con*fronted him at the theatre, I did not much mind him; I even wrote a long letter to my Sister, and the above remarks on 'Don Juan' just after the circumstance.

I had been out on Wednesday night enquiring after J Gibson, who was poorly and was surprized to find on coming in this notice in the message book (a book where all mem: messages are entered).

'T. W---t not to leave the Surgery on any pretence without giving information'. My companion Greenwood had either not chosen to hear, or had been inattentive to my observations on going out, that I was 'going to Mr Moores to see J Gibson.' Completely vexed at the public sort of way in which the above was written, I immediately wrote underneath 'TGW has *invariably* observed this rule'. Mr McI was as I expected not a whit the more appeased for my making this addition to his *papal thunder*, when he saw it next morning. I, of course, insisted upon having left word, whilst Greenwood admitted he was very busy reading at the time, and might not have paid attention. Finding his flow of anger there stopped, Mr McI began to pour forth upon another subject, my not informing him after having seen patients; and instanced *unluckily* two whom I had the day before seen (the burnt men at Heaton) and concerning whose state he had made *particular enquiries* when I came home! He however denied this stoutly and to help himself thro' told a few other abominable f–l w–ds. He worked himself into a terrible passion, and told me if I 'did not behave otherwise he must get some one else' &c &c. He must think me either a complete fawning sort of Scotchman, or else profoundly ignorant of both his character and the behaviour and faults of my predecessors in office. I am sadly too open & candid for him; – he has been accustomed to be wheedled & truckled to (as e.g. Mr C-h-e [*probably Cochrane*]) or to be gulled by cunning & lies; and be cheated on all hands, – not a very difficult job, but one which I either cannot, or do not chuse (which you think likeliest) to practise.

The only reason I can find for the dislike Mr McI has evidently

---

meeting where the work was described by one member as 'a profane and licentious poem': see MacKenzie 1827, p. 464.

taken to me, is, that his *hauteur* does not inspire me with so much *awe* as he would wish. All this will blow over however. The time, I trust, *will come* (at least I have ambition to hope so,) when I shall be able to hold my head as high in society, and perhaps higher in *professional* & *scientific* society, as Mr McIntyre. Who lives to see that, will observe a very different aspect on *his* brow, should we meet, to what is here depicted. Mr McI has not one spark of soul, – of intellectual feeling, – about him; – he indeed inherits the worst qualities of a Scotchman, without even his *industry* or his *love of music*, and I fully believe Shakespeares remark to be a just one that

> A man who hath not music in his soul
> Is fit for treason, stratagems and spoils.[15]

[*Patient numbers*]

April 1 2 3 [*Sunday – Tuesday*]
I have managed to write what would about compose a *decent* sized volume in six months. Well – that is as much as could be expected from me circumstances considered. I have not, – as many journalists, a tour, – a voyage, or a revolution, nor yet am I in the army or navy, – to form the subjects of my remarks; – nothing but the constant humdrum routine of a surgeon's country practice. There are 'tis true cases to describe and now and then a few 'accidents and offences' to relate, but no field in which brains so dull as mine can call amusement for a work of this kind – for I beg, gentle reader, you will bear in mind my assertion in Page 1st that I *wish* to make this volume more '*interesting*' i.e. if possible worth your reading. I have long thought of establishing a receptacle for miscellaneous papers unconnected with the *business of the 'Diary'*; into which I may perhaps be able occasionally to *compress* something '*amusing*'; Articles such as, *were they worth it*, might find place in a magazine or other periodical; hence I shall give this department the title of *Magaziniana*.

As I have before said this is only for the perusal of a few friends and hence to them (as 'Recollections' & 'Reminiscences' are the fashion of the day) brief epitome of my own life, *connected with*

---

15 Compare: 'The man that hath no music in himself,/ Nor is not moved with concord of sweet sounds,/ Is fit for treason, stratagems, and spoils': Shakespeare, *The Merchant of Venice*, Act 5, Scene 1.

myself, may not be uninteresting. This therefore will be one subject of my 'Magaziniana' papers; to be got up by scraps, &
resumed just as inclination may supply materials. One provision
however I will make before I begin *viz.* that not *one word* of it
shall be written (or indeed of any articles of the kind) but when
I am in perfect good humor.

Our Heaton burnt patients [*Bell and Patterson, 27/3/27*] are all
doing well – one gone to work. The cases of scarlet fever I mentioned are convalescent. Fracture at Wallsend [*Thornton, Vol 2, 11/
12/26*] going on well.

I have seen a patient [*Miss Fabeus*] this morning with a chronic
'white swelling' of two month's standing in her left knee. Mr McI
has had her under his care about a week, and has applied the
Liniment Sapon to the limb. It is to be placed too on one of our
ever useful splints! I should like very much to try the effect of a
moxa or two upon the disease. The Soap Liniment however *has
made it no worse*, but if Mr McI gets it bent upon the splint he will
find it an awkward job, should anchylosis supervene, to get it
back into its present straight position. I have lately heard an
account *from the patient himself* (an old schoolfellow & intimate
friend) of the inconveniences resulting from the limb being
allowed to anchylose in a semibent posture.

The English surgeons are said to *kill their patients*, whilst the
French ones *let them die*.[16] Now Mr McI, being as aforementioned
a Scotchman, and that nation from long ancient intercourse with
the French having picked up a number of *their* notions, has apparently acquired an *affinity* to them in this respect also. Certainly as
a physician his treatment is far from *bold*, approaching sometimes
to complete *humbug*.

April 4 [Wednesday]

I have just returned (3 PM) from as pleasant a ride as I ever took.
The day is *too fine* for the season; it is quite like June. There only
wanted the foliage which is just beginning to sprout forth, instead
of being in full leaf, to make one mistake it for the middle of
summer.

---

16 A similar quip, 'The British kill their patients; the French let them die', is
quoted by E. W. Ackerknecht, *Medicine at the Paris Hospital, 1794–1818*
(Baltimore, 1967), p. 129.

Some time ago in reading a new work 'Essays on Opinions'[17], I was very much consoled to find that talent is of two kinds, practical & speculative; and that these two are *rarely* combined in one individual. This afforded me a nice corner to creep into, by excusing my want of *ideality* on the plea of being one of the *practically talented* persons and among whom rank some of the greatest philosophers of all ages. In poring over Stewart[18] this morning, I was delighted to find a passage which I shall not use as an *excuse* but be proud of quoting ' – *and hence the effect which long habits of philosophical speculation have in weakening, by disuse, those faculties of the mind, which are necessary for the exertions of the poet and the orator, and of gradually forming a style of composition, which they who read merely for the amusement, are apt to censure for want of vivacity and of ornament*' Vide p: 180 Vol 1.

The title of 'poet' I have little idea of laying claim to; that of 'orator' is more easily acquired; but one might almost suppose that Mr Dugald Stewart had written the last clause purposely for me. Henceforward then let it be known, and I here proclaim it, that I now aspire to the great and glorious title of – *Philosopher!* Let no captious critic censure *my style*, for he is only thereby raising my dignity. Any sentence which he cannot understand let him credit to the account of his own *stupidity*, and my *philosophy*. Let him learn that the mazes & depths of philosophical dedication, & metaphysical argument, – of logical reasoning and theoretical speculation, are too abstruse for the shallow capacity of his uncultivated intellect; and let *his* ornamental style, and vivacious descriptions be taught to bow before the profundity of *philosophical knowledge!*

'*By disuse*' says my quotation; and hence I shall also endeavour by preventing '*disuse*' to encourage the *speculative* department of my understanding; that I may if possible (my ambition being *unbounded*) be one of those who combine both talents.

I had determined not to begin my 1st Mag: till I had taken a ride to clear my faculties & refresh my memory, and had therefore fixed upon this date for the commencement of the undertaking. Since I wrote the preceding page, however, an untoward cir-

---

17 Possibly a reference to Samuel Bailey, *Essays on the Formation and Publication of Opinions, and on other Subjects,* 2nd edition (London, 1826), which is included in the Supplement to the Lit. & Phil. catalogue of books for 1826.
18 See note 11 above.

cumstance has occurred which has served to clog my *writing* as well as other appetites – I have got my dinner.

The *morning*, especially after a pleasant walk or ride into the country air, is by far the most eligible period for intellectual labours; tho' I find a very different hour also advantageous particularly in calling forth ideas or in composing verses, – 'tis when I am just going to sleep, – when imagination is beginning to rouse herself & preparing for her *dreamy* exertions of the night.

6 PM I have just looked into one or two of the new periodicals at the reading room and meeting there with a friend have learned that Mr Wood, lecturer on History & Architecture – whom I had the pleasure of hearing some four years ago, is about to deliver a course at the Turk's Head Long Room. This news has rather given me the *vapours* for it is connected with another story beside an architectural one; so I have taken up my pen to amuse myself – yes, – in Mr Wood's lecture room, during the course I attended – I saw, for the last time – but more of this anon; for further particulars see – a future Magaz:[19]

There is an interesting and apparently feasible paper in Blackwood this month by two Capt[ns] R.N. on 'Steam Navigation', and the advantages which would result from a navy being worked by steam.[20]

Mitchell has *injudiciously* inserted some remarks on the late changes in the Lit. & Phil. Society in a paper on the Mechanics Institution – part of the last Newcastle Mag.[21]

April 5 [*Thursday*]

As I see no likelyhood of my getting a ride this morning – almost as pleasant as yesterday, I will e'en stick down to my Diary a bit.

I expect the pleasure of seeing my F & M to spend the evening and part of the following day here tomorrow. We shall, I expect, go to the Theatre. Mr McI will *not* be there as Mrs Buddle an old

---

19 There is no information in any existing *Magaziniana* to elucidate this remark.

20 A letter on Steam Navigation from anonymous 'Captains R.N.' was published in *Blackwood's Edinburgh Magazine* (April 1827), p 393.

21 In *Newcastle Magazine*, XVI(4), pp. 175–7 an article entitled 'The Mechanics Institutes of this District' includes the comment that the Lit. and Phil. subscription had been raised by ten shillings and sixpence to 2 guineas to give members access to the museum 'which some do not want'. The article points out that 'subscribers can become members of the Literary, Scientific and Mechanical Institute for 12/- per annum.'

friend (and under the rose an excellent patient) is to be buried tomorrow. Destitute of feeling as Mr McI is he cannot, in common decency, go; I care little however whether he does or not, only that he does not prevent me going.
[*Magaziniana No 1 Autobiog Chap 1*]

April 7 [*Saturday*] [*Patient numbers*]

April 14 [*Saturday*]
I was at the Theatre with Father & Mother on Friday week to see 'Education' & 'Midas' for Butler, the stage manager's benefit: – a very full house.[22]

Mr McI & my Mother had a long confab the next morning when our late disagreements were fully discussed much to my satisfaction. All was very amicably & pleasantly explained so there the matter I hope ends. Since then I was at church on Sunday.

Had an accident on Tuesday evening a boy got a severe cut on the thigh. I inserted two sutures and the wound when I dressed it yesterday was looking remarkably well. Mr McI took occasion in my mentioning the accident to him to remark that 'sutures are very seldom useful'! Mr Liston on the other hand whom Mr McI himself denominates 'the first surgeon perhaps in the Kingdom' never uses 'one atom' (as Mr L says) of adhesive plaster. He unites all his wounds by means of sutures!! I made no reply however to Mr McI.

A man came in this morning from Walker with a long tale that 'a person at Biggs Main had got his foot nearly taken off'. Accordingly the horse was ordered into the gig though at 4 AM – and the amputating case &c &c put ready. To give every advantage to Greenwood, Mr McI took him up at the town end, and we all three proceeded down to the place. As I fully expected, the hurt was slight. The man [*Moore*] had a cut upon his foot the size of my finger nail!! To dress which (he might have done it well

---

22 An advertisement in the *Newcastle Chronicle* on Saturday, 31/3/1827 reads: 'Theatre Royal. Last Night of Acting till Easter Monday. Mr Butler (Stage Managers) benefit on the 16th fashionable evening Friday April 6. Comedy written by T Moreton Esq Author of *School for Grown Children* &c called *Education, or, The Yorkshire Farmer and the Shipwrecked Frenchman*. The Whole to coincide with the Burletta of *Midas*. . .'

enough himself) *three* doctors were arrived! In coming up again about ½ past 5, I sung in *thought* the following *stanzas*.

Stay though. I will not hide them in a corner this way, – let them have all the advantage they can get, and recollect they are *almost* extempore; composed as I was *stuck* in front of the gig half on Mr McI's knee & half on Greenwood's. They embody pretty much of the story usual upon such occasions.

Stanzas
Air 'When first I came to London Town'
　　Behold! Three doctors coming now,
　　In a gig, sir, In a gig, sir,
　　Heres three doctors coming now,
　　For to see a patient!

　　Oh! Sir, ye might hae spared yor horse
　　(Nay dinna now begin to curse[23])
　　It's well, an sure 'at its nae warse!
　　Don't ye think sae now ye're set sir!

　　We were sairly flaid, there was summat wrong
　　About his anklet; 'bout his anklet;
　　His banes ye see's not verra strang
　　He's but a smally lad, sir

　　A coal fell frae the roof, ye ken;
　　It struck upon his knee; and then,
　　It *shived* right down by his shin bane;
　　What a wonder it's not broken!

　　When we sent away, – it teuk five men,
　　Indeed it did; indeed it did, Sir!
　　It teuk four putters[24] & wor Ben
　　To lift him out o' danger

　　To get the coal frae of his foot,
　　And into 't cairt to get him put,
　　We expected nought but it was cut,
　　It's a marcy he's not killed, Sir.

After three weeks attentive study (i.e. for about an hour a day) I have finished Stewart's elements. I dare not engage with Vol: 2 yet awhile; but must get some lighter works for a week or two till I have got my present intellectual banquet digested.
[*Patient numbers*]

---

23 [*TGW footnote*] A feeling very natural to some people upon such an occasion; tho' I do not say such was committed this morning.
24 [*TGW footnote*] One class of workers in a coal pit.

We are all crying out for something to do just now. Some epidemic or *instructive* accident.

April 20 *[Friday]*
Bells are ringing for the Duke of Northumberland's birthday.

Wish a bad wish and the Devil is sure to grant it. I was only last night wishing for 'something to do' when a man made his appearance all in a foam to fetch 'the doctor' down to a woman who was dying. Mr McI could not find in his heart (his love of the sex is so great) to go; and accordingly *I* set off with all convenient speed to Ouseburn. A woman [*Mrs Archbold*] near 'confinement' of her first child had distressed herself with the idea of her husband being in a consumption, in consequence of Mr McI's having ordered him a sea voyage in the morning. She had come up from Walker Gate, her residence, to her Mothers at Ouseburn. There she was seized with *Puerperal Convulsions*.

She was in one of the paroxysms when I got down. I called for a bason & bandage immediately to bleed her. A Mr Wilson, Druggist &c &c of the village, who had been sent for in the interim (till someone from head quarters should arrive) had however saved me the trouble, and given her some antispasmodic medicine. As nothing further could be done while the fit lasted, I made the best of my way back to see Mr McI and sent him down; not wishing to have the responsibility of the case on my own shoulders. He went down. The person has continued in a succession of convulsive fits thro' the night; being so much worse about 12 oclock that they called us up, and got some change of medicine. She has had no return since 9 AM, and Dr Headlam[25] who has just seen her (12 PM) has ordered her some aperient medicine and considered her out of danger. A slight degree of sensibility was perceptible when the messenger came away with the D^{rs} prescription. Mr McI is gone off to a consultation at Penshah[26] and has not therefore seen her since last night. I was called

25 Dr Thomas Emerson Headlam (1777–1864) was a leading physician in Newcastle.
26 In the MS this was originally written as Penshaw but this was crossed out and Penshah substituted; TGW also spells it Painshaw and Pensher. The present-day spelling is Penshaw – a village west of Sunderland, now noted mainly for its prominent Grecian-style monument to the first Earl of Durham erected in 1844: see *BED*, p.371.

up to an accident at 5 this morning and precluded the necessity of Mr McI's called upon our patient till he returns from Painshaw by seeing her then. A more deplorable sight I think I have never witnessed than the distortion produced with this poor woman's convulsions.

This does not end the *consequences* of my wish. *Consequences* mind, properly means 'events following' whether accidental or otherwise.

I was, as I have said, called up to an accident – and a terrible accident it was. A man [*Gordon*] had got struck by a stone falling from the roof of the pit (he belongs to Heaton Middle Pit) which first hit his head, and falling upon his legs had fractured the fibula of one, and cut the other down in a flap from a little below the knee to nearly the ancle, laying the shin bone bare for about 6 inches. When this wound was closed by three *sutures* & adhesive plaster, it presented the appearance of an angle of about the following dimensions

[*Here, a very small rough sketch shows the lower leg and foot, with what appears to be a V-shaped wound with the lengths of its sides indicated as 5 and 8 inches*].

I put it up very carefully but if it unites by the first intention, I shall consider it almost a miracle. It is the most extensive flesh wound I ever saw. After I had dressed it my patient complained very much of the other – the fractured limb. I of course could only apply lotion to it and lay it in a proper position. No leeches are to be had.

Having now done with the doleful we will try something of a lighter *caste*. Reader what do you say to

[*Magaziniana no. 2: 'My Autobiography', chapter 2*]

April 21 *[Saturday]*
I have forgot to mention that our new apprentice [*Gray, 4/1/27*] has returned from school and gone to Backworth, to our drill sergeant there; while we have got the youth he has had in hand this last year to occupy the junior station in *our* establishment.

Mrs Archbold – our hysteric patient – is decidedly better this morning. [*20/4/27*] She was worse again yesterday afternoon but has had no return of the fits. She is sensible this morning and able to swallow a teaspoonful of liquid at a time. Her tongue was so much swollen yesterday she could not be got to take the smallest quantity of her medicine.

April 24 [*Tuesday*]

On Saturday as I was coming home from Heaton I was called to a person [*Kidman*] who had drunk some caustic soap-ley (a poison) in mistake. She has scarcely swallowed any, but the little she had taken was sufficient to bring on inflammation in the Stomach & Throat by the following day when Mr McI (who saw her *then*) bled her and ordered her some leeches. She is almost well again today.

On Sunday I remained altogether at home. In the evening we drank tea and had some good plumbcake [*sic*] with Miss McIntyre.

This morning about 7 AM I was called to a man [*Sopwith*] who had got his foot bruised at Benwell and had just got home and breakfasted when a woman came in requesting her husband [*Bell*] might be seen who got his side hurt last night at Heaton. Scarcely had she got out of the shop with a promise that he should 'be seen' before a horseman brought word that two men were 'desperately hurt at Heaton'. 'One had his hand ta'en off' and the other's head was very badly cut. Both horses were ordered and I set off to the Middle Pit where it was said the 'head-cut' patient resided and Mr McI was to meet me at the other person's on my return. *My* first patient however was lying in bed not wishing for or expecting any doctor; his side was slightly bruised. I proceeded of course with what speed I might to the other sufferer & found there something better worth the trouble of coming out for. The end joint of the thumb was *nearly* 'off' – the bone shivered to pieces and the part split up the middle. This man (Yule) had also a cut on *his* head but very trifling. I had with some pains & care succeeded in putting up this thumb to my satisfaction when Mr McI came. The man would not be satisfied without it was taken off now if there was any chance of it having to come off at all. I told Mr McI how I had managed with it but the patient seemed to wish to have it amputated reason or none, and to pacify him Mr McI opened out the dressing to look at the wound. He put it up just in the same way again but (low it be spoken) not half so neatly as before. As soon as Mr Mac was gone & whilst I was washing my hands the folks *rated* Yule soundly for being 'sic a feul as have it opened out agaen when it was put up sae bonnie' they 'sure'd it was not deune half sae cannie 't second time' – To which the patient agreed.

I opened out Gordons cut leg at the Middle Pit yesterday (vide

20th). [20/4/27] It has united *close*!! From the bruise however one or two sloughs will have to come away on the upper part. Mr McI thinks both bones of the opposite leg are fractured. The tibia close up to the joint but so transversly that it is scarcely perceptible. I indeed have not yet discovered it. I have been told and that by a surgeon a friend of my masters that Mr McI sometimes 'makes fractures' (Do not start, dear reader, I of course only mean '*in verbo*') and tho' with all allowance for his greater experience and hence more delicate '*tactus eruditus*' I am in this instance very much inclined to turn infidel. I will ask him however particulars as he has never told *me* of it but this I learn from the patient. The limb was formally laid upon a splint yesterday. It is terribly bruised.

But surely we had an accident yesterday. Oh aye – one at Walker. A rolley in going over a boys hand laid the whole of the palm bare down to the bone leaving a flap laid back. Mr McI & I were both there.

An incessant snow storm yesterday and ditto mixed with rain & hail this the quarter part of today have made my rides rather uncomfortable; but the zest which a renewal of 'plenty of business' gives to them far more than counterbalances unpleasant feelings.

I was in G Field Place with my flute an hour or two last evening.

April 26 *[Thursday]*
I was down at Heaton &c yesterday. All there doing well. Opened out the boy's hand at Bigg's Main which is not doing so well. [*Todd, 24/4/27*] The flap in the palm of the hand is undergoing the process of mortification and I doubt will all come away. This be it remembered was Mr McI's putting up though I by no means attribute *all* the consequences to that.

This morning I was called out to Felling to a patient [*Bailey*] who had been kicked down & sadly bruised by an unruly horse. His face head & chest had suffered severely. I bled him and hope he will do well. After breakfast I set off to see my Benwell patients who are better; and then proceeded to Heaton, Byker & c &c seeing in all upward of 20 patients. This though at one time not an unusual number is from the great plenty of that useful commodity to most folk and plague of our Profession – *health*. (Mem: I must write a paper someday 'On the disadvantages of

Health'!). 20 patients, I say is at present rather an unusual number. I hope however we shall go on increasing in our sick list till I again arrive at or outdo that glorious & memorable day when 'I saw 43 country patients' (for which vide memoranda pocket book Sept 15 – 1826).[27]

Not (as I have often had occasion to remark) that I wish people to fall sick on my account but I would have those who in spite of Hygeia do fall back from among the number of her votaries – to come with all convenient haste to *me*, who will gladly 'give them a lift' and assist them up the hill to overtake their more fortunate fellow worshippers.

I have not done yet with accidents though of which a greater *congregation* have occurred this last week than I ever recollect since coming to Mr McI. There were two yesterday which I have not mentioned as they were slight. One man had his wrist sprained by the fall of a corf full of coals. The other was hurt on the shoulder from a blow. Both were able to come into town.[28] A man also was killed at Elswick this morning but as he was dead when found the folks had the sense not to send for 'the Doctor'. A coal was laid upon his head which had most probably fractured his skull.

Today when I was just sitting down to dinner with Mr McI & Miss M[*Mary*] a horseman summoned me off to Walker to a person whose foot & leg were bruised by the fall of a coal. This accident however was not very severe. NB I did not go till I had got aboard a good cargo of fish roast pig & bread pudding. A surgeon should never go to a patient with an empty stomach else the chance that whilst his fingers are upon his patient's pulse or exercising their 'tactus' on a broken bone – his eyes are wandering into the cupboards or towards the bread loaf (mayhap a spice cake) and teapot which are generally in the way when a lamed man is brought home.

The weather has resumed its proper spring-like appearance

---

27 Presumably the pocket book, referred to in 'My Autobiography', chapter 15, in which TGW made notes on his time in Edinburgh. The date of the marathon round was about a month after TGW returned to Newcastle after being in Edinburgh.
28 That is, for the patients to attend the surgery in Newcastle rather than be visited at their homes.

again today. The snow has disappeared and the verdure all the
fresher for the rain. The charm is broken by the change of the
long fixed North East wind to West so I hope as the Moon too is
renewed today this fine weather will be permanent for a while.

April 28 *[Saturday]*
Mr McI directed me last night to see the Heaton & Walker
patients early this morning and rang his bell at $6\frac{1}{2}$ AM for me to
fulfil my orders. I had a very pleasant ride it being a beautiful
morning. Patients doing well.

Received this morning a supply of new music from my Sister
by Father who to my agreeable surprize is here today to teach at
Colⁿ Gilmores. And to crown all, Mother has sent me with her
love the most tasteful elegant & valuable watch equipage. A key
in the form of a lyre with a handsome seal & ring to correspond.
All this has made me in a very pleasant & *gratitudinally* (grateful
won't do) sort of humour and expelled the vapours under which
I slightly laboured last night. The cause of these latter was thus.
Mr Taylor Gibson's had a very large & *swell* party last [*missing
word*] – 70 or 80 folks it is said – to which I was *not* invited. Mrs
Gibson has always been very polite in asking me to go there often
in an evening when I had the leisure but though I have never
acted upon her general invitations I would have had no objections to a particular one. This is the second party they have had
this winter and I have been at neither. Mrs G *may* suppose that I
should not like to meet Mr McI but at any rate the invitation card
would be a compliment. Mr McI too was in Edinburgh at the
time their first rout was held.

JG [*John Gibson*] was capering & careering about before their
windows in coming home yesterday afternoon when his horse
slipped & fell upon him. His knee is very much bruised but his
leg is fortunately not broken. I was unwilling to call upon him
(as he is laid up at his Fathers) this morning but luckily saw his
F at the door and had the opportunity of making enquiries. It
would spoil his dancing last night – a great disappointment no
doubt to Miss T – [*Taylerson?*] who I hear was there. Miss & Mr
McI of course were of the party.
[*Patient numbers*]

A blank week here occurs from my sending the Diary to Sunderland for my Mother's perusal.

May 5 *[Saturday]*

I am so much behind hand with what I have to relate that I hardly dare begin; and, (especially as I have something new *in pickle*) I must therefore be as brief as possible in running over the memorabilia of this last week.

On Tuesday afternoon I went to Bells Close (about 3 or 4 miles up the Tyne[29]) to see a boy belonging to Benwell [*Nicholson?*] who was hurt by some rolleys. His head was severely cut and he was otherwise much bruised. In the evening I went to see J Gibson, who had wondered I never called to see him, and was called away from there to a severe accident at home.

Mr & Miss McIntyre were down at Tynemouth and about to return home when in taking off the horse's bridle (a wrong one had been put on) whilst both were in the gig, the horse set off at full speed without any bridle on. Mr McI having directed his sister to sit still leapt out and attempted to seize the horse's head but was thrown down and the wheel passed over his body. By this his arm was severely bruised also his side and his brow & nose deeply scratched. Miss McI fared worse. The horse carried her – now on the footpath & now on the road – about a mile making some turns very cleverly. At one sharper than the rest Miss M was projected out and most fortunately for in a hundred yards more the gig was overturned and the horse thrown quite on to his back with great violence breaking the gig & harness very much.

The lady's side was severely bruised and her face but slightly. After being leeched & bled in consequence of an attack of inflammation in her chest she is able to sit up today. Mr McI does not shew himself much on account of his piebald face, which I have to dress night & morning; otherwise he is quite well again.

On Thursday morning a boy [*McDougal*] got his arm broken in St Nicholas Ch. yard. Mr McI went down in a hackney coach and we set it *secundum artem*.

I saw my patient at Bells Close [*Nicholson*] and was happy to find instead of a large flap upon his head merely two red lines where the edges of the united wound were.

Yesterday I was on a longish round in the country – by Heaton, Wallsend, Walker &c and had just got into our yard

---

29 Bell's Close is to the west of Newcastle, near Lemington.

when a man on horseback followed me to announce an accident at Walker. I was very hungry tho', so having despatched the messenger back I *got my dinner* and then saw my patient [*Rowland*]. A rolley had run quite over his leg which was cut and severely bruised.

J Gibson was out yesterday and purposed being on horseback again today.

My Mother says this last song of mine is not as good as the former one. I have notwithstanding ventured again and were a higher flight. I have sent her 'a Flute Song' set to music with an original air and a flute obligato accompaniment duly written out with flourished Title page and blank lines left for Father to add a Piano forte accompaniment which is beyond my powers of musical composition. Observe it is intended to display the tones of the flute which in skillful hands may be made to produce tones such as described in the song and which are given in the fl: account:

The following are the words

> *Flute Song*
> 'How sweet at eve the lover's (f)lute[30]
> Sounds, when the groves are still and mute' Lady of the Lake

> How sweet at eve when all is mute
> To hear the dulcet warbling flute,
> Smoothly in melodious lay
> As distant echoes melt away!
> When all is mute
> Sweetly the flute,
> Warbles forth its mellow strain!

> But hark! it changes now its Sound,
> As fife so lively thrills around,
> Like the lark's matin song on high
> Its rapid notes swell thro' the sky
> With thrilling sound,
> It trills around
> And carols blythely on the plain

> Again that all is hushed & lone
> Here the hautboys martial tone,
> With pompous pride scarce yields its note,
> To that which peals from brazen throat

---

30 [*TGW footnote*] I have ventured here to add a *letter* which I hope does not impair the beauty of the line, or make the quotation much less *literal*.

With mock alarms
It calls 'to Arms'!
And boldly rings thro' all the glen!

[*Patient numbers*]

May 7 [*Monday*]
After a ride in the country I took a walk of about 6 miles yesterday evening by Jesmond a very romantic and almost the only
pleasant walk about Newcastle.

This morning I had to see a gentleman a regular patient of *Mr
McI* [*J Redhead?*] who had got sprained in leaping.

We had summer weather last week immediately after a snow
storm and this morning had all the damp raw feeling of
unhealthy October.

May 8 [*Tuesday*]
A very pleasant ride this morning has put me in a writing
humour and lest 'my life' should be too much of a good thing if
continued without intermission we will try a different subject.[31]
[*Magaziniana no. 3: About a flute*]

May 12 [*Saturday*]
On Wednesday morning I went by special invitation to play a
game at cricket with a club composed partly of old school fellows.
We met at 5 AM and played till 8 In consequence of this violent
exertion I have felt stiff ever since, but none the worse otherwise.

We have had two or three accidents. A man got burnt at
Elswick and two got hurt at Walker. One also at Heaton none of
them severe.

We have for some weeks expected our Edinburgh Collegiate
my fellow *foreman* Mr King but he has at length arrived. He is I
am happy to see greatly improved, brimful of Anatomy; and
bearing very creditable trophies from his late Teachers, particularly from my friend Dr Knox under whom he has dissected.

May 14 [*Monday*]
I had a very pleasant ride to Backworth &c with Mr McIntyre
yesterday and dined or rather lunched with Mr Cochrane. We
went to dress a comp^d fracture of Mr C's.

---

31 The previous *Magazinianas* (nos. 1 and 2) are autobiographical.

In riding with Mr McI we had a good deal of conversation – professional of course and amongst the rest I asked about the fract[d] leg of Gordon's mentioned in April 24 and was glad to find that I had been misinformed by the patient. Mr McI said the tibia was *not* fractured as I had all along persisted. The knee no doubt was injured and the fibula fractured but still the principal bone was tho' damaged not broken. I told Mr McI I thought the fibula was fractured in two places. He said very probably it might.

I have had a beautiful ride to Bells Close this morning and will now try my hand at a continuation of my life.

[*Magaziniana no. 4: 'My Autobiography', chapter 3*]

May 22 [*Tuesday*]
In consequence of my Father having sprained his back whilst lifting some packages at Croft and wishing to see me concerning it, I went over to Sunderland by Mr McI's leave on Friday evening and staid all night, returning by Saturday afternoon's coach.[32] I found [*Father*] a great deal better and left him almost well.

This and a regard for not wasting paper very little of which is left for the rest of this month are the causes of this blank of a full week in memoranda.

I have had a pleasant opportunity of renewing with an old friend when we lived at Stockton – a gentleman who used then to be a frequent visitor of my F & M's home and who always took much notice of me tho' then but a child – Mr Frank. Some business regarding property at Stockton[33] has given rise to our correspondence and Mr F has written to me in answer to a former letter of mine. I replied to his yesterday.

Nothing remarkable has occurred in a professional way lately. Patients are all doing well.

May 24 [*Thursday*]
Ascension day and 'par consequence' the day on which the Mayor of Newcastle sails round the boundaries of the port in

---

32 The Wellington, coach to Sunderland left from the Turf Hotel, Collingwood Street, Newcastle, at 8 AM and returned at 5 PM passing through Boldon: see PW, I, p. 136.

33 In an obituary of TGW (*Wakefield Express* 4/6/1898, p. 5) it is stated that before his birth his parents had purchased a pair of houses on the Green, adjoining the Vicarage in Stockton. Possibly they had retained ownership after leaving Stockton in 1818 and returned to live there. In 1827 they were

his state barge and followed by a concourse of boats. The day is hereabouts known as the 'barge day'. This mayor being a great general favorite his barge day was expected to be more splendid than usual and I have just come up from viewing the procession. There are boats, and barges, wherries, gigs, luggers, steam vessels, *keels*, and every description of nautical pleasure boat, with flags of all colors sizes & shapes, the rowers chiefly in their peculiar uniforms. The mayor's & the custom house barges of course formed the most conspicuous objects but the gaudy painted gigs and steam boats greatly aided to enliven a very busy and interesting spectacle. Three or four bands of music were in different parts of the river. The officers of the troops at present in the barracks had their galley with six oars and cut rather a prominent figure in their straw hats, striped shirts with black handkerchiefs, blue jackets & white trowsers. Among the prettiest of the gigs were the 'Venus', 'Harmony', 'Britannia', 'Caledonia' & 'Tyger'.[34]

I have these two days made at attempts at a very learned matter no less than an essay on Attention to prove that it can only be directed to one point at one time. It is too long for insertion in this filling four closely written folio pages!!

May 26 *[Saturday]*
My Father is here today and enquires for the next volume of the Diary but I find I have been so lazy that I shall hardly get it filled up by the end of the month. I must try another Magaz. tomorrow to fill up as I have promised the completion of this volume on the 31st.

My Mother has made a most valuable present today and one which I have often wished to have a sight of, *viz.* the MS of her opera – Rusticity. She thought every paper concerning it had been committed *ad flammas* but luckily here is an old copy of the whole

---

lodging in Sunderland but, at the end of the Diary in May 1829 (Volume 12), TGW mentions returning home to The Green when he left Newcastle.
34 There are several published accounts of the Ascension day celebrations in Newcastle, see e.g. Mackenzie 1827, p. 744 and Middlebrook, pp. 222–3. The barge procession of 1827 is depicted in a well-known painting by J. W. Carmichael, *Ascension Day on the Tyne*, painted in 1829 and first exhibited in 1830. The original painting is in the Bowes Museum private collection: see Diana Villar, *John Wilson Carmichael 1799–1826* (London, 1995), p. 20.

in existence which Mother has been kind enough to send me. [35]
[*Patient numbers*]

May 27 [*Sunday*]
[*Magaziniana no. 5: 'My Autobiography', chapter 4*]

May 28 [*Monday*]
I have this morning been examining a well-marked case of hip
disease. Mr McI saw the patient on Sunday week and I saw him
for the first time on Saturday. I then ordered him a powerful
blister which has 'risen' very well but little change is so far perceptible in the complaint. The hip joint is nearly immovable. Mr
McI made an issue in the thigh last week which has not yet discharged any *pus*. The patient – a boy – is very much emaciated
but otherwise of healthy constitution.

By the bye I forgot to mention that Mr McI set off for
Edinburgh on Saturday morning and is yet from home so that
I am once more *'charge d'affairs'*. Miss McI has this afternoon
gone down to Wallsend where, from her shaking hands, invitations, good byes &c to us I conclude she will remain some
time.

We have had but one accident and that a very slight one since
Mr King came from Edinburgh and are therefore rather slack at
present. My co-partner – King – has not been on horseback once
since his return and never by Mr McI's orders before.

May 31 [*Thursday*]
Miss McI went down to Wallsend on Monday afternoon. I had
an accident [*i.e., attended an accident*] at the stables close to Mr
Buddle's the following day and of course called upon her ladyship. She was not up but gave me an audience in her bedroom. I
had a note for her which had been left that morning.

I was down again this morning and merely sent in my respects
and enquiries after her. She however requested I would go in to
see her. I did so.

---

35 An unacted opera, 'Rusticity' written by TGW's mother (Elizabeth Wright
née Foxton) in 1800, with music by his father, Thomas Wright, is referred to
in Thomas Richmond, *Local Records of Stockton and Neighbourhood*
(Stockton-on-Tees, 1868), p. 154, and G. Grove, *The New Grove Dictionary of
Music and Musicians*, 20 vols (London, 1980), XX, p. 541.

The accident at Wallsend was not severe – a bruise on the foot. Mr McIntyre has not arrived at home yet but we half expect him tomorrow – that is Miss McI and I do. By the way Miss McI's looks are greatly improved by this accident of hers – it is whispered that she is likely to remain permanently in this neighborhood, and Mr Buddle our great professional friend – the celebrated colliery viewer – in short the well-known *Mr Buddle* is said to be endeavouring to engage her assent to the above resolution. Mr McI will I dare say have no objection. As this is the last day of the month I must prepare for a conclusion and in the *last* place therefore to our usual list of the patients ultimate fate.

March 11	*Pratt*	BykerHill	head cut – well
	Pyle	Benwell	do do
	Boddison	Walker	leg cut do
	Davison	Benwell	bruises last time I saw this patient he was weak but still improving. This was about 3 weeks after his accident.
	Dodds	Wallsend	fractured breast bone – did very well
	Gray	Heaton	no doubt did well (I forget this patient)
March 27	*Widdrington*		Scarlet fever – soon arrived in the destined port. I have all along had a succession of cases of scarlet fever which have *all* without exception terminated favorably.
	Bell & Patterson		burnt – soon got well again.
April 3	*Thornton*	Wallsend	This I hope will be my last mention of this unfortunate man. He is now at work and bears his labour very well.
	Miss Fabeus		white swelling. This young person is considerably improved and is now

			able to walk a little by the help of crutches. Mr McI *had* recourse to the more powerful treatment I recommended.
April 14	*Moore*	Biggs Main	Was not very many months off work.
April 20	*Mrs Archbold*		Convulsions. This person had a miscarriage a day or two after which terminated the cause of the complaint and of course *eradicated* the disease and terminated our attendance being then consigned to the midwives hands.
	Gordon	Heaton	He is now rapidly improving, There was every reason to suspect a collection of matter in the fractured limb. By persevering in the use of white liniment the fluctuation has disappeared. He is still able to walk. The cut leg is just about well.
April 24	*Sopwith*	Benwell	bruised foot – soon got well
	Kidman	Heaton	cured
	Bell	Heaton	Side bruised – only slightly injured
	Yule	Heaton	Cut thumb. This case has done remarkably well. He is now able to work.
	Todd	Walker	cut hand. A large slough came away and the wound has now healed very prosperously. It is now *all but* closed.
April 26	*Bayley*	Felling	done well

May 5	*Rowland*	Walker	cured
	Nicholson	Benwell	soon well
	McDougal	Newcastle	fractd arm – done well
May 7	*J. Redhead* Esq		Sprain better
May 22	*Mr Wright*		Sprain better

Only one patient *of mine has died lately* I think, a child of Hydro-cephalus; it was incurable even the parents had almost given up hope when I first visited it.

V O L U M E 4 (June 1, 1827 to July 31, 1827)

June 1–2 *[Friday – Saturday]*
In return for the kind attention of my friends, I have this time treated them with an improved paper. Whether the subject of the ink may correspond is not for me to judge. For this I expect to receive the thanks of all my spectacled readers and of – the stationers; as I have already, through the transmission of the sense of touch, received those of my fingers & pen. You will perhaps say the tributes of the latter are but gooseish and by analogy foolish; but those who are much accustomed to writing will be able to appreciate their due value.

I intend to make a vow against painting, as well as superfluous poetry; that kind of painting, I mean, which is done 'by rule of thumb', and of which I have given numerous specimens lately. As a Surgeon I ought to be more addicted to the use of the knife, but my vow not being yet registered before a magistrate, a *lapsus pollicis* may occasionally be committed. Bad habits are not quickly abandoned.

I think I cannot make my bow better in again introducing myself to my readers than by quoting the following passage as an excuse for my sometimes tedious remarks, which will serve at once as a mot-to and a mot-ive for the continuance of this Diary.

'Some people have not the talent, some have not the leisure, and others do not possess the requisite industry for keeping a private diary or journal; and yet there is probably no book which a man could consult with half so much advantage as a record of this sort if it presented a faithful transcript of the writers fluctuating feelings and opinions' H. New Monthly Mag:[1] To which may be added this from Jefferson Hogg's preface to his *Two hundred and nine Days on the Continent* before quoted from.[2] 'The more

---

1 The author of this quotation, 'H', is later identified by TGW as Horace Smith: see 14/7/27.
2 Hogg is referred to in 'My Autobiography', chapter 4, note 11.

dignified critics are frequently offended at the minute observations that abound in Diaries; but the more particular the details
the more engaging is the author at least in my opinion'

Without further remark I shall leave these passages to speak for
themselves; hoping that the authorities will have some weight – I
shall proceed to ordinary subjects.

June 4 (Mon) *[The day here is written in the MS in pencil]*
On Thursday night (31ˢᵗ) about 10 PM I was called to an accident
at Heaton. [*Marley*] The patient's right great toe was dislocated at
the first joint. The swelling was exceedingly tense all over the
foot; and, having no proper assistance I was after three or four
vain attempts for want of mechanical force compelled to leave
the luxation unreduced and apply leeches and fomentations. Next
morning I got Mr Church – House surgeon to the Infirmary – to
accompany me in my visit to the patient, and by our united
strength together with that of another man we got the joint at last
put right. Mr Liston says he would rather reduce a dislocated
thigh than one of these above named cases; he thinks it is best to
spend little time in vain attempts at reduction, but to cut down
at once on the lateral ligaments and divide the opposing bands.
In justice to myself I might say that both Mr Church & the patient
agreed that it was impossible I should have reduced this bone
(especially while unassisted) the night before.

On the morning of the same day I was sent for to a child
[*Robson*] who was severely scalded on the neck breast & belly by
boiling water. The child is doing well. Mr McI put it under King's
care yesterday.

In the evening of Friday, Mr Cochrane came in with his mare
in a foam. Mr Church was requested to go out with him. I with
difficulty made out what was matter – a compound fractᵈ skull.
Mr Cochrane I saw did not wish me to have anything to do or
say in the matter but I cared not for that, and after consulting Mr
Church who was desirous I should accompany him I ordered
both horses to be saddled and off we three set to near Backworth
about 7 miles from hence.

Had Mr McI been at home he would most probably have given
King the advantage of going with him but as Mr King did not
entertain an idea of going and even refused when I mentioned it
to him I was determined not to lose so good an opportunity for
improvement for any small matter. As Mr Church justly observed

to me in returning that night 'One operation where you have
your finger in, – are assisting and can examine the parts for yourself is of greater advantage than *seeing* half a dozen being merely
a spectator, and that perhaps from a distance'.' The case was a
very severe one – Mr Church trepanned the patient and large
pieces of bone were taken away – the fracture extended about 4
inches. The parietal bone was principally injured but the temporal shared in the fracture. The patient yesterday was doing
well. He being within Mr Cochrane's jurisdiction I of course
having nothing to do with his treatment and can only report progress occasionally. On the night of the operation the chances
seemed to be calculated at about 3 to 1 against his recovery.

On Saturday evening I drank coffee at John Gibson's to meet
Messrs Henzel, Brockett & Pyle. We had a game at whist – 6d a
game – I won two games then lost the same number which I
thought a very appropriate time to return, being about 12 oclock.
Mr McI had fortunately not come in himself so I got very snugly
into bed.

I should not have minded his knowing of my being out, but I
intend to go to the Theatre on Thursday evening to see Miss
Foote.[3] I had resolved to go no more this season and have resisted
the appearance of two 'stars' but never having seen Miss F I
cannot resist going to hear & see her. She is almost the only celebrated performer I have not met with except Madame Vestris. I
have seen Kean, Young, Kemble, Macready, Wallack, Farren,
Liston, Matthews, Harley, Braham, Horn, Sinclair, Murray (Edin),
McKay, Denham, Rayner &c. &c. Mrs W. West, Miss ONeil, Mrs
Bunn, Misses Stephens, Love, Tree, M. Tree, Goodall, Mesdames
Catalani – Caradon, Misses E. Paton, Travis, Noel, Cubitt &c. &c.
but M. Vestris, Misses Foote, Paton & Povey I have [*not*] been so
fortunate as to hear.[4] Mr Webb too the Irish comedian is to play
on Wednesday and Thursday nights along with Miss Foote.

3 The actress Miss Maria Foote was about 29 when Thomas saw her. She had
  made her debut, aged 12, at Plymouth in 1810 and appeared at Covent Garden
  in 1814. She was noted for her beauty, although her acting was said to be
  mechanical and lacking spirit. While playing in *The Belle's Stratagem* at Chelten-
  ham, she captivated Colonel Berkeley, who married her when he came into
  his title of Earl of Harrington in 1831, making her Countess of Harrington: see
  H. Oswald, *The Theatre Royal in Newcastle upon Tyne* (Newcastle, 1936).
4 The list of actors includes some seen in London and Edinburgh, as well as in
  Newcastle: see 'My Autobiography', chapter 11 and 20.

I went with a friend on Saturday to see the seasons exhibition of paintings.[5] It is thought to be the best yet produced. There are some very fine pictures. Parker's 'Pilots on the look out' is justly considered the most admirable. Ewbank has one large one of the King's entry into Edinburgh and he excels in this kind of landscape where thousands of figures are represented; I have before seen and admired 'Alexanders triumphal entry into Babylon' by the same artist.

In the Edinburgh painting the view of the Castle in the background seems the only defective part of its *locality* but in the distance of 'Portrait of a Lady by Nicholson' we have a beautiful view of this fortress. G. Watson RSA has some very fine heads in this collection 'The Hermit', 'The Recluse' & 'Head a Study' are most conspicuous and seem to be *perfections* in their style. I do not think Richardson (the manager of this institution) shines very much this time. His 'Storm scene at Tynemouth' is very good as a whole but will not bear individual examination which last quality gives such a share of finished beauty to its neighbour the first mentioned picture.

Mr Syme, Surgeon & lecturer Edinburgh has two very good pictures exposed. Both portraits and they are the only good paintings of this kind in the room unless we consider Lewis' 'His Majesties Deer Keepers buck-shooting in Windsor great park (portraits)' of the above class.

In comic pictures – Farrier's '1ˢᵗ of September' & 'bob-cherry' and several little scenes by Heath are excellent. Watson Gordons 'Returning from a foray' Fradelle's 'Olivia and Viola' well deserve attention but to enumerate all were endless; at least compared to our space of paper & time. Suffice it to say there are only two which my friends & I derided and they are certainly very poor and are put together seemingly to bear each other company these are 'The Widows Lament' Bouet and 'A view of the

5 The Northumberland Institute for the Promotion of Fine Arts, established by the Newcastle artist Thomas Miles Richardson (1784–1848), held its first annual exhibition in 1822. TGW appears to have viewed the sixth exhibition held in 1827, which was the last one to be held in the room that Richardson built onto his house in Brunswick Place for the purpose of exhibiting his own work. Paul Usherwood, *Art for Newcastle: Thomas Miles Richardson and the Newcastle Exhibitions 1822–1843* (Newcastle, 1984) gives the background to the establishment of the exhibitions as well as details of several of the works and artists mentioned by TGW.

Building of the Lit: & Phil: Soc' by Richardson who cannot have *seen* properly when sketching this picture.
[*Patient numbers*]

June 6 [*Wednesday*]
A man at Wallsend received a severe concussion of the Brain on Monday afternoon. Mr McI was passing and saw the patient though not till after the messenger had set off to Newcastle. I went down too late therefore to have any dictum in the matter or I should have bled him *secundum artem*. Mr McI has not done so – he saw him yesterday again but still no venesection – and today I was ordered to see the patient and if his pulse was full – to bleed him but if not merely to apply leeches to the temples! I should have bled exactly in consequence of the small pulse but as it was this morning very feeble I obeyed my directions by leeching only. Mr McI's mode of treatment, I think, has changed since our last case of concussion mentioned in Vol: 2 (somewhere about Dec 16) which see. [*Hunter, 2, 19/12/26*]

As soon as I had returned from my morning round I was called back to Walker Henry Pit which patient I saw after dinner; a cut on his foot with a bruise forms the *sumucrum* of his injury.
Marley's dislocated toe [4/6/27] is doing well but the patient still complains of pain. The swelling is considerably less.
Gordon's cut leg is quite healed but the other still remains very weak. [*case list, end Vol 3*]
Batey's son Heaton New Pit came into the surgery last Sunday a week [27/5/27?] with a spontaneous dislocation of the patella. His knees have been giving way under his weight, from his scrophulous diathesis are very much bent inwards; while bathing, most probably from some sudden exertion of the muscle on which the patella is fixed, this bone slipped quite off its articulation to the outside of the joint. I would explain this as follows. In the natural position of the limb the knee pan is as it ought to be mechanically considered in a direct line between the origin and the insertion of its attached muscle the 'Rectus femoris' as in the 1ˢᵗ Figure. When the knee became bent as in Fig 2 the case in point the line of direction of the muscle would not properly pass thro' the patella but have a tendency to draw it, at every exertion of this muscle to the outside of the joint which circumstance it has eventually accomplished.
[*Here the MS includes 3 rough sketches, labelled: a The Patella, b The Rectus muscle, c its origin*]

NB Please to consider the intent not the execution of the above diagrams.

I saw the patient today the swelling has abated and the patella tho perfectly moveable at pleasure into its former position will only remain in its new one being kept so by the muscle. The lad is able to walk a little and is ordered off to the seaside for the benefit of his general health.

June 7 *[Thursday]*
I have not been on horseback today so I can give little account of patients. Mr McI has blistered the concussion patient [6/6/27] who is said to be much the same.

I attended the monthly meeting of the Lit & Phil Society on Tuesday evening and heard an interesting paper read on the antiquity of the arch in architecture by Mr McGregor.[6] Mr Adamson the junior secretary read it very ill but the essay (one of a series on the same subject) was interesting from the detailed account contained in it of the rise progress and fall &c of Carthage and the latter part of a similar view of Egypt. Four new members were admitted but not one proposed! Only ten members present at the meeting – a few more were of necessity called down from the reading room to constitute a quorum for voting – a dozen. These did not stay for the essay.

After the meeting, Mr Pyle whom I met in the room insisted on my going to sup on cold lamb with Brockett & Henzell. I went; but Henzell had been there and gone before we got from the library, I staid till a little after ten.

After a due consideration of the playbills I have determined on not going to the Theatre tonight. If no obstacle presents itself I will see about it tomorrow evening when Mr Webb & Miss Foote each play in two pieces. A wag says the performers are now *Webb-Foote-d*!

June 9 *[Saturday]*
I was at the Theatre last night and saw the two last acts of the Rivals,[7] The Weathercock and the Irish Tutor. Miss Foote neither

---

6 This lecture is mentioned briefly in the Annual Report of the Lit. and Phil. (1827).

7 *The Rivals* by R. B. Sheridan (1751–1816) had remained popular since its first production at Covent Garden in 1775.

surprised nor disappointed the expectations I had formed of her. She is certainly beautiful both in person & figure and her dancing is exquisite. She is a person too who grows more fascinating the longer you look at her.

I had never seen the Rivals and was glad to see I had formed so just a conception of the characters. Mr A. Wright, the Captn Absolute wants power of voice but is otherwise a good actor. I think I should play the character (as well as his other part last night, young Fickle) tolerably, especially to Miss Foote's Lydia Languish. Mr Webb is excellent as Dr OToole though I did not think so much of his Sir Lucius O Trigger. I only went in at half play but passed a very pleasant evening. One of the fullest houses I ever witnessed in Newcastle theatre since I came with F & M to see Mr Macready & Miss O Neil about 9 years ago who performed here then for two nights both of which we were among the audience.

Not out in the country since Wednesday Mr McI's mare being lame. Fract^d skull doing well I believe. Concussion patient very ill yesterday [7/6/27]. Mr McI bled him!
[*Magaziniana no 6: ' My Autobiography', chapter 5*]
[*Patient numbers*]

June 11 [*Monday*]

On Saturday morning I was ordered 'to horse and away' to Wallsend. Mr King was to hold himself in readiness to mount the driving box of a hackney coach and in half an hour we found ourselves, i.e. Mr McIntyre, Mr Church, Mr King and myself, found ourselves at the Wallsend Pit.[8] Word had been sent from Hunters that the boy continued much worse and our intent was to propose an operation to the friends. On examining the skull I had not disturbed the patient by doing so before being told (Mr McI said it was not fractured) there was a feeling like the edge of a fissure on the opposite side of the head to that on which the blow was received. The patient was insensible. He had been rather furious but as the compression on the brain became more powerful he subsided into the torpid state in which we then saw him. The Father after an argument of near half an hour with Mr McI & Mr Church would on no account allow any operation to

---

8 This appears to be the case first referred to on 6/6/27. The name of the patient is not mentioned, nor is it in the case list at the end of this volume.

be attempted so we were obliged to leave the lad to the inevitable fate which the operation of the trephine it was then thought afforded a *possibility* of averting.

Yesterday morning the father came to the Surgery to say that the young man died about 4 AM and that if Mr McI wished he might now examine his head. I was down the Shields road at the time but King met me on my way home and we turned back. We were in about an hour followed by Mr McIntyre. On opening the head no fracture or fissure of any kind was perceptible in the place we suspected but the temporal ridge was very prominent and has afforded the feeling above described. The brain was gorged with blood and great extravasation was visible in all parts of it. The ventricles were distended with fluid and a small quantity of pus was visible on coming down upon the *sella turcica*. Below this the injury shewed itself there was a complete and severe fracture of the basilar process of the occipital bone. The sella turcica and the clinoid processes of the sphenoid were quite shattered. A sharp spicula with a point like a lancet projected into the brain and this had divided a blood vessel causing great extravasations at this part and from hence Mr McI supposes proceeded the blood which he vomited and which oozed from his nostrils.

Dr Knox says this fracture is much more common than is generally suspected and is uniformly fatal. *I* was not therefore so much surprized at discovering this case though very much pleased at meeting with one. The operation I need hardly say would have been productive of no benefit on the preceding evening.

The Fracture near Backworth [4/6/27] is doing extremely well; the patient was sitting up on Friday!

June 12 *[Tuesday]*
Mr Abernethy in one of his last weeks lectures (*vid Lancet'* June 9, 1827) says 'there are some cases of injury to the head which would puzzle the devil himself I believe; and those are the cases of fractures of the base of the skull'. This exactly bears upon the above instance. The patient had all the symptoms of concussion – so Mr McI did not bleed – but he had also evident signs of compression on the brain which called for venesection. As Abernethy says again 'those cases are attended with a train of symptoms that would puzzle anybody. They are a mixture; sometimes like

concussion sometimes like compression'. I merely quote this in vindication of *our* character in being rather puzzled by the afore-mentioned case.[9]

June 15 *[Friday]*
I had the pleasure of getting my Mother over yesterday to see the Exhibition of paintings &c in *our* Museum.

In the evening I spent a few very pleasant hours at Mr Brocketts to tea and a game at whist, meeting Henzell and a Mr Cleghorn and Morney and being introduced to the two Miss Brocketts. I omitted mentioning that Mr Pyle came up for me on Tuesday evening to go to his lodgings on the purpose to meet Mr Losh Jun[r], son of the counsellor[10] our vice president at the Lit: Society. He is a very fine youth and has been some time abroad but pleased me by his shewing none of the more disagreeable qualifications of a traveller. Henzell & Brockett as usual were there and on that evening I had the good luck to come away *plus* sixpence from the card table. On both these last occasions I got home at 10 oclock and nothing wanted.

I saw the lad *[Dixon? 3, 28/5/27]* with the diseased hip joint yesterday. He has been applying the Tartar emetic ointment since the blister healed but it has brought out no eruption. Upon the whole I think the patient a little better: the joint seems freer than before.
[Patient numbers]

June 18 *[Monday]*
The cannons woke me this morning in announcing the anniversary of the battle of Waterloo which I suppose will in many places be fought over again today at the dinner table. The Tyne Huzzar Yeomen are to be up on duty for eight days commencing this morning. My friend Henzell is a cornet in that regiment.[11]

---

9 John Abernethy (1764–1831) gave a series of lectures on operative surgery at St Bartholomew's Hospital, London, which were published verbatim in *The Lancet*: the one referred to appears in *The Lancet*, XII (1827), pp. 289–96. It is interesting that TGW quoted from this publication three days after its publication date.

10 The 'counsellor' was James Losh, see Volume 3, note 2.

11 The Northumberland and Newcastle Volunteer Corps of Cavalry, also known as the Tyne Huzzar Yeomen, was formed in December 1819, during a period of unrest following the end of the Napoleonic war, to provide a force that

I had a very pleasant ride after a shower of rain yesterday morning in the course of which I called upon Miss McIntyre at Wallsend. She is better but still far from strong. She was going down to Tynemouth and I suspect her brother has been there too for he has just come home (2½ PM) after being away since yesterday morning.

I do not expect to be on horseback today but I have a patient to see in the *suburbs* which will be a pleasant walk.

I was applied to on Saturday regarding a case of Epilepsy with great constitutional tendency to disease in the head. The boy [*Hindmarsh*] about 4 years of age has a large head and in consequence of repeated attacks of this disease one of the eyes has become inverted. He has not regular fits, i.e. convulsion fits, but experiences intense pain in the head at certain intervals which generally happen once or twice during the afternoon. His tongue is much furred bowels constipated, he picks his nose a good deal and when the paroxysms come on his face becomes flushed and even livid while his [*missing word*] are excessively affected with a tremulous motion which they have a little at all times. I gave him a brisk purge yesterday which had slightly opened his bowels. Another of the powders was to be given in the evening and repeated if necessary. They were Calomel: gr iv P: Jalapa; gr viij . As no word has been sent in today I conclude that the patient is relieved.

June 20 *[Wednesday]*
My patient mentioned yesterday [Hindmarsh, 18/6/27] whom I have not visited till today is so much relieved as to be nearly well. The fits have left him and tho' he is still rather epileptic in an evening the complaint is in a great measure removed.

Mr McIntyre after at home about an hour on Monday set off to Pensher[12] to see a patient of his who is staying there just now and got home yesterday about 3 PM. A message awaited his arrival regarding an engagement for his going with a friend down to

---

could be used to assist the Civil Powers to maintain law and order. It was the direct forerunner of the Northumberland (Hussars) Yeomanry, established as a regiment in 1876. The tradition of annual training for eight days on the Town Moor continued until the 1870s:. see Howard Pease, *The History of the Northumberland (Hussars) Yeomanry* (London, 1924); Henry Tegner, *The Story of a Regiment* (Newcastle, 1969).

12 Probably Penshaw, see Volume 3, note 26.

Shields. He just snatched a dinner and departed again. He has returned this afternoon.

A patient of his took ill last night, Miss Aveling – once before mentioned in my first volume I think. [*1, 22/11/16; see also 2, 24/2/27*] She was relieved a little this morning and Mr McI has since seen her and repeated my medicine.

Regarding this Miss Aveling I feel myself in gallantry bound to correct a mistake I made in before mentioning her name. She *is* a young lady and no relation to the Mrs Atkinson I spoke of. I had not seen her when I made my former assertion of her being an old maid but have since had frequent opportunities of convincing myself to the contrary.

[*Patient numbers*]

June 30 [*Saturday*]

Something more than common must have happened to cause this long silence and something more than common *has* happened I must assure you gentle reader.

On Sunday last I and my horse with all the paraphernalia of saddle, bridle &c came down upon the hard road with considerable impetus. Whether it was that the horse trod upon a sharp stone which pricked his conscience or that the sanctity of the day alone caused the deed, but certain it is that this said animal suddenly took it into his holy head to kneel in such a way as to cause great detriment both to his holy knees and to my elbow. I gave him a very righteous pull but only succeeded so far as to pull the pious animal over onto his side and on to my leg. The curve of the saddle formed an arch over my limb which saved it from harm, but I received as aforesaid 'a contusion of the arm with a slight abrasion of the cuticle' which is not yet quite healed. Luckily there has been no accident till yesterday morning and as my patients are all well or doing well they have found no want of me. I walked down to Wallsend & Heaton on Tuesday. Mr McI desired me to ride so far in a Shields gig and return by the same conveyance; but the day was so pleasant I preferred walking down, and as I could not meet with a gig back I was obliged to trudge it both ways.

Yesterday I mounted my Bucephalus[13] again who is as spruce as ever with the exception of a momento on his *off* knee.

---

13 Bucephalus was the war-horse of Alexander the Great hence a popular name for a horse often, as here, used ironically.

I have again written to my F & M today however and having resumed my penmanship again I shall continue my usual routine in this department.

Yesterday I received by the Hylton Joliffe (the newly started steamer from Newcastle to London)[14] a parcel from my sister containing among other things a large plumb [sic] cake – a very excellent specimen of Islington confectionary;[15] which fact is visibly demonstrated by its rapid dissolution. Mr John Gibson is still very poorly but rather better. Miss Aveling is convalescent. [20/6/27]

The Cavalry are very busy parading about this week amongst them of course *Cornet* McIntyre.[16] Yesterday morning a man one of the troop [*Forster*] was thrown from his horse while on duty on the moor and his horse falling upon him his ilium was fractured at the spine and his hip severely bruised. Surgeon Moore and Assistant Surgeon McIntyre have attended him and after prompt leeching he is today doing well.

A child [*Story*] received a concussion of the brain by falling out of a window. I was not in and Mr McIntyre was at mess, so Mr Church, Mr King and Greenwood attended. I have since with King visited the patient who is doing very well – is nearly recovered indeed.

A man [*Roseby*] was severely bruised at Wallsend on Friday week who is doing well.

[*Patient numbers*]

The Hay Harvest which has been partially commencing for these last two weeks is now pretty general in this neighborhood.

---

14 The Hylton Joliffe, a steamship with two engines of 100 hp capable of carrying 30–40 passengers in 'very comfortable accommodation', was the largest steam vessel that had then been seen in the Tyne. When it arrived in June 1827, to begin a regular service between London and the Tyne, it excited great interest, with the quay and the Tyne bridge being 'thronged by very great numbers anxious to catch sight of her': see *Newcastle Chronicle*, 16/6/27; Middlebrook, p.184.

15 This suggests that TGW's sister was living in Islington at this time.

16 See note 11 above. James McIntyre was promoted to Lieutenant in the Newcastle Yeomanry Cavalry in March, 1829: see *NYB*, p. 275.

July 3 *[Tuesday]*
Our Newcastle races[17] began yesterday which will of course cause
a little gaiety in the town this week. Mr McI, according to custom,
offered me the use of the horse I usually ride, which I, according
to custom, accepted; as he has only been one day out of the stable
since he and I happened our accident he was proportionally in
high trim, and cut by no means a sorry figure among his numer-
ously assembled brethren. There were two very prettily contested
races yesterday; the other the Produce stakes was 'won easy'. Six
horses started for 'The Tyro Stakes' which a son of the renowned
Dr Syntax won. He was not the favorite but a grey filly took such
a wide turn, or as it is technically termed *'bolted'* by which she
lost more ground than it was possible to make up again. The last
race 'the Gosforth Stakes' was a neck and neck matter from the
distancing post – only two horses ran.

Mr McI is gone to Tynemouth on my steed and will most likely
not return till near race time. Mr King (William) would perhaps
have the option of riding today but not having yet been on the
saddle he prefers the safer way – going on foot. As the horse will
not be so fresh I shall walk too.

There has been an accident this morning at Walker. A boy *[Shi-
elds]* got his wrist dislocated and the head of the radius fractured.
It was easily reduced and will I doubt not do well.

July 4 *[Wednesday]*
The horse was not at home for either Mr K or me yesterday. Mr
McI not returning till evening. We walked therefore and King
having the offer of the horse today has ventured to mount and
luckily came home with no injury more than a fright or two. I
rode the steed about 10 or 12 miles this morning and took a little
of the *shine* off him in compassion for Mr K.

Mr Powlett's *Gazebo* (a horse I bet upon by chance for the *Plate*)
won the King's £100 yesterday which is a four mile job and with
very heavy weights. When the horses for the Stakes appeared
to my great surprize my favorite *Gazebo* was again among the

---

17 Horse races were run on the Newcastle Town Moor from 1721, and after 1751
  it became customary to hold a race meeting there during the week nearest to
  midsummer. A grandstand was built by public subscription in 1800: see R. J.
  Charleton, *A History of Newcastle upon Tyne* (Newcastle upon Tyne, 1894,
  reprinted Newcastle upon Tyne, 1989), pp. 355–6.

candidates and after a severe contest won both heats of this race!!

Today I laid out my profits of yesterday in bets and chose first the field against two horses neither of which ran and of course won. I also wagered a bottle of porter with Brockett upon the horse which won the Silver cup! All the heats today have been sharply contended for and hence the sport has been very good.

July 9 [*Monday*]

On Thursday I went on horseback to the Races and enjoyed the sport highly. The crowds of people were immense and the racing tolerably good. As usual the horse on which I bet won the Gold Cup!

With all my winnings however I am not a farthing the richer. My wagers were in bottles of Porter, Pop &c and the only one I staked in money was left unsettled as to the amount and by that means my opponents Tyler & J Gibson slipped off. Indeed I shall never have the *face* to ask a person for a bet in money; and hence had better not speculate any more *in spece*. In anything else too I have to *treat* as much as I have been *treated* with hence I get little profit in that way either.

Mr McIntyre went down to Tynemouth in the evening and staid till Saturday morning, again he set off yesterday morning and I dont expect him back till tonight. Miss McI is to leave Tynemouth today so that this will [*be*] his last trip to visit her.

On Friday evening I went to sup at Pyle's upon pickled Mackerel, Lambs fry & green peas. Henzell, Brockett a Mr Ellwood & Mr Row were there; we spent a very pleasant evening.

Mr McI very justly observed he never knew business as slack as it is at present. There is nothing doing at the Collieries almost and our town patients are very few. The same complaint is general among the profession.

My patient at Walker is doing well. [*Shields, 3/7/27*]
[*Patient numbers*]

I thought I had previously mentioned a case which I have particularly watched and which I am now half afraid will turn out less favorably than could be wished. My friend John Gibson has now been laid upon the shelf three weeks with a diseased elbow. Mr Moore & J Gibson's uncle Mr Westgarth – also Dr Headlam – have attended him. He has felt pain in the joint for these four months past but paid little attention to it till he got his accident by the horse falling with him. He had then a blister on, which was not healed when he fell and as his weight chiefly centred upon his elbow he at that time complained more of this joint. His leg was principally hurt however and this got well in ten days. He never after did anything to his arm in the way of care till by degrees it got so much worse that he was necessitated to use a sling and in a day or two was confined altogether to the house.

There is evidently a collection of fluid in or near the joint but the usual symptoms of the formation of *pus* have been wanting. It appeared at first decidedly an enlargement of some *bursa*, but now seems to be an affection of the joint itself. The principal symptoms are intense pain on the least motion of the bones, & soreness in the course of the bones. During the last week the pain grew less violent and the patient could bear a sling instead of the pillows he usually had it supported on; but on Friday and Saturday it worsened and the latter day confined him for the first time to his bed for the whole day.

The treatment pursued was in the beginning 20 to 30 leeches every night for a week which has been followed by two blisters the last of which is not yet healed.

The disease seems to me to be a collection of glairy serum in the cavity of the joint with a chronic inflammation of the parts around produced partly by a scrophulous diathesis and partly by some mercury which he has been using with sarsaparilla (by Mr Moore's discussion) for some blotches on his face, the exciting cause being his fall from horseback and too constant use of that arm (the right) in hard riding.

J Gibson wishes the lancet to be dipped into the part affected or some active treatment to be employed. I proposed *moxa* which I think might prove efficacious. As yet nothing decisive has been done and poor Gibson is getting quite melancholic with the prospect of losing the use of (or the member altogether) so important a limb.

July 12 *[Tuesday]*
Two men were hurt at Walker on Monday night and two severely bruised on Tuesday morning. [*Armsley, Donal, Hall, Shields*] The former were only slight injuries of the foot. The others are doing well.

I have not seen J. Gibson these three days but hear he is much the same and has had another blister on.

Miss McIntyre returned here yesterday from Tynemouth, she is *almost quite* well again.

Mr Crawford called upon me this morning with an invitation to tea there this evening to meet Mrs & the Miss Jacksons – with my flute. I have brushed up my flute and shall shortly wait upon the party.

July 14 *[Saturday]*
Just as I was putting on a pair of trowsers, clean collar &c preparatory to going up to Mr Crawford a man & horse came trotting down the yard to my great annoyance with the news that a boy at Walker [*Armstrong*] had been run over by some rolleys and that his foot was cut. He lives at Biggs Main about 3 miles off. I quickly arrived at the place and found a more serious accident than I had anticipated. The cut extended from between the second and third toes of the left foot through the joint of the latter one completely dividing the two bones and then continued back between the 3rd and 4th metatarsal bones as far as their union with the tarsal ones. On the underside of the foot the cut was not so extensive as above. There was a quantity of small coals & dust in the wound so that though I took considerable pains to make the parts clean I am afraid it will scarcely unite. The boy was doing tolerably well yesterday but I shall not open out the dressings till tomorrow.

I spent a pleasant hour or two at Mr Crawfords. Mrs & 3 Misses Jackson, Mrs Shields and a Miss [*missing word*] were at the party. Collingwood Jackson who plays the flute well, and with whom I wished to be acquainted was prevented from being there. Miss Sarah Jackson recognised me as once a playfellow with her at Stockton some 12 or 14 years ago. Their party left about $9\frac{1}{2}$ oclock, and as I saw them home I was in before 10, without anything more being wanted.

My readers will begin [*to think*] I am getting tired of my life and that it has suffered an untimely death but I beg to assure them such is not the case and that the Maga: though in a slumbering state just now will shortly be revived – and indeed why not now? I have caught an idea by the tail and having a little leisure will try to dress it up on the spot. Almost every subject has been laid hold of by an essayist from the Spectator downwards to the answering production of the H (Horace Smith) M.O.W. & Co in the New Monthly; but I think I have one which has escaped

notice, and hence has the merit of being an original idea at any
rate: after thus establishing any claim upon this important point,
any one is welcome to make what improvement he pleases
upon it.
[*Magaziniana no 7: On Mottos*]
[*Patient numbers*]

July 16 [*Monday*]
There was an alarm raised on Saturday afternoon by the news
being brought in that a boy at Elswick [*Eliot*] had both his legs
fractured, to the great joy of Mr King as Elswick and Benwell
Collieries are to be under his management and this is the first
accident at either since he came from Edinburgh. Mr McI ordered
me to mount and accompany him while King and the youth Spearman were to join us at the house of the patient. Mr McI got off
first and I had nearly overtaken him in Elswick lane when a man
told me that the boy's injury was only a cut upon one leg instead
of both being broken and that Mr McI desired him to tell me that
we might all turn back – he would go to dress it himself. The real
nature of the accident is however that the fibula of one leg is
probably (Mr McI thinks it is) broken and there is a considerable
wound also. King has dressed it today and is very *large* as to the
size of the incision. The solution of continuity according to his
report is about 18 inches long by 5 or 6 broad but as it is unlikely
that Mr McI would leave that width unclosed I should suppose
that by dividing the above length by 4 and the breadth by 6 we
may arrive at somewhat of the true dimensions.

I opened out the boys foot yesterday which was injured at
Biggs main on Thursday last. [*Armstrong, 14/7/27*] It has healed
as much as I could reasonably expect. The internal part of the
wound is united firmly I hope but the edges being a good deal
contused (as must have been the case in an incision made by the
blunt edge of a waggon wheel) are suppurating and throwing off
the black coal dust &c which the sponge and warm water would
not before remove. The patients health keeps very good.

Dysentery has begun to make its appearance; two or three cases
have occurred this last week.

J Gibson continues much in the same state. I assisted to get him
up for an hour or two on Saturday evening and both this excita-
tion and his getting to bed again were productive of great pain
(and took up an hours performance each) He had a blister (the

fourth) laid on last night which is to remain four & twenty hours before the sore is dressed. The pain is more violent than it was and excited by the most trivial motion in the arm or shoulder.

July 18 *[Wednesday]*
Having seen my patients yesterday I have had nothing to do today but spend a few hours at the Society reading Anderson with a few of Persin's satires. I have read 40 lines of Homer too this morning which I found a very laborious task having in a great measure forgot my Greek. In short I have determined to revise the classical lore I once possessed and have besides the above looked over the Greek verbs. Latin I have kept more familiar with occasionally translating an ode of Horace or a Chapter of Sallust or Livy but I am sorry to find how greatly I am deficient in knowledge of Greek. The elements and principles of the language I cannot forget after being thoroughly drilled in the Grammar at school but in translation I have lost ground. A little diligence will soon I hope make up all and I intend Latin & French to follow or accompany Greek.

During our slack of business lately I have had leisure for more attendance than usual at the Society; sometimes spending two or three hours in the morning. My studies have been very miscellaneous, being composed of any subject that chanced to catch my eye while ranging around the shelves. I intend shortly to take out for home study the Anatomical and Medical departments of the *Encyclopédie Francaise* a most extensive work begun about 40 years ago and of which the 96 vol: is lately published.[18]

July 20 *[Friday]*
I had a long*ish* round yesterday morning which occupied me from $\frac{1}{2}$ past nine to about 2 oclock. I went to the Jane Pit Walker from thence to Biggs Main and Heaton Middle Pit and in coming home met Mr McI from whom I learnt there was an accident

---

18 A new and enlarged edition of the *Encyclopédie*, which was first published in the 1750s under the direction of Denis Diderot, was initiated in 1782. Plans for this new edition, which originally was intended to have 26 parts, and to be completed by 1787, were revised in 1788, increasing the proposed number of volumes to about 124. Publication was actually completed in 1832 with the appearance of Volume 166, 50 years after the appearance of the first volume. See *Encyclopaedia Britannica*, 14th edition, 24 vols (London, 1963), VIII, pp. 368ff.

which required me to proceed immediately to Felling; making *in toto* a journey of 16 or 17 miles. The day was cloudy and by consequence the more pleasant for riding. Today unless an accident happens I shall remain at home and by way of occupying an half hour I will resume my narrative.
[*Magaziniana no 8: 'My Autobiography', chapter 6*]

July 25 [*Wednesday*]
My patients are all going on well most of them quite recovered again.

The boy at Biggs Main [*Armstrong, 14/7/27*] had stolen out of the house when his Mother was absent and by running about had made a change for the worse in the appearance of his foot. I applied a poultice for two days and the wound is now looking extremely well.

J Gibson is now I hope past the worst; his arm though *little* changed in appearance or feeling is decidedly better. I have been trying to get him a splint contrived for resting the limb on and have procured one that was made for Mr McI once as an experiment. It is for the left arm however and consequently not the *right* one. I shall shew JG it this afternoon and hear how he likes the plan of it.

Miss Taylerson is staying there just now and is of course very assiduously attentive to him. The Gibsons have been very polite and civil to me lately (as indeed they have never had reason to be otherwise) but, though I am inclined always to court good society I cannot altogether forget the slighting way in which I was treated by them in Winter.[19] There may however be sound reasons for that though but I am at a loss to divine them.

As this Vol: is only to last out this month and I wish to get on with my life I will crowd a chapter or two rather closely upon each other to forward both my designs; and hence proceed to –
[*Magaziniana no 9: 'My Autobiography', chapter 7*]

July 27 [*Friday*]
I have extremely pleasant rides these two days, indeed the fineness of the season has rendered horse exercise particularly

---

19 TGW commented on not being invited to parties at the house of Mr Taylor Gibson in Volume 3, 28/4/27.

delightful for this month past. The wind has not raised such clouds of dust as I was exposed to at the beginning of Summer.

I went round to Willington &c with Tyler yesterday as well as I saw my own patients at Heaton Walker &c and this morning an accident called me down to Wallsend. A man had had his foot bruised by a fall of coal.

A patient [*Brown*] came into the surgery last night in an awkward predicament. He had fallen from the scaffolding at the side of a hay stack and come into contact with some forks below – one had gone nearly through his wrist another had slightly penetrated his thigh while a ladder in falling struck him on the head and neck which were bruised in consequence. He had walked into town from Walker and was in the hay field this morning *superintending* the stacking. I ordered him fomentations & poultices by which he is relieved.

A great number of new works laid upon the Society's reading room table just now, which I have dived into a little these few days. Among them are conspicuous Sir W Scotts *Life of Napoleon* 9 vols, McCries *Hist of the Reformation* Vol 3, Transac: Hortic: Soc: London – DeRoos *Journal in America* and three or four vols of travels. *The Military Sketch Book*, T Dibdin's *Reminiscences*, Sir Jonah Barrington's *Sketches* &c which &c includes some six or eight works *exclusive* of the monthly periodicals.[20]

Having skimmed into the *Military Sketch Book* at J Gibsons lodgings one day I was so much taken with it that I popped down its title and my name in the 'Recommendation Book' and to my great satisfaction it was ordered by the Committee at their next meeting. The Monthly Review has the bad sense to assert in its

---

20 The works mentioned are listed in the Annual Report of the Lit. and Phil., 1828, in the Supplement to the 1819 General Catalogue: Sir Walter Scott, *Life of Napoleon Buonaparte Emperor of the French*, 9 vols (Edinburgh and London, 1827); Thomas M'Crie, D.D., *History of the Progress and Suppression of the Reformation in Italy* (Edinburgh 1827); *Transactions of the Horticultural Society of London*, VI (parts 4 and 5) and VII (part 1); Lieut. The Hon. Fred DeRoos, *Personal Narrative of the Travels in the United States and Canada in 1826* (London 1827); William Maginn, *Military Sketch-Book: Reminiscences of Seventeen Years in the Service Abroad and at Home, by an Officer of the Line*, 2 vols (London 1827); Thomas Dibdin, *The Reminiscences of Thomas Dibdin: of the Theatres Royal, Covent-Garden, Drury-Lane, Haymarket, &c.*, 2 vols (London 1827); Sir Jonah Barrington, *Personal Sketches of his Own Times*, 2 vols (London 1827).

critique on this work that it is inferior to its prototype the *Naval Sketch Book*!!²¹

My sister in writing to me advised me (in speaking of new works some time ago) not to waste my time by reading the Naval Sk: Bk: on which account, as is usually the case, I directly set off to the library for the work which full justifies Mrs Green's observation. My opinion and the same I have heard from all who read the two works in question, is that the *'prototype'* as the reviewer calls the Naval – tho' they are both of course on the plan of the Washington Irving's productions – is not to be compared in *wit*, elegance of language, and *good sense*, to its admirable successor.

So much has been said by critics on the life of Napoleon that little voice is left for anyone in the matter. I have not patience (or leisure perhaps) to read the work systematically through but in the detached way I have dipped into it the composition seems to me worthy [*of*] its subject (which I take it is a very high encomium) and worthy of the author of Waverley. It is written in a *novel* style for a biography though and bears evident marks of haste in the formation of many sentences. A succeeding edition may shew these *lapses* corrected, but that can hardly have been effected in the *second* edition which has already appeared though the first has not been out a month yet.²²

Sir Jonah Barrington's *life* is I am told excellent but I have not even looked at the title page. A leisure half hour just now however is a temptation I shall not resist to finish the Military tales and commence Sir Jonah's feast – So for the present good reader adieu – I will tell you all about it when I come back.

July 28 *[Saturday]*
I was prevented reading what I wished yesterday afternoon by another gentleman's having engaged the work so I took up

---

21 *The Naval Sketch Book; or The Service Afloat and Ashore*, 2 vols (London, 1826), by Captain W. N. Glassock, RN (1787–1847) is listed in the Annual Report of the Lit. and Phil. Society, 1826, Supplement to the 1819 General Catalogue.

22 Sir Walter Scott's *Life of Napoleon* was published in June 1827. It was written at a time when Scott was under severe financial pressure. Although started in May 1825, it has been estimated that the work, equivalent in length to five of his Waverley novels, was actually written in only 12 months. TGW's comments about the deficiencies of the edition accord with what seems to have

Dibdin's *Reminiscences*[23] and have this morning put my name down for the first volume of these to read instead of a sermon tomorrow. I wished to have had Moores new tale *The Epicurean*[24] which has just come in but it was engaged for tonight.

I find by a letter yesterday morning that my Father and Mother, who have been five weeks in Yorkshire, are to return to Sunderland, their present *home* on Tuesday. I had till now taken up a slight idea of a jaunt to the sea this summer as we were so slack in business. My Mother had it at one time in contemplation to go to Scarborough for a week to meet a young lady whom she wished to be near and who was out of health. The lady however did not visit Scarborough so the project dropped.

If my Mother had gone she wished me to have met her there and taken a few day's holiday. Though my F & M did not quarter themselves there I expected – their great partiality to the seaside is such – that they would have taken lodgings at some seaside place in my Fathers route and *had they done so* I should certainly have offered my services in the way of looking to their health (!) while there but I durst not say a word of my intent lest I should induce any alteration in my F's arrangement which I wished particularly to avoid. My expectations however have not been realised in the way of 'a Trip to Scarborough' or elsewhere but this not having taken place will give me a claim for a holiday afterward with a better grace. I always like to deduce some saving clause from the *most* untoward circumstances.
[*Patient numbers*]

July 29 [*Sunday*]
NB I have now – i.e. have had for these three months since King came back, a smaller number of patients on account of having only four collieries instead of six to attend to. King has Benwell & Elswick with the three or four *sick*[25] that belong to Benwell and one or two town patients.

It has happened however that these pits have had almost nothing for us to do amongst them this six months – they seldom

---

been a general opinion, although the work was very successful and profitable for the author, who sold it for £18,000: see *DNB*, XVII, p. 1018 ff.
23 See note 20 above.
24 *The Epicurean* by Thomas Moore (1779–1852) was published in 1827.
25 'Sick' were subscribers to the practice: see Introduction.

have much. Though I do not enter these patients in my numerical list I shall relate any particular cases from King's reports. The sum total of his practice so far does not exceed 13 patients – if so many! – of whom 4 are on the books.

July 30 *[Monday]*
I was at Mr Turner's chapel[26] yesterday morning and heard a good sermon as well as read J. Dibdin's life. This latter is very amusing and written in an exceedingly pleasant style. But I must leave room for my usual list of patients mentioned in this volume and as tomorrow is the last day of the month and today I find is publication day for the New Magazines I will make a finish of this and publish it also today. I have before observed I like to conform a little to fashion or if you will – custom.

Eventual situation of cases mentioned.

June 4	Marley Dislocated toe – his foot is still very stiff and painful but it daily receives strength from cold affusion &c
	Robson's child scalded – cured – fractured skull – did very well
June 6	Batey's son goes to work as usual, the patella still retains its new situation
June 18	Hindmarsh Epilepsy – remains well
June 20	Miss Aveling has returned to her home near London tolerably well
June 30	Myself's arm is long since well
	Forster NNV Cavalry – is no longer on the books
	Story's child Concussion of the brain – cured
	Roseby Wallsend – convalescent
July 3	Shields boy fractured arm – at work
July 9	Mr J. Gibson is now I am happy to say decidedly convalescent
July 12	Armesly Donal, Hall & Shields are all at work again – Walker patients.
July 14	Armstrong – injured foot. This wound is looking remarkably well and when I last saw it – five days ago – was cicatrizing over.

---

26 For comment on Turner, see 'My Autobiography', note 61.

July 16   Eliott Elswick. This cut leg is reported to be doing very
            well
July 20   Haddrick Jane Pit Walker. This was a case of abscess
            in the leg from a cut which had been neglected by the
            lad's friends – He is quite well again.
July 27   Brown who was hurt by the hay fork is doing very
            well.

There are few medical cases just now. Several females are complaining of dyspepsia produced by the relaxing heat of the
weather and for which they are all ordered to the seaside. There
they soon recover their health.

July 31 *[Tuesday]*
I was reading at the library last night when I met Brockett & Pyle
with whom I went to the latter's lodgings and had an hours chat
over some excellent black currant preserve & bread.
I have read the Epicurean but must reserve remarks till next
month.
[Patient numbers]

V O L U M E 5 (August 1, 1827 to September 30, 1827)

August 1 – *Wednesday*[1]
As it is my intention to proceed vigorously with my autobiographical papers and I expect to have some rather interesting
ones ere long, I have manufactured this volume (for you must
know good reader I am not only printer and publisher but also
stitcher, book-binder &c &c of this bantling, and may therefore
like Tom Dibdin[2] add P.P.P.P. to the rest of my titles; viz: printer,
publisher poet & prose writer). I have, I say, manufactured this
volume of greater thickness than usual – a whole quire of folio
paper having been employed in the formation of it, – though I
only intend it to serve me for two months memorandums. Prepare therefore for long sentences and short intervals, and if you
should remark at any time in perusing this that more blank paper
is left than is accordant with strict economy or that the type is
wider than usual or that a few sentences of nonsense should
happen to creep into so learned a work i.e. a few lines more than
the allowed and allowable number – I beseech you set it down
to the account of my having been called up the night before, or
not being well and having taken a dose of my own physic, or to
indigestion, or to haste, or a patient waiting, or – in short excuse
for me in any of the thousand and one ways which may happen
to enter your mind, *all but one*, which I pray by no manner of
means may be taken into consideration – the desire of filling up
my paper. Should such a reason be even in the slightest manner
alluded to, it would be so great a slur on our editorial capacity
that I implore ye instantly to exclaim with Paul Pry 'I beg you
won't *mention* it! I beg you won't mention it!'[3]

1 [*TGW footnote*] I think the mention of the day will be an improvement. [*The
   day of the week was not included in the earlier volumes.*]
2 Possibly Thomas Frognall Dibdin (1776–1847) a writer and publisher: see *DNB*,
   V, p. 907.
3 Several passages from *Paul Pry*, an extremely successful play, became popular
   as catch phrases: see 'My Autobiography', note 79.

Besides though it is now customary in printing to place (I believe I have before alluded to the simile) an island of type in an ocean of margin – I here decided to differ from *custom* and the worst you can say of my productions will be that there may occasionally arise an island of margin (pardon the solecism) in an ocean of print.

> And of the two ways, 'tis best I should think
> To have least of the margin and most of the ink

There is another charge which I wish to refute before *progressing* further, *viz* that *vanity* has a large place in the production of this work. That it has this large *share* I most flatly deny; but that it may have a *small*, *tiny* share in its formation, – that a little *authorial* conceit may have got mixed up in the composition, as it somehow or other gets itself shoved into most human undertakings, I most readily admit being possibly the case here. Lord Byron says

> 'Sure 'tis sweet to see ones name in print
> A book's a book although there's nothing in't'[4]

and this some folks may be ill natured and unjust enough to apply to me; but as I before said I deny the imputation which it conveys. Besides there is neither print in the work; nor, as far as I know (in consequence of my great – m – m – m – modesty!) has my name yet appeared. The above therefore is totally inapplicable; indeed I wonder what could possibly make it come into my ideas just now!

As I have no critics to contend with (and I begin to think it rather a misfortune) you observe, gentle reader – I am necessitated to *fancy* aspersions cast on my work – to turn critic myself. A man would never have opportunity of laying his perfections and accomplishments *genteelly* before the public if he had not the excuse of self defence to support him; and I being the sole actor upon this petty stage am reduced occasionally almost to *'point nonplus'* to exhibit myself to full advantage; – I am obliged to raise enemies and then kill them, to conjure up spectres and afterwards exorcise them – I cannot use the *argumentum ad hominem* and I therefore employ *argumentum ad me ipsum*.

---

4 The quotation is from Byron's poem, 'English Bards and Scotch Reviewers', lines 51–2.

August 2 *Thursday*
I have not been on horseback yesterday or today so far; business is getting rather scarce again. Two or three cholera morbus cases though have been the fore-runners of what must shortly be the rage.

I have just finished translating Moschus' first Idyll *Cupid the Run Away*[5] and find I am a little improved or rather *improving*. I accomplished the above (29 lines) in about an hour and had not *quite* every word to '*seek up*' in the Lexicon.

In *my* last month I mentioned having read *The Epicurean*.[6] The gentleman who recommended this work – a friend of mine, – did so upon the understanding that it was in the style of Moores former production *Lalla Rhookh*[7] – i.e. a little prose and a large proportion of poetry. Such had been the idea conveyed by a notice of the former work in one of the reviews. This opinion however proves to be quite erroneous. *The Epicurean* is a *prose* tale with two or three original songs in it. I am on the whole disappointed in the work. After reading the beautiful, nay, heavenly conceptions of this poet in his verse, I fancy he falls far short of them in prose compositions.

The description of the Athenian sect from whom the tale takes its name, and the exposure of the grand mysteries of the Egyptian worship are sublime. The principal part too is tolerably sustained but the personages bear the least important feature in the work. The songs too are not worthy [*of*] the author of the Irish Melodies though they are advertised in the work as sold with music.

I have taken out of the library the two vol: of letter press and one of plates forming the *Systeme Anatomique* of the *Encyclopédie Francaise*.[8] The work is a dictionary of Anatomy – and it is a mere dictionary – is in no way superior to our own works on the subject and the plates very poor indeed: but I wished through it to observe the

---

5 Moschus was a Greek poet of the second century BC.
6 For comment on *The Epicurean*, see 28/7/28 and Volume 4, note 24.
7 A note on a loose scrap of paper found between the MS pages reads: 'The Epicurean and Lalla Rhookh are among the many delightful works I am anticipating the happiness of re-reading someday, my love.' *Lalla Rookh*, a poetic work by Thomas Moore (1779–1852) on a fashionable Eastern theme, published in 1817, was very successful, rivalling works by Scott and Byron in popularity: see *DNB*, VIII, 827 ff.
8 For comment on the *Encyclopédie Française* see Volume 4, note 18.

difference between the English & French nomenclature and to accustom myself a little to French description – as I hope some day to hear a few lectures in the metropolis of that country.

August 3 *Friday*
I had written a letter to send home yesterday afternoon and was just returned from a walk down street and a visit at the library when I learnt to my 'agreeable surprize' and astonishment that my Father and Mother were in the house with Mr McIntyre!! In a few minutes they came out and I had the pleasure of a few hours conversation with them. F had unexpectedly come over on a little banking business and Mother took the opportunity of accompanying him. I had intended taking a leave of absence for a day or two next week and transported myself over to Sunderland, but it seems Father has to be in Yorkshire in about a month and I have gladly instead accepted an invitation to accompany Mother and him in a fortnights tour then. I must therefore be getting on with my Magazinianas as I shall not be able to write any of them while in Yorkshire though I shall take this with me. [*Magaziniana no 10: 'My Autobiography', chapter 8*]

Afternoon. I have just now added another star to the galaxy of my train of titles, (which I am almost afraid to give in full lest like the foreign count I should be considered as a *host* instead of a single unpretending individual) – I have to add two more P's and N.C.I. – P.P.N.C.I. – to my regiment of letters viz. I am now a perennial pupil to the Newcastle Infirmary for which honor I have paid the sum of five pounds five shillings good and lawful money of – my kind Father. Titles don't cost nothing gentle reader whether bought or got by merit. I shall soon have all the letters of the Alphabet pressed into my service – I have already, you observe, many repetitions of one letter.

I (it is difficult to avoid egotism when talking of nobody but *myself*) – I am now a member of two great public libraries – the infirmary – an excellent professional one being open to my perusal.[9] I have brought out 'Laennec on the Stethoscope' to begin

9 The Medical Library at the Newcastle Infirmary, established in 1819, comprised 940 volumes by 1827. The full subscription was one guinea annually; students who were under medical officers at the Infirmary paid half of the full fee: See PW, I, p. xciv.

with.[10] It makes the fifth volume I have out of the two libraries at present.

The number of cases the Infirmary will afford as subjects of remarks obliges me to fix upon some plan of distinguishing the patients which may be as clear and concise as possible. I do not think I can adopt a better symbol than that of a number to each patient in the order they happen to occur; prefixing the initials to the first mention of the case. The observations on these with the operations &c &c will contribute very usefully in filling up this Diary though it will throw more matter into *my* (or rather I ought to say *our*) editorial hands than we shall be able to do justice to.

In the miscellaneous plan of reading I have adopted at the Lit: & Phil: Society I have in very few instances thought it useful to take notes of the works I have read but I must, now that I have so much medical & surgical literature before me, bring out from its snug retirement my 'Medical Extracts' (MS) book as I make it a practice when reading any permanently useful work to have always a pen and a blank book at my elbow in which to make systematically arranged notes of what I think essentially important or particularly curious.

My hand and pen must now indeed be those of a ready writer.

August 4 *Saturday*
I went down to Gibson rather earlier than usual last [*missing word*] to see if he would get up – and staid tea there. JG [*John Gibson*] still keeps improving he intends to sit up two or three hours this afternoon. [4,25/7/27]

I have changed my resolution regarding the Infirmary case remarks being noted in this work; they will be much better to be by themselves. Any particular operations or accidents I will cursorily mention here but I must have a case book made for particular mention of such patients as I think worthy of the honor. Besides the details I shall necessarily have to make will not always be proper to enter into such genteel circles as I intend this Diary to move in – therefore all these things being taken into account I shall immediately set about manufacturing a blank book for a 'Hospital Case Book'. The entries to commence next Monday.

---

10 Probably an English translation of R. T. H. Laennec, *De l'auscultation médiate* (Paris, 1819), see also Volume 2, note 5.

I went along to the Infirmary this morning but there is nothing very particularly worthy of note today. The wards are but thinly filled – the surgeons wards at any rate. I shall make my entry into the physicians department on Monday which is their receiving day.
[*Patient numbers*]

August 5 *Sunday*
Yesterday morning we were treated with some of the heaviest rain I have seen for a long time the water literally poured down in torrents. The showers continued (with a good deal of thunder) at intervals all day and through the night. Luckily I had to go nowhere in the country but I expect a ride today though the clouds look still threatening rain. Mr King took his second journey on horseback yesterday afternoon to Benwell. 'Better day, better deed' I will begin this now and finish it through the day as I get time.
[*Magaziniana no 11: Beauty*]

August 6 *Monday*
After going round the Infirmary surgical wards this morning with Mr Smiles and his dressers[11] I heard Dr Bulmans outpatients received and went round the medical wards with him and Mr Church. I saw nothing worthy of note except two very severe cases of burn which I shall duly enter in the proper place.[12]
    Called at Greenfield Place on my way home.

August 7 *Tuesday*
I got to the Infirmary this morning only in time for half of an operation by Mr Moore and afterwards saw a case of strangulated hernia of Mr Baird.
    By the bye, in using their names so often I should mention that the four surgeons to this Institution at present are *Messrs Leighton, Moore, Baird* & *Smiles*, the four physicians Drs Headlam, Smith, Bulman & McWhirter, the house surgeon Mr Church and the house-pupils Messrs Holt, Reed & Carter.[13]

---

11 Mr Smiles was a surgeon at the Infirmary. The dressers, usually apprentice doctors, assisted in the operation and bandaged the patients after surgery.
12 Presumably this means TGW's Hospital Case Book: see his comments 4/8/27.
13 Further details about the running of the Infirmary and the personnel are given in Hume, p. 43.

I have sent a quire of folio paper demy size to be quarter-bound in quarto for a case book and as I expect it home in a few minutes I shall begin my register.

J Gibson was sitting up for six hours yesterday afternoon. His arm is less painful but he complains much of the *stiffness* of it. He felt much relieved and more comfortable on getting into bed than he has done since he took ill. [4/8/27]

Evening I was called away as soon as I had laid in a good dinner to ride down to Wallsend by way of a digestive. A man [*Rosely*] has got a cut on his head this morning. I went down and with some little difficulty found my patient who was walking about. On opening his head out I was surprized to find a scratch of three or four days standing evidently evinced by the suppuration being well established. The truth was he had received a slight cut four days ago and sent word to the colliery that he 'wished to see some of the gentlemen the first time they were down'!!

On coming home I was stopped by a lad who had received a cut on his foot at Walker. It is not serious and will be well as soon as the above patient.

August 8 *Wednesday*
Last evening being the monthly meeting of the society[14] I attended to hear my friend Brockett's notice of a motion to be brought forward next month for a sub-committee to be appointed to see after the new catalogue being proceeded with which has been in the printers hands these three years. A letter too was read accompanied by a model of a way for two waggons to pass each other on a single line of railroad. Neither the members present nor myself could discover anything new however in the invention as the model is precisely similar to the plans of rail-roads now in common use.

It is worthwhile noticing that I have observed in being in the library this afternoon a part of the Catalogue; about one half being all that is printed laid upon the table as a specimen I suppose.

I was at the Infirmary this morning as usual and heard Mr Moore (with whom I went the round of the wards) Mr Leighton, Dr Smith and Dr McWhirter receive their outpatients.
The patient who was operated on is doing tolerably well.

---

14 Newcastle Literary and Philosophical Society, see Introduction.

August 9 *Thursday*
A summons this morning called me about 9 AM down to Wallsend to a boy [*Dawson*] who was reported to have had his arm broken. I went down seeing a patient or two on my road and found the accident not so bad as I, in truth, wished it to be. The radius was bent but not fractured the ulna uninjured. I dressed it in the usual way and have no doubt of the boys doing well. I rode sharply home to be in time for Infirmary and made the pupils look round at my apparition in white smalls & top boots – the first time I have shewn myself there in that dress.[15]

August 10 *Friday*
I had a ride more than I expected yesterday Mr McI having desired me to see my patient at Felling after dinner which as we did not dine till 5 oclock made me a very pleasant evening ride. I had not seen this case for 3 weeks [*Dixon, 4, 15/6/27*] and found the youth (this hip disease before described) as well as he could possibly be expected to be. There is very little motion in the joint but he is free from all pain and can go about with one crutch and a stick. The knee however is still very weak though his general health is good. I recommended sea bathing as the only remedy (with patience) now requisite.

There was an interesting *sect: cadaveris* at the Infirmary this morning which I of course was present at. The case proved to be a similar one to the Ex-Emperor Bounapartes – cancer of the stomach.[16]

Talking of great people – this morning brought the news of the death of our present greatest statesman Mr Canning.[17] What a confusion this will create in the Cabinet!

I *must* write home today but before I begin I will try another Chap: of my memoirs which are flagging.
[*Magaziniana No 12 My Autobiography Chapter 9*]

I was up at Greenfield Place with my flute last night and was surprized in the middle of a piece of music by a carriage drawing up a Mrs Bowes quite unexpectedly making her appearance.

---

15 Smalls were breeches, fastened below the knee and worn with stockings.
16 Napoleon Bonaparte died in 1821. The cause of his death remains uncertain, with cancer being only one of the possibilities.
17 George Canning (1770–1827) was British Foreign Secretary from 1807 to 1809 and again from 1822 until he became Prime Minister, five months before his death.

J Gibson continues improving but very slowly. [7/8/27]
[*Patient numbers*]

August 14 *Tuesday*
Two accidents happened in my *'beat'* on Saturday. One boy
[*Gibson*] was just brought home when I was at Biggs Main
severely crushed on the abdomen. I feared worse symptoms but
by the prompt application of leeches and a brisk purge, he was a
great deal better yesterday. The other case was a very bad
sprained knee at Heaton. I ordered leeches and cold lotion but
there was little change in the patients state yesterday. The cut on
the foot at Biggs Main [*Armstrong, case list, end Vol 4*] now presents only the appearance of a narrow red stripe.

One of *our* great fairs began on Saturday and yesterday was
the horse market day on the moor. I went to Heaton &c on my
old friend the black horse but on coming home found a man
waiting to take him away for good and altogether. Mr McIntyre
was at the moor[18] all day with his groom looking out for a new
gig horse as I understand. They had made some sort of exchange
between the black horse and a little brown mare which was
accordingly *installed* in his *place*, but I hope not in his *office* of
carrying me. I did not exactly relish the idea of lowering my seat
of dignity (no offence gentle ladies) from my tall and somewhat
handsome black steed to the stumpy low tho' not badly 'set on'
beast that I now saw in the stall usually appropriated to my
riding nag. I thought it was unlikely the animal before me would
be able to trail the heavy gig which its master required in one of
its station of life. These cogitations were dispelled however by
the appearance of a tall chestnut colt towards evening.

The little mare no doubt is for Mr Cochrane who has been on
the lookout for a new one, and the chestnut 4 year old a genteel
looking affair and which I shall forthwith christen 'Bayard' will
have the honour of serving under me. He is a foreigner but if
anything like equal in spirit and activity to his predecessor the
Flanders mare he will be sure to gain my favor and good-will.

As I am so much on horseback and will not plead entirely 'not
guilty' of a smattering of vanity when on a fine animal I hope I
may be excused taking a particular interest in what I am to ride

---

18 Presumably Newcastle town moor.

on without being considered a horse jobber – a character I by no means emulate. As I have had no occasion to be out of town yet – I can say nothing of the roadster virtues of *Bayard*.

August 16 *Thursday*
Mr McI went off to Backworth early yesterday morning and returned about noon; he shortly after mounted his mare and left no word where he was bound. A message came here at 2 to request Mr Redhead of Walker might be seen immediately. From report he had a attack of cholera morbus. I put some of the usual remedies in my pocket and mounted the chestnut (who had been with the groom at Backworth also) arriving at Byker Turnpike-gate I learnt that Mr McI had passed through about an hour ago and further along the road was told he turned down Walker Lane the direct road to Mr Redheads. I now concluded that he had gone to his patient and was on the point of returning when I met Mr R's nephew who informed me Mr McI was *not* with his uncle! I accordingly set forward and had been about a quarter of an hour with our patient when Mr McI made his appearance. He had been paying a professional visit at a house close by. We rode home together and canvassed the merits of my new steed. This beast, – he is unworthy of the name I gave him and I therefore *unchristened* him, – is good for nothing but carrying a dutchman, to which occupation he has most likely been accustomed. He *splanders* (if I may be allowed this expressive word) out his fore-legs as if he wished to throw them away and can trot full *four miles an hour without a stop*!! Mr McI says 'he goes very well for a young horse' – 'Yes Sir' replied I 'but he takes an immense deal of driving'. My 'yes' however went a little against my conscience I only wish Mr McI to ride him one journey. I am satisfied the animal would never have the honour of carrying its owner again.

After two days delay in being too late for the coach I have got a parcel sent off to Sunderland. I wrote a letter on Tuesday but one which I was to enclose from Miss Gibson to Miss Bel G. was not ready. Yesterday I did not get home from Walker till after five oclock but I gave it in to go by an early coach this morning, with its precious charge of the above letter enclosed 'politely con-veyed by Mr T. Wr – '.

The sheriffs show yesterday was I understand the most splen-did one seen for many years. I did not see it but am told there were a long line of carriages and about 800 horsemen. I saw the

judges come up to open the county courts in the sheriff's splendid equipage.
[*Magaziniana No 13 My Autobiography Chapter 10*]

August 17 *Friday*
I have today had the pleasure of seeing & hearing for the first time one whom I have long wished to hear & see, viz. Mr Brougham.[19] The public opinion regarding him and the power & eloquence of his speeches as reported in the papers of the day had raised in my mind great expectations regarding him. I only heard his pleading on a trifling cause, an assault case, yet I felt assured from what I did hear of what his force would be had he a full scope for his talent in an important subject and a crowded senate.

Mr Scarlett[20] of course being no longer on the circuit was not here but I have before had the pleasure of listening to his mild and good tempered pleadings. He should always open an action while Mr Brougham's proper sphere is on the side of the defence. To hear Mr B to advantage a person should be out of sight of his face at any rate; while Mr Scarletts winning smile and polite demeanour are strong incentives in favour of his cause. The two however whom I should have liked most of all to attend would have been Messrs *Canning* and Brougham opposed to each other in the house of commons in some of their great and immortal debates. That pleasure is now never to be enjoyed for on this very day are the remains of the above statesman to be laid near those of his glorious predecessors Pitt & Fox.

Once I was gratified by the sight of this man and heard his voice in a few words on the London Bridge question;[21] but the reading [*of*] his speeches in the papers had so completely won

19 Henry Brougham (1778–1868), created Baron Brougham and Vaux in 1830, was called to the Scottish Bar in 1808. In 1810, he was called to the English Bar and became an MP. In 1828 he helped in the foundation of London University. He was Lord Chancellor 1830–34. See Volume 12, Memoranda (3–22/12/1830) for TGW's notes on his involvement in presenting a congratulatory address from London University students to Lord Brougham on his elevation to the Woolsack.
20 James Scarlett (1799–1844), later the first Baron Abinger, came to eminence as a barrister on the Northern circuit in the 1820s.
21 See TGW's comments on his visit to Parliament, made on 16/6/1823, in 'My Autobiography', chapter 11.

upon my feelings especially in his late contentions under the change of the ministry and had impressed upon me so profound a respect for his great talent that in what little I did consider of politics his words were law.

The newspapers abound with eulogising upon him just now therefore I need not attempt to increase the number; but am struck with the aptness (which I cannot refrain from expressing) with which the lines he himself composed on his friend and patron Mr Pitt apply to his own loss:

> And shall not his mem'ry to Britons be dear
> Whose example with envy all nations behold,
> A statesman unbiased by interest or fears,
> By power uncorrupted, untainted by gold?
> When, *Canning*, the course of this greatness is o'er
> Thy talents thy virtues we loudly recall
> Now justly we praise thee, whom lost we deplore
> Admired in thy zenith beloved in thy fall!

August 18 *Saturday*
This day twelvemonths I re-entered Mr McIntyres establishment after an absence of about 10 months, or rather this day I made my first visits among my patients in my new capacity having come back the evening before.
[*Patient numbers*]

August 20 *Monday*
I received a parcel of Apricots from my Grandfather yesterday morning and an unexpected parcel from Sunderland this evening which latter I have with great difficulty got answered this afternoon. I had to follow the coach over to Gateshead to overtake it so as to have my parcel forwarded.

I did not go to see J Gibson last night the first day I have omitted seeing him for some weeks. [*10/8/27*] He finds my assistance necessary indeed for getting into bed in the evening. His knee has been for some time threatening to be affected in the same way as his elbow and he applied some leeches to the former on Saturday night. What effect these have taken I have not yet heard but shall go to see tonight – the idea of having his troubles to begin again in a series of applications to the knee is very disheartening to him but I hope the leeches will subdue the little tendency to Inflammation and that no further care will be requisite in that quarter. The elbow is still improving but slowly.

August 21 *Tuesday*
I am now in the midst of a series of letter writing which I heartily
wish I had accomplished. I have written five in as many days and
long ones too and must have a still longer ready for my Father
to get franked[22] at Sir John Lowther's for my sister the latter end
of this week. I have to add one more to my certainly not numerous list of patients dead under my care, this week. A child affected with the complaint I described in the first volume of this
Diary. [1, 4/10/26] More might have been done for this patient had
medicine been earlier resorted to but the disease had got too
firmly established before I was called in to allow even much
amendment to take place.
There is an interesting and well-marked case of epilepsy on the
books just now arising from worms. The boy [*Ainsley*] about 7
years old some time ago got rid of one large worm but lately has
been attacked every night and frequently during the day with
fits. He has partially lost the use of the left side. Mr McIntyre
ordered him some Jalap & Calomel last week with a Rhubarb &
Magnesia mixture which being taken without effect. I yesterday
prescribed the following on the supposition that more worms
remain which are causing the disease.

Pulv: Scammon: gr vj; Sacchar: Alb: gr iij; Calomel: gr iij; Ol:
Croton gutt $\frac{1}{4}$ mane sumendus

August 23 *Thursday*
Spent last evening very pleasantly with a party at Mr Piles being
invited two days ago 'to tea & cards'. The junta consisted of
Messrs Lang, Henzell, Elwood & Pow of the old quorum and two
new friends of Mr Flood a Norwegian merchant who has been
sometime in Newcastle and is to leave it tomorrow – also a Mr
Tebey. Henzell did not join us till late and as we could not till
then make up two whist tables we drew cuts for who were to
compose the complete game and the other three who were to
form a three handed party. It fell to my lot to be of the latter class
and I took as a trial the playing of the dumb hand for a partner.
My opponents were Mr Flood and Mr Pow. If I won I got double
stakes but this advantage was more than counterbalanced
(considering I had never played two hands before) by my liability

22 The procedure of franking mail is described in the Introduction.

also to pay 'shots' for myself & partner should I lose the game. Stakes were as usual at our meetings sixpence per game. I won the first and second but lost a third when Henzell became my partner and he and I were victors again before supper was announced. I therefore was in the end *plus* 1/6. With toasting singing & speechifying the evening as I have said passed very pleasantly. I was the only one whose song (such as it was) was encored.

August 25 *Saturday*
Just got a letter sent off by coach to Sunderland enclosing one for London for Father to get franked when at Sir John Lowthers next Sunday. My day-book had got sadly behind hand in way of being *posted* a good part of which labour I have also got accomplished so that I have only to enumerate a few accidents here and make two or three remarks in Infirmary case book to be all right and straight for finishing the week in comfort.

A boy with a bruised leg & a man with D° back living at Wallsend but working at Walker. A lad severely bruised on the leg & shoulders; a man whose leg is bruised & cut both at Wallsend and a boy from Benwell whose dislocated wrist I reduced (he would not allow King to do so) are the sum total in the accident line worth mentioning. They are all doing very well.

My horse has got a bad cold and par consequence is unfit to be ridden just now but I hope to be able to mount him again tomorrow. I have had therefore to travel on 'Shank's Nag' or by a Shields gig for these last four days. On Thursday I borrowed Mr Gibson's poney but just as I got home (Mr McI was away at Tynemouth) a summons met me to call me to Wallsend – Miss McI was going down there in half an hour with the groom in her brothers gig and kindly offered me a third seat which I of course accepted and was to have come back in a Shields stage. None being on the road at the time however I walked up.
[*Patient numbers*]

August 26 *Sunday* (morning)
My horse is so much better that I am prepared for riding on him my rounds today as I have some distance to go.

The epileptic patient mentioned [*Ainsley, 21/8/27*] has found great benefit from the use of those Croton Oil powders. The paroxysms when I saw him on Friday – when he had taken four powders – had returned less frequently and the dejecta were extremely unnatural and tar-like. Thinking that 6 g^{rs} of Calomel a day might be *too* powerful for a boy of his age I ordered the medicine to be repeated in a rather different formula.

> ℞   Pulv: Scammonia gr v
> – Jalapae gr v
> – Rhei gr x
> Ol: Crotonae gutt $\frac{1}{4}$ bis die

The other powders had not been very powerful.

August 28 *Tuesday*
I rode the chestnut both Sunday and also this morning. He is a good deal better but still far from strong again.
Ainesly's boy (Epilepsy) [26/8/27] is better in regard to his original disease but I find his tongue very foul this morning but of a different appearance to the fur at first exhibited and which last had almost disappeared. This today shewn is a thick softish white coating whilst the former one was brown & dry. I should judge the stomach now to be weakened by the severe medicines it has been necessary to use and have accordingly prescribed for him tonic medicine

> ℞   Infus: Gent: c ℥ vj
> Aqua Menthae ℥ i ss
> Tint: Jingiberis ℨ iij;
> Pulv: Rhei ℨ j Carb: Sodae ℨ ss Sum cochl ij ter dei

The last powders I ordered were sufficiently powerful taken once a day.

August 29 *Wednesday*
I have not been out nor do I expect to be in the country at all today; so far (2 PM) not one patient requires my attendance.

August 30 *Thursday*
My expectations yesterday were not fulfilled as a messenger hurried me down to a distant part of Wallsend to a man whose ancle was bruised. Today I have been at Heaton only. Horse almost well again.
[*Patient numbers*]

September 3 *Monday*
Recopying an essay, posting in ledger and filling up a leaf or two in Miss Bel Gibson's Album have completely occupied my pen every leisure moment for the last four days and I am likely to be kept busy*ish* for a day or two longer in consequence of Mr McIntyres being absent and as usual leaving me his *own* patients additional duty.

Mr McI has gone off this morning with his gun to enjoy a few days shooting (some would say to kill birds instead of men) at a friends about 30 miles from here. He is a keen sportsman and I understand 'a good shot' but his professional duties have prevented him from firing a gun these ten years almost.
[*Magaziniana no, 15: 'My Autobiography', chapter 12*]

September 5 *Wednesday*
I was summoned down to Wall[*send*] to a bruised ancle [*Moores*] yesterday morning and rode down the turnpike with Mr Henzell who wished to look at my 'Bayard' which we are now wishing to be rid of, he not being strong enough for *our* gig. The accident was not serious but misfortunes never come single in our practice. During the night King was called out to a burnt man at Benwell [*Ryle*] and this morning I have just been to Felling to a lad [*Pearson*] who has received a violent kick in the side from a horse.

It is reported that a number of men have been killed by a blast at Fawdon.[23] I forgot to mention that I dined and spent a very pleasant afternoon with Mr Henzell on Sunday.

J Gibson was out in a chaise on Sunday, and is to proceed to Tynemouth this afternoon. [*20/8/27*]

September 7 *Friday*
On Wednesday evening I went by appointment to give Mr Henzell a first lesson on the flute; adding *'music master'* to the rest of my multifarious professions; and last evening meeting with Mr Pyle I accompanied him home and played a game at whist.

Today I have been at Felling and should no more accidents

---

23 'An explosion of gas took place at Fawdon colliery, near Newcastle, when 3 young men were much burnt, two of whom shortly afterwards died': see Sykes, p. 209.

intervene I shall be able to leave the books nearly clear of my patients against Monday, when I hope to proceed to Sunderland there to join my Father & Mother preparatory to our seaside trip.

September 8 *Saturday*
A man [*Kingsley*] belonging to Heaton – Johnsons Houses – having received a nip on the thigh required my attendance, but the case is not at all serious.
[*Patient numbers*]

September 9 *Sunday*
Spent last evening with Mr Henzell over another lesson on the flute; – my pupil is making rapid advancement.

I have this morning been round among all my patients and only for two or three have I had occasion to prescribe any thing. The morning being very wet I got a complete ducking which however I take very contentedly in the hope the rain today will supersede the necessity of more tomorrow.

King's patient the burnt man [*Ryle, 5/9/27*] at Benwell is doing well. The burns were only superficial and of no great extent.

September 24 *Monday*
Arrived home again by the Express coach on Saturday and have just now for the first time been able to take up my pen for amusement. I intended to have registered my excursion in a regular and continuous manner and took this volume along with me for the purpose, but I was so entirely occupied during my fortnights ramble that not one entry has been made. A short description of my tour may now however be accomplished but it must be a *very* brief one.

Monday 10 I went down to Tynemouth seeing one or two patients in my way. At Shields I overtook Miss Taylerson bent on the same errand as myself so dismissed the gig I was in and walked to our destination Mrs Gibson's lodgings. It was a lucky circumstance that I met Miss T: at that time for I had entirely forgotten at whose house the Gibsons were. After dining there I crossed the water and coached to Sunderland. Called in the evening upon Mrs Hall for my Mother.

Tuesday 11 Took seats in the Pilot[24] and were set down at Sheraton a village about 5 miles from Hartlepool our intended place of sojourn for a few days. After breakfast Mother and I commenced our *walk* to the latter place which we greatly prolonged in going round by the sands, – in the end however we arrived safely at the King's Head Inn and found our quarters there very comfortable.

Wednesday 12 Heavy rain which caught me in a walk towards Seaton, and superseded the necessity of a cold bath that day had I been in the habit of bathing. One object with me and a main one in *my* wishing to go to Hartlepool was that I might have the opportunity of seeing and being introduced to a certain young lady who was then at Seaton. As this part of my business concerns only myself I shall say no more of it here than that I *did* see the lady and *was* introduced, though it cost me a little trouble at first; and that I received a cut from the said lady the following day that yet remains a complete mystery to me, having no rational mode of accounting for it, – but young ladies always appeared to me unaccountable creatures and I must in this instance leave *time* to explain all.

Thursday 13 Walked to Seaton. Called upon Mr Frank whom I have once before named [24/5/27] and who has a summer residence there.

Friday 14 I had yesterday taken places in the Car which runs from Seaton to Stockton and appointed that the vehicle should take Mother & me up at the end of the lane leading from Hartlepool. The car however came past us quite full through negligence of the man whom I had desired to keep places. We walked to Wolviston and after resting there Mother proposed that instead of sending to Stockton for a chaise as was at first intended we should enjoy the afternoon by continuing our walk to Stockton! This I gladly agreed to as I am always a bad traveller inside a close vehicle. According we got to Stockton towards evening having walked about 14 miles that day altogether.

Saturday 15 The arrangement was that we were to meet Father this afternoon at or near Neasham. After breakfasting at Stockton

---

24 The 'Pilot' mail-coach for Leeds left from the Sun Inn in Newgate Street, Newcastle every day, except Sunday, at 4 am, travelling via Sunderland and Stockton: see PW, I, p. 134.

the railway coach[25] took us as far as the Fighting Cocks public house from whence we walked through Dinsdale spa[26] to Neasham and not meeting with F proceeded towards Croft to which place we had just approached when he came up. As no beds were at liberty at Middleton and tolerably comfortable lodgings offered at Neasham it was determined that we should settle there for a few days. At Mrs Gunson's then (dealer in Tea, Coffee, Tobacco and Snuff, with bacon, eggs, and *other* vegetables) we unpacked and fixed our quarters.

Sunday 16 At Dinsdale church and walked to the spa in the evening.

Monday 17 Neasham

Tuesday 18 My F had to look after the piano-fortes under his care at Raby Castle and as I had never seen the place I most readily accepted the proposal for me to accompany him. We called at Dr Sherwood's Snow Hall[27] on the way. The Castle and grounds were in first rate order as the family were expected in a day or two. The housekeeper ordered lunch for us which I tasted for curiosity sake but we dined at the Queen's Head Inn Staindrop. I was highly gratified with my day's drive and returned to Neasham in the dusk. While my Father was tuning in the different rooms at Raby I had excellent opportunity of seeing all the curiosities by roaming about the apartments. One piano is in Lady Arabella's room and there also she has her private library which I took the liberty of glancing into. Among other volumes was her Ladyship's Album containing many original and pretty pieces.[28]

---

25 The railway coach was probably on the Stockton to Darlington Railway, opened in 1825, the world's first public steam railway.

26 Dinsdale Spa near Darlington, also known as Middleton Spa, had a spring discovered in 1789 that was believed to have useful medicinal properties. A bath house and hotel were built there for visitors to the spring in the 1820s. The Spa is described in *A Guide to Croft, Dinsdale, Middleton, Darlington &c* (Darlington, 1834) and T. D. Walker, *An Analysis of the Waters of Dinsdale and Croft* (Durham, 1828).

27 For comment on Snow Hall see 'My Autobiography', note 91.

28 Raby Castle was built in the fourteenth century, with the interior being substantially remodelled in the eighteenth and nineteenth centuries, see *BED*, pp. 382–9. At the time of TGW's visit in 1827, it was the seat of the third Earl of Darlington: see 'My Autobiography', note 45. Lady Arabella was a daughter of the Earl by his first wife, Katherine Margaret.

Wednesday 19 Went up to Darlington in the afternoon and drank tea at Mr Bowes.

Thursday 20 Neasham

Friday 21 Walked with Mother to Croft; took coach there to Ferryhill near Durham where we staid all night. I was to have come forward to Newcastle that night but my Mother was unwell so I proposed to stay with her till the coaches passed the following afternoon.

Saturday 22 Walked to Bp [*Bishop*] Middleham and called upon Mr Will: Gibson. In returning we met a party of schoolboys, amongst whom was one of the *little* Gibsons to my & his own great surprize. Walked through Mr Surtees gardens at Mainsforth[29] and returned to Ferry Hill to dinner. Jumped on to the Express at 5 P.M. and arrived in Newcastle about $\frac{1}{4}$ past 9.

Sunday 23 I had scarcely been home $\frac{1}{2}$ an hour last night when a summons came for Mr McI to go to Seghill. As the case was immediately urgent he promised to go off at 6 this morning. Accordingly I was called up to accompany him in the gig.

A girl fell backwards on her head about a fortnight since and symptoms of phrenitis had come on with a great puffiness of the scalp. Mr McI intended if circumstances required it to use the trephine. After making a crucial incision the bone was found uninjured and further operation was deemed unnecessary. Mr McI and I processed to Wallsend where the groom met us with Mr McI's mare. We went on to Tynemouth and I drove the gig home (the groom with me) and saw my patients by the way.

Monday 24 evening I have just returned from visiting a patient [*Hall*] of Mr McIntyre's at East Boldon upwards of 8 miles from hence and only 3 from Sunderland. I am sorry to say the patient will not require much more attendance being in a dying state. He appears to me to have a schirrous pylorus or in common language a cancer in the stomach.

September 28 *Friday*

So much other business presses on my hands just now that I am afraid I shall have little time to pay attention to my Diary so as to finish this volume with the Month. As however it is now my

---

29 Mainsforth Hall, 1 mile west of Bishop Middleham, Co. Durham, was the home of Robert Surtees (1779–1834), Durham historian. The house was demolished in 1962: see *BED*, p. 109.

intention to be very [*brief*] in my remarks in future I will reserve the remaining blank paper (after the customary observations to the end of the month) for completing my autobiographical papers. They will thus be out of the way in the next number and as I have found that undertaking a much more extended one than I at first contemplated that will be no unpleasant matter.

Some interval may elapse before the next years vol: is commenced but the time will be occupied during the leisure I can afford in filling up the *appendix* to this, and writing (custom requires it) an address at the completion of our twelve months editorship.

I was called up yesterday morning about 7 AM the first time I have been disturbed from my bed by an accident these four months, I believe. A young man [*Wrightson*] at Heaton Old Engine has received a severe cut on the ancle penetrating the joint, an extensive wound of the scalp with other injuries. I dressed him in the usual way and Mr McI will I expect see him this morning. No further hearing from Boldon. [*Hall, 24/9/27*]

The general topic of conversation just now is the Duke of Wellington's visit to Newcastle.[30] He is to come in about 3 oclock this afternoon and to review the cavalry on the moor; after which there will be a great dinner at the Mansion Ho: and ball at the Assembly rooms. The newspapers are so full of all the regulations &c that it is quite throwing away time for me to say much about the business here.

My horse unfortunately fell lame a day or two ago which will preclude the possibility of my riding him to the moor this afternoon and the day is unfavourable for walking.

September 30 *Sunday*
The great day has passed over and nothing particularly grand took place. An immense concourse of people was assembled but the afternoon was very unfavourable. I was in a window looking out to the Sandhill and with my companions at that window received a most polite bow from the Duke as he passed and on our kissing our hands to his Grace.
[*Patient numbers*]
Event of cases herein mentioned

---

30 The Duke's visit is described in detail in Sykes, pp. 210–12.

August 6	The two burns named as Infirmary cases are progressing toward recovery but slowly.
August 7	The man operated on was perfectly cured.
	Rosely Wallsend went to work next day.
	The cut foot at Walker I suppose would do well but I do not now recollect the Patient.
August 9	*Dawson* Wallsend Curvature of Arm. After going to work too soon and receiving another bruise upon the same part the case was eventually quite cured.
August 10	*Dixon* Felling Hip Disease remains in status quo.
August 14	*Gibson* Biggs Main – did very well.
	Hall Byker – cured. The ligament of the knee had been severely sprained and the patient was a proportionately long time off work.
August 14	*Armstrong* Biggs Main cut on foot. This rather severe case has done very well the limb being perfectly free in motion &c.
August 16	Mr Redhead cured in a day or two.
August 21	Ainesly's boy Epilepsy. I rather pride myself on the treatment of this case which required to be pretty brisk. The boy is now perfectly well.
August 26	The accidents here lumped together all did well.
September 5	*Moores* Wallsend done well.
	Ryle at Benwell King's patient is cured.
	Pearson Felling cured.
September 8	Kingsley Heaton well.
September 28	Hall Boldon I have heard nothing further from or of this man since I saw him.
	Wrightson Old Engine The wound on the ancle has united partly by the first intention which dissipated all fear of the limb being in danger. The cut on the Head is quite close (Oct 1).

[*The MS here includes an appendix of about 17 pp. containing Magaziniana nos 14 to 17 (My Autobiography, chapters 13 to 17) and a list of the Magaziniana and their contents. The following entry appears after the list.*]

N.B. I beg to take this opportunity of requesting the reader to take no further notice of some hints and promises made in different parts of the foregoing papers. Some of the intended plans *may*

yet be carried into execution but others never will. This system
of exciting expectation I shall certainly avoid in the future, and
hope my kind readers will take my word that I am acting wisely,
under the reflection that 'second thoughts are always best'. I must
henceforth recollect also to '*think* twice before *writing* once'.

> Address to the Readers
> 'What more I have to say is short
> I hope you'll kindly take it
> It is no tale; but if you think,
> Perhaps a tale you'll make it'
>
> Wordsworth[31]

Ladies & Gentlemen,

I set out in this undertaking by professing my submission to
that great authority, – custom, and, by the same authority, – the
time is now come when I am to address a few words to you
personally; when after appearing publickly before you as an
author, (if I may use the term as applied to 'myself') I am privil-
eged to speak with you privately as a friend, in a snug, quiet,
sousy sort of a way.

'Time will try – the best resolves may fail' was the motto under
the shelter of which I commenced the fulfilment of my resolution.
Time *has* tried – fairly, duly, truly tried, and here is my undertaking so far from abandoned, that the next volume is already begun.
Some thanks are certainly due to my friends who have encouraged me in proceeding; but I think *I* have a just claim to credit,
who, like most youths, am not in general extremely obstinate and
persevering in what I take in hand, – for this continuing was to
be as much for my own gratification and advantage, as for the
amusement and edification of my nearest and dearest relations
and friends.

In the first *volume*, or perhaps it would be more appropriately
called *number*, I have endeavoured to give a general idea of my
daily professional occupations; the usual distance and direction
of each days rides; and the reception I met with amongst my
patients. In the second volume trivial domestic casualties, and
other more important concerns are alluded to. In the third, cases
and local public occurrences are, I believe, (I speak from memory)
to be principally met with; while the fourth and fifth numbers

---

31 The quotation is from William Wordsworth's poem, 'Simon Lee, the Old
Huntsman', lines 76–80, first published in *Lyrical Ballads* (London, 1798).

are chiefly conspicuous for these magaziniana papers; which, so far, almost entirely consist of chapters of my *autobiography*, (if such trifles are worthy of the name).

The system I shall henceforth adopt will be much more leisurely to continue my remarks on the same plan; but, as other pursuits and new occupations are constantly presenting themselves, and there is now no necessity for daily or minute observations (the objects of making them being fulfilled) my Diary will be in future rather a receptacle for any thing new or amusing that strikes my fancy, and for the relation of any extraordinary occurrences, than strictly a 'Diary'. The establishment of a regular 'case book' has precluded the necessity of registering professional subjects; so that except as anything particular may be mentioned, the 'Diary' (for such it will remain in its appellation) will no longer be at all occupied with treatments of cases, which in many instances can be but imperfectly detailed in a general work of this sort.

Regarding the grammatical merits and composition of the language I must be allowed a few words in extenuation.

I have a habit, perhaps it is not a good one, of being very fidgety and restless during the interval which divides the formation of a purpose or the suggestion of an idea from the putting these in actual practice. This tends in many respects to a laudable end, but it has this disadvantage when the object is a scriptorial one, viz that the language is often incorrect, for the most part inelegant, and always by omissions blots &c bears evident marks of the haste in which it was performed. This I am afraid is eminently exemplified in this Diary, but, as I can seldom have patience to read over anything immediately after it is written, the omissions and inaccuracies are frequently left uncorrected. An incessant anticipation of being called away, no one knows how soon, may tend to heighten this despatch.

Egotism is another charge to which I must plead guilty, and one to which most young scribblers are liable. In my reminiscences it is hardly possible I conceive to avoid it. My aim in future however shall be to use the pronoun and its equivalents more sparingly.

For the penmanship I must offer the same apologies as for the language. With all its disadvantages I throw it and *myself* upon the mercy and kind consideration of the reader, in the full confidences of his or her lenient judgement allowing its merits (and

I am fain to hope it has some few) allowing its merits, I say, to gleam out and gradually to dispel from his observations the cloudiness of its imperfections, and, in the end, securing for us a *favorable reception*.

T.G.W. Newgate Street Oct 11 1827

V O L U M E 6 (October 11, 1827 to May 30, 1828)

October 11 *Thursday*
Though the Appendix which forms the concluding part of my last volume is not yet filled up, I must make a beginning of this new one in order that it may be open for the reception of anything very important that occurs.

As I have endeavoured to make last year's volumes perfect in themselves and of course this one must be connected with them, it behoves me here to warn the reader, (though the caution is mentioned in my concluding 'address',) that the extended remarks adopted in former numbers will not and cannot longer be continued in this and hence that in future my annotations will be – 'few and far between'.

A Magaziniana paper may occasionally appear, but the principal end of their institution has been fulfilled. They will be still a convenient *vehicle* (as we say in medicine) for exhibiting a dose of anything amusive that fancy may dictate.

Though a diminution should take place in the number of accidents noted the reader must not conclude that business is on the wane. By no means! But unless the pen is in my hand I shall not care particularly to record every trifle that happens. If the reader has perused the other volumes he will be pretty well acquainted with the general routine of our practice, if not, – to them I beg leave to refer him should he be very anxious for information on that subject. So much for promises now for performance.

On the second of this month, – being the month's meeting of the Lit: & Phil: Society I sent a paper to Mr Turner, stating that 'should nothing more important press upon the attention of the Society at their next monthly meeting' I intended doing myself the honor of laying before the members a model of a machine invented by my Father for drawing coals up the pit &c.[1] My offer was very flatteringly accepted Mr Turner saying that the Society would feel obliged by any information regarding that subject and hoped I would bring the machine before them when convenient.

The writing, correcting and re-copying a paper to be read at our next meeting is one sufficient reason why little attention or leisure can be devoted to my Diary during this month.

Mr King is out at Backworth, to assist Cochrane who is unwell, for a few days; and in consequence I have his collieries to attend in addition to my own. There have been no less than five calls out there during the five days he has been absent. One man [*Rutherford*] has received an injury in the spine and will I am afraid require visiting twice a day for some time. I have been out this morning in the midst of a heavy rain. My patient who only got hurt yesterday is as well as can be expected. His case will be entered in my 'case book'.

[*Patient numbers*]

October 14 *Sunday*

I was on Wednesday called in to a person at Wallsend [*Soulsby*] who was reported to have swallowed a bone while supping some mutton broth last Sunday. I examined her throat with my fingers but could not go down as far as the point where she complained of pain. Mr M'Allum, surgeon, Wallsend, had been called in on Sunday and had maintained that no bone was in the passage but that it might perhaps have scratched the Pharynx in its way down. From symptoms *I* judged a portion of the bone *was* stuck fast but desired the woman (about 65 aetate) might come to Newcastle to have the requisite instruments used for investigating the subject. Mr McIntyre however went down with me in the gig next day and after fruitless attempts to extract any bone or to get a probary passed in consequence of the great swelling of the parts and the contraction of the passage. Mr McI desired she might come up to the Infirmary. Mr Leighton examined her there on Friday morning but upon hearing she was our patient (he and Mr McI are not upon good terms) determined that no bone was

---

1 TGW mentioned this invention when he wrote about searching some Journals for information about the premium which should have been awarded to his father, see Volume 1, 12/11/26. For TGW's account of the presentation of his paper, see 4/11/27 and 14/11/27.

there – that, forsooth, an abscess had formed in the pharynx causing the present symptoms. The patient had felt the bone on
Monday with a quill and in her efforts had pushed it a good deal
further down her throat. Mr McI thought he felt it at one time
deep in the oesophagus but being surrounded and enclosed by
swelling could not lay hold of it with his forceps. Today, – the
eighth day from her tasting food, the utmost extent of what she
has taken through the week being about a cupful of liquids, – I
took down the stomach pump and after Mr McI had passed a
small flexible gum tube down the oesophagus I injected first
about a pint of coffee and afterwards a similar quantity of sago.
The patient had felt little hunger during her long fast but
expressed herself 'comfortable' when the boiled sago had been
given. She is taking a solution of Muriatic acid to attempt to dis-
solve the bone, upon the supposition that a piece is lodged still
in her throat.

King has returned from Backworth to relieve me of his share
in the business. I have been called out no less than five times to
his collieries during his absence though he had been summoned
only twice all the previous months since his appointment. The
patient [*Rutherford, 11/10/27*] whom I mentioned as to be seen so
frequently is now reduced to an allowance of one visit a day. He
is doing very well.

When told of the numerous accidents King exclaimed 'Well,
Wright, you are the luckiest that ever was; you are always getting
accidents!' – *luckiest fellow*!!'. *Proh pudor*! [*i.e., For shame!*]
[*Patient numbers*]

October 17 *Wednesday*
Mr McIntyre questioned me a few days since on the progress
the 'young men' were making in professional attainments and
requested that I would look after their studies and 'go over' some
anatomy with them. In consequence of this I proposed to my
junior companions that I would, – if they liked the plan, deliver
'a course of lectures on Anatomy' as the best way of communicating to them that practical sort of knowledge they principally
required. The suggestion was highly approved and I was
entreated to act upon it. This I have done. On Monday night I
commenced the course with an introductory lecture on General
Science, shewing the extensive connection of our profession with
almost every branch so as to point out the indispensable necessity

of a liberal education and diligent study in various departments of Knowledge. This lecture lasted three quarters of an hour and was delivered merely from a small page of notes etched out for the purpose.

October 18 *Thursday*
Last night was delivered my second lecture on Anatomy. Organic life; the view of Human Anatomy; as regards the solids, fluids and different textures were the subjects concluding with a general glance at the Skeleton and formation of bone. The course is to consist of about 30 lectures. *My colleague* (!) Mr King is to take in hand the mere descriptive parts, as the muscles &c. and after this week is to make his demonstrations on Wednesdays and Fridays; while I hold forth on Monday and Thursday evenings. I continue the Osteology this week so as to get a frame work put together on which Mr King can build his structure of the soft parts.

Lecturer on Anatomy &c. is now therefore to be added to my list of 'styles'. This system will be a good exercise in spontaneous composition and at the same time a pleasant method of rubbing up my anatomical acquirements so that I do not doubt of its being of as great utility to the lecturer as to his audience. *Strict attention* and *regard to privacy* are the only regulations enforced upon the pupils'. So says my syllabus.

The woman at Wallsend [*Soulsby, 14/10/27*] who swallowed the bone is considerably better: a probany was introduced on Tuesday and the bone dislodged. Since then the patient has been rapidly convalescent.

Rutherford, Benwell is improving as fast as medicine can make him. [*14/10/27*]

October 20 *Saturday*
The bones of the head formed the subject of last nights lecture which lasted an hour all but five minutes. As I have a very good collection of well prepared bones I am enabled to give this part of the course with full effect. The soft parts must be illustrated by plates.

I had a very curious dream last night which will form the subject of a Magaziniana paper the first opportunity.[2]
[*Patient numbers*]

---

2 Probably *Magaziniana* no. 21, 4/11/27, 'On Dreams'.

October 29 *Monday*

Yesterday not having to go into the country I went to hear Mr Turner in the morning who gave us one of his usual excellent practical discourses.[3] Miss McIntyre upon learning that I had been at the Unitarian Chapel wished very much at dinner to enter into a theological conversation upon the impropriety of the tenets of this sect. I however was not disposed to follow up any argument and observed that *I* went to their chapel merely on account of knowing Mr Turner personally and being partial to his discourses which seldom even allude to any particular tenets. Of these I know no more than just that they disavow the doctrine of the Trinity as founded of the Scriptures. And by the way from an excellently written article I *once* read in the Edinburgh review attempting to prove that the only verse in the bible where this trinity is distinctly asserted – is an interpolation, I am rather inclined to agree in this opinion.

My religious sentiments, and they have not been adopted without due and serious consideration are perhaps rather peculiar; but I shall I trust, never build my hopes of happiness hereafter on foundations of bigotry to any one sect or church.

In the afternoon I went to St Nicholas anticipating a good sermon from Mr Griffiths the evening lecturer. Another gentleman mounted the pulpit, and after commencing by enforcing a new and certainly ridiculous idea to say the least of it – *viz*: that Christ's expressions towards his Mother were always harsh and not in his usual mild style of discourse – from which the lecturer concluded that our saviour had a foreknowledge of and wish to obviate as much as possible the idolatrous worship paid to her by the Romish church (!!) This clergyman gave us a tolerable discourse upon the necessity of constant attention to religious duties. One expression may shew however to what an extent some persons carry their zeal in these matters. In speaking of the importance of the above duties they were contrasted with worldly enjoyments – one antithesis was 'the pursuits of literature and science which bring only pleasure but not profit'!!!! This coming from an enlightened minister of the Church of England certainly made me lift up my eyes in amazement.

---

3 Turner was minister at the Newcastle Unitarian Church: see 'My Autobiography', note 61.

Lectures get on swimmingly. Patients doing well.
[*Patient numbers*]

November 1 *Thursday*
I spent a very pleasant evening at Mr Brocketts and came away
from the whist table about 11 PM *minus* 1/-.
A little after two AM I was called to an accident which had
happened at Heaton. A man [*Ramshaw*] was said to have received
a fracture of the leg. Mr McIntyre was in the way but ordered
both horses to be saddled; his mare for me and King was to
accompany me on the chestnut. To Byker Hill therefore we went
and there a severe compound fracture presented itself! After
examining the injury so as to ascertain its exact extent I
despatched King (having well weighed the measure in my mind)
into town for Mr McIntyre. My reasons for this were manifold,
but need not be particularised here. *Inclination* was against the
measure but *reason* dictated the opposite. Lest however Mr McIntyre *should* suppose I had sent for him from inability to manage
the case alone, I, as soon as King was gone, reduced the fracture
having cleaned the wound and taken away with the help of my
scalpel two tolerably large splinters from the tibia, laid the leg
upon the splint thus leaving all open for Mr McI's inspection, and
yet having only the bandages to be put on should the position &
c be approved. When Mr McI came he (under the idea I suppose
that the people had wished him sent for, though to my surprize
they never once asked for him till I named his being brought)
said it was *very well reduced* and rather pouted at having been
called out! We got the patient put to bed and though he today
complains of severe aching in the knee, evidently proceeding
from injury to the tibial sleeve, he is doing 'as well as can be
expected'.
My F & M sent to Mr McI a paper of mine upon his splint to
read not long ago and though he took little notice of it and rather
poked me upon the subject at the time; I cannot help observing a
material change in his behaviour – never anything less than civil
and attentive but now approaching to a degree of familiarity his
reserve never before permitted. Some circumstances have most
fortunately combined, of late, to put my conduct while in his
establishment before him in a favorably contrasted light. Those
together with a secret, private matter I am able to serve his *interest*
in just at present all combine to produce the good effects I have

noted. My only wish on the subject is that the impressions on both sides may be rather more lasting than has so far been the case.

[*Patient numbers*]

November 4 *Sunday*
Having sent my paper to Mr Turner got my model ready and all prepared for the Society,[4] I will occupy a little leisure this morning in making up the deficiencies in my Diary.

Tuesday night will be an epoch of great importance in my calendar. My *ambition* is to be admitted into the class of *philosophers*; and to take a standing, humble though it be, among scientific men. This will be my first attempt in public – my *debut* upon the stage of learning and art; and, as first impressions are always most powerful, my *anxiety* regarding the reception of this 'address' is, of course, great. I have been careful not to allow my expectations too high a flight which will render an unfavourable issue less unpleasant to my feelings. The subject treated is one of first rate importance in this neighborhood and the Society professes itself mainly attentive to anything connected with the coaltrade. Circumstances being thus far in its favor, the machine must either be devoid of merit – an assertion I cannot by any means allow, – or the fault must rest with my delivery of the address and failure in making myself properly understood. If, then, the invention fades into obscurity *I* attribute the blame only to myself; if any honor is obtained my claim to a small share of the credit will, I am sure, not be unappreciated.

Wallsend patient [*Soulsby? 14/10/27*] doing well. Fracture [*Ramshaw, see below*] as well as can be looked for.

[*Magaziniana no. 21: 'On Dreams'*]

Evening, Mr McI, King & I have been at Byker Hill dressing Ramshaws leg. Mr McI promised to meet me at $2\frac{1}{2}$ PM but as he had not arrived at $4\frac{1}{2}$ I proceeded to open out the dressings. The bones had slipped from their apposition the apposthis surfaces being very small after the splinters had been extracted. I re-reduced the bones and having dressed the wound put on the bandages with additional cards & splints so as to prevent if possible the recurrence of any displacement. When all was done and I was set get-

---

4 See note 1 above.

ting a 'dish of tea' Mr McI arrived i.e. *only* three hours behind his appointed time. He unloosed a small part of the bandage but finding 'all right' proceeded to no further examination.

A man [*Todd*] at Biggs Main still required seeing, and while visiting him I had the opportunity of seeing my old patient [*Armstrong*] mentioned July 14 Vol: 4. This severe injury is not now distinguishable except by a small scar along the top of the foot and the loss of power in one of the toes. This case was altogether my own. No one ever saw him but myself excepting one visit from Mr McI when the boy was recovering.

November 14 *Wednesday*
The Society business & bustle has passed over and still I see no prospect of having more leisure for my Diary remarks. My time is now more fully occupied than before with a new and extensive undertaking *viz* the making out of the years accounts. This will be a source of constant employment for me for the remainder of the year and will be about as much *writing* labour as I shall care for. Nevertheless it will be a hard case if I cannot squeeze a word or two now and then into my Journal.

Last Tuesday evening passed off very much to my gratification at the Society's meeting.[5] About 35 members were present forming the most numerous monthly meeting I have attended. Mr Boyd the Banker was president for the night and I was called to his and Mr Turner's right hand, taking possession indeed of the secretaries desk – to read my paper. I have had the pleasure of hearing nothing but compliments from all who were present and I must say *I* was very well satisfied with *myself* on the occasion.

With the exception of the foregoing, no further notice has been taken of the machine. It has stood on the Society's table ever since the meeting and has been examined by many persons but *I* have not been applied to by any. A friend (Mr Charnley) warned me of the inventions failed to be adopted unless it was supported by the *patronage* of some great viewer as Mr Buddle &c. Mr B has not seen it; but Mr McI who thinks the model 'very ingenious'

5 See note 1 above. The Lit. and Phil. Annual Report, 1827, states 'Mr T.G. Wright read a Paper describing the ingenious invention of his father, for raising water, coals &c without changing the direction of the power employed, or in any way endangering the safety of the workmen.' For the comments of some of the coal owners and managers on the machine, see 18/1/28.

says he is to see it as soon as I get it from the library. My debut
(which I before spoke of) has, therefore, been very fairly to my
satisfaction, and seeing *I* acquitted myself sufficiently well there
is no cause left for any future neglect of the machine, according
to the reason I used three pages back. Should the invention be no
more heard of I must adopt Mr Charnley's opinion and conclude
the desideratum wanted was *Patronage*.

I cannot take leave of the subject however without here
expressing my thanks to my Mother for her effective assistance
in modelling and correcting the 'Address' I read to the Society.

Ramsay [*previously spelt Ramshaw, 4/11/27*], *Byker Hill* is now
doing pretty well. A pair of forceps have been contrived and
made for preserving the apposition of the fractured bones, which
answer the purpose tolerably. Another fractured leg [*Todd*?] has
occurred at Biggs Main which improves every day. The Patient
has had no pain since the fracture was reduced on Friday and I
had him out of bed yesterday. Both bones are broken but Mr McI
has never had occasion to see the man since the day we were
called out to him
[*Patient numbers*]

November 28 *Wednesday*
A short month this, gentle reader, but I hope you are not disappointed for you know it is only in accordance with my promise
that I have these large gaps. A half hour just now however gives
me opportunity for inserting a remark or two on a few conspicuous events in these last three weeks.
Imprimis I have just now got into regular working trim a new
mare and the chestnut horse I before spoke of has been sold. He
was offered and shewed and displayed at two fairs but no dealer
would (according to their expressions) 'look at him'. At last he *is*
sold and a pretty little black nag Mr McI had bought nearly a
month since but so far used entirely in the gig has now become
my steed. By careful tuition and kind treatment I have brought
this one already into a degree of docility I hope yet to improve
upon. Though I have only ridden her 10 days the animal will
follow me along the road without any hold of the reins and stand
at the patients doors till I come out following me from one to
another like a dog. As yet I dare not place much confidence in her
fidelity but in a little while these qualities will be found extremely
useful in a surgeons steed. The former practice too is useful on

frosty days when a walk in pleasant to relieve the cold inactivity of the saddle.

After puzzling my head in vain for a classic appellative for this favorite I at length fixed upon plain *'Fanny'* by which she is conscious of being spoken to.

On Sunday afternoon I attended service at All Saints to hear the sacred music then and there to be performed by the 'Gateshead Choral Society'. About fifty formed the band. The opening chorus was very well sung and hence I anticipated a treat throughout. The church was as closely packed with people as the wood-work (the only space left not occupied by human beings) would permit; and the congregation could not be far under 4000 people. The effect of the hundredth psalm in which most of these joined was sublime in the extreme, and I was in one of the best situations in the church for enjoying it. I anticipated a climax of rapture with the Hallelujah chorus of the Messiah which was to conclude the whole but never was any one more grievously disappointed. The counter tenors shouting, for roaring is too mild a term – bellowing is perhaps more expressive; and the altos and trebles squalling with the basses *howling* (those these last did acquit themselves the best if any) were altogether much too *powerful* for my ears and almost enough to destroy the effects of the previous music. Dr Gibbs of Durham preached a sermon for the benefit of the Church Missionary Societies and a plentiful harvest would be secured by the collectors I should think, though I have not yet heard the amount.

Lectures prosper. I have just finished 'the viscera' and tomorrow commence 'the organs of sense' by a lecture on the *eye* which I hope to make the most brilliant part of the course.
[*Patient numbers*]

December 2 *Sunday*
A fractured clavicle was added to the list of broken bones on the books at present. The boy [*McKid*] who got the accident on Friday night is my patient and will, I doubt not, do well.

Ramshaw's leg [*14/11/28*] is assuming more of a settled appearance than at all since his accident. The granulations have so far filled up the previous loss of substance as to retain the fractured bones nearly *in situ*. The forceps I mentioned though they assisted in keeping them steady seldom were able to prevent displacement from one dressing to another; the fracture was literally

therefore to *reset* most every day. Though the ends of the bone are not so correctly in apposition as one could wish they are so far straight as to allow good hopes that no deformity will be perceptible and that the limb will be of the same length as full as strong as the other. Notwithstanding the strumous habit of the patient and a previous weak state of health the suppuration is healthy and the wound rapidly cicatrizing. The Mg^d Petrolee[6] has had a very good effect in this case causing the granulations, as Mr McI observed, to sprout up like cauliflowers
[*Patient numbers*]

December 13 *Thursday*
It is now a matter of surprize to me how I ever found materials for filling up a daily annotation. When during a lapse of weeks and in full occupation I now meet with nothing important enough to be noted.

In the course of the next week I expect my Father & Mother will arrive in Newcastle to spend here part of the winter – probably three months. I have succeeded in engaging for them extremely comodious lodgings – in appearance, and within a hop step & jump of our own door so that I hope to spend many a pleasant leisure hour with them in an evening.

The course of lectures which have engrossed good part of my spare time for this month or two are to be concluded tomorrow night, which will happen very *apropos* for my F & M coming. My speechification has of late been a full hour or hour and quarter. I have derived great benefit from the practice and I have been gratified on examination nights with the progress my pupils have made under my tuition.

Ramshaw's leg is now uniting, the wound nearly healed; but extensive abscesses discharge a quantity of pus which leaves the patient still in a very weak state. His general health remains tolerably good but his constitution never was a healthy one. [2/12/27]

I have had a galloping fortnight with accidents but no bones broke. A number of severe medical cases on the books just now, too, keep me and my mare in full employment.

J Gibson is better now than for some months past but he is still unable to get downstairs. His elbow admits of a very trifling degree of motion. [5/9/27]

---

6 Probably an ointment of petroleum jelly and magnesium oxide.

Besides all I have mentioned as subjects of business and employment there has been the annual hubbub of the accounts writing out. All these are I am happy to say (with the exception of one colliery bill) ready made up to the last day of entry in the ledger so that a fortnights labour as soon as the new year comes in adding up and finishing off will complete this disagreeably tiresome job.

[*Patient numbers*]

December 26 *Wednesday*

My Father & Mother are now comfortably settled in Newcastle for a few weeks. This is another arrangement which will have the effect in diminishing the number and length of my Diary remarks. Indeed the office of Diarist is now almost a sinecure and it is probable the succeeding leaves will continue in a blank state for some time. The return of Spring along with its other vivifying effect may restore some degree of animation to my quill but I am afraid it will have to continue in a very torpid state during the winter.

[*Patient numbers*]

1828

January 1 *Tuesday*

Many happy returns of this day to you, dear reader, and may each succeeding one bring a renewed supply of causes for contentment and happiness. This seems to me to be the best wish I can present you with; and if you, as I hope will be the case, return the compliment I shall further pray that both may be fulfilled.

The arrival of new year's day is calculated to awaken feelings of various *castes* in any individual according to circumstances but as I am *inclined* to regard the season more as the old fashioned Xmas of innocent mirth & revelry than that in which the gloomy zeal of religious fanatics so prevalent in this age, is to be at its darkest pitch, I would if I could commence the year with a few lines of rhyme but as unfortunately

> 'The God of Verse & Physic too' – only
> 'Inspires me twice a year'

and this it seems is not one of the inspiring moments; we must e'en wait for that till some more favorable hour. Instead either of saying more in plain prose I find business calls me away at present.

January 4 *Friday*
What will not perseverance industry & method accomplish! The accounts for finishing off which I had set apart at least a week or ten days are already completed
'Credat Iudaeus Appella!'[7]
[*Magaziniana No 22: 'Rides in the country', no 1, chapter 1*]
[*Patient numbers*]

January 8 *Tuesday*
On Saturday night I had the pleasure of hearing Mr Vandenhoff play Hamlet and also in a new piece – Cardillac in the Goldsmith.[8] The former part was fine but the latter piece, tho' Mr V made the most of his character, was paltry after the Shakespeare.
[*Patient numbers*]

January 18 *Friday*
I have before had occasion to hint at the insubordination and irregularities of my juniors in the Surgery, but it is a long time since I gave up the practice of reproof or any sort of remonstrance. I left things to take their course hoping that Mr McIntyre would eventually have his eyes opened to their conduct. It was not till eight days since, and then in consequence of an appeal from me, that this wished for event took place; A pretty sharp verbal correction was the consequence; but that very night affairs instead of being amended took if anything a worse turn. The following morning Mr McI made strict enquiry of me 'how the youths had behaved, and who was out last night?' Spearman the youngest and most incorrigible was packed off at five minutes warning and the other admonished to beware of a similar fate.

Mr McI has since unadvisedly taken the expelled back again under promises of amendment. I say unadvisedly because no

---

7 'Ap[p]ella the Jew may believe it': Horace, *Sermones*, 1.5, line 100. TGW implies that his achievement seems incredible.
8 This was the actor Mr Vandenhoff's benefit night, his final appearance at the Theatre Royal. Miss Jervis played Ophelia. The after-piece, *The Goldsmith*, never before acted in Newcastle, had been performed in London 'with unbounded applause . . . upwards of 36 nights. . .': see NRPB.

signs of amendment or alteration are at all manifest in the scoundrel.

I spent a very pleasant evening on Tuesday last at my F & M's lodgings to meet a few friends at a game at 'Pope'[9] and a little music. Miss McIntyre, the Miss Crawfords, Mr C & Mr Brockett were of the party. I asked Mr Henzell; but he was prevented joining us.

Yesterday in my round I called with a message upon Major Johnson of Byker; and after a very obliging invitation partook of his excellent roast hare and wine.

After a tedious month since last report [2/12/27], Ramshaw's leg continues little improved. A severe attack of erythematic inflammation has been got the better of and the limb after free incisions is again on the road to recovery.

A child severely burnt at Byker and two extensive burns at Felling all requiring daily attendance are doing well.

Mr Buddle, Major Johnson & Mr Carr – three great colliery managers & owners have seen and examined my model[10] and all agree that the idea is highly ingenious and the machine 'very *natty*' but would be too complicated and expensive for general use. The pitmen too they find do not like innovations especially mechanical ones which shall lessen the demand for manual labour.

[*Patient numbers*]

January 26 *Saturday*
Well might I say it was 'unadvised' in Mr McIntyre to take back the youth he expelled when he had occasion to pack him off or rather to send for a police officer to him after ten days further trial. But what remark I am to make on the fact that he has again been reinstated in his office I know not. After what I have borne and the treatment I have received from both this young man and his colleague it is impossible I can ever be on any terms but those of the most distance and contempt. I still have it in my power to be comfortable & independent in my situation *et me suffice a moimême*.

Today has brought intelligence of a mournful event in the sup-

---

9 Pope was a round game of cards, also known as Pope Joan. Charles Dickens describes a lively game of Pope Joan in *Pickwick Papers*, chapter 6.
10 See notes 1 and 5 above.

posed shipwreck of a cousin of mine on the 7th ult: I have never seen the youth these twelve years; but relationship makes his melancholy fate an object of more than ordinary sorrow to me. He was about my own age.
[*Patient numbers*]

February 4 *Monday*
Going – Going & gone seems to have been Mr McIntyres motto on taking back our worthless sub the last time. Indeed an agreement was I understand entered into then that if the youth ever more offended it should be the last; and from an expression dropped by Miss McI I conclude that her brother was pretty well aware of the truth that this would soon happen. He was last night so drunk he absolutely could not stand – the third or fourth time since he returned but the first Mr McI has observed. Today he was set off and I hope for the benefit of all parties concerned it may be for the last time, and that this page may be the last I shall have to sully with mention of him.

I went up to Mr Crawfords on Monday last to meet Miss Halls, their Aunt & a Miss Clarke all of Westgate Hill. Just as we were beginning to get acquainted and feel social I was called away to take a ride in the country.

Ramshaw is improving [*18/1/28*]. Burns all cured, i.e. those previously mentioned; but a very severe case has occurred next door to us of a young woman [Jackson] who set herself on fire and which will be a tedious case.
[*Patient numbers*]

February 13 *Wednesday*
When mentioning a diminution of our establishment in the number of juniors I did not anticipate an increase of seniors in so short a time. A young gentleman who happens to be an old friend of mine Mr Sang[11] has been engaged as assistant in conjunction with myself. He is to take the town department and attend Midwifery cases while I retain as usual my country & colliery practice. As bringing me an agreeable companion I am very much

---

11 John Sang was born in Scotland c.1807. He was in general practice in Newcastle from about 1834 until after 1875: see Tyne and Wear Archives Service, DX 56/1.

pleased by the change and as taking from my shoulders a part, at any rate, of the odium in managing the juniors I also have good reason to be thankful. I shall have more leisure therefore for study and reading than formerly (perhaps a little more for filling up this volume which still looks very blank & blue upon it) without losing any material part of the practical advantages belonging to my situation.

Under the rose I do not think our new assistant is intended to remain long in the department at present assigned him but meanwhile I have an agreeable companion.

[*Patient numbers*]

February 29 *Friday*
On Saturday night last I went over to Mr Brocketts for an hour or two and found an assemblage of gentlemen very busy emptying the decanter on occasion of his birthday.

I forgot to mention having had the pleasure of seeing Messrs Pyle, Brockett, Henzell & Sang to play a game of whist about ten days since at my Father & Mother's lodgings.

On Tuesday I dined *by invitation* at Mr McIntyres table to meet my F & M. Mother was poorly and could not come. I underline 'by invitation' because I think it should not be needful at any time whether there was a dinner party or not for the young gentlemen of the establishment to have any invitation to what ought to be a matter of course. Nor do I like the arrangement which separated my fellow pupils from table though I was *invited*.

Pursuant to an invitation through Mr Sang I on Wednesday evening accepted an appointment to join a party and dance at Mr Burnups – friends of Sang , and with whom the latter is likely to be more intimately connected. I met about 30 and we kept up the dancing till an *early* hour. To enumerate all present were needless but not to mention the names of my partners were ungallant. Among them are Miss Burnup & Miss Ann D°, their cousins Misses Fanny & Mary Burnup, Miss Rogers, the Misses Morris – Sangs cousins, Miss Mary Sang, Miss Allan &c &c

I danced quadrilles for the first time and did not find it a very difficult matter to get through. My only declining two dances proves how much I enjoyed the occasion and I felt less fatigued yesterday than I expected.

[*Patient numbers*]

March 10 *Monday*
Last Tuesday was the annual meeting of the Lit & Phil: Society
when a number of motions were made opposed and carried or
negatived. Mr Rayne figured away as before and we had a very
neat speech or two from my friend Mr W. H. Brockett. I voted
with the majority on every question. Mr C. W. Bigge in the Chair.
On Wednesday evening I went to a card party at Mr Bracketts
and played a very pleasant game at Pope. About 26 ladies &
gentlemen were there – who I know not. But I do know I got
set between two nice lassies at the card table, enjoyed myself in
laughing with them till my sides ached; and was obliged very
reluctantly to tear myself away from pope and the pretty Miss
Rutherfords about eleven oclock.
[*Patient numbers*]

March 31 *Monday*
A daily journey to Newburn [*Patterson*] about 6 miles from hence,
and very frequently the visit repeated twice in the twenty four
hours has so far kept me employed that I have no leisure to think
about anything but business, otherwise the inclination to resume
my Diary remarks more at length is I find returning (as I
prophesied) with the coming in of Spring.
My Father & Mother leave next week after which my time will
be more at my own disposal and will require some occupation to
fill up my leisure.
Mem: I have today been hiring a violoncello for a few weeks,
having taken a desire to learn the instrument in addition to my
flute. I hope to have my first bass lesson tonight.
[*Patient numbers*]

April 11 *Friday*
My Father took his final departure from Newcastle this day week
and my Mother proceeded to join him at Sunderland on Tuesday.
I am now once more therefore left to my own resources and
though I may feel time hang rather heavily on my hands for a
day or two and miss the accustomed walk down street every
leisure hour to which I have been for four months daily accustomed I hope to be able as I feel strongly the inclination to make
good use of the more secluded state I now enjoy recalling to my
aid my old and for some time past neglected companions my
books and pen.

This trifle shall experience the change if my brains will bear me out in my resolution and as after a cold and variable season Spring has this week fairly commenced I gladly remember my former hint and *resolve* to start seriously, vigorously, & diligently to refresh my memory of my old and add fresh stores of new information literary & scientific in the fullest sense of the words i.e. comprehending all known knowledge *de omnibus rebus et quibusdam aliis*.

Ramshaw after one or two very severe & dangerous attacks of inflammation is still unable to get on to his crutches. He sits up an hour or two daily. [4/2/28]

The case of severe burn I mentioned [*Jackson, 4/2/28*] died after three weeks care.

A very serious case of comp^d fracture of the leg in an exceedingly stout intemperate man happened on the 1st at Wallsend to Mr Towns a butcher and terminated fatally on Wednesday.

The patient at Newburn [*Patterson, 31/3/28*] is considerably better and only requires a visit once in two or three days.

J Gibson has been in the country at his uncles for three months and is recovered sufficiently to get out a little in the gig, – but mends very slowly. [13/12/27]

[*Patient numbers*]

April 14 *Monday*

I went last evening to hear a very popular lecturer at St John's[12] and a most extraordinary sermon was delivered in which the preacher predicted the destruction of the world by fire as very close at hand. The subject was taken from the words 'As it was in the days of Noah so shall it also be in the days of the son of man.'[13] These words, which at first sight would seem to apply to the days of our Saviour, we were told allude to the second annihilation of the world and that as the present age (such was evidently the purpose of the discourse) has arrived at the same stage of wickedness, irreligion and scepticism, which preceded the flood the accomplishment of a similar catastrophe was to a certainty near.

---

12 St John's Church in Westgate Street, Newcastle: see MacKenzie 1827, pp. 342–57.
13 Matthew 24, 37.

The clergyman's style of eloquence is peculiar and very powerful, calculated to strike forcefully on the feelings of his audience; but his influence is over the fears by terror and dread rather than over the opposite passions by inspiring sentiments the most pleasing to a Deity – those of gratitude and love. The former however seems to be the prevailing style of the day. A picture of the flood with its preceding events was given in last nights discourse in a truly sublime manner and was itself enough to inspire a high opinion of the author's power and induce me to take the next opportunity of hearing another of his lectures. *Then* I shall perhaps notice more particularly Mr Taylor's method of reading the Litany which indeed is that of most clergymen and is far from accordance with the sense and tenor of the words.[14]

April 15 *Tuesday*
I have this afternoon tried upon a poor odontalgic damsel the effect of Mr Fay's summary method of tooth drawing by nipping off their bodies with his awful looking forceps. Mr McIntyre got a set of these lately and used them unsuccessfully upon a lady's jaw nor have I so far better reason to think favorably of the plan.

By reason of my mare's being lame having fallen with me about a fortnight since – and in consequence of my frequent visits west-a-way[15] – I have been seldom among my Heaton patients lately who were full of congratulations on my having found the way back again. Though they like Mr Sang 'varra weel' and as a varra canny young man but they think he looks young like and they like to see someone with mair experience. Now though in the matter of experience this may be true enough; yet the taking me for Sang's senior in age – who is twelvemonths older and a member of Apothecaries Hall[16] to boot makes me pull up my collar and look *very* wise upon the subject.

---

14 TGW presented more of his views on the litany in Magaziniana 24, Volume 6, 4/5/28.

15 'West-a-way' probably means visits to patient at Newburn: see 31/3/28.

16 This implies that, unlike TGW at this time, Sang had a Licence awarded by the Society of Apothecaries, i.e., he was licensed to practice medicine. See Introduction.

April 16 *Wednesday*
I am very glad to have to recant the assertion I made yesterday
of Mr Fays apparatus. The patient then mentioned today declares
that as soon as she got home the tooth became quite easy and has
not troubled her since. Should the plan be effectual it is
undoubted a less painful operation than the extraction of the
whole tooth.
[*Patient numbers*]

April 21 *Tuesday*
Mr Sang who has been for some time past complaining of palpitations of the heart & sundry other nervous affections left us last
Wednesday to breath for a while his native air among the vales
of the Tweed. His stay is indefinite; indeed if another more prom-
ising situation should offer his return here at all will be unlikely,
a stipulation to that effect being made on Sang's coming to Mr
McI. It may seem a little odd indeed for the latter gentleman to
make so loose an agreement or to take an extra assistant at all;
but this may be accounted for by a number of reasons; though be
it observed altogether unconnected with *me* but rather dependent
on Mr Cochranes movements & intentions.

From some conversation Mr McI held with J Sang on his
coming to this situation I was to hope that a plan I had very
much at heart would be accomplished *viz* my being present at
the opening of the new London University and being enrolled
among its first students.[17] Mr McI has however more lately told
my Father that he is afraid he cannot spare me so soon (October)
and if Sang leaves us altogether I shall be still more unlikely to
get released till my full term is expired. Be it at its longest however – somewhat short of eleven months is a brief future to one
who has spent already nearly five years in this junior department

---

17 The University of London opened in 1828, with medicine as one of the subjects
    taught. Before this, England had no university-type medical schools like those
    in Edinburgh and Germany; apart from Oxford and Cambridge, which were
    open to Anglicans only, medical teaching was confined to teaching hospitals.
    The University of London, which had no religious entrance requirements and
    no teaching of religion, did not have a royal charter and was unable to award
    degrees. In 1836, the original University of London became University College
    in a new University of London, which also included King's College, founded
    in 1829. Under the new charter both colleges could grant degrees. See N. Harte,
    The University of London 1836–1986 (London and New Jersey, 1986).

of the profession, though time seems to lag as the final period approaches.

April 25 *Friday*
The great guns of the Castle and sundry vollies of small arms together with ringing of bells and drinking of wine, announced Wednesday to be the birthday of this present Majesty.[18]

Today the first which could be called Spring since the quarter came in. I have had a pleasant ride to Felling. As the wind appears to be settled in the west I prognosticate a continuance of clear weather though the season has so far been very disagreeable and very unhealthy. We had so large a taste of Spring in January that we naturally must look for a slice or two of winter in this more genial season.

Some two or three months since I applied to a patient a French remedy I had seen used by Dr Knox with considerable relief and was happy in obtaining a similar success. Having mentioned the circumstance to Mr Church, and recommending to him the perusal of a work on the subject with which I have been much interested (Wallace on Moxa[19]) he requested me to operate on a patient in the infirmary who is in every way a fit subject for the experiment by way of making trial of the effects. The operation consists of burning a piece of pith or rolled lint upon the skin with a blowpipe and is very successfully employed by continental surgeons.

Prejudice is the only assignable cause of Moxa not being in general use among English practitioners, but it is scarcely known among our *materia chirurgica*.

I shall watch with solicitude the case [*McDermot*] at present under treatment and should it succeed I shall have had the honor of first introducing the operation into the Newcastle Infirmary,

---

18 The reigning king was George IV, who had been Prince Regent from 1811 until he ascended the throne on the death of George III in 1820. He died in 1830, aged 67.

19 The work on Moxa referred to is probably William Wallace, *A Physiological Enquiry Respecting the Action of Moxa, and its Utility in Inveterate Cases of Sciatica, Lumbago, Paraplegia, Epilepsy, and some other Painful, Paralytic and Spasmodic Diseases of the Nerves and Muscles* (Dublin, 1827). Moxa, or moxibustion, is a method of disease treatment in which a moxa, i.e., a small cylinder or cone usually made from dried mugwort leaves, is burned over the skin, with the aid of a blow-pipe. It is still used in traditional Chinese medicine.

as I have already been the only one who has ever employed it in the north of England.[20] You, gentle reader, shall have early notice of my success.

[*Magaziniana No. 28 Rides in the Country Chapter 2*]
[*Patient numbers*]

May 3 *Saturday*
I was prevented on Sunday from even commencing my intended remarks but they will find vent if I have leisure tomorrow, being upon rather a Sunday subject.

John Gibson whom I have often had occasion [*11/4/28*] to mention as a friend and patient now comes to be named here I hope for the last time. He has left England for a sojourn in a milder climate (Bordeaux) and will not probably return ere I leave NCastle. Though for his sake and on account of our former friendship I looked over, but could not forget some unpleasant occurrences the winter after my leaving Edinburgh. I could not possibly remain in any degree of intimacy with the family after the slights offered to my Father & Mother this last winter. Not a word of an unfriendly nature has passed between any of us, but John first left the town and now has left the country without my seeing him; nor have I been in the house these 3 months.

It would be tedious as well as disagreeable here to enter into all particulars of what has passed. I am sorry for it as I must say many pleasant evenings I have spent with the family. The cause of their behaviour to me I cannot divine but it differs lamentably from the professions of obligation I have always been accustomed to receive from them and is equally unaccountable and ungrateful both to me and to my friends, who had also at my request shewn kindness to one of the young ladies when opportunity offered.

'Fanny' continues lame – her lameness being produced by a blister put on after her fall. She was used in the gig immediately on the application of this and the consequence was an inflammation of the whole limb and subsequent infirmity. I have had a pit

---

20 [*TGW footnote*] From the remedy being so little known and so many enquiries being made of me concerning it, also from never having heard the name mentioned among provincial surgeons I was led to the conclusion I have here expressed. Since then however I have been informed of one solitary case in which Moxa was used with success by Mr John Fife of this town.

galloway[21] on trial for a day or two; but on my unfavourable report being seconded by the groom's, it was returned as deficient in action. I shall be sorry to lose my old favorite and hope she may by time and gentle usage get sound though she never will be safe.

I just popped in last night to see the first representation of a drama by an acquaintance of mine, a young Cantab – Mr John Forster. The piece was announced as an attraction for the benefit of Mr Stuart the principal tragedian of the company. This gentleman did his part ample justice, and though there was no great talent in the composition it was sufficiently creditable to a lad as a first attempt. After repeated plaudits during the acting three rounds of applause were at the fall of the curtain given to the author of 'Charles the 2nd' or the 'Cavalier of Wildinghurst'.[22]

Mr Mitchell the Editor of the Newcastle Maga: has produced a very successful drama from the story of Pierce Shea in Tales of the O'Hara family this season but an interlude (in the last no. of the Maga)[23] was the other night 'indulgently damned'.

May 4 *Sunday*
I have been twice to hear Mr Taylor since I remarked on his style and still retain the same sentiments as before expressed. I shall however take this opportunity to say a few words on the manner of *reading* the forms of prayer usually adopted by the clergymen of the church of England, and which forcibly apply to the above gentleman at present the most popular preacher in this town. I did intend to express here also my sentiments on the doctrines of the present day but as they extend to more lengthy reasoning I will endeavour to throw my ideas together in a separate essay on the subject, in which give a more rational & pleasing aspect to devotion – for such only can true devotion be and to excite it

21 The pit galloway was a small, strong, breed of horse, largely used for work in the coal-mines.
22 The full title of the play was *Charles at Tunbridge, or, The Cavalier at Wildinghurst* described as 'a new petite Play in 2 Acts, written especially for the occasion by a Gentleman of Newcastle' – the author is not named in the playbill: see NRPB.
23 The text of Mitchell's 'interlude' was published in the *Newcastle Magazine*, April 1828.

rather by the prospect of a heavenly paradise than the dread of the opposite abyss.

[*Magaziniana No 24 On the Litany*]

May 10 *Saturday*

After what I have said of the Gibsons I am forced to recur again to the subject and was surprized yesterday to receive a box ticket to the Theatre enclosed with 'Mr Taylor Gibson's comp^ts to Mr Wright'!! I was at first tempted to return enclosure and all and was for ten minutes really *vexed* about it. I soon set myself down however to pen & paper and reenclosed the ticket on the plea of being engaged. The affront, for such I cannot but consider it, will explain itself, and was quite unnecessary in the present state of affairs.

All the family were at the Theatre last night I hear. It was Mr Nicholson's[24] benefit (a customer of Mr G's) and the last night of the season.

[*Patient numbers*]

May 16 *Friday*

I threatened to write a sermon, gentle reader, and I *have* written one a real veritable full half hours sermon! One which I shall be happy, on the offer of a pulpit and the express wish of the congregation, to preach without a fee. It is entitled 'A discourse on true Devotion as the means of real happiness' and the text is from Psalm xix verse 14 – 'Let the words of my mouth and the meditations of my heart be acceptable in thy sight O Lord, my strength and my redeemer'.

We have had a severe case of internal bruise at Heaton. The patient [*Holmes*] was seen three times each day at first and was then most dangerously situate but is now doing extremely well. Fanny's lameness almost well.

Though my opinion of Mr Forster's play (mentioned May 3) was favorable to one or two of the parts I could not but see a sad discrepancy in others not at all in semblance with the rest. From a severe critique in the following Tyne Mercury[25] I find – and state it here in justice to Mr F's authorship, that while Mr Stuart played *well* in his character few of his brother performers knew

---

24 Mr Nicholson was then manager of the Theatre Royal.
25 See *Tyne Mercury*, 6/5/28, p.2, column 4.

their parts – Some did not repeat six words allotted to them and
the principal personage the chevalier was quite an altered being
from what the writer depicted him. Those who have seen the
M.S. speak very highly of the production but I have unfortunately
never once met Mr Forster since that important night.
[*Patient numbers*]

May 23 *Friday*
I was called from the infirmary yesterday by a visit from my
Mother who had come over on some shopping concerns which I
had been making enquiry about for her. Two accidents happened
while she was in town to one of which I paid attention and
returned just in time to see the coach off in which she was passenger.

Mr Sang is expected back tonight and if circumstances will
allow I hope to cross Sunderland bridge and spend a night or
two at F & M's lodgings before they proceed to Stockton which
will be in about 3 weeks hence.

Hazlitts Life of Napoleon[26] has provided me a fund of delightful occupation of late and having previously read with great
interest O'Meara[27] & Antonmarchi's[28] journals. Mr Hazlitt's style
and principles are exactly to my taste independently of the large
stock of excellent general observations with which his work
abounds. Sir W. Scotts voluminous Biography of the Emperor
seems to be entirely under government direction and support[29]
that after perusing it Mr H's unfettered and clear reasoning car-
ries conviction in every case by its impartiality. Les Oevres de
Molière – the vols containing his comedies have, with Bell's
Observations on Italy[30], furnished me with *light* reading since my

26 William Hazlitt (1778–1830) began his *Life of Napoleon* in 1827. TGW must be
referring to the first and second volumes published in 1828; the final two volumes were not published until 1830: see *DNB*, IX, p. 317.
27 Barry Edward O'Meara (1786–1836) published several works on Napoleon,
starting about 1817.
28 Probably *The Last Days of Emperor Napoleon* (London, 1825) by Francesco
Antommarchi (1780–1838).
29 [*TGW footnote*] To say nothing of its hasty composition and numerous blun-
ders. [*For comments on Scott's Napoleon see also 27/7/27 and Volume 4, note 22.*]
30 *Observations on Italy*, an account of travels in Europe by John Bell, surgeon,
FRCS Edinburgh (1736–1820), edited by Rosina A. Bell, was published in 1825
(Edinburgh and London).

F & M left while Johnson on the Stomach,[31] Wallace on Moxa,[32] Bell's plates of the nerves[33] &c have been my professional occupation. Violoncello has not been forgot.

May 25 *Sunday*
As this volume and the month are speedily approaching their last moment I must hasten to conclude – tho' in a hasty way – the 'journey' I have undertaken; more especially as materials are sketched out for another subject to begin with the next volume. The *sketches* are more quickly, though not more easily formed, than detailed and time & inclination rarely occur in affording opportunity for giving a shade to the outline.

I am extremely well pleased to observe the small space which intervenes between this and 'Finis' – or rather the space I intend that Latin conclusion to all English beginnings to occupy – for I am heartily tired of this long used number. I believe if I get not quicker forward with the next I shall be obliged to put only a $\frac{1}{2}$ dozen leaves in each that at any rate I may have a new title page and clean back to look at occasionally.
[*Magaziniana No. 25 Rides in the Country Chapter 3*]
[*Patient numbers*]

May 27 *Tuesday*
Many a week has passed since I have been treated with a 'ride in the country' by night; but at midnight's fearful hour or rather just after the clock struck one this morning, I received a summons to see a man [*Pethy*] at Wallsend belonging to Walker colliery. The night was very rainy but armed against the weather by a stout great coat and old hat I set out for my place of destination. On the road I learned from the messenger that though the good man had happened his accident before 10 PM he was so very *considerate* i.e. had taken such a length of time for mature deliberation as to the exact nature of his injury, that the doctor was not sent for till three hours had elapsed and I had fallen into a sound, – sound sleep.

---

31 Probably *An Essay on Morbid Sensibility of the Stomach and Bowels* (London, 1827) by James Johnson, MD (1777–1845).
32 See note 19, above.
33 Bell's plates of the nerves were probably *A Series of Engravings, Explaining the Course of the Nerves,* by Sir Charles Bell (1774–1842). The first edition was published in London, 1816.

Before I reached the house the patient had further considered that he might as well take a nap till the doctor came. Accordingly, himself, the wife and the family were with difficulty roused from their slumbers. Upon discovering the true state of the case, I found that my patient had received a severe, deep-seated *fright*, but had fortunately sustained no other injury except a slight bruise on the ancle. In consequence I had no further trouble than merely remounting my horse and riding back the same four miles I had already come in the same soaking incessant rain, and with the pleasant addition of being so completely wet through my great coat that I had even to *wring* the sleeves of my shirt on getting home. 'Oh! the pleasures of a ride in the Country'.

Our extra assistant Mr Sang who had been absent about 7 weeks returned to his post this morning. He is nearly restored to perfect health which I hope from interested as well as disinterested motives may long continue.

May 29 *Thursday*
Mr McI has been away at Tynemouth all night – no uncommon thing of late – and told me yesterday that he is going from home tomorrow for about a week. I expected to have made a short visit to Sunderland today or tomorrow but must now therefore delay my visit till Mr McI returns. His route I suspect to be Harrogate as Mr Gray (his late partner) & his lady are at Tynemouth on their way to that former place.

I had a pleasant sail by steam down to Howdon, about 6 miles off yesterday.

My last task now remains to finish this number and no unpleasant one it is on that account *viz.* to review the cases briefly herein mentioned.

1827

Oct 11	*Rutherford* Benwell had needs be well!	
Oct 14	*Soulsby* Wallsend	D°
Nov 1	*Ramshaw* Heaton This poor man is still in a bad state. Another large opening was made on Sunday the effect of which can yet be scarcely ascertained. His constitutional health is better than for some years past but the limb continues obstinately intractable under every application. Patient sits up an hour or two daily and a chair is in preparation to enable him to get the fresh air out of doors. [11/4/28]	

Nov 14   *Todd* Biggs Main was out of hand in about 8 weeks
Dec 2   *McKid* Smashers Row This fract: clavicle did very well.
1828
Jan 18   *Dixon* Byker and two men at Felling were all good
           cures
Feb 4   *Jackson* Newgate St. died [*11/4/28*]
Mar 31   *Patterson* Newburn convalescent [*11/4/28*]
Apr 25   *McDermot* Infirmary dismissed the following fortnight
           'relieved'
May 16   *Holmes* Heaton Doing well
May 27   *Pethy* Wallsend is doing *pretty well*

[*Patient numbers*]
Magaziniana in this number [*Dated list of Magaziniana*]

V O L U M E 7 (June 13, 1828 to August 1, 1828)

June 13 *Friday*
Friday the thirteenth and not a syllable written yet to begin the month! but I have a good excuse, gentle reader. My writing desk has not been within many miles of its owner for a week out of the thirteen days and Mr McIntyre's previous absence from home and my consequent extra throng of business filled up the remaining six. By the size of this number, however, it does not appear that I shall be more regular or frequent in my scribbling than during the six months contained in the last volume. The prolonged dates and slow progress of that sufficiently accounts for the brevity in form of this which I hope to get through *publication* in somewhat less time than was the case with the former one.

As, without becoming tediously monotonous I find the subjects for general remarks get scarce*ish*, I shall endeavour to collect matter for filling up this deficiency by an additional number of detached papers. The space allotted to each of these has usually been about six pages, but as such *when read* appears very brief we must endeavour to fill eight pages in future with each Maga: number.

I have been a week at Sunderland with my Father & Mother prior to their return to Stockton next week. On Monday I was invited to dine with my old master Mr J. Cowan[1] but not being able to go in time I made my appearance there after dinner and spent a very pleasant evening in company with Mr Cowan of Glasgow and his lady – Lt Colonel Aird – Scots Greys from Edinburgh, Mr Robinson & his son from India, Mr Patterson a clergyman &c. Dr Brown was to be of the party but could not attend. I however had the pleasure of an introduction to him & Mrs B. in making a call there with Mother yesterday. Col: Aird – I & a

---

1 Mr J. Cowan was one of TGW's schoolmasters in Darlington: see 'My Autobiography', chapters 5 and 6.

bottle of Mr Cowan's fine Bucellas grew very friendly on the above evening.

On Tuesday my Mother and one or two friends had an excursion up the Wear in a boat to Lambton Castle,[2] which we had an opportunity of seeing through all its apartments and departments. After dining romantically enough (had we only had a few *younger* ladies with us) in a glen we returned to Sunderland to tea. An extra pair of oars afforded me good exercise. My name was put on the list of visitors at the News room & library by the kind attention of Mr Tanner, whom I met at a visit to Miss Beckwith's on Wednesday evening; and yesterday I was employed principally in assisting to pack. This mornings coach had the honor of my conveyance back to Newcastle, and now at 2 PM *me voila*!

Mr McIntyre returned from his trip to Edinburgh on Friday night and on coming home today I find him on a few days visit at Tynemouth on pleasure! If any surgeon but himself were to run away from his business as he does there would soon be a blank day book to look at, and an empty ledger to cash up

June 16 *Monday*

Yesterday I rode as far as Walker with Mr McIntyre who was again on his way to stay all night at Tynemouth. He very courteously asked me to keep my seat in the gig if I wished to see any friends at Shields or Tynemouth, which I having no acquaintance in that direction declined. This morning at 5 AM however I had a jaunt to these places without choice, for a message came from Penshaw requiring Mr McI's attendance at Mrs Burnets instantly; and, as upon consideration, I thought *I* had best be the communicant, I rode the grey mare to the Star & Garter. After calling Mr McI up and breakfasting he set off across the water, and thro' Sunderland to his destination. I took a half hour's stroll along the banks, (it being then after eight oclock) and drove pleasantly home seeing the patients along the way.

And now let me resume my compository exercises, which I

---

2 Lambton Castle is a mock castle built around the core of Harraton Hall, established as the Lambton family seat when inherited by William Henry Lambton in 1794. The building of the castle continued, with interruptions, until 1828. Significant rebuilding and reconstruction took place in the latter half of the nineteenth century: see *BED*, pp. 345–9.

intend to do by making an attempt at telling a story. This is, I know, the kind of composition in which (if I scribble worse in one line than another) I shall least of all make a respectable appearance; but for that reason only I make such my subject. 'Practice–improve' and hence it is in those departments of writing which I know I am most deficient in that will now form, principally, the fields of my endeavours. Thus I shall gain advantage and amusement and my friends I hope will not lack partiality enough to make up deficiency in interest. With this preface I begin my tale, only premising that after a dozen imaginary sketches the author can no more than you, gentle reader, state what will be the precise development of it.

[*Magaziniana no. 26: 'The Fisherman's Grave', chapter 1*]
[*Patient numbers*]

June 19 *Thursday*
I have got up to the ears in Metaphysics again being busily employed with Brown's lectures[3] on this subject. Having only read through two lectures I cannot yet judge of his opinions but am very partial to his style of composition.[4]

June 23 *Monday*
A few months ago[5] I recorded the unhappy shipwreck of my cousin and now I have the melancholy task of naming the death of an uncle – the father of the youth before mentioned. He died after a few days illness on Saturday noon, having been in good health the Tuesday previous.

June 27 *Friday*
My hopes of being free in October are completely set at rest in the negative; and I must quietly prepare myself for passing a winter more than I intended in this smoky neighborhood. Mr McIntyre has directed me to acquaint my Father with the above decision, and I have been able through collateral channels to elu-

---

3 'Brown's Lectures on metaphysics' possibly refers to a work by Thomas Brown, who was successor to Dugald Stewart as Professor of Moral Philosophy in Edinburgh, 1828.
4 [*TGW footnote*] The period allotted at the library elapsed before I had leisure to get through more. (July)
5 See Volume 6, 26/1/28.

cidate a number of previously unintelligible appearances which have been lately scattered around our little political horizon.

Mr Sang is now in treaty and likely to come to terms with Mr Dixon of Bp: Auckland as partner & successor. His departure therefore is now determined on though from what Mr McI said to me *he* evidently did not intend to keep Sang long had no cause of separation been on his (Sang's) side. The intention of his coming to us was rendered abortive from Mr Cochrane changing his mind about spending a month or two in Edinburgh, and other changes are in contemplation in which Mr S's participation will be doubly needless.

Mr McIntyre has decided on taking a partner and Mr Church had the first offer of the engagement. The terms were considered too exorbitant for that to be successful, but I have had it hinted to me that another negotiation is pending. A few weeks will try the issue.

[*Patient numbers*]

June 30 *Monday*
Sang left Newcastle this morning and will not I expect return to our establishment in a professional capacity. Nothing further *is fixed* however about the Bp Auckland engagement nor do I hear more of Mr McIntyre's intentions.

[*Patient numbers*]

(7 to 10 Removing)

July 14 *Monday*
Last Monday morning at 2 AM we commenced the arduous task of removing all the goods and chattels from our late abode.[6] I was sent forward to take charge of the things as they arrived in the new house, and by seven oclock (a little before which Miss McIntyre came over) we sat down to a comfortable breakfast in a well furnished dining room. Almost all the furniture came over that day and on Tuesday I was busy superintending the putting up of shop fixtures &c. Wednesday was employed in sending over the contents of the cellar which was left to my care.

On *Thursday* we *all* found time to spend a few hours on the

---

6 This is the first mention in the *Diary* of the move of Mr McIntyre's residence and business from Newgate Street to Eldon Square. More details are given 24/7/28 and in *Magaziniana* no. 27.

moor to see the gold cup run for; but it was not till Saturday night that I could sit down in any sort of comfort in the new house. By that time I was completely worn out and have hardly recovered from the over fatigue of last week, and a complete drenching yesterday, which dose was repeated today. I was with Mr McIntyre in the gig yesterday to Backworth, Whitley, Cullercoats, Tynemouth & Shields and though a fine day when we set off the rain was heavy and incessant the last twelve miles of our drive. Great coats and 2 umbrellas with difficulty kept us from being wet to the skin. This morning in a ride to Newburn I was as fairly soaked as if I had fallen into the Tyne on the banks of which my road lay.

July 17 *Thursday*

Mr McIntyre set off to Edinburgh on Monday and has not yet returned. In his absence I have had five accidents at the Collieries one of which caused my detention in the country all day on Tuesday. I did not get home till 8½ oclock. The boy [*Chaytor*] (aetat 16) has his thigh fractured and very severe wounds on the scalp. On the first day I suspected fracture also at the base of the skull which would have been fatal to a certainty, and I was glad to have Mr Henzell's approbation of the treatment I had pursued when he called with me to see the boy as he was on the road. Mr H. seemed to hold out less hope to the friends even than I had done, of the patient's recovery. During the first 12 to 24 hours from the accident it is difficult if not impossible to distinguish fracture at the base of the skull from compression or concussion – or the two latter from each other. I bid the friends of my patient watch for a change in that time and accordingly in 14 hours it took place.

I will not say my pleasure exceeded or even equalled that of his father & mother, for he is the youngest & favorite son, but it was extremely great to find my patient next morning in full possession of his senses and in high spirits. I reduced his fractured thigh and now have tolerable confidence in his ultimate recovery. Danger is not altogether over, but the first & most violent shock has been successfully bore up against. Full two pints of blood were taken away on my first visit and about eight ounces more today whilst the strictest quietness is enjoined.

The other accidents have not been of so serious a nature though rather severe. They are all doing well.

We have now got pretty comfortably settled in our new domicile and so far it is by much preferable as regards my personal arrangements to the last situation. I have been so fully employed not to say harassed with business since Mr McI left I have not had time to take the notice I intended of our change. I shall begin something on the subject this evening and finish it when I can.
[*Patient numbers*]
[*Magaziniana no. 27: 'The Removal'*]

July 24 *Thursday*
Chaytor, Wallsend [*17/7/28*] is I am happy to say still going on well. He is now out of danger.

Ramshay [*probably the patient also spelt Ramshaw[7]*] has had a severe attack lately of inflammation in his limb but it is today considerably abated. He gets out a little just to the door in an arm chair but is not able to use crutches.

A new oil cloth has this afternoon been laid down on 'my room' floor; which now gives us a very respectable appearance, i.e., one befitting the *dedication* of the place, and the *gentleman* who inhabits it.

Instead of our late *office* (as it was termed), a dirty smoky hole with a black ceiling – (from the gas); walls which could not upon a moderate computation have been papered or cleaned within the last century; a window seldom disturbed by brush or duster, and through which, if you could see any thing, it was only to count the stones in the opposite blank wall about three yards off, – for a glimpse of even sky much less *sun* you could hardly get; a fire-place which my antiquarian research opines me had once been black, but had been improved in course of time to all colors *but white*; a thing which I believe once had been a fender; but without irons or other appurtenance except what an old coal-rake shank stood instead of; a few old bookshelves which the dust and the flies had painted with an imitation of anything but wood; and finally the room hung around with a few pictures varnished with grease and glazed with soot and dirt.

Such, kind reader, is the abode where your friend, 'myself', resided since we became acquainted, and for some years before. 'Tis there he laboured for your amusement; 'tis there he toiled

---

7 See the list at the end of Volume 6.

many a long night for his own instruction: and in looking back to those hours he can with pleasure advert to the past.

The well inked uncarpeted floor bears witness to his industry, when illuminated often *all day* by the light of the gas – (often not illuminated at all,) he has sat for hours upon the *hard* solid wood chairs, poring over and extracting the sweets from some gem of science; or penning some lighter articles in his Diary.

Now at any rate I have a comfortable rush bottomed arm chair to sit down in (one or two to spare for a friend also) and the light of heaven and sunshine to enliven me; though I still cannot boast much of improvement in regard to prospect, a joiners work yard and saw pit being my vista, wood, & water. A pair of globes, pray take notice, ornament my sanctum, and all bears an air of comfortable usefulness. I must not omit to add that a good genteel set of fire irons and fender with a respectable grate and black marble chimney piece form part of our arrangements; and that good inside folding window boards have assumed the place of a queer dingy, black–brown, quondam green gauze blind with sundry rents and peep holes, which was all the protection our last settlement afforded. The new surgery, though, like the room above it small, is at last conveniently arranged; and when *it* gets its finishing coat of paint and I get my room *papered*, this part of the great house will have a genteel appearance not unworthy of the rest of the building.

July 25 *Friday*
[*Magaziniana no 28: 'The Fishermans Grave', chapter 2*]

July 26 *Saturday*
I have received orders to prepare for a campaign in the country next week. I am to assume the command of the Backworth division in the absence of its present officer; and I expect to take the field there tomorrow or Monday. Woe then to the disease that dare oppose me within the extent of the district. Some of *my own* patients have assured me that if anything goes wrong I may look for a summons even there to attend them; And this from more than one family today.
Chaytor & Ramshay both doing well. [24/7/28]
I *myself* was a patient last week from a return of my old bilious complaint which I have till now kept clear of for upward of two years. I was at supper at Mr Pyles to meet some gentlemen from

London, Mr Nicholson & Mr Walton, in addition to the old set of
Messrs Fairs, Henzell, Brockett & Ellwood. We had roast ducks
among other good things for supper, and though I took a sip of
brandy at supper, and merely a glass of shrub & water after it, the
compound was more than my stomach would bear; previously
weakened with a harassing week's work. Two days brought me
out again and a ride in the gig on the 3rd Sunday made me quite
well.

[*Patient numbers*]

July 28 *Monday*
(3 PM) Here I am fairly domesticated at the Surgeon's house
Allotments – lately christened Northumberland Place, Backworth, in the very midst of inclines, coal pits, waggon ways &
steam engines.

Our Backworth establishment is pleasantly enough situated for
a summer residence being about 2 miles from the seashore. The
country is flat but scattered with more picturesque hamlets than
are to be found in the older established coal districts. Many of the
pits too are not much seen among the thick woods of several pretty
estates around us; And the blue expanse of ocean forms an always
beautiful boundary to a tolerably rich *champagne* of country.

Mr Cochrane left me this morning at 6 AM to join the steam
boat at Shields on its way to Leith[8] and though the bar was then
so rough that vessel could not venture out to sea, the day has
turned so much finer and the weather so greatly calmer since that
hour that I make no doubt but she is by this time many miles off
at sea.

I have this morning been at Earsden, Murton, or rather perhaps
Mertown, Holywell & Backworth Collieries, Benton Square &c. In
my late district I had frequent visits to Egypt without crossing
the Mediterranean but now I have even New York and Philadelphia to visit which last place I was at today. Wapping is also
within a short distance. Cullercoats and Shields are about 3 miles
each distance from me, Tynemouth rather more; Newcastle is
marked 7 miles.

---

8 A steam-boat to Leith, the 'Rapid', sailed from Newcastle to Leith every
   Monday morning, leaving the quayside at 5 AM. It called at Berwick-on-
   Tweed if weather permitted. The fare to Leith was £1 for the best cabin: see
   PW, I, p. 136.

July 29 *Tuesday*
I have spent this morning in visiting patients at Backworth &
Earsden, Seghill & Cramlington Collieries, Seghill village &c and
rode half a mile out of my way to gain a nearer view of the pretty
woods of *Seaton Delaval* the ancient residence of the baronial
family of that name. The present edifice was burnt to the ground
in late years and the conflagration was very generally understood
to have been purposely caused under the sanction of the owner;
the now notorious *Sir Jacob Astley* of Crim: Con: celebrity.[9] The
structure was a beautiful one but little remains are to be seen
and those left just in the state they were thrown by the accident;
otherwise the woods seem fine and the estate *might* be made one
of the greatest provincial ornaments of the country.

Backworth Hall[10] a large genteel mansion enclosed in a wood
is within a mile off. The proprietor the Revd King resides there.

I am delighted after the mechanical monotony of my *own* district to meet with real English farm houses and fold yards, and
real English villages and green – real green (not dingy smoky
brown) fields again.
[*Magaziniana no. 29: 'The Fisherman's Grave', chapter 3*]

July 30 *Wednesday*
I had scarcely ended my last page and taken a comfortable cup
of tea when I was called away to Cramlington High Pit about 5
miles off and the most distant of our pits. A boy, aetat 11 years,
had fallen down the shaft a depth of 126 feet and strange to say
was actually sensible when brought home.

This case presented a striking contrast to the one I mentioned
at Wallsend. To an inexperienced eye the patient presented nearly

---

9 Seaton Delaval Hall, built 1718–29 by Vanbrugh, was severely damaged by
fire in 1752 and in 1822, see *BEN*, pp. 561–4. Sir Jacob Astley inherited the
Delaval estate in 1813. A Crim: Con: (Criminal Conversation) case involving
Sir Jacob's wife, Lady Astley, and Thomas Garth is mentioned in an article
dated 16/3/1829 published in the *Newcastle Courant*, 21/3/1829. This article is
concerned mainly with rumours then circulating that claimed that Garth was
the illegitimate son of Lady Sophia, a daughter of George III and a sister to
the Duke of Cumberland. More information about this scandal is given in, for
example, Elizabeth Longford, *Wellington: Pillar of State* (St Albans, 1975), pp.
263–6.
10 Backworth Hall, built 1778–80, is now Backworth Miners' Welfare Hall: see
BEN, p. 152.

similar appearance but, instead of reaction taking place, he gradually sank under the effect of a severe *'star* fracture' of the frontal bone with extensive wounds; and though I sent for instruments and assistance in Mr McIntyre to give him a faint chance by operation, his pulse grew weaker, his breathing ceased, and in this state he lay corpse-like, my finger never leaving his pulse, till about 9 PM (three hours after the accident) when it was at rest for ever, life was extinct!

Mr McIntyre was dining at Shields, wh[*ich*] I accidentally heard of, but had left it before the messenger arrived. A gentleman by coach took the note to Newcastle and this morning Mr McI came out!

I had gone into the country and have not yet seen him (1 PM). My round today has been Benton Square, Wapping, Willington Square, Merton Row, Backworth &c. and a more judicious arrangement of my time than I am able to make at NCastle enables me to have an abundance of leisure for reading and my Diary.

$8\frac{1}{2}$ PM As my head is *queerish* with reading about midwifery, [*illegible word*] and the cases in 'the Lancet' I will een take up my pen to try to amuse an hour in another spell at my story. I hardly know however what to make of my *dramatis personae* in conducting them to the finish, *and* shall work my perplexities in a future paper for the benefit of my indulgent readers.
[*Magaziniana no 30: 'The Fisherman's Grave', chapter 4*]

July 31 *Thursday*
After finishing this chapter of Dicky Bronting[11] which observe is 'to be continued' I am called upon by the date to finish this volume of the *Diary*. I have no paper to make a new one however and intend this to serve me till I reach NCastle again or at any rate have opportunity of procuring some of the required materials. By leaving the conclusion of this story till next number, – in true magazine fashion,– however I shall leave paper enough here to contain all I have to say for a week to come and we must not mind much about the formality of the dates tallying exactly with the change of the month.

This morning I made my ride thro' New York, Philadelphia,

---

11 A character in TGW's story 'The Fisherman's Grave', part of which appears in existing *Magaziniana* nos. 26, 28–30.

Merton, Monkseaton, Earsden Village, Holywell & Backworth pits. I rode down to the seashore thro' Monkseaton merely for amusement as the day is the first fine one there has been for the last three weeks. The east winds have continued to blow incessantly since I came here.

The curve of the coast between Monkseaton and Hartley is not very dissimilar to that in the county of Durham,[12] only instead of the sweep of six miles of fine even sands there is not half a mile together worth rolling a carriage on to. The villages are very unlike their namesakes still the association of ideas carried my fancy 30 miles further along the shore and

> While still as Monkseaton's green banks met my view
> I could not help wishing 'twere *Seaton Carew*!

But 'thereby hangs a tale' and as it is not connected with Dicky's adventures we will e'en drop the subject and 'let that flee stick to the wa'!
[*Patient numbers*]

August 1 *Friday*

By way of *Appendix* I will here add some observations to fill up these remaining leaves, for, having found some of the same paper, I can very conveniently commence my new number; which during the leisure I have here I shall be able to do more at length than would be the case were I to confine my remarks while at Backworth to the space I have left before me.

Last night about 7 PM a messenger called me away to Earsden pit to visit a man who in carelessly managing the rolleys had contrived to get two ribs fractured and his shoulder severely bruised. I have today bled the patient who is so far doing well.

It is a question which has often been put to me, and may readily be asked by the reader, how I should like to fill the situation of assistant at this department of Mr McIntyre's practice. One of *my* predecessors at Newcastle (Mr Rhodes) lately asserted he would not remain here for £500 a year. He is now surgeon to an Indiaman and may afford to use strong language.[13] 500 a year

---

12 [*TGW footnote*] Between places of a synonymous appellation.
13 By the 1820s the position of ship's surgeon, a relatively humble one in the eighteenth century, had become respectable and lucrative, see, for example, Christopher Lawrence, *Medicine in the Making of Modern Britain* (London, 1994), pp. 24–5.

would enable *me* to keep such a genteel house as to draw my friends around me in the lone winter months; and to take a standing in the first society of the district. At *such* a salary, I *would* become stationary here, for a few years, but not for much less. It would require a handsome remuneration to make up for the total want of company which this dreary spot presents.

Annoyed by the incessant rattle & din of a colliery incline both before and behind it – the surgeon's house faces the north-east, and stands in the midst of a group of pitman's cottages flanked by a little shop[14] and the Northumberland Arms public house. The cold damp east & North Easters are so well known on this coast as hardly to require mention here. They blow upon average one half the year, I dare say; and beat upon this exposed situation with a bitter effect. Exposed indeed the spot is as the name of a farmhouse opposite – 'Prospect Hill' would imply, and I may safely aver that

> 'If you search the country round
> This you'll find the highest ground'

Sitting as I am while writing this at Mr Cochrane's bedroom window, the wind having got into the WSW and the sky clear & fine, the look out is pleasant enough. The stone farmhouse prettily covered with green – a dry bridge crossing the rail road, and the smoky but new stone engine house – form the foreground. A green field between them and the spectator. In the centre of the middle distance, crowning the only piece of rising ground, stands the village of Earsden, with some larger stone houses rising among the trees, belonging to Mr John Taylor, Mr Thos^s Taylor (brother) and Mrs Marshall. In the background of a general slope to the sea is Hartley to the right of Earsden, and the woods of Seaton Delaval to the left. Groups of houses shew their red roofs here and there but the coal pits are most of them discernible only by their smoke issuing from among the trees. On the extreme left is the high ground towards Alnwick &c. and beyond it bounding the horizon the faint range of the Cheviots.

This house being visible in almost all parts of his district I propose that the surgeon here resident should have a flag staff attached to some conspicuous part of it, for warning him when

---

14 [*TGW footnote*] Mr Cochrane's sister who kept his house married the owner of this shop. The brother & her have not spoken since.

in the country if anything required his instant attention, this might save sometimes a vast deal of unnecessary riding. A set of signals for each of the five collieries might easily be framed, and should a call from 'a lady in the straw' be the message one sign to that effect might answer every purpose, as the doctor would easily know from whom to expect the summons. This I am convinced must be of great assistance in the ordinary run of accidents; in extraordinary cases of course the usual method must avail.

Another hint and I am done. Instead of the present residence and establishment of Mr McIntyre's representative here, were *I* as full of practice and as *big* a gentleman as him, I would plan this way. On some pleasant green slope to the south of Earsden (or on any other spot that was cheap & convenient) I would buy, lease or rent an acre or two of land and on it build a neat genteel snug little country box with pleasant gardens, stables, surgery & c. With a paddock and a piece of kitchen garden this would require a trifling annual expenditure. A man & woman servant (some steady body say & his wife) might keep it in order. Two assistants should be procured – one might suffice if I did not run off to Edinburgh, and all over the country very often; – *members of the College*[15] and with genteel salaries perhaps 100 a year with board & lodging *in the family*. One of these gentlemen to reside in the country and one at Newcastle. Three apprentices divided between the two places would be sufficiency. The 'commander in chief' to spend his time at one or other domicile as suited his pleasure or inclination; each being fitted to receive him or even a wife and family if necessary, in the summer season. The increase in practice which would follow such a step would amply repay the little extra expenditure; though an annual income amounting nearly to thousands ought to support an establishment which would then be decidedly the first surgical practice in the North! NB in pursuing the idea of the above subject I have been led to sketch a plan for a complete detached surgery &c with a description of which I shall commence my next volume.[16] A review of my patients closes my task here.

July 17 *Chaytor Wallsend* – was when I left Newcastle doing

---

15 Member of the College probably meant Member of the Royal College of Surgeons, i.e., well qualified to practise medicine.
16 One of the missing volumes of the MS, unfortunately.

extremely well. By the abatement of the swelling and consequent slackness of the bandages, the bones were a little displaced on my last visit. I reduced them to a proper apposition however and have no doubt this will be 'a good job'. [26/7/28]

July 26   *Myself at home* – Doing pretty well I thank ye!
Ramshay [?*Ramshaw, 26/7/28*] was better the day before I came here and will now be probably as well as before this last attack.

[*List of Magaziniana with dates*]
[*Patient numbers*]

[*There is a break in the Diary MS from September 1828 to March 1829, with Volumes 8, 9 and 10 apparently missing*]

V O L U M E 1 1 (March 3, 1829 to March 31, 1829)

March 3 *Tuesday*
Mem: This paper looks rather thin for the job but it seemed to me finer than the last; and that you know, gentle reader, is a greater recommendation with me on your account, as I wish to make up for the little value of my observations by putting them down on the very best *outsides* I can procure; and really is not what I am writing on excellent foolscap for 9ᵈ a quire? It is Mr Charnley's,[1] and I shall be most happy to supply any of my friends from his stock at the same price; – with a reasonable percentage for commission, of course.

This is intended as the last volume but one of my journal, and as I hope 'ere long to leave the scenes and subjects we have of late discussed, I shall have, dear readers, such a *vast* to say, and such a *deal* to do before we finally wind up our accounts, in order if possible to take a few mites from the heavy surplus on the debtors side of my books, that you must excuse me if I continue rather verbose through this and the following months. Remember at the end of that period we part – our old acquaintance the *Diary of a Doctor* expires, and with it ends the medium of that happy sort of conversation we have, so pleasantly to the writer, maintained for upward of two years and these perhaps the happiest of his life.

Tonight the annual meeting of our Literary & Philosophical

---

1 Probably Mr Emerson Charnley, Bookseller, Bigg Market, Newcastle: see PW, I, p. 18. Emerson Charnley succeeded his father in the bookselling business in 1803. He was an active member of the Lit. and Phil.: see Watson, p. 112.

Society a very crowded assemblage of the members is expected, as some questions of great moment to the welfare of the institution are to come under discussion, a due report of which I shall give tomorrow.

March 4 *Wednesday*
At the Society last night a very animated debate took place upon the motions previously given notice of. The first related to the disposal of the Society's museum, which an embryo 'Natural History society' offered to pur[*chase*] upon liberal terms. The pleas for its disunion from *our* Institution were that there is not sufficient room to exhibit the specimens and by no means enough funds to enlarge or maintain it. This new Society would have built their museum in a yard belonging to the old Institution and for an annual payment allowed free access to its members.[2]
James Losh Esq. VP in the chair.[3]
The report of the committee for the past year was read, and a general vote of thanks to Sir JE Swinburne (President) for his munificent donation of his own portrait (by Phillips) unanimously acceded to.[4]
The Revd. J. Collinson (Gateshead) brought forward a string of resolutions on the museum question *viz.*

1. That the committee appointed this evening be empowered to treat with the members of the Natural History Society, – should they be called upon to do so, – for the sale of the Society's museum; and that the said committee shall make a report of such treaty to a general meeting assembled for the purpose, which meeting shall be authorised to decide upon the terms proposed by the committee.[5]

---

2 For background to the discussion of the Lit. and Phil. Museum and the Natural History Society, see Watson, pp. 305 ff.
3 James Losh mentioned the meeting in his diary, but more briefly than TGW: 'Went to Annual meeting of Lit Soc in the evening. I was in the Chair and there was some sparring about the Museum everything went off tolerably well.' See the entry for 3/3/29 in E. Hughes ed., *The Diaries and Correspondence of James Losh*, 2 vols, Surtees Society, 171, 174 (Durham, 1962–3), II.
4 Sir J. E. Swinburne of Capheaton, on resigning as President of the Lit. and Phil., a position he had held since 1798, presented the Society with a portrait of himself by T. Phillips, Esq, R.A.: see Watson, pp.105.
5 [*TGW footnote*] The above is the substance tho' perhaps not exactly the words of the resol:

2. That all donations which have been received into the museum be transferred to the purchasers of the original collection, with an express understanding that any such presents are to be returned to their respective donors if claimed within twelve calendar months after their transfer.
3. That in consideration of an annual payment of the sum of – from the funds of the society, its members shall have free personal admission to the future natural history museum. (Mr Losh being called out Wm Bigge Esq., VP was voted into the chair.)

Mr Collinson in introducing these made a few remarks which seemed taken at random from his last sermon; but bore no weight on the subject at issue.

Mr Fenwick, in a very energetic and eloquent speech, implored the members to ponder and consider well the measure now brought before them; and not to be hastily persuaded to part with so useful and ornamental a moiety of their property. He even ventured to question the legality of disposing of the museum, especially its donations. He suggested that if room was so great a desideratum, tables for the display of the minerals &c. might be placed in the great library, as was the case in many other institutions. Mr F reminded the members of the high character they had attained in the annals of science as a scientific body; and of the great advantage of a museum of natural history attached to such a society possessed in the rich district around them and in conclusion entreated that they would not allow an establishment of which every one connected with it might feel proud, to degenerate into a mere circulating library, reading room, or book-club.

Mr Bruce[6] briefly reviewed the rise and progress of the Society during the 30 years he had been connected with it; and, having been greatest part of that period on the committee, he could answer for the uniform intention of the members that their care should be bestowed on forming an institution worthy of the advantages for natural history which the county afforded; and hence a museum was a part of that original plan. Mr B traced in detail the efforts and successes of the principal supporters of the society till the opportunity was afforded them of purchasing a

---

6 [*TGW footnote*] This gentleman spoke before Mr Fenwick.

collection, then unique in value in the Kingdom (as private property) when the Turnstall Museum was removed to its present owners. Many of the oldest members, especially those at a distance who could not be supposed to make use of the library, became subscribers purely as giving support to a generally scientific undertaking, and could not be expected to continue their patronage if a mere literary club was formed; hence the economy so much spoken of in favour of the motion was not so apparent.

Mr Fenwick moved the original question.

Dr McWhirter in seconding Mr Fenwick adverted to the extra half guinea in the subscription, which was levied avowedly for the support of the Museum, and which must, therefore, – or the members would subject themselves to the charge of obtaining money under false pretences, – be dispensed with if the Museum was sold. Thus in 650 members (as was at present on the list) 325 guineas per annum would be lost to the Society; and as the Museum was only allowed £60 a year, the odds were greatly in favour of the museum being retained on the score of economy.

Mr H.A. Mitchell considered the primary object of a man's private life to be to keep out of *debt*; and as every individual should be expected to possess a few grains of sense, 650 individuals should by computation be expected to possess a few grains more. He *did* think therefore that so learned and sensible a body should not be exempted from the ties of a private individual, but that *they* should feel it a primary consideration to keep out of *debt* likewise. The society was already burthened with a load of *debt*[7] and the question for the gentlemen to consider was not are we to be a book club, or are we to be anything else, but how are we to get rid of our *debt*. Can we with proper care for paying our *debts* carry on the Museum, or are we to persevere in our extravagance and plunge deeper and deeper into *debt*?

Mr Wilson (Mr Bruce's usher) said, the Museum was objected to by many on account of its affording gratification only to a certain few of its members while the expenses had to be borne by all. He

---

7 [*TGW footnote*] Mr M always laid uncommon stress on this important monosyllable.

granted Natural History might not be the favorite study of perhaps a majority of the members; but if this argument held, the
works in Italian or Spanish or the class of foreign languages generally might come under the same objections, were they too to be
dismissed, – treatises on mechanics or mathematics might next
follow, till the Society was despoiled of its choicest treasures, and
dwindle down to a repository of works of fancy alone.

Mr C Rayne was glad the members had an eligible opportunity for
disposing of what had long been so expensive an appendage to the
society; and when the gentlemen of the proposed new society
offered such almost equal advantages as the members now possessed, he hoped they would not hesitate in ridding themselves of
the incumbrance. (This gentlemans language has in general more
of impertinence than argument, which first I do not choose to
notice here).

Mr John Fife in a very tame address, entreated the gentlemen to
refrain from a measure which must, he knew for a fact, diminish
their numbers, and destroy their high fame.

Mr W H Brockett begged to contradict the assertion which had
been made on the subject of the extra half guinea. It was *not*
levied solely in aid of the Museum, nor was that held out as a
principal inducement. The subscription was increased for a very
good and plain reason – we should have been in the Gazette[8]
without it! The Museum was a greater expense than the present
funds of the Society could support, and they must either lessen
its expenditure or they must dispose of it altogether. The latter
he conceived to be the wiser plan: the society would thereby get
£400 or 500 to pay off a part of their debt; and 60 pounds a year
more to buy books; an expenditure which was now of necessity
very limited. A great stress has been laid on the term book club
and circulating library – these Mr B considered very honorable
designations as much so as the more high sounding titles the
gentlemen on the other side of the house had made use of; – at
any rate let us not attempt to support a hollow reputation; if we

8 The official journal the London Gazette, issued twice a week, included the
  names of bankrupts, hence 'to be in the gazette', i.e., to be published as a
  bankrupt.

cannot afford to be a 'Scientific Institution' let us be a 'Book Club only', but let us pay our debts and apply our income in the most prudent and economical manner possible, though we should be without either a museum or bankruptcy.

After Mr B. sat down, loud cries of 'Question' obliged the Chairman to call for a shew of hands, when the resolutions of Mr Collinson were negatived by a large majority, amidst long continued, and violent plaudits.

This decision was as welcome as it was unexpected, for Prospectuses of the Nat: Hist: Society have been published, and the Lit: & Phil: gentlemen all seem to fear the Museum would be lost. What the Nat Historians will do now is not known.[9]

Mr Turner proceeded to move on behalf of the committee that Mr Brocketts motion of last anniversary be rescinded; which motion was that 'all books on Nat: History (except periodical ones already subscribed for) be purchased out of the funds of the Museum'; and the Rev^d secretary proposed to alter this to a resolution 'that the Committees of future years be enjoined by the members to preserve no more than a due proportion of works on Natural History amongst the allowed subjects in the Society'. Mr T supposed this would sufficiently convey to the Committee the meaning of Mr Brockett's injunction without rendering it (as was the case at present) impossible for them to order a single publication in this wide branch of science. The sum appropriated to the Museum, besides a considerable private subscription, was found inadequate to support the establishment, and hence as no surplus remained, as the law now stood, Natural History was a proscribed subject in this Society.

Mr Bruce contended that the committees of past years had not exceeded a due allowance in the purchase of works on Natural History and referred to the catalogues in proof of his assertions.

Mr Rayne supported the original order.

---

9 The Natural History Society (NHS) was finally set up at a meeting held at the Lit. and Phil. on 19/8/1829. By 1834 the NHS had erected their own building on ground purchased from the Lit. and Phil., which eventually held the museum specimens belonging to the Lit. and Phil. This arrangement, with matters of finance and access having been agreed between the two societies,

Mr W H Brockett did not exactly agree with Mr Turner as to the import of his last year's injunction. The intent of it was *bona fide* to lessen the sum devoted to the Museum in one way or other. He would now endeavour to meet the wishes of his excellent friend Mr Turner, and the same time do what he considered his own duty to the Institution, by putting his intention in another form. The friends of the Museum had stated that the collection of British birds was very nearly (within 5 or 6 species) complete, – not much more *'stuffing'* would be wanted; the curator's salary he thought might, considering the low ebb of his patrons' finances, with his (the curator's) own consent be reduced; and the collection was represented to be in so flourishing a state from donations &c. that surely less expense might serve its purposes. Mr B therefore proposed to support Mr Turner's resolution, but with the following amendment – 'that the sum annually devoted to the Museum be £45 instead of £60'. Seconded by Mr Rayne.

This amendment was lost; and Mr Turner's motion carried almost unanimously.

Proposed by Mr Turner and seconded by Mr Winch that the thanks of the meeting be given to Mr Bigge for his obliging conduct in the chair. Carried with great acclamations, after which the meeting dissolved; and the [*illegible word: votes?*] in the [*illegible word: vase?*] for choosing a committee were scrutinised.

N.B. I observe one mistake in the foregoing *viz*: the first obs: on the 'bankruptcy of the society' was made by *Mr Fenwick*, who remarked on the accounts being read over previous to the report, that the statue of Milo has cost the Society nearly fifty pounds 'If', said Mr F., 'we receive many more such splendid donations, we shall soon be in the Gazette!'

March 5 *Thursday*
I endeavoured during a little leisure yesterday to give the substance of the debate on Tuesday. I shall not answer for the language I used being that of the respective parties as it is but a very brief summary of course; but the intent and character of each address is, I am sure, correct, so far as brevity will allow.

I am pleased to observe on the committee of this year, as

---

continued until 1884 when the NHS moved to the present Hancock Museum at Barras Bridge: see Watson, pp. 305 ff.

chosen by vote the other night, my good friend Mr Brockett for the first time. The rest are principally old councilmen. Messrs Charnley, J T Brockett, W A Mitchell, Dr McWhirter, Mr Murray &c are among the number.

This morning I resigned my membership as about to leave town. Those who have read the former numbers of this will believe how reluctantly I gave in my name, and separated myself from this excellent Institution.

I shall yet be allowed (by courtesy) to make use of the reading room and to take a peep at my old friends on the book shelves now and then till I actually do go away.

Yesterday I was lucky enough for the first time this season to meet with the hounds during my ride. They were passing near the Benwell stables and though I had to breast the hill to get into their track I soon overtook the rest of the sportsmen, and had a pleasant run as far as Denton Burn near Scotswood, where they lost scent and I left them. The pack (harriers) belonged to Mr Burdon, Sanderson and were attended by Mr Clarke, Fenham, Mr Hazle, Denton, and about $\frac{1}{2}$ a dozen other gentlemen. My young charger agreeably surprized me by his willing exertions. He was certainly fresh and in good trim, but from his shyness on the road I hardly expected him to face a hedge or a ditch, and began to funck for the respectability of my appearance when we should come at any obstacle of that sort; but Nebuchadnezzar had only to be turned to the fence, and he was over it in a trice not did he refuse a single leap during our short run. Had he been prepared (by having no water &c) for a good wind and a brisk chace I should certainly have indulged my horse and myself by keeping the field till the last. As his wind was rather short from his morning's water I reluctantly, and to the no small disappoint-ment of Nebby, evinced by many a prancing wish to turn back, – brought myself away, home, having seen my patients before I met with the dogs.

A wretch has taken her trial today for the murder of her Mother; and it is reported that the monster killed her Father and two illegitimate children before this. She belonged to the Keel-mens Hospital in this town where she perpetrated the crime for which she has this afternoon been condemned. I could not obtain access to the crowded court but I am told by one who was there that the unfortunate creature is condemned to execution on Satur-day morning and to be given to Surgeon's Hall for dissection. If the latter part of the sentence be correctly reported I shall most likely partake of the benefits accruing therefrom.[10]

March 7 *Saturday*
The poor woman was hung this morning at the old place of execution near the barracks. The procession passed along this street and within sight of my window but I had not the curiosity to join the assembled thousands who crowded to the last scene of her existence. The body will I suppose be exposed to public gaze for a few days when she will be anatomised by Mr Fife.
[*Patient numbers with following footnote added*] Mr McIntyre now takes subscribers (i.e. 'sick') at one or two more collieries though the new ones are not very numerous.

March 11 *Wednesday*
Mr John Fife on Monday noon gave a very good demonstration on the brain of the criminal who suffered on Saturday. There is to be a course of lectures on this *subject free* to surgeons &c, but open to the public on payment of a fee – half a guinea the course and 2/6 a lecture.[11] Mr Fife as I have said acquitted himself well in his place as lecturer, and had a good opportunity, from the freshness of the brain before him, to exhibit its parts and structure in a clear manner, more so than usually falls to the lot of an anatomical teacher. Mr Geo: Fife holds the office of assistant to his brother. The audience altogether might be about 50 of whom almost one third were non professionals.
  About 10 AM yesterday I set off on a round to Backworth and returned by Wallsend Heaton &c.
  My errand at Backworth requires a slight comment. Though I have so frequently been obliged to employ my pen in speaking (unwillingly enough) of disagreeables, yet I feel that I ought not

---

10 For details of the trial and execution of Jane Jameson on 6/3/1829, see Sykes, pp. 244–6; the execution, the first hanging of a woman in Newcastle for 71 years, was reported in the *Newcastle Courant*, 14/3/1829. The legal provision of bodies of executed murderers for dissection, its effects on attitudes to dissection and the consequences of the Anatomy Act of 1832 are fully discussed in Ruth Richardson, *Death, Dissection and the Destitute* (London, 1988). For TGW's description of the dissection by Fife, see 11/3/29, 18/3/29.
11 An advertisement for the lectures in the *Newcastle Courant*, 14/3/1829, states that the fees for the public were 'for the sake of preserving order and defraying the necessary expenses'; the surplus was to be given 'towards the support of the Eye Infirmary'.

let any circumstance remain unnoted here which may serve to exemplify to my friends at present and to put me in mind here-after, of the data whereon to estimate Mr McIntyre's sentiments and conduct towards me in the truest light we are able to arrive at. His reserve makes it impossible to judge of these from *viva voce* avowal or any audible expression of feeling whatever; and while I remain under his roof, my sanguine, perhaps I may wish with some truth confess it – to be vacillating, – judgement, is so easily biased by every little event that occurs, and which at the moment weighs more than a due importance in the scale, that it will only be by reference to the evidence contained in my notes when every trace of partiality has subsided, that we may attain to a just picture of my present master; master as yet, but before this volume closes master of mine no longer. Whether a true por-trait may be *serviceable* to me or to my friends hereafter, it remains for future years to decide; the drawing cannot fail to be worth the space of canvas it occupies, and must be at least interesting to the kind readers of my *Diary*.

It is now more than a month or six weeks since an accident, the most severe in its nature not to be attended with fatal con-sequences, that has happened since I was of Mr McIntyre's house-hold, occurred near Backworth. A child [*Stephenson*] about 8 years old fell amongst some waggons which passed over her and caused a compound fracture of the skull, and a yet more violent compound fracture of the leg. Mr Cochrane at the time trepanned the skull and reduced the fracture; which last was so splintered and the bone so much injured together with a large lacerated wound that it was subsequently found necessary to *saw off a por-tion from each end of the bone*. This operation was attended with the happiest effect and the patient is doing remarkably well. The wound on the scalp perfectly united and loss of substance in the limb filling up wonderfully quick. So far highly to the credit of the surgeons employed – Mr McIntyre and Mr Cochrane.

Of this remarkable and interesting case I heard nothing till some time after the second operation had been performed. My first knowledge of it indeed, was communicated by Mr Robt Mackreth (the artist)[12] bringing home a drawing of it, which he

---

12 Robert Mackreth (1766–1860) worked in Newcastle from before 1820, employed as an Inspector of Taxes until 1833, and he exhibited his paintings regularly in Newcastle and elsewhere. Between 1828 and 1831 he was commis-

let me see before it was sent into the house, and to my surprize related to me the brief history of the subject of his pencil. Mr Church had been out once or twice in the gig with Mr McIntyre to see it and Mr Mackreth as often it seems, but as I knew nothing of their errand, and the mere fact was not unusual, I took, of course, no alarm at finding what ought to have been *my* seat thus filled. If the gig was occupied, still with a stud of four horses surely one of them should have been at my service. I have gone out with Mr McIntyre to less urgent cases at Backworth when I was a junior apprentice and every horse was thus employed.

After first hearing of the case I waited a day or two in the idea that Mr McI would certainly mention it and fix a day to go out with me, but no! not a word from either him or Dr Morson![13] Finding that I should gain nothing by silence I appealed to Mr McI and requested he would allow me to ride out some day soon when he could arrange for me seeing the patient dressed and reminding that I had never yet had such opportunity afforded me. In his usual distant (I would almost say *sulky*) manner he told me I might ride out any day when I was in the country. I declined this loose sort of arrangement whereby I might have called, a stranger at the house, asked a question or two but without opening out the bandages and thus rode off from my eight miles of journey nearly as wise as before, and hoped that Mr McI would fix some early day when I might join either himself or Mr Cochrane in visiting his patient. After another profound silence of a week or ten days, Mr McIntyre was at Backworth on Sunday and was graciously pleased to order me out yesterday as before stated.

Is this further neglect of me, and of Mr McIntyre's own real

---

sioned by the Marquess of Londonderry to record the building of the harbour at Seaham. See Paul Usherwood, *Art for Newcastle: Thomas Miles Richardson and the Newcastle Exhibitions 1822–1843* (Newcastle, 1984).

13 This is the first mention of Dr Morson, who apparently had joined Mr McIntyre as a partner in his medical practice after August 1828. There is no information about his background in the existing *Diary* MS but it is known that Walter Skerret Morson, MD, was born in Antigua, West Indies, in 1802 and died 27/9/1832 at Newcastle. He came to England at the age of 17, being adopted and educated by a Mr Underwood. He married Jane Jamieson at Edinburgh in 1822, and three of their 6 children were born at Newcastle: Margaret Emma Morson (7/2/1829), Alexander Kinnear Morson (17/3/1830) and Christina Morson (before 23/1/32).

interests the result of forethought and intention, or is it the off-spring of a proud heedlessness of all actions which do not *seem* to point to the goal of *self*?

A public meeting was held yesterday in the Spittal for the pur-pose of petitioning Parliament in favor of the Catholics.[14] A scene of uproar and confusion ensued. Dr Headlam, Mr Ord & Mr Losh – barristers – were the principal speakers for the petition; while Mr Clark, printer; Mr Taylor, parson; and Mr Fenwick banker were its most violent opponents. These last carried the day by about 5 to 4 I am told, (I was at Backworth at the time) which the *liberals* consider a triumph sufficiently great, in spite of the immense exertions made by the Methodists in *and out of the church*, to bring up riotous forces. As far as I can judge from reports on both sides the victory seems to have been more that of the Methodists over the church, than of the Church of England over the Catholics.

[*Magaziniana no. 45: 'More Miseries'*]

March 12 *Thursday*
A man & horse in breathless speed summoned us to Backworth last night just about 10 PM to 'two women [*Ann Graham and Eliz Ord*] who had their legs broke' by leaping from some waggons which had run amain during Mr Cochrane's absence from home. Mr McIntyre, Dr Morson & I set off in a chaise as soon as possible, but met another messenger near Benton who informed us that Mr C had arrived and finished the job by that time.

I have been out there this morning and find one woman with a compound fracture of the leg; but the other has fortunately escaped with a sprained ancle.[15]

[*Patient numbers*]

March 17 *Tuesday*
Another severe accident occurred at Backworth last night. Mr McI & Dr Morson went out in the gig and my horse was from home or I dare say I should have accompanied them. Mr McIn-

---

14 Long and detailed accounts of the meeting at Spittal about Catholic Emancipa-tion are given in both the Newcastle Chronicle and the Newcastle Courant, 14/3/1829.
15 [*TGW footnote*] I give Mr Cochranes report of the latter case which I did not examine.

tyre explained the nature of the injury to me this morning. The horsekeeper [*Spence*] had fallen under some laden waggons and received so terrible a compound fracture of the arm that the condyles of the humerus with the articular surfaces of the radius and ulna are all removed, but the man would not submit to what must eventually have to be done in all probability – amputation.[16] The other fractures are doing well.

I shall now take notice of a correspondence I have had regarding my right to a free ticket for the course of lectures about to be given at the Society of which I *was* a member.

It commenced by my presenting Mr Brockett with the following note, which I wrote in a formal style that he might, *if he thought proper*, consider it as an official paper and treat it accordingly.

'Mr T G Wright begs respectfully to enquire of Mr Brockett as one of the members of the committee of the Lit: & Phil: Society, whether the course of lectures which commence this evening[17] (and which were given notice of last October as to begin immediately after Xmas) do not properly belong to *last* year's business of the Institution? If so, are not members who resigned at the late anniversary entitled to a subscriber's ticket? A chief regret in the prospect of leaving Newcastle is that he is deprived of the happiness of being connected with the Society, Mr TGW is therefore unwilling to lose an iota of privilege which may *honorably* remain to him, though he cannot avail himself of it beyond attendance at a few of the first lectures. The librarian has informed him that he has no claim whatever upon a free ticket for the ensuing course. He will be much obliged by Mr Brockett's advice on the subject.
                    To W H Brockett Esq Monday Mar 16[th']

Mr Brockett, whom I saw at the time I left my letter, was of the opinion that I ought to have a ticket, and thought the committee, a few of whom he should see during the morning would have no hesitation in agreeing upon the subject without a necessity for calling a meeting for the purpose. In the course of the afternoon I received his answer as follows.

'Dear Sir, I have spoken with one or two of the committee & am afraid they differ with me on the subject of the lectures, by saying

---

16 A note written by TGW on a scrap of paper, found inserted between the MS pages, reads: 'Condyles' – 'humerus', 'articular surfaces', 'ulna' – all these will be familiar terms to my love by & by I guess.

17 [*TGW footnote*] The opening has been postponed to Thursday.

that no *non*-member can be entitled to the privileges of a *member*. This may be law, but I confess I think it a hard one, and perhaps you had better make another statement to me requesting me to lay it before the committee and I will do so. You can mention that the Society's subscription to the lectures being paid last year you consider yourself entitled. Mr Hudson may be impartial but he ought to be civil also.[18]

Believe me Dear Sir, Ever truly yours, W H Brockett *Monday*.'

Immediately on the perusal of this I determined upon my answer to Mr B but did not write it till this afternoon – I was in the country all the morning – a copy of it is subjoined.

'My dear Sir, I am very much obliged to you for the friendly interest you have taken in the question I proposed to you yesterday, but as there seems to be more than one opinion on the case, which would hence cause some discussion amongst the committee (an event I hardly anticipated) I beg to save you and your colleagues further trouble on my account by withdrawing my request.

I am not at all the less convinced of the soundness of your opinion; but I feel that *I* cannot handsomely persist in urging the point, because, having been elected in Nov^{br} 1826, I have already attended two courses of the Society's lectures, during the two years and four months I was enrolled in it.

If, however, you or any other member of the committee wish the question should be discussed as a debatable point in the laws of the Institution, I will gladly present you with my memorial for *that* purpose (of introducing the subject to the meeting) but shall in such a case decline accepting a ticket though the votes prove in my favor.

I remain dear Sir, Yours sincerely, TG Wright Eldon Square, Tuesday.'

I had just finished the above when I was called to receive a visit from the Rev^d lecturer himself – Mr Turner. He had had a note from Mr Brockett detailing the peculiarity of my case, and Mr T did me the honor of calling to say that he perfectly agreed with Mr Brockett and myself as to my *right* of free admission, but as there was no time for summoning the Committee to decide the question at a special meeting he proposed to settle the matter by requesting my acceptance of a ticket. Sir J. Swinburne subscribes 5 gns annually to these lectures and places his five tickets in the disposal of the lecturer, and it was one of these Mr Turner offered to my service. I only thanked my kind friend, read him my

---

18 [*TGW footnote*] I had mentioned the ungracious way in which *the librarian* treated my enquiry to Mr Brockett.

answer to Mr Brockett, explained, and accepted his obliging present.

A PS tacked to my note informs Mr Brockett of this circumstance which however I have not yet sent down to him, but shall communicate early tomorrow. The lectures are to be on the Vegetable Kingdom, and the first part, the physiology of plants will be very interesting to me.

March 18 *Wednesday*
Mr Fife continues demonstrating the *subject* at Surgeon's Hall [11/3/29], and I have attended two or three of his lectures. They may be very useful to the tyros of the profession and highly interesting to a general audience but they do not contain any information as *anatomical* lectures. Mr F's manner of delivery is so deliberate and slow that the whole of his orating, leaving out repetitions (as the table goes round) amendments and directions to his brother, might easily be compressed into one third or a quarter of the time it occupies. The brain was fresh and the dissection of it therefore interesting from its distinctness. (Erratum – lectures finished on *Monday*)

I have finished my study of Dr Clutterbuck's interesting work on the seat of fever,[19] and before I allow his opinions to engraft themselves too strongly on my understanding, I have obtained for perusal (also thro' Dr Morson's kindness) M Broussais' counter opinions on the subject.[20] This latter work being in the original french is a source of much pleasure and improvement in acquiring the language *professionally*.

Called at Mr Brocketts instead of sending my note and explained the event of the negotiation to him. He seems determined to bring the question before the next committee however, though of course *my* motion is ended.
[*The following section of the Diary (two MS pages) has a black-inked border*]

March 20 *Friday*
'We have this morning a melancholy pleasure in announcing the demise of 'Papyra' second wife of Thomas Giordani Wright Esq;

---

19 Probably *An Enquiry into the Seat and Nature of Fever* by Henry Clutterbuck (1767–1856). A second edition of this work was published in 1825.
20 The fourth edition of *Histoire des phlegmasies, ou, Inflammations chroniques*, by F. J. V. Broussais (1772–1838), was published in Paris in 1826.

she *expired* last evening at about 40 minutes past four oclock; a happy release to herself who has just joined the race of eternal nonentities, and doubly happy escape to her late husband – now a joyful widower. She had been for some time past in a gradually declining state, and when the period of her existence terminated she yielded herself without a groan and with quiet resignation to her inevitable fate.[21]

Mr W's first wife was united to him in 1823, and but twelve months before his second marriage. She however died suddenly of a palsy stroke in the eighth month of a conubial engagement, which at its onset promised fair for much consequent happiness; but proved a source of great discomfort. A divorce ensued and a few days after the bride was found dead.

The late second spouse of Mr W was of rather prepossessing appearance, thin figure, square features, sallowish brunette complexion and jet black eyes (i s); her temper and character was stiff and formal and enabled her to exercise a strict control over her 'pupil' as she was wont familiarly to denominate her husband. He, therefore, has some cause to rejoice in the dissolution of a bond whose yoke was somewhat galling.

This worthy couple had been united precisely five years during which time, it is a singular fact, that Mr W had not once beheld his wife! The marriage was performed in the temple of the Sun[22] by special license and the articles drawn up by Phillip Stanton Esq[re] and immediately after the ceremony had been signed and sealed, the bride passed into the protection of rightful guardian Mr M– through whose intervention all correspondence between the parties was carried on.

The will of the deceased, or rather of her executors, is, that her remains shall lie in state (*qu: statu quo?*) for a short time, after which, a certificate of her demise having been duly registered, they are to be carefully preserved by her loving widower for the benefit of himself, and of society in general!; –

Requiescat in Pace! (From the NCastle Courier)[23]

---

21 Being apprenticed is likened to being married, with the apprenticeship to Mr McIntyre being TGW's second wife. See also Volume 2, 1/1/27, and 'My Autobiography', chapter 12, where the same comparison is made. The appearance of the 'spouse' referred to below is presumably that of the indenture document.

22 [*TGW footnote*] Sunroom Turks' Head Inn.

23 This is apparently a fictitious newspaper supposedly reporting the demise of the apprenticeship.

I have received rather alarming intelligence of the illness of my dear Grandfather this morning, but hope another day or two may bring happy news of his recovery.

Called up at 7 oclock this morning to accompany Mr McIntyre to Backworth where we visited all the important cases. They are going on very well so far. Mr McI, though we had most of the leading topics of the day discussed, did not once allude to the individually most important topic to ourselves – my 'freedom'; nor has his partner at all touched upon the subject though I told him the other day that my 'wife' was 'poor thing, *in articulo mortis*'.

Dr M has Mr Frost with Mr & Miss M to dinner on occasion of his baby's christening today – but not me!

[*Patient numbers*]

March 22 *Sunday*

The late bleak March weather and the prevalence of measles to a great extent with an ephemeral epidemic fever (principally amongst the females) has rendered our list of patients more than usually numerous. I am happy to say that one solitary case is the only instance of fatality in any of the above complaints – one child died in the measles. Those who had any tendency to weaklings have been sorely tried in the last three weeks and very many cases of lingering consumption terminated their career for ever.

A few days ago I first set in force my newly acquired rights as a *free* Englishman, by signing the *pro*-catholic petition of the Inhabitants of Newcastle to Parliament.[24] It was to lay open for signatures till last night and then closed for presentation to the houses as the prayer of 2146 individuals.

Mr Turner commenced his lectures on Thursday evening with a summary of the objects advantages and pleasures of the Science of Botany, to a numerous muster of members and subscribers.

[*Magaziniana no. 46: 'Whimsical scraps' no 2*]

March 23 *Monday*

I once thought much of seeing 43 country patients in one day at two rounds and on two horses. That was certainly a longer round than my ride today, but I will note down the number *at present*

---

24 The pro-Catholic petition is referred to in the accounts of the emancipation meeting: see note 14 above.

on our books to show the state of health in this part of the country just now.

The first column of figures denotes the number of those whom I have nothing to do with – i.e. are attended by Mr McIntyre or Dr Morson without my participation at all. The next is the sum of those whom I visit either altogether alone or in conjunction with those two gentlemen. The relative proportion of town & country patients is also given.

[*The MS here includes Table 2: see Appendix*]

March 24 *Wednesday*

Had a pleasant letter from home today. G Father reported better.

It may be thought strange that while every tongue has been employed in discussing the late horrible murders in Edinburgh; whilst the name of Dr Knox has sounded from one end of the empire to the other with all the opprobrium which public hatred could attach to it, I, his friend and pupil should so long have maintained a profound silence in not even alluding to the subject. The reason is that I entertained different opinions from most of the world, and even from my friends, therefore while public feeling was so highly excited, considered silence – wisdom.[25]

I am happy to see in this morning's paper a letter from Dr Knox enclosing the report of a committee which sat expressly to investigate the Doctors conduct in the late transactions; and which so exactly verifies the views I had confidently formed, and wished to lay before the public, that I now almost regret having kept them back.

Before F & M left NCastle I penned a letter intended for pub-

---

25 TGW, when a student in Edinburgh (1825–6), had become friendly with Robert Knox, who was one of his teachers (see 'My Autobiography', chapters 15–17). The case referred to is that of Burke and Hare, who murdered at least 15 people in Edinburgh during 1828 and sold the corpses of their victims for medical dissection. Burke was tried, found guilty of murder, hanged and publicly dissected; Hare turned King's evidence and was released. The case was widely reported in the Edinburgh press, and the Newcastle papers published lengthy extracts of the Edinburgh reports, together with extensive comment: see, for example, *Newcastle Courant*, 3/1/1829 and 10/1/1829. The Burke and Hare case and its effect on Robert Knox, whose school of anatomy had purchased at least some of the bodies, has been the subject of much discussion over the years: see, for example, Isobel Rae, *Knox the Anatomist* (Edinburgh and London, 1964), and Richardson, *Death, Dissection and the Destitute* (note 10 above), pp. 131–41.

lication in that week's Newcastle Courant, espousing the cause
of my friend (for I hope I may still call him so) and endeavoured
by a simple statement of facts to shew some grounds whereon
the public (the non-professional public) might form a correct
judgement on Dr Knox's case. As the contrary sentiments were
so loudly and universally vociferated and my single voice against
a host of opponents would not gain me in favour in their eyes or
be of much avail in argument I adopted the advice of my best
advisers, and relinquished the publication of my epistle, partly
from personal motives, and partly from the silent example of the
Doctor himself.

I shall not say more on the matter at present, but shall try to
leave room at the close of this number for the insertion of the
letter alluded to, which will sufficiently explain the ground of my
sentiments, and, I hope, have some weight in my client's favor
with my readers.[26] Spent a pleasant evening at Mr Crawford's,
having been especially summoned to meet Mrs & Mr Holland
with Miss Phillipson.

March 29 *Sunday*
I am surely fated to be the mark of thievery just now for here
is another most vexatious loss of mine attributable to no other
cause.

On Friday week I was off early with Mr McIntyre to Backworth &c whence we did not return till afternoon, and not requiring my breastpin I in my hurry left it sticking in the corner of
my dressing glass, a place where indeed it often was kept for
convenience. On going to my room at night I observed it to be
wanting and made enquiry amongst the servants next morning.
One girl had left the day before and she was said to have been
last in my room so to her I sent word that if she did not return
my brooch, a constable and search warrant would be applied to.
She came into town yesterday to answer the charge and firmly
asserts that the trinket was on my dressing table when she left
the room that morning. Her, I confidently suspect of the theft; as
certainly as I charge the cook who left last term with the taking
of my other breast pin and silk handkerchief. I cannot, however,

---

26 TGW copied his unpublished letter about Knox as an 'Addenda' to this
volume of his diary: see below.

devise any plan of regaining the lost goods as they will be securely enough disposed of by this time.

This brooch is more valuable both in intrinsic worth and if possible on account of the donor (my dear Mother) than the last one I had stolen – an agate set in gold.

If any excuse for my not putting the brooch into a more safe place be wanted or allowed, I may state that I have in this large, new, *in*convenient house, neither closet, drawers, or wardrobe of any kind to keep an article in. My trunks are occupied by my linen and other vestments, so that two open wash stand drawers are all I have upstairs to put anything of that kind into, and my writing box downstairs (four stories from my dressing glass) is an inconvenient receptacle for such ornaments.

I have not quite given up all hope – it is barely possible the brooch may have been mislaid or found in some way or other but such chance I fear is so slight as almost to amount to despair.

March 31 *Tuesday*
I am also engaged in a letter to my sister today but I must endeavour to spare a little time to wind up this number. No news of my brooch, I am grieved to say.

I have to record one more death amongst my numerous patients. A man has just called to request my certificate that his child died of measles last night. I am about to set off to the country and pray that I might not find many more the worse for yesterday's raw, cold, unhealthy rain.

A man at Felling received an extensive wound on the knee joint on Saturday afternoon at 1 PM. On visiting him I found the internal condyle of the right femur exposed and the joint in a small degree opened. I dressed it and desired to hear from my patient at 6, when if necessary I would see him again in the evening.

Mr McI, after hearing the report in the evening, (which included a request from the Colliery agent that the man should be visited immediately as he was worse) reproached me for arranging another journey that night and asked me what I intended to do by going out. I represented to him that some authors insisted on the necessity of immediate amputation if the knee *joint* was wounded, which maxim was put in force after a very slight wound in the notable instance of the Marquess of Anglesea at Waterloo;[27] and reminded Mr McI of the constitutional irritation likely to follow the injury of so important an articulation. I repeated that bleeding would at any rate be promptly necessary. Mr McI went out more through fear of Mr Grace's message than the patients welfare or my wish I am persuaded, – and did bleed the man. He has continued very ill, with symptomatic fever and was again bled by Mr McI and myself yesterday, with an order that if not relieved before night the venesection was to be repeated.

Dr Morson is now (10 AM) out to see him for the first time. I shall give his report when he returns. 4 P.M. reported to be doing well.

Event of Cases

Mar 10   *Stephenson* Backworth – girl. The remarkable case is going on extremely well, and rightly merits the attention it has received in a correct drawing by Mr Mackreth.

Mar 12   *Ann Graham* and *Eliz. Ord* Benton. Both these turned out to be fracture cases. They are going on well.

Mar 17   *W Spence* Backworth This severe injury is recovering very favourably so far; but, I am afraid the arm will ultimately be lost or if preserved will certainly be quite useless.

I find my own patients today doing well but fresh cases of measles spring up by wholesale in every hitherto healthy family. [*Patient numbers*]

ADDENDA

Dr Knox

To the editor of the Newcastle Courant Jan 23, 1829.[28]

---

27 The incident, where Lord Uxbridge, later Marquess of Anglesey, lost his leg after being hit by a cannon shot, is described in most accounts of the battle of Waterloo: see, for example, Elizabeth Longford, *Wellington: The Years of the Sword* (London,1969). The account of Uxbridge's injuries and treatment given in G. C. H. V. Paget, Marquess of Anglesea, *One Leg: The Life and Letters of Henry William Paget, 1st Marquess of Anglesea* (London, 1961) does not support TGW's description of the wound as 'very slight'. However, it is possible that TGW had learnt some details of the case from Robert Knox who, as an army surgeon in Brussels, attended the wounded after the battle of Waterloo.

28 This letter is referred to by TGW (24/3/29): it was not sent to the newspaper.

Sir, At this period when public feeling is strongly excited by the late horrible disclosures of a system of cold-blooded villainy rarely to be met with in the annals of any country, much less our own, the tide of public prejudice and indignation has set strongly against all individuals whose names may be in the most distant or fortuitous manner connected with these diabolical transactions.

My friend and much esteemed preceptor Dr Knox is one of those unfortunately implicated, and I am anxious through the medium of your widely circulated journal to contribute my mite towards stemming the adverse current of general opinion by a plain statement of a few facts.

The unprofessional part of the community are by the very nature of the system most inadequate judges of occurrences in a dissecting room, as profoundly scientific men are generally the most ignorant in the ways of the world. But let those who violently traduce Dr Knox place themselves in his situation and see how easily they may be imposed upon. The general outcry is that the doctor and his dissectors *must* have instantly detected the murdered subjects so barefacedly brought to them by the marks of violence upon the bodies.[29] I was a dissector in Dr Knox's rooms in 1825–6 and can most readily answer that assumption in the negative. Let it be considered how the *usual* supply of *materiel*

---

29 [*TGW footnote*] Burke's confession and the report of the select committee with Dr Knox's accompanying letter must have been read by every one and afford a pleasing confirmation of the opinion I had (previous to that) advanced in the above letter. There is one more evidence of no less authority than Dr Christison, Professor of Medical Jurisprudence in Edinr., whose observations may not be so well known. A short extract from his 'reports of cases of legal evidence' in the Edin. Surgical Journal Mar 1829, will conclude my remarks –
'In the body of the woman Campbell', says Dr C., 'no person of skill *whose attention was pointedly excited by being told* that from general circumstances murder was probable but the manner of death unknown, could have failed to remark signs that *would raise a suspicion* of suffocation. But if his attention had not been roused, if for example he had examined it in the dissecting room of an anatomical theatre of an hospital without knowing that suspicions from general circumstances were entertained regarding it, *he might have inspected it even intimately and yet neglected the appearances in question.* Nay, a person of skill and experience would have been more likely to do so than another; because every one who is conversant with pathological anatomy must be familiar with such or similar appearances as arising from *various natural diseases*'. [*This footnote clearly was not in the original 'letter', and probably was added when the copy was entered into the Diary.*]

from the burying ground is obtained – that the coffin lid is knocked in, and a rope fastened round the neck of the corpse by which it is dragged from its resting place (such I have been informed by the resurrectionists is the plan pursued) – it is then disfigured about the face to prevent recognition, the teeth are generally broken out as perquisites of these human wolves, and the stiff carcass is tied with ropes and beat into shape for package in a small box or trunk; – let these usual appearances of a subject, I say, be considered and it must cease to be a wonder that *external* signs of violence pass unnoticed.

It may reasonably be asked, however, is surgical [*knowledge*] of no more avail than that a murdered subject should not be recognisable by *internal* appearances. The *postmortem* evidences of apoplexy and strangulation are so closely allied, if not precisely similar, that amongst so many subjects a few with turgescence of the brain & call for no particular scrutiny; especially when it is known that persons of the lower orders who had dropped down dead from hard drinking are occasionally picked up.

The freshness of the bodies is also urged as a circumstance which ought to have excited suspicion. I myself dissected a decapitated head which had not been dead to all appearances above a day or two and had assuredly not been buried, without surprize being expressed by anyone present; and I know that a traffic is carried on by the body snatchers in purchasing the poor immediately after death, nor do they scruple to steal these during the night if they cannot prevail in any other way.

Further it may be stated in support of the Doctor's unsuspecting ignorance of the horrid traffic he was engaged in, that he rarely if ever sees the subjects when first brought to his rooms. This is usually at night: they are taken in by his assistant or door keeper and the men proceed to a known house near his residence to receive pay for their goods.[30] Had a murdered body been even brought warm to the rooms overnight it would by next morning when stripped and laid out upon the tables have assumed the appearance of an ordinary *subject*.

---

30 [*TGW footnote*] Such is the carelessness of the Janitors that a human figure in a sack was one night (of the session I attended) deposited in the rooms and would have been paid for but fortunately the Doctor was engaged from home. The disappearance of the *living subject* next morning disclosed the attempted hoax.

All these points considered, the doctor's studious habits and arduous duties as lecturer, demonstrator, editor, author and physician being also taken into account, the strongest charge which *can* be laid against Dr Knox is that of *negligence*.

Of his doorkeeper Patterson I know nothing nor do I wish to become his apologist in the slightest degree for it appears to me that his connection with the murderous gang has been more intimate; that he has cast a cloak, to say the lightest of it, over their then suspicious proceedings. But I hope the space this may occupy may not have been unprofitable if I have in any measure contributed towards relieving the character of a valuable member of the scientific world from unjust aspersion and unmerited disgrace.

[*Signed with Greek nom-de-plume*]

Newcastle upon Tyne, January 21, 1829
Finis

[*Note written on cover*:] Vol 12th and last will finish on the 1st of May.

V O L U M E 1 2 (April 2, 1829 to April 30, 1829)

April 2 *Thursday*

How long and how ardently I have waited for this month – the coming of April eighteen hundred and twenty nine,[1] when I should be at liberty to prosecute my studies in a nearer approach to the ordeals of professional qualification, when I should be at least open to any new engagements or prospects that might advance my interests and set me independently afloat on the stream of public occupation! By this time I once hoped to have made considerable progress in my academic pleasures and even ventured to imagine myself passed at least one of the two college examinations I am destined to submit to; but the month has arrived and I am still at my old and now almost veteran station.[2] I am still at my round of patients and business, my old haunts and occupations around me, the same trial of temper and unfeeling reserve (or rather worse than reserve – indignity) from my superiors, the same gratifying respect and attention from patients – one perhaps being a salutary check upon the self-conceit which might arise from the other; the same field for study and improvement, and the same heartfelt devotion to my profession which I have now experienced for so long a period.

In the kindness of my friends, and my happy lot in life, as related to them; in my good fortune which has cast in my path so many advantages not to be lightly appreciated; and further in the pleasurable practice of essential services to society in general, I always find materials for self-congratulation; and being blessed with the disposition to look instinctively at pleasantest aspect of affairs, I seldom lay my head on my pillow without feeling that

---

1 This was legally the end of TGW's 5-year apprenticeship with Mr McIntyre. See 'My Autobiography', chapter 13, for the events leading to and the signing of the indentures.

2 TGW had hoped to be released from his apprenticeship before its full term to enrol as a student at London University in its first session in 1828: see Volume 6, 21/4/28.

I have superlative cause for contentment; and, making allowance for little ebullitions of youthful indiscretion, am as nearly approached to the *summum bonum* of *happiness* as even favorable circumstances will permit.

The commencement of this my last number brings with it feelings, something akin to sorrow in the prospects of leaving the scenes I have been engaged in so long. I am not much disposed to moralize; but I may be allowed to indulge a little in that 'charm of melancholy' which forms one of the most pleasurable emotions of life; sometimes to vary my 'pondering' (if only for sake of variety)

'from grave to gay
from lively to severe'

I feel just now in the situation of an exile about to quit the spot he has made his second home, anxious for the period of his departure which is to restore him to freedom and among his friends, but half reluctant to leave behind him the nest he has feathered and the labour he has daily been accustomed to; impatient – but my thoughts are more subject for private reflection than verbal annotation. I will adhere to my motto and be silent.

Last night about ½ past 7 I joined a party of about 30 at Mr Burnup's to tea and a dance, and enjoyed a very agreeable evening. The company consisted of several known faces and some that were new to me. Among the former were besides the Miss Burnups – their cousins Misses Fanny and Ann Burnup, Miss Row, Mr Sang (who was in town for the day and called upon me in the morning) Mr & Mrs Burnup, Messrs Nichol, Richardson, Wm & R Atkinson, Bilton &c; and of the former I only made myself acquainted with Miss Ann Hutton a pretty dark-eyed girl with whom I danced, I believe, four times; her sister Miss Phyllis; Miss Sillick a perfect little mountain whom I durst not engage for a partner through fear of some catastrophe, and who only did get a mate in one or two dances; and Mrs Nichol. Quadrilles, country dances, 'the Coquet' and songs set off the evening till 'past one' when the ladies broke up and I having set Miss AH home made the best of my way back to Eldon Square.

April 4 *Saturday*
I have not often had occasion to complain of being despicably mounted, but yesterday I cut an uncommon large swell upon a

barb that would not have disgraced the champion of England. Mr McIntyre bought him at Durham fair a few days since, and not finding the animal carry his weight so well as he expected, will I hope frequently turn him over to me till he is disposed of. This bucephalus is a tall iron grey, – said to be five, but more like four years old, young, frisky, and rather foolish, but very showy shape (*ladies* and ignorant (?) gentlemen will think so, though the horse dealers may not be quite so positive about that) – a long sweeping tail, and pretty head & eyes. He has something of the foreigner in his paces, but his other qualifications amply make up for trifling faults in my estimation. He would make a beautiful lady's nag or an elegant looking gig horse.

My bay charger improves greatly and is becoming an exceedingly useful steed. As for our old friend Fanny; she has suffered a woeful change thanks to the Doctor's gig and hard driving. I rode her a short time since, and was very sorry indeed to find her paces so broken up, though she is in good condition and looks well.

As I was lounging up Dean Street this afternoon and ogling attentively towards some windows on the other side of the street, I was obliged to turn my ideas forward to avoid being run over by the very lady my optics were in search of – Miss A Hutton. We were both turning the same corner in opposite directions, – her eyes seemed to say in a glance 'fairly caught' – mine had no objection to plead 'guilty', and almost before I could make my [*illegible word*] she was out of sight, and I went laughing home. Some person was with Miss Hutton or I should have stopt to parley a while; but whether it was man, woman or child I'm sure I cannot tell.

Just been at the post with a letter for Stockton which I had wished to get written for every post this week past. After post hour had gone by last night I sat down to communicate to Mr Mitchell a hint for remedying an inconvenience I have often felt and was particularly annoyed by at lecture on Thursday evening – I penned the following letter.[3]

'To the editor of the Tyne Mercury
Sir, Your valuable paper is always so readily open to receive any suggestion which may contribute to the public utility or accommodation, that I am emboldened to lay the following hint before you for insertion if you think proper.

---

3 Published in the *Tyne Mercury*, 14/4/29, p. 3, column 1. See also 10/4/29.

I am of those, who, not being eagle eyed, cannot bear to look the sun or its scarcely less brilliant semblance, a gas light, 'full in the face'; and hence, during an evening service at any of the churches or chapels, or a lecture at the Literary & Philosophical Institution am considerably annoyed by the unobscured lamps which blaze on each side of the lecturer. It is always desirable that the eye should rest on the features of the speaker while listening attentively to his discourse, and I am sure many must have felt the inconvenience of these burners glaring directly in the way of their vision.

No doubt all of the light possible should be thrown on the subject; but would not semi-cylindrical shades similar to those used by Mr Matthews 'At home'[4] (if I may be allowed to speak of the church and stage as parallel examples, *profana componere sacris*) in some degree obviate the disagreeable effect complained of by guarding the eyes of a majority, at least, of the audience, while they would permit the same illumination of the lecturer and his text as at present? I for one, should thankfully appreciate the comfort of such an arrangement. Newcastle April 3 1829' [*signed*] W

[*Patient numbers*]

April 7 *Tuesday*

The nasty, raw, moist unhealthy weather which has obstinately prevailed for ten days past is exerting deplorably fatal effects on my poor little measles patients. Happy it is for those who got through the disease before the worst of these frequent atmospherical changes came on.

Two more children are dead, though I have spared neither pains myself nor consultation with my seniors to master their bad symptoms. Today also I am maintaining a determined and desperate struggle for another little patient in the same disease.

I opened the jugular vein this morning and have followed up the treatment by emetic, warm bath, & blister but almost despair of subduing the derangement which has taken place both in the head & chest.

Another child who was dangerously ill yesterday, I am delighted to find much better today.

April 10 *Friday*

I found my little patient alive yesterday but in so feeble a state that I have no hopes of its recovery.

---

4 This appears to be a reference to *At Home*, a one-man show, devised and performed by the popular actor Charles Mathews: see 'My Autobiography', note 75.

Mr McIntyre read me part of a letter a few days ago (from whom he did not say but I think) from either the Marquess of Londonderry or Mr Buddle for the Marquess – in which the writer desired an average list of accidents at Mr McIntyre's collieries in order to estimate the comparative liability of pitmen to danger. This will form a desideratum in the enquiry into the state of the coal question now before a select committee of the House of Lords.[5] By a weary study of the day books for 1827 page by page through the twelve months I have accomplished my task for that year and as soon as I can obtain the only remaining want – the number of workmen in each colliery at that time I shall copy the summary which concludes my labours into the Diary.[6]

Yesterday I sent off the first of my homeward-bound packages of luggage; about 50 volumes of my library with some music & c &c. My bookshelves present a pitiable appearance now that they are despoiled of a load under which they have smiled for a long time. The dozen volumes remaining seem to grieve for their companions which they will I hope shortly rejoin in a better and happier situation – the writer's *sanctum* on the Green,[7] there to enjoy many a pleasant hour of future intercourse.

Mem: Tyne Mercury April 7th 'W. on gas lights in lecture rooms, churches and chapels in our next.'

[*Patient numbers*]

April 12 *Sunday*
Mr McIntyre had a state dinner party on Friday at which I was present and the most stylish affair we have had of that kind in the new dining room. The company who sat down 14 were Mr McI & Dr Morson at the top and bottom as usual, Dr Ross surgeon to the 7th D Guards in the garrison here (full uniform) and Mrs Morson, Mr Reed, I think from the barracks and his 3 (plain) daughters, Mr Hedley and Miss Hedley, Mr Stable, Miss Jamie-

---

5 The Marquess was the owner and Mr John Buddle the Viewer (Manager) of the Wallsend colliery. John Buddle gave evidence to the Select Committee on the Coal Trade on 6/5/29: see Introduction, note 18.

6 The table showing the numbers of accidents in 1827 is included in the *Diary* MS on 17/4/29; it is reproduced here as Table 3. The number of miners employed is not given in the MS.

7 This refers to The Green, Stockton, where TGW's parents had returned to live. Their impending return to Stockton is mentioned: see Volume 7, 13/6/28.

son, Mr Robt. Mackreth and myself. I was on Dr Morson's left and next to Miss Hedley who has just arrived from London (whither her sister Miss Anna before named as a partner of mine, has gone) has been in Edinburgh, was once at the manor school in York and there last week, knows some friends of my Father's in Wensleydale, and having met before at Mr McIntyre's table we soon got into busy conversation.

Dr Morson had an evening music party whither we found the ladies adjourned when we went up to the drawing room but *as I was not specially invited* I, of course, did not intrude myself nor did the Dr or Mrs M take any notice of my absence by sending out for me.

Mr McI's dinner was set out in splendid style at 5½ PM, and was composed of an abundance of 'bachelor's fare' of which all particularly the wines – Champagne, Claret, Hock, Madeira, Constantia [*pencilled in*], Clary, *white* Port (a new wine or rather, I believe, and old one revived), red Port – pronounced to be the very best that need be drunk, – and Sherry, were highly extolled.

April 13 *Monday*
Since commencing the above notice Dr Morson has apologised for his seeming neglect of me on Friday night by saying he fully expected I had joined their party which he was sorry to find had not been the case. He hoped I would have gone in with the rest of the gentlemen and was so engaged with his music that he did not pay sufficient attention to his guests and did not perceive my absence till too late in the evening. I leave his *amende* without comment which would lead me into a longer discussion than I have at present time for.

William Gibson a brother of John and who has lately come home to settle in the town as a surveyor has been very importunate with me for a long time to visit him. He has frequently called upon me and I firmly declined his invitations till I had related to him every circumstance of the situation I stood in regarding their family. He avowed to know nothing of any disrespect which had taken place and was inclined to attribute such partly to John's caprice and illness, and part he was at a loss to account for, but he agreed with me that the situation I must feel in to prevent me from visiting at the house were by no means such as to make a visit pleasant in my meeting the whole family. I promised him that I would go to see him some day before I left town and yester-

day was fixed because all the family [*would be out*] except Mr
Gibson (for whom Will totally disclaimed any share in or knowledge of what I had detailed) himself, and two of the younger
sisters.

I went; Miss Bell & Dorothy were there; no allusion to my painful subject was made and the evening passed off tolerably cheer-
ful.

Mr Buddle has got the list I mentioned to fill up himself with
the remaining numbers of pitmen to each concern, and as the
document may not again come into my hands I shall copy just
what I can [*of*] the summary from a pencilled list I reserved for
the purpose; as also a few obs: I drew it up to fill up a blank
column by way of report but which Mr McIntyre thought it was
unnecessary to insert as the column might be wanted for another
purpose.
The measles patient at Byker died on Friday evening.
Patient at Felling doing well. Ramshay – Byker – [*Ramshaw?, case
list end Vol 7*] is yet much in the same state as he has been for the
last six months.

April 14 *Tuesday*
The first appearance of spring weather in the delightful sunshine
this morning added to a good breakfast gives me courage to
undertake a task which has been long before me, *viz* that of communicating to my Diary the only remaining paper of mine which
it has not seen or heard tell of, one which has yet to be drawn
from the most secret recesses of my writing desk, but which *must*,
according to rule, be presented in some shape or other to my
readers, though the key of explanation to the blanks here must
be returned uncopied to its former hiding place.
[*Magaziniana No. 47: 'Confessions', no 2, chapter 1*]

April 17 *Good Friday*
Mr Turner, in his lecture last night made allusion to the letter
wh[*ich*] appeared in Tuesdays Mercury relative to 'Gas Lights'.
Mr T has ordered shades similar to those proposed by the writer
and on next night will try their effect. If the plan is generally
approved they will, of course, be continued. I thought once to
have reminded the lecturer that the shades, as there are no lamps
in the body of the room, should be semi-transparent; but upon
second consideration I remained silent.

The next lecture does not take place till Thursday on account of the Easter holidays.
[*Patient numbers*]

April 20 *Monday*
At Backworth yesterday with Mr McIntyre visiting all the important cases which are doing remarkably well. Mr McI uncommonly civil and amongst other news told me that a young man from Kelso was engaged as assistant in my place and he expected would arrive in the course of the week.

This afternoon while I was in the country this youth came, but having gone out again before I got home I have not seen him (9 PM). As he is to sleep here I expect him in every minute and am all in fidgets to behold my intended successor.

Dr Morson *has* invited me to join a dinner party at his table tomorrow though I am only asked to join after dinner, want of room, attention to business &c *may* be pleaded as an excuse, and we will not stick at trifles considering that when I get there it will be my first appearance in his dining room since the house was inhabited. – But here comes our new factotum.

April 22 *Wednesday*
An agreeable party last night which I joined at $7\frac{1}{2}$ PM and found that there really would not have been room for me at the dinner table. Company present were besides the host, hostess, Miss Jamieson, the partner Mr McI and man Friday Mr Wright; Dr Ross, Mr & Mrs Gouthwaite, Mr (but not Miss) Hedley, Mr Donkin, Mr Jamieson and Mr Winstanly. This last gent: retired early; and after tea two whist tables were formed while the Doctor, Miss J. & I set to work with music; some songs, duets & trios were sung and we finally broke up about $11\frac{1}{2}$ PM. It is justice to say that Dr M chid me for not joining them sooner, and altogether made me feel very much at home during the evening.

Mr Leith, the newly arrived, departed to Backworth yesterday noon while I was in the country. What can be the meaning of this I do not pretend to divine.

He is a raw-ish looking scotch youth fresh from Edinburgh, where he has been two winters under Dr Knox. As I have had little conversation with him I can say little about his attainments. *Apropos* of Dr Knox. [*see Vol 11, 24/3/29 and Addenda*] I find he has had so large a class this season that he has been obliged to devote

two hours to his morning lecture from want of room i.e. to deliver
the same discourse twice to two crowded roomfuls of pupils. He
has not either as was reported been absent from his students
during one lecture, notwithstanding the reports that were abroad
of his temporary banishment from Edinburgh.
[*Patient numbers*]

April 26 *Sunday*
On Friday I dined with my old schoolfellow J Watson at Bensham
where I had long promised to pay him a visit; and in the evening
I went down to sit an hour with Mr Burnup. This morning I *drove
Miss Jamieson out to Backworth* where we were joined by the rest
of the party and Mr & Mrs M., Mr McI & Miss J went to Tynemouth while I rode home and saw my patients. I was to have taken
pot-luck with Mr Pyle at 2 P.M. but luckily sent him word not to
wait dinner for me. I joined him to have a glass of wine about 4
oclock.

As 1827 appeared too favorable an estimate of the extent of
danger to which the pitmen are liable Mr McIntyre requested me
to make up a short summary of those in – 26 which he thought
would be nearer the average. I have done so and copied my document into the foregoing page.[8] Both will accompany Mr Buddle
to the House of Lords next Saturday.

April 27 *Monday*
Busy this morning writing to persuade F & M to allow me to
purchase the grey horse lately mentioned, to ride during the
summer; and also as a bit of a speculation which I fancy I can
make a few pounds of after I have done with him. Mr McI wants
him sold and will let him go cheap.
[*Magaziniana no. 48: 'Confessions', no 2*]

April 29 *Wednesday*
So much remains yet to be done before I leave NCastle, and only
two days before me to accomplish my tasks that I must leave
my Diary in a somewhat unfinished state till I have time and
opportunity to wind up my accounts with my readers. If the
muse would have condescended to inspire my rhyming propen-

8 Reproduced here as Table 4.

sities I wished to have closed with a poetical address but one is not yet 'to the fore', though I hope to take my leave in genteel prose.

April 30 *Thursday*
All ready to leave in the morning by Express coach. Mr McIntyre will not sell the horse, though F & M most kindly gave me leave for the purchase.
[*Patient numbers*]
Summary of Patients wholly or partly attended by me since Aug 18, 1826 as given in the 12 volumes of this Diary: 2896
In 1826 the total number of subscribers to the 'Sick' were Heaton 62 Benwell 2.
In April 1829 the amount was Heaton 69 Elswick 34 Benwell 30 Walker
about 50 families paying to Mr McIntyre.

Concluding Address
'Moriturus'
Reader my *Diary* is no more! The manuscript through whose friendly interposition we have carried out our correspondence, and the manufacture of which has been productive of much pleasure and profit to the writer as is was intended to be amusing to You, has returned to its primary non-existence. Whatever may have been its faults and imperfections its author lays down his pen with regret in now closing the last number of his first juvenile attempt at scribbling, and containing all he has hitherto attempted in this literary apprenticeship.

He now enters upon another act of the great drama of life. New characters, new incidents, new plots and counter plots, a change of dresses, properties, decorations and personification are to be encountered. A fresh round of tragedy, comedy, opera & farce are to be met with and the revision of an old play for the present to be got up. One part, the library scene only remains unchanged, and here *the doctor* 'will often be found *At home*' if not with his *Diary* before him he will never be at a loss for some means of communicating to his friends anything very particular that befalls him; and should he enter upon voyages, tours or travels, he will perhaps keep a future *Journal* of his principal excursions. These preparatory steps of book-keeping gone through he hopes in the end to be rewarded with a full Cash Book and well assorted Ledger.

Having made up the accounts of the Day Book he will not longer detain his kind and esteemed readers, than till he makes his very *very* best obeisance, and subscribe himself the much obliged writer of the

Diary of a Doctor

The Green Stockton May 3, 1829

[*2 pages blank*]

MEMORANDA

1829

May 1	Durham (races) Sedgefield
2	Stockton
14	Thirsk (16 Carlton Ponds)
18	York (Mr Newtons)
19	Philosoph Hall &c &c
20	Thirsk
23	Ottrington & Mannby
25	Richmond
Jun 5	Rokeby
6	Barningham – Merrick – Richmond
9	Whorlton (bridge foundation stone laid) Rokeby Richmond
11	Middleton One Row
13	Darlington
16	Stockton
18	Mr Hills concert
Jul 1	Middleton
4	Miss Ann Bowes (Richmond) on a fortnight's visit
8	Ormesby
10	Middleton
11	Ormesby &c
14	Stranton, Hartlepool, Seaton on board the Brompton &c Tees Bay
20	Miss A Bowes left Stockton
29	Mr Pyle declines (from pressure of business) an invitation I had given him to spend a few days with me. He mentions too in his letter this morning that Greenwood my late *sub* at Mr McIntyre's who was to return from Edinburgh shortly after I left NCastle, has attempted to poison himself after one of his con-

tinued debaucheries. He has finally been dismissed from Mr McIntyre's!!

29	Asbull's concert
Jul 30	Thirsk – 31 Borrowby &c
Aug 1	Ottrington
4	Stockton[9] again
6–8	Races (excellent sports)
9	My Father called upon Mr McIntyre & Dr Morson on Wednesday (5th). The former not in; but the latter was so importunate in begging I would go over for a few days that, though I have taken lodgings at Seaton for 2 or 3 weeks, I make a pleasure of attending to the request and set off to NCastle this afternoon. 7 PM Arrived once more at my old quarters 1 Eldon Square. Mr McIntyre had written this evening to Stockton to urge the same proposal as Mr M had made. Mr Leith has ruptured a blood-vessel and gone away ill. The books hardly meddled with since I left them. My friends very glad to see me.
Aug 10	Called on Brockett, Pyle &c. Posting ledger. Dined with Dr Morson. Mrs M. & family at Cullercoats.
11	At Walker with Dr M. Posting. Called at Mr Crawfords
12	Called upon J Watson, D Oliver &c
13–15	Posting, Posting, finished. Duets with Dr M about every other night.
16	Hanover Square Chapel. Mr Rodgers preached. Dined with Mr Pyle
17	I had met Mr Turner at the Lit: & Phil: Library (Mr Brockett introduced me there and at the News room) and been invited to dine with him (Mr T) today which I did, meeting there Miss Turner, Mr & Mrs Rogers from Norwich and Mr Wood. Saw the exhibition of paintings. Spent the evening in G Field Place.
18	Benwell with Dr M. Calls &c Mr McIntyre who has shewn me the kindest attention during my visit made me a present of a superb silver lancet case, enclosing 3 pearl lancets, and inscribed (JM to TGW)

---

9 [*TGW footnote*] Miss J.B. (No 11) married to J.Y. Pe – k Esq[qr] Aug: 3

19	A passenger in the Pilot to Sunderland and the Mail from thence to Wolviston. Walked to Seaton where I hope to remain for a week or two.
20	[*shorthand entry with a footnote in pencil:*] First spoken to A Wray and joined her evening walk]
25	Hartlepool – 26 Stockton
28	Miss Bowes & Miss Eliz: B. – came on a weeks visit
30	Stranton Church (Sunday)
Sep 3	Hartlepool
4	Castle Eden Dean, Black Rocks, Hartlepool &c.
5	Miss Bowes left Seaton
12	Returned to Stockton

1829	**Memoranda contd (1831)**[10]
Sep 19	Left Stockton pr Mail; and on the 20th arrived in Cloudesly Sq, London
Oct 1	London University opened for the session
24	Dinner to the Medical Professors by the students at Freemasons Tavern
Nov 21	Attended poor Duckham's funeral; a medallist of the L.U.
24	[*Here, pasted onto the MS page, is a cutting from a newspaper, around which a black border has been inked. It reads as follows:*] {'On Tuesday, the 24th instant, after a short illness, at Wycliffe Rectory (whither he had gone on a professional engagement) Mr Wright, music master, of Stockton on Tees, aged 66, extensively known and esteemed for 40 years past in this county and the North Riding of Yorkshire, as an able and scientific teacher, and highly endeared to his family and friends as an ingenious and most worthy man.'}. *The newspaper cutting in the MS is probably from the Durham Chronicle as the wording is identical to that of the notice from that newspaper as quoted by Thomas Richmond,* Local Records of Stockton and Neighbourhood (*Stockton-on-Tees,1868*), *p. 154.*]
26	Left London per Mail and reached Stockton the following evening.

---

10 Presumably the date when the following notes were written.

Nov 29	Followed the remains of my beloved Parent to their last resting place in Norton Church Yard.
Dec 30–31	Returned from Stockton to London
1830	
Jan 5	University opened after Xmas recess
Feb 18	Passed my examination at and became a Licentiate of Apothecaries Hall[11]
Mar 27	My intimate friend Wm Reed died after an illness of four days during which I was almost constantly at his bedside.
31	Poor Reed's funeral: attended by his brother (who came up the day before) Mess: H Thomas, W Johnson, R Shute & myself
Apr 10	University Easter recess till the 13th. I went down the Thames to Margate with Mr Neil. On the 11th (Sunday) we went to Chapel at Broadstairs; then walked on to Ramsgate, and returned to Margate to dinner. Evening at Margate New Church.
12	Returned by steamer to London
May 4	Examination week at the L.U. Intend to compete in 3 classes only, which are on the 4th, 6th & 8th
May 14	Adjudication of Honorary Certificates at the L.U. Attended a splendid quadrille party at Professor Davis. Misses Turners (sisters of Prof: T) and Miss Johnson (daughter of the Editor Med: Ch: Review) the most agreeable partners I met with in the rooms, which were crowded.
15	Public distribution of Honors to the Medallists. Sir J Graham in the chair; from whom I had the gratification to receive as the prizes due to my motto '*Quis hic loquitur*' a silver medal in the Class of Physiology, another in that of Midwifery; and an honorary Certificate in Surgery.
19	Left London & 20th Joined my dear Mother on a visit at Mr Newtons, York.
26	Thirsk to visit Aunt & Uncle Pick

---

11 A List of Licentiates of the Society of Apothecaries of London, published in 1840, shows Thomas Giordani Wright of Stockton-on-Tees became a Licentiate on 18/2/1830. The significance of the LSA qualification is commented on in the Introduction.

Jun 12	Drove my Mother to *Castle Howard* and after viewing the house and grounds of this magnificent residence, we went forward to *Malton*. A fellow student Mr Copperthwaite whom I met in the street supped with us at the Inn.
Jun 13	*Malton, Snainton, Scarborough.* Evening at the New Church.
14	Left Scarborough at 1 PM and drove by Snainton, Pickering &c to Kirby Moorside.
15	On our road from K. Moorside we peeped into the Kirkdale Cave and reached *Helmsley* to dinner. It was a tempestuous day, and the rain poured down in torrents so that though we left Helmsley we were only able to get so far as the Blucher Hotel on the top of Hembleton instead of reaching Thirsk that same night.
16	Set out from the Inn at 6 AM and got to Thirsk to breakfast. A very high flood in all the brooks and rivers
24	Went down with M to *Redcar*.
25	Into lodgings at Mr Thomas Thompsons. We remained at Redcar through the whole of this summer, during which I enjoyed a very agreeable vacation. The village was generally full of visitors most of whom I knew; and as I was beau general to all the young ladies – some of them very pretty and all very pleasant – I was seldom without abundance of occupation. Thus busy I took no notice of time and can only measure it by incidents not days and months; hence I shall group such events as I wish to note under the head of

Redcar Reminiscences, or Seaside Scraps

La belle Blonde A day or two after we came to Redcar I met with Miss H and her friend Miss Hixon on the sands. There were very few visitors then at Redcar, and though I presumed it *might* hence be agreeable to both parties to become acquainted yet as we had not renewed our childish acquaintance when I was at Stockton last summer I did not at first wave when we passed. After some exchange of glances I saw Miss H go up the long lane alone, I walked that way too, and we returned together the best friends in the world. During Miss H's stay, which was six weeks after our arrival, I spent many agreeable hours in her company, and with her lively friend Miss M– we had several long walks to the Tees Mouth &c.

Miss H is the 'fairest fair' I have seen: her beauty is even too pale when her features are at rest; but so soon as a smile (or more frequently a laugh) lights up her countenance a glow of color tinges her cheek too lovely to remain there, & her soft blue eyes with a light almost celestial, beam from among a cluster of bright sunny flaxen ringlets. On her departure I wrote some verses in her Album headed 'La belle Blonde' and hence the appellation by which I designated the lady.

The Coates, Mrs Whitehead, Walkers, Faulks and two Miss Browns were at Redcar at the time Miss H. left so that I was soon in a full round of occupation with another set of young ladies.

A pleasant family from Leeds the *Hubbards* were also down. I first got acquainted with them through Mr John a youth of my own age. We soon became intimate. I went excursions with them to Lofthouse, Saltburn &c. Their party consisted of Mrs H (Mr H was down for a few days) Miss H & Miss Sarah, John, and two fine children. Mr J. played the flute well and was an agreeable duet companion.

Miss Hubbard[12] was another Redcar beauty. With the diffidence of a schoolgirl of 16 or 17, she possessed a figure and features that promised in a few years to be highly beautiful. As I gazed on them it seemed as if a Madonna of Titian, or a chef d'ouvre of some master hand was before me in all the loveliness of form and color, but endowed with life; a placid 'harmony of soul and face', and now and then a playful archness – in a year or two this Miss H may become a yet more dangerous associate than her almost namesake 'La Blonde'. On leaving Redcar the Hubbards gave us pressing invitations to visit them in Park Place: I shall not be loath to accept when opportunity offers.

Miss Oates and her little flock of nieces and nephews was another agreeable Leeds acquaintance with whom I took some excursions.

In riding one day with J Hubbard to Snaiths I called at Boltby to enquire after my cousin F Foxton.[13] I found her ill in bed with

---

12 Elizabeth Hubbard (Eliza) became TGW's wife in 1835, see Introduction.
13 Foxton was the maiden name of TGW's mother.

Inflammation on the chest. I went several times afterward to see her; and eventually she recovered, was brought to Redcar for a day or two, and I set her down at Stockton.

Aug 16th Went to Darlington. Stayed all night. Next day called at Snow Hall, and at Wycliffe Rectory. Returned to Darlington and next day to Stockton.

Mr J. Hubbard met me at Stockton for seeing the races, and we went back to Redcar together.

Ten days after this Mr Sowray of the Red Lion Hotel was attacked with a violent Enteritis. Mr Bailey his surgeon, sent to request my assistance in consultation and this lead to a renewal of old Kirkleatham friendship with him and Mrs B. By a severe struggle Sowray recovered from his attack, but was left in so weak a state that he never regained full health and died of consumption this summer (1831).

Was two or three times up at Wilton visiting Mr C Lowther.

Towards the end of the stay Mrs and Miss Skelby & Miss Robson came down to Redcar. They were intimate with the Miss Browns and I was their beau in several excursions to the Tees Mouth &c. One day we made a party to Eston Nab: Miss Hobson rolled into a ditch, Miss Brown sank in a rut: we dined on the summit: the ladies were determined to cross a stout wall about 8 feet high through which there appeared no ordinary mode of passage; this was accomplished with some difficulty: we went down by Wilton grounds by Lady E's leave; had some songs in Lady Eliz: bower; and returned to Redcar to tea.

Mrs & Miss Sherwood & Mr Wm were at R about this time. I was often with them; and accompanied them to Lofthouse and Saltburn.

One afternoon I went over to Seaton, took tea with Miss Lambs; spent the evening at Dr Wrays, and returned to Redcar via Stockton next day, singing 'Adieu, my love, till I return Adieu!'

1830

Sep 24	Left Redcar for Thirsk
27	By Willington to London
29	Cloudseley Square
Oct 1	Lond: Univ: opened for the session. I became a pupil for a $\frac{1}{2}$ session
8	Elected president of the LU Med: Soc:
11	Went to lodge with Mr H Thomas at 6 Gower Place

Nov 3   First Univ Conversazione

11   Mother went to lodge at Hampstead

24   Received intelligence of dear Grandfather's death on 22nd. Mother went down to Thirsk. I was laid up for 3 or 4 days at Cl: sq: with cont^d fever.

Dec 3   A meeting of the students of L.U. (called by Messr Macaulay, Herdman & myself – by permission of the Warden) in one of the great theatres to consider of sending a congratulatory Address to Ld Brougham on his elevation to the Woolsack. About 300 students present. A committee of delegates appointed to arrange matters. A vote of thanks to me as the originator of the measure.

Dec 5   Second L.U. Conversazione

6   Election of a member of committee by each class. I was returned for the largest class in the Univ: Professor Bennetts Anatomy.

7   From some informality the elections of yesterday in the Medical classes were declared void. At a new election I was again returned for the same class in spite of some smart canvassing against me. What was still more gratifying I was not present during my election and did not canvas a single vote & yet was in a large majority about 72 to 48.

8–10   Meetings of committee about 4 hours a day. The most agreeable and intellectual discussions I ever attended.

11   Meeting of Students to adopt the address. Six deputies were appointed to present it to his Lordship. Mr Eisdell and I were elected for the Medical department.

22   Breakfasted with Mr Adall and the deputation went in two carriages to Lincoln's Inn where we had the honor of shaking hands with the Lord Chancellor and gave our address.

1831

Jan 7   Was examined by the Court of the Royal College of Surgeons (chiefly by Mr Guthrie) and received my diploma as MRCS. Met Mr Nasmyth who was examined the same night.[14]

26	Mother arrived in London. I returned to lodgings at 6 Gower Place.
Feb 1	Removed with M to 16 Alfred Place
2	3rd L.U. Conversazione
Mar 23	Down to Dover
24	*Rye, Hythe* &c to *Hastings*
Apr 8	Left *Hastings* for *London*
9	Breakfasted with Prof: Grant
10	Left *England* per *Batavier*[15]

Vide 'My Note Book' Vol: 1

---

14 A List of successful candidates for the Diploma of Membership, MRCS, recorded by the Court of Examiners of the RCS(London) in the Examinations Book, 7/1/1831, includes Thomas Giordain (*sic*) Wright, Stockton upon Tees, and Alexander Nasmyth, George St., Hanover Square.

15 *Batavier* was probably the name of the vessel on which TGW travelled. A description of a steamboat *Batavier* and its passengers departing from London is given by William Thackeray in his novel *Vanity Fair*, chapter 62.

APPENDIX

MAGAZINIANA

The numbers and titles of the non-autobiographical *Magaziniana* are shown, with their position in the original manuscript.

No.	Title	
3	About a Flute	Vol 3, 8/5/27
7	On Mottos	Vol 4, 14/7/27
11	Beauty	Vol 5, 5/8/27
21	On Dreams	Vol 6, 4/11/27
24	On the Litany	Vol 6, 4/5/28
26–30	The Fisherman's Grave – A Story	Vol 6, 16/6/28
27	The Removal	Vol 7, 17/7/28
45	More Miseries	Vol 8, 11/3/29
46	Whimsical Scraps 2	Vol 11, 22/3/29
47	Confessions 2 Chapter 1	Vol 12, 14/4/29
48	Confessions 2 Chapter 2	Vol 12, 27/4/29

MEDICAL GLOSSARY

Symbols and abbreviations

The symbols and Latin abbreviations used in the prescriptions that appear in the Diary text are listed. For a more complete description of the pharmaceutical conventions used in the early nineteenth century, see e.g., M. P. Earles, 'The prescription records' in Richard H. Ellis (ed.), *The Case Books of John Snow*, Medical History, Suppl. No. 14, Wellcome Institute for the History of Medicine (London, 1994).

ℨ	drachm (60 grains)
℥	ounce (480 grains, 31.1 g)
℞	Recipe, take
aa	ana: of each

bis die	twice a day
c	cum: with
Capt or Capt	capiat: let him take
cochl	cochlea: spoon
ft, f^t	fiant: let it/them be made
gr	grain (64.8 mg)
gtt or gutt	guttae: drop(s)
h	hora: at the hour of
Hss	haustus: draught
M	mane: in the morning
Mist or Mis^{tr}	mistura: mixture
Mitt	mitte: send
Pulv	pulver: powder
q.q. hora, 4ta q.q. hora	quarta quaque hora: every fourth hour
2nd q.q. hora	secundus quarta quaque hora: every second hour
ss	semisse: the half
sum, sum^d	sumendus: to be taken
ter	ter: thrice
T^r	tincture

Quantities are usually written in lower-case Roman numerals, with j substituted for the final i.

Medical and pharmaceutical terms

Drugs, treatments and medical conditions mentioned in the Diary are listed here in alphabetic order, with brief definitions. The terms as they usually appear in the Diary are shown in bold type, followed by alternative names or spellings in normal type. For the terms that are no longer in use, or have changed in meaning, the early nineteenth century usage is indicated; where it seemed appropriate, the modern usage is also given.

The main sources for the older usage were Robert Hooper, *Medical Dictionary* (London, 1801); Robert Hooper, *The Physician's Vade-mecum* (London, 1812); R. G. Mayne, *Lexicon of Medical Terms* (London, 1860). The modern definitions are based mainly on Peter Wingate, *The Penguin Medical Encyclopedia*, third edition (London, 1988).

aloes. The deep red or brown and very bitter juice of the aloe plant (*Aloe perfoliata*). This was used as a laxative, and consid-

ered to be the best one for women with irregular menstru-
ation.

anchylosis. A stiff joint.

angina pectoris. Pain, usually in the centre of the chest, accompanied by difficulty in breathing. Usually there was a grad-
ual worsening of the condition ending in death. It was recognised that there was usually ossification of the coronary
arteries of the heart, and accumulation of fat around the
heart in sufferers who had died of the disease. The pain is
now known be a result of metabolic changes in the heart
muscle due to shortage of oxygen caused by restriction of
the coronary arteries.

antimon tart, antimony tartrate. This was taken internally in
single large doses as an emetic, or in smaller regular doses
to induce perspiration (i.e., as a diaphoretic, or sudorific) in
the treatment of fevers.

antimonial wine. This was made by digesting antimony with
white wine. Like antimony tartrate, but believed to be milder
in its effects. It was used to treat fevers.

aorta. The principal artery carrying blood from the heart.

aqua menthae. Mint flavoured water.

articular surfaces. Surfaces of bone joints.

atrophia. Shrinkage, wasting of an organ or tissue.

Atrophia lactorum. This seems to be a name invented by Thomas
Wright for the disease in children that he describes. His
nomenclature is in line with common usage at the time, e.g.,
Atropia famelicorum was wasting caused by famine and *Atropia cacochymica* was wasting due to 'corrupted nutriment'.

auscultation. Diagnosis by listening to the sounds from the heart
or breathing.

axilla. Armpit.

blister. This treatment was based on the principal that irritation
of the skin causes congestion of the parts immediately below
the skin, which relieves congestion of deep seated organs.
Irritants, such as acetic acid, tartaric acid, ammonia, mustard
or cantharides, were applied to the skin, usually held in place
by a cloth or piece of leather, and left in place until a blister
had formed.

bloodletting. Removal of blood was widely used in the practice
of medicine from very ancient times, and its efficacy considered an established fact until about the middle of the nine-

teenth century. The most common technique **venesection** was to tie a bandage around the arm so a vein of the forearm would swell up and then open the exposed vein with a sharp knife or lancet. The blood was collected in a bowl or basin. Alternatively, **cupping** was used to draw blood to the surface: a cupping-glass was heated and inverted over a cut made in the skin. Sometimes, particularly if the patient had been subjected to much bloodletting, the blood would become viscous, and difficult to draw, and was referred to as being 'cupped'. **Leeches** were also widely used to remove blood.

bursa. A membranous bag for secreting and containing a substance to lubricate tendons, muscles and bones. Now defined as a pocket of fibrous tissue lined in the same way as a joint with a slippery synovial membrane.

calomel, hydrargyrus submuriate, subchloride of mercury, mercurous chloride, mercury (I) chloride. A purgative, extremely popular in the nineteenth century but now known to be toxic and never used internally.

carb ammon, carbonas ammoniacae, ammonium carbonate. As a solid (*sal volatile*) or liquid solution (*spiritus salis ammoniaci*) was used as 'smelling salts', to arouse a fainting patient. It was also used as an antacid and in the treatment of various complaints, including typhus, ataxia, atonic spasms, arthritis and rheumatism. It is no longer considered to have any useful effect in any of these conditions.

carb sodae, carbonas sodae, sodium bicarbonate. Used as an antacid.

castor oil. Oil from the seeds of a plant (*Ricinus communis)* used as a laxative. Now usually used only externally, in ointments.

chlorosis. This term was first used in 1681 to describe a disease causing yellow or greenish pallor, which was particularly common among young women. It was also known as Virgin's Disease and Green Sickness. Its cause was not known at the time of the *Diary*, but it is now believed to be severe anaemia resulting from lack of iron.

cholera (Cholera morbus). At the time when the *Diary* was written, the terms cholera or *Cholera morbus* were used for a condition that had been known throughout history, characterised by violent bilious vomiting and diarrhoea, often with spasmodic contractions of the extremities and convulsions.

Its cause was not known, but sometimes different names were attached to the condition, depending on the supposed origin of the disease, e.g., *C. spontanea*, for cholera occurring in warm weather, without manifest cause, and *C. accidentalis*, for cholera due to acrid matter in the stomach and intestines. The pandemic disease now usually known simply as cholera, but sometimes called Infective, Indian, or Asiatic cholera, did not spread to Western Europe until the 1820s, and there was no outbreak in north east England until after 1831.

cinchon, cinchona bark, bark. See **quinine.**

clavicle. Collar bone.

clinoid process of the sphenoid. One of the 4 bony projections (processes) on the wedge-shaped bone at the base of the skull (sphenoid).

coats. Membranes.

condyle. Rounded end of a bone, e.g., a knuckle.

conjunctiva. Delicate membrane covering the inside of the eyelids and the front of the eye.

consumption, phthisis, pulmonary consumption. Was indicated by a persistent cough, emaciation, debility, often with blood-spitting and night sweating. It was usually fatal. The disease is now recognised as tuberculosis of the lung, caused by infection of the lung by the tubercle bacillus.

cranium. Skull.

creta, chalk, carbonas calcis, calcium carbonate. Used as an antacid and particularly in the treatment of diarrhoea and dysentery. It was also used as an antidote for arsenic poisoning.

croton oil. Oil from the seeds of *Croton tiglium*. Used as a purgative. Its purgative action is so violent that it is now recommended that it should not be used internally.

cupping. See **bloodletting.**

cystus duct (of the gall bladder). Urinary duct.

dejecta. Excrement.

drachm. Apothecary's measure equal to 60 grains (1/8 ounce).

dropsy, ascites. An excess of tissue fluid, often collecting in the belly cavity. Various causes are now recognised, including heart or liver failure.

dysentery, flux. A condition marked by fever, nausea loss of appetite with griping and stools chiefly of mucus with sometimes blood. The cause, not always recognised, could range from food poisoning to cancer. It is now a term for the disease caused by infection of the large intestine by protozoa or bacteria.

dyspepsia. This was a condition recognised by its symptoms which included loss of appetite accompanied by nausea, vomiting, flatulence, constipation and stomach pain. Among the possible causes were: a glandular tumour, an ulcer, poison, worms, chlorosis, pregnancy, gout, inflammation of the kidney. The term is now sometimes used for indigestion.

enema tabaci. Tobacco enema.

effusion. Leakage of fluid into a body cavity due to inflammation or congestion.

epilepsy. Disorder characterised by fits, in which there can be disturbance of sensation, movement or consciousness. In Cullen's **Nosology**, 9 species of epilepsy were recognised, with different causes, including head injury, pain, worms, and masturbation. The cause of the condition is still not always well-understood, but is recognised as being due to disorganised and excessive activity in some parts of the brain.

erythematic inflammation. Reddening of the skin.

extensor. A muscle that extends or straightens any part of the body.

extravasation. Leakage of fluid (e.g. blood) from a vessel into the surrounding tissues, as a result of injury.

femur. Thigh bone

fever. The term 'fever' was used for many of the common illnesses encountered by ordinary doctors. Although opinions and theories abounded there was little, if any, understanding of the causes of these illnesses, and 'fever' covered many different conditions, distinguished at the time mainly by their symptoms. Particular forms of 'fever' were given names such as **typhus** or **synochus**, but more often a condition would be referred to by a description such as 'slow fever', 'malignant fever', 'gaol fever', 'putrid fever'. It is now believed that the illnesses called 'fevers' could have been very different diseases, including typhus, typhoid, and malaria.

Typhus fever was first clearly distinguished from typhoid fever in 1837, and it is now the name given to a group of infectious diseases, caused by bacteria of the genus *Rickettsia*, often transmitted by body lice. All forms of typhus cause a prostrating fever within a two weeks of infection. Skin rashes are common and many sufferers develop a kind of pneumonia. Typhoid fever is an infectious disease due to *Salmonella typhi*, passed from person to person by contaminated food or water.

fibula. A slender bone in the outside of the lower leg.

fibular artery. An artery in the lower part of the leg.

first intention. A term used to describe a procedure used in wound management. In treatment by first intention, the wound was closed, either by suture, or using sticking-plaster, and healing allowed to take its course. Often, infection of a wound caused serious inflammation and suppuration, which could not be treated because the wound had been closed, and healing was retarded or prevented. The alternative was to keep the wound open, and try to deal with any inflammation by treatment during the healing process. Controversy about the techniques of wound management continued for many years, even after recognition, during the latter half of the nineteenth century, of the causes of wound infection and the need for sterile conditions.

fomentation. A cloth (e.g. flannel) used to apply warmth to or bathe a wound.

fontanelle, fontanel. Space between the bones of the skull of a young child.

gamboge. Obtained from the juice of the gamboge tree and administered as a powder or syrup, a drastic purgative, sometimes used to remove tapeworms.

gastralgia. Pain in the stomach.

granulations. Granulation tissue is composed of tiny blood vessels and fibres, formed at the site of a wound or infection as the first stage of healing.

heamorrhois, haemorrhoids. Distended (varicose) veins near the opening of the anus.

hemiplegia. Paralysis of one side of the body.

hepatitis. Inflammation of the liver, was recognised by high temperature, accompanied by nausea, tension and pain in the region of the liver and highly coloured urine. Now several types of hepatitis are recognised, with different pathogens.

hernia. A protrusion of an organ from one compartment of the body into another. The commonest form is the inguinal hernia, in the groin. The hernia is said to be **strangulated**

when a loop of intestine is pinched at the entrance to the hernia. This can be a dangerous condition and nowadays is usually dealt with by prompt operation. In the early nineteenth century, when surgery was usually not possible, a strangulated hernia often led to infection, with symptoms such as vomiting and fever, and could be fatal.

hirudrius. Medicinal leeches

humerus. The bone of the upper arm.

hydrocephalus. This now means a condition of enlargement of the head by accumulation of fluid, known to be due to a blockage of its normal circulation in and around the brain and the spinal cord. Earlier, the term was used for two diseases found under two different classes in the **nosology** of Cullen. One of these diseases was characterised by symptoms similar to those now recognised for this condition. The other, placed in the Class Neuroses (nervous diseases), was largely confined to children and characterised by symptoms of languor, inactivity, loss of appetite, vomiting and head pain, sometimes with convulsions.

hydrothorax. Water on the chest. Characterised by difficulty in breathing, swelling of the legs, scarcity of urine, and palpitations.

illium. The haunch bone, part of the pelvis.

infus rosae. Infusion of rose petals, rose water.

infus senna. Infusion of senna plant (*Cassia senna*) leaves, used as a relatively mild laxative.

in spicula. Bandage applied with successive turns crossing each other; figure of eight bandage.

integument. An external covering.

ipecac, ipecacuanha. An extract of the root of a Brazilian shrub. Used mainly as an expectorant.

jalap. Obtained from the root of the shrub *Convolvulus jalapa,* and administered as a powder or tincture, was used as a drastic purgative.

julep. A liquid medicine, usually sweetened with honey, syrup or sugar.

lime water. A solution of calcium hydroxide, used as an antacid.

liniment sapon. Soap liniment.

linteum ammoniated. Lint treated with ammonia.

luxation. Dislocation of a bone joint.

magnes calcine, magnesia, magnesium oxide. Used as an antacid.

marasmus. Extreme emaciation, particularly in infancy. Now taken to mean wasting as a result of gross malnutrition.

metatarsal bones. Bones of the foot, between the ankle and the toes.

mist purg. A standard mixture, e.g. of castor oil and antimony tartrate, used as a purgative.

moxa, moxibustion. As still used in traditional Chinese medicine, a small cylinder or cone made from dried mugwort leaves, is burned over the skin, with the aid of a blow-pipe.

mur ferr, ferric chloride. Used as an iron supplement. Now superseded by less toxic alternatives.

muriatic acid, hydrochloric acid. The dilute acid was used as a gastric antispasmodic and sedative.

nitr potassae, nitre, saltpetre, potassium nitrate. Used to induce sweating and as a diuretic.

nosology. The branch of medical science dealing with the classification of disease. In the late eighteenth and early nineteenth centuries this field was particularly influenced by the work of William Cullen (1710–90), Professor of Physic at the University of Edinburgh, who published a treatise, *First Lines of the Practice of Physic* (1778–84). In this he attempted to classify particular diseases by a system along the lines of that used by Carl Linnaeus (1707–78) to classify plants, animals and minerals.

occipital. Of the back of the head.

occipital bone. The occipital bone is the back of the floor of the skull and forms a moveable joint with the backbone.

oesophagus. The gullet; the downward continuation of the **pharynx.**

ol croton. See **croton oil.**

ol ricini. See **castor oil.**

ophthalmia, conjunctivitis. Inflammation of the membranes of the eye.

papaver. A preparation from a poppy (*Papaver somniferum*), i.e., the plant from which opium is obtained. The syrup, prepared by infusing the flower heads, was used as a soporific.

paregoric. A tincture of camphor and opium, used as a soporific, often to calm fretful children.

parietal. Of the wall of a body cavity as opposed to its contents. With reference to the skull, it refers to the side of the cranium or brain box.

patella. Kneecap

periosteum. Fibrous coating of a bone; now known to carry nerves and blood vessels essential to the nutrition of the bone. Fractures do not heal if the periosteum is destroyed.

phalanx. A segment of the digit, or the bone of the segment. The thumbs and big toes have each 2 phalanges, the other fingers and toes have 3.

pharynx. Muscular back wall of the nose, mouth and throat, extending from the base of the skull to the entrance to the **oesophagus**.

phrenitis, phrenzy, inflammation of the brain. A condition characterised by strong fever, violent headache, and delirium. It was regarded as symptomatic of several diseases including **worms** and hydrophobia (rabes). The word is no longer in use.

pil rheice. Rhubarb pill.

pledget. A wad of lint or cotton.

puerperal convulsions. Convulsions associated with childbirth.

pulver (pulv). Powdered.

pulv sacchar. Powdered sugar.

pus. Usually a thick yellow fluid, but may be watery or almost solid. It is a by-product of inflammation and, in the early nineteenth century, it was generally regarded as a bland substance produced as a necessary and desirable part of the healing process. It is now known to be formed as a result of the action of certain bacteria and to contain fluid and white blood cells, leaked from blood vessels, together with dead and living bacteria and fragments of tissue damaged by the inflammation.

quinine, sulphate of quinine. This plant alkaloid was first isolated in 1820 from **cinchona bark** and replaced the cruder bark preparations in therapeutic use as it became readily available after about 1825. The bark, used by native Peruvians as a cure for fevers, was first brought to Europe in the seventeenth century. Used to treat malarial fever, quinine is probably the first drug to be discovered that is specifically effective against the cause of a disease. Although it is now known to have no value against non-malarial fever, quinine continued to be an ingredient in medicines used to treat all kinds of fevers until recent times.

radius and ulna. The two bones of the forearm.

rectus femoris. Vertical muscle at the front of the thigh.

rhei. Rhubarb.

sacchar alb. White sugar.

sarsaparilla. Extract of the root of *Jamaica smilax*, used as a tonic.

scammon. Powder from resin of the shrub *Convolvulus scammonia*, used as a purgative, usually together with other substances.

scarlatina. Now regarded as the same disease as scarlet fever.

scarlet fever. Begins with fever, sickness and sore throat, a flushed face with the skin around the mouth remaining pale. A day or two later a rash of tiny raised spots spreads over the body. Now known to be caused by a bacterium and to be spread by coughing, contact and by contaminated milk or other food.

scirrous pylorus. A hard tumour on the pylorus, i.e. the interior aperture of the stomach that opens into the intestines.

scrofula. Now recognised to have been tuberculosis of the lymph nodes at the side of the neck with ulceration of the over-lying skin. In the early nineteenth century it was described symptomatically as a disease characterised by chronic swelling of glands in various parts of the body, particularly the neck, behind the ears and under the chin, tending slowly to imperfect suppuration and sometimes referred to as the King's Evil.

scrofulus diathesis. A predisposition to **scrofula**.

secundum artem. According to the art.

sella turcica. Literally Turkish saddle – small depression within the 4 **clinoid processes of the sphenoid bone** on which the pituitary gland rests.

serous. Relating to or containing serum (the clear yellow fluid that separates from clotted blood) or resembling serum. Serous membrane is a smooth transparent membrane lining certain large cavities in the body.

sinus. This is used in the pathological sense i.e. a burrowing ulcer in the form of a blind-ended tube which is usually a track by which pus formed at the blind end reaches a body surface.

solution of continuity. A term for breaking down, or division, of the skin and other textures by a blow, a cutting instrument or ulceration.

spiculae. Sharp, needle-like, splintered bones.

sternal end (of clavicle). End (of shoulder bone) nearest the breast bone.

sternum. Breast-bone.

stethoscope. An instrument, used to examine the sounds from the chest or the heart. It was developed between 1816 and 1819 by the French clinician René Théophile Hyacinthe Laennec (1781–1826), and became widely used after about 1825.

strangulated hernia. See **hernia.**

strumous. An adjective used to describe an appearance similar to that of **scrofula.**

submaxillar glands. Glands below the upper jaw

sudorifus. A medicine taken internally that promotes sweating.

sulpht magnes, magnesium sulphate, Epsom salts. Used as a purgative.

syncope. Faint. Sudden unconsciousness now known to result from lowered blood pressure in the arteries of the brain.

synochus. See **fever.**

tactus (*tactus eruditus*). Sense of touch. Before X-rays this was often the only method of detecting the position of a fracture.

tartar emetic, antimony tartrate. Used to bring about vomiting, but now known to be toxic, resembling arsenic compounds in its effects.

temporal of the side of the cranium (temple). The **temporal artery** runs in front of the ear and over the scalp; the **temporal bone or ridge** is the part of the skull around the ear.

tibia. The shin bone.

tincture. A solution of the active medical ingredient in ethanol (rectified spirit) or in ethanol-water mixtures.

tintura iodi. Iodine and potassium iodide in alcohol.

tintura opii, laudanum. Powdered opium dissolved in alcohol (spirit).

trepan. A very ancient instrument for cutting a round hole in the skull. The operation of trepanning was used from the times of the ancient Greek surgeons to relieve pressure on the brain from bleeding after severe head injuries.

typhus. See **fever.**

vaccination. At the time of the *Diary* this meant deliberate infection with cow-pox (vaccinia) to confer immunity against small-pox, as introduced by Jenner in 1796.

vena saphena. Two conspicuous superficial veins of the leg.

venesection. See **bloodletting.**

ventricle. Anatomical term for a cavity of the heart or brain.

ventricular valve. Valve controlling blood flow from a major compartment of the heart (ventricle) to the lungs or the rest of the circulation.

viscus. Any organ (plural viscera).

worms The worms referred to were probably intestinal worms: the round worm (*Ascaris*), the threadworm (*Enterobius*) or a tapeworm, *Taenia saginata* or *T. solium*. It is now believed that these worms rarely cause any symptoms.

zingiber. Ginger, obtained from the ginger plant (*Amonum zingiber*). Used as an antispasmodic and carminative. Usually prescribed in combination with other medicines.

TABLES

Table 1. Numbers of Patients

The Table shows the numbers of patients recorded at different dates in the *Diary* MS. The column headed 'Entry date' gives the dates in the MS where the numbers of patients are listed. TGW often made a list of numbers at the end of a month, sometimes repeating the numbers already given weekly. These monthly lists have been omitted here, but have been used to derive weekly values if these were not given.

Vol	Year	Month	Entry date	Coll & Private	Sick	Total	Note
1	1826	Oct	4	116	48	164	1
			7	11	5	16	
			15	18	6	24	
			21	26	7	33	2
			29	22	6	28	
		Nov	4	7	8	15	
			12	17	11	28	
			17	10	9	19	
			27	12	16	28	3
			30	8	4	12	
2	1826	Dec	11	6	7	13	
			11	19	5	24	
			27	9	21	30	4

Vol	Year	Month	Entry date	Coll & Private	Sick	Total	Note
			27	5	11	16	4
			27	10	14	24	4
	1827	Jan	8	5	9	14	
			13	9	4	13	
			20	16	3	19	
			27	14	10	24	
			31	10	3	14	
		Feb	3	5	8	13	
			20	12	11	23	5
			20	19	10	29	
			26	13	10	23	
			28	3	5	8	4,6
3		Mar	3	13	4	17	
			9	10	8	18	
			11	10	10	20	7
			24	11	6	17	
			31	10	11	21	
		Apr	7	14	2	16	
			14	14	8	22	
			21	16	8	24	
			28	23	11	34	
			28	0	2	2	4
		May	6	26	7	33	
			14	18	18	36	
			14	10	3	3	7
			26	11	4	15	
			31	21	13	34	4
4		Jun	4	1	2	3	
			9	6	13	19	
			15	7	14	21	
			20	22	11	33	
			20	12	2	14	
		Jul	9	8	1	9	
			14	16	7	23	
			31	14	9	23	
			31	10	3	13	4
			31	6	3	9	4
5		Aug	5	2	5	7	

Vol	Year	Month	Entry date	Coll & Private	Sick	Total	Note
			10	17	8	25	
			18	11	6	18	
			25	12	7	19	
			30	14	6	20	
5		Sep	8	16	7	23	
			30	19	6	25	4,8
			30	0	1	1	
6		Oct	11	19	6	25	
			14	14	12	26	
			20	14	16	30	
			20	14	11	25	
			29	4	4	8	
		Nov	1	3	5	8	
			14	11	12	23	
			14	15	7	22	
			28	7	7	14	
		Dec	2	2	1	3	
			2	15	12	27	
			13	14	4	18	
			13	10	6	16	
			26	5	14	19	
	1828	Jan	4	3	6	9	
			8	10	7	17	
			18	10	9	19	
			18	12	11	23	
			26	9	5	14	
		Feb	4	6	8	14	4
			4	8	8	16	
			13	3	9	12	
			13	8	12	20	
		Mar	(29/2)	1	2	3	
			(29/2)	13	14	27	
			(29/2)	9	11	20	
			10	6	7	13	
			10	9	2	11	
			10	0	101		
		Apr	(31/3)	8	6	14	
			11	7	10	17	

Vol	Year	Month	Entry date	Coll & Private	Sick	Total	Note
			16	13	11	24	
			26	12	5	17	
			26	7	5	12	
		May	(27/4)	5	1	6	
			10	5	8	13	
			16	14	7	21	
			25	9	7	16	
			31	11	10	21	
7		Jun	16	16	7	23	
			16	2	5	7	9
			16	4	10	14	
			30	5	2	7	
		Jul	(30/6)	5	3	8	
			(30/6)	0	1	1	10
			17	24	3	27	
			26	10	9	19	
			31	39	21	60	11
11	1829	Mar	7	13	12	25	
			12	4	19	23	
			20	19	24	43	
			31	12	28	40	
			31	8	21	29	

Notes to Table 1
1. Covers the period 18/8/26 to 4/10/26.
2. [*TGW note*] 8 children vaccinated rather increased the list of private patients this week.
3. [*TGW note*] Coll 0 Priv 12
4. Numbers from the monthly list.
5. The *Diary* had been left at Sunderland: see 19/2/27.
6. This entry was crossed out.
7. Appears to have been recorded just before next *Diary* entry.
8. Away from Newcastle: see 21/9/27.
9. Away from Newcastle: see 13/6/28.
10. Moving to Eldon Square: see 10/7/28.
11. At Backworth from 28/7/28 (possibly includes all patients in July).

12. First entry after missing *Diary* volumes, i.e., since 30/7/28. Includes TGW footnote: Mr McI now takes subscribers i.e. 'sick' at one or two more collieries though the new ones are not very numerous.
13. Last entry before leaving Newcastle.

Table 2.

List of Patients on the books of Messrs McIntyre & Morson, Ncastle. Mar: 23rd 1829

	J M & WSM	Do & TGW	Total
Town Patients	9	9	18
Country Do			
1. Private	12	8	20
2. Collieries	—	43	43
3. Sick	—	72	72
Total	21	132	153

Number seen in my *country* round this morning
Colliery & Private 35 Sick 56 Total 91
T. G. Wright Assistant to Messrs McIntyre & Morson, Surgeons &c

Table 3. Summary of Accidents in 1827

[From Volume 12, 13/4/29. The Table lay-out has been changed.]

Accidents	Heaton	Walker	Wallsend	Benwell	Elswick	Felling	Total
Fractures compound	1	2	1	—	1	—	5
Fractures simple	2	2	4	—	2	—	10
Dislocations	1	2	—	1	—	—	4
severe wounds lacerations	7	8	3	4	3	4	29
bruises sprains &c	14	20	10	4	5	3	56
burns	3	—	—	1	2	—	6
Minor accidents wounds &c	9	17	10	6	3	5	50
Contusions &c	17	14	11	9	8	5	64
Injuries of the eye (specks &c)	—	2	—	—	—	—	2
Ophthalmia*	1	20	1	1	2	1	26
Total	55	87	40	26	26	18	252

*From the noxious effluvia while sinking &c. Some of the men were attacked three or four times with this disease

Report [*on Table 3*]

Numerous cases of comparatively less moment, – sprained wrists, lacerated fingers &c are omitted here, because it is imposs-ible to ascertain with sufficient accuracy the amount of this class of injuries. Some workmen especially at the pits in the vicinity of the town apply for surgical assistance in the most trivial cases, while others at more distant collieries depend frequently on their own skill for care of more severe accidents. Those patients alone who were unfortunately compelled to seek advice have been entered in this list and generally speaking they were such as required instant attention.

The great number of medical complaints which arise from inhaling the foul gas, generally more or less mingled with the underground atmosphere, it would be vain to guess at. They are all left out here: but several instances of Ophthalmia requiring the surgeon's care and which was prevalent this year at Walker where a new shaft was sunk, are detailed on account of their frequent occurrence. It is unnecessary to mention the event of each individual case which would be a useless repetition of the same term through the whole column. Not one death is to be recorded of any of the patients named in the foregoing who, with the exception of a dreadful compd fracture Nov 1st (Ramshay) are again following their usual employment in robust health and vigour. No capital operations were found necessary nor was a single limb lost. The cases of burns have not been many this year, but as usual were speedily cured under Mr McIntyre's improve-ment on Dr Kentish's system of treatment. In the fracture of the lower limbs Mr McI's double inclined splint was invariably employed.

T G Wright Assistant to Mr M'Intyre Surgeon

Table 4. Summary of Accidents in 1826

From Vol. 12, 26/4/29. The Table lay-out has been changed.

Accidents	Heaton	Walker	Wallsend	Benwell	Elswick	Felling	Total
Fracture simple	3 (a)	4 (b)	4 (c)	4 (d)	2 (e)	2 (f)	19
Fracture compound	3 (g)	1 (h)	2 (i)	—	—	—	6
Dislocations	1 (j)	—	—	1 (k)	1 (l)	—	3
Wounds abscesses &c	30	22	23	16	14	7	112
Bruises &c	42	35	47	17	44	17	202
Burns	2	1	—	9 (m)	5	—	17
Injuries of the eye	1	2	—	—	—	—	3
Ophthalmia	3	3	1	—	4	1	12
Total	85	68	77	47	70	27	374 (n)

a Ribs Spine Thigh. b 3 Legs, spine & sternum (sent to the Infirmary where he died after some weeks). c 3 leg (one of these was [*illegible word*]) d 2 Arm, Thigh, Clavicle. e Leg. f Skull Ribs. g Fingers (portion removed) Arm (amputation) Leg. h Fingers. i Toes Leg. j Shoulder. k Collar. l Wrist. m For the severe accidents at Benwell this year see the various parts of the Diary especially the explosion on Oct 27. n Died 2 the rest all cured.

INDEX

Medical and surgical treatments are indexed under 'treatments and procedures', specific medical conditions under 'medical cases', and substances used in treatments under 'medication'. The names of patients are indexed under 'patients'. In the Diary MS usually only the surname of a patient is given without any other means of identification: some of the names indexed may represent more than one individual. Unidentified individuals named in the Diary, other than patients, are indexed under 'people'. The letter 'n' refers to editorial notes accompanying the text of the Diary.

Fife, Mr (later Sir) John (surgeon)
289, 293, 299
Fighting Cocks public house
235
flute 208, 224, 232
food/meals 92, 95, 105, 110, 111,
114, 118, 119, 135, 137, 150,
155, 175, 180, 184, 185, 197,
203, 204, 206, 223, 224, 228,
230, 232, 235, 236, 245, 258,
271, 278, 313–14, 317
Forest Hall 157
Forth Banks 116
Foundling Hospital (London) 53,
53n, 54
fox-hunt 292
Foxton, F (cousin of TGW) 324,
324n
Fry, Master (pupil at Quaker
academy) 45
Fry, Mrs (first patient at
Darlington) 48

gall bladder specimen 147, 166
gas lamps 277, 312, 313, 315
Gateshead 228
Choral Society 252
Gibb, Mr DR (Durham) 252
Gibson, Mr Benjamin 154
Gibson, Miss Fanny 95n, 139,
154–5, 226
Gibson, Miss Isobel 95n, 154–5,
226, 232
Gibson, Mr John (assistant to
McIntyre)
accident/illness 183, 185, 204,
206–7, 209–10, 211, 215,
221, 223, 225, 228, 232, 253,
260, 264, 314
background 60, 62–3, 63n
professional behaviour 63, 101,
103, 138, 140
social relations with TGW 63,
90, 91, 98, 99, 133, 139, 146,
149–50, 154–5, 157, 167,
183, 212, 264, 314
Gibson, Mrs 157, 167, 183, 211,
233

Gibson, Mr Taylor (wholesale
chemist and druggist) 147,
154, 183, 211, 266
Gibson, Mr Tom 146
Gibson, Mr William 236, 313
gigmen 78
gigs 93, 99, 109–10, 122, 123, 130,
169, 176, 177, 203, 184, 230,
232, 233, 236, 251, 263, 272,
311
Gillan, Mr (usher at Quaker
Academy) 43
Gillmore (Gilmore), Col (Barrack
Master) 73, 73n, 88, 91, 104,
114, 139, 183
Glasgow 70–71
Goulding's music shop (London)
52, 52n, 53
Grace, Mr (colliery agent, Felling)
305;
grandfather (of TGW) 33, 113,
228, 301, 326
Gray, Mr James (apprentice to
McIntyre) 139, 140, 179
Gray, Mr (ex-partner of McIntyre)
269
Green, Mr (brother-in-law of
TGW) 51, 51n, 53, 73
Green, Mrs (sister of TGW) 28,
35, 40, 46, 51, 72, 73, 104, 119,
132, 151, 152n, 171, 183, 204,
213, 204n, 229
Greenfield Place 161, 162, 167,
181, 211, 224, 320
Greenwood, Mr (apprentice to
McIntyre) 17, 62, 103, 106,
118, 124, 130, 134, 140, 148,
167, 168, 171, 176, 177, 204,
319
groom 83
Guthrie, Mr (Examiner at Royal
College of Surgeons,
London) 326

Hanover Square chapel
(Newcastle) 320
Hardcastle, Mr (surgeon) 147
Harrogate 269
Hartlepool 234, 321

Hartley 281, 281
Haughton-le-Skerne 33
Hawkes, Sir Robert Shafto
	(industrialist) 62, 62n
hay harvest 204
Headlam, Dr Thomas Emerson
	(physician) 178, 178n, 206,
	222, 296
Heaton 80; *see also collieries*
Heaton Hall 82, 82n
Heaton High Pit *see collieries*
Heaton Middle Pit *see collieries*
Heaton New Pit *see collieries*
Heaton Old Engine *see collieries*
Henzel, CR (surgeon) 146, 167,
	195, 197, 201, 229, 230, 232,
	233, 256, 258, 275, 278
Hexham 60
Higham Place (Newcastle) 156,
	156n
Highflyer coach 49, 49n,55
Hogg, Thomas Jefferson 31, 31n
Holt, Mr (house-pupil at
	Newcastle Infirmary) 222
Holywell 278, 281
Hope, Professor (lecturer in
	Chemistry, Edinburgh) 67
horse market 225, 313
horse races 205, 205n, 206, 275,
	320
horses
	accidents involving 86, 99, 181,
		183, 184, 203, 261
	dealing in 86, 105, 106, 169,
		225, 318
	lack of 103, 104–5, 109, 130,
		205, 230, 261, 295, 296–7
	lameness of 96, 102, 104, 109,
		130, 230, 261, 264
	pleasures of riding 173, 183,
		186, 211, 224, 225–6, 292,
		310–1
	training of 96, 134, 205, 251–2,
		264–5
Hosegood, George (surgeon) 110,
	110n
House of Commons 55, 55n
House of Lords 55, 55n *see also
	Select Committee of House of
	Lords*

Hubbard, Elizabeth (later wife of
	TGW) 23, 24n, 324, 324n
Hubbard, Mr J (brother of
	Elizabeth Hubbard) 324,
	324n
Hudson, Mr (usher at Quaker
	Academy) 43
Hunter's Houses 82, 89
Hunter, Mr Ritchie (horse-keeper)
	113, 116
Hunter, Mr John (apprentice to
	McIntyre) 62, 139, 179
Hunterian Museum (Glasgow) 71
Hylton Joliffe 204, 204n

inclines (at colliery) 278
Indiaman, surgeon on 281, 281n
Infirmary
	Edinburgh 67, 67n
	Newcastle
		cases at 223, 224
		house surgeon consulted 194
		patient sent to 244
		perennial pupil at 222, 223,
			267
		staff at 222, 222n *see also
			doctors/medical
			practitioners*

Jackson, Mr (lecturer at
	Darlington) 45
Jameson, Jane 292, 292n
Jesmond 184; *see also collieries*
Jesmond Bridge 83
Johnson, Major (colliery owner)
	125, 256
Johnson's Houses 82, 92

Keelmen's Hospital 78
Kelso 316
Kenton 94
Killingworth 157
King George IV (birthday of) 263
King, Rev (Backworth Hall) 279
King's Head Inn (Hartlepool) 234
King, Mr William (apprentice,
	later assistant to McIntyre)
	background of 24, 60, 61, 97,
		205

waggonway 122, 122n, 223, 278
Walker *see collieries*
Walker Henry Pit *see collieries*
Walker Jane Pit *see collieries*
Walker Lane 226
Walker stables 133
Wallsend *see collieries*
watchmen 140, 149
Waterloo (anniversary of battle)
    201, 304
Wear, river 272
weather 50, 91, 107, 110, 113, 120,
    123, 136, 145, 148, 150, 181,
    182–3, 186, 202, 203, 211–12,
    215, 221, 232, 244, 260, 263,
    268, 275, 301, 304, 312, 315
Wellington coach 63n
Wellington, Duke of 237
Wilson, Mr (druggist, Ouseburn)
    178
Westgarth, Mr John W (surgeon,
    uncle of Gibson, Mr John)
    206
Westgate Hill (Newcastle) 257
Whitley Bay 275
Willington *see collieries*
Willington Square 280
Windy Nook 157
Winter theatres (London) 52, 52n
Wolviston 234
Wood, Alderman (MP) 55n
Wood, Mr (surgeon, Gateshead)
    45, 94, 94n
Wooler 153
Wright, Elizabeth (mother)
    advises TGW 47, 48, 57, 59, 63,
        112, 165–6, 176, 251
    comments on
        amorous relationships 165–6
        Diary 162
        music 185
        quack medicine 132
    communicates with TGW 111,
        113, 147, 150, 183
    health of 32, 40, 49, 150–1
    holidays with TGW 214, 234–6
    residences of 29, 31, 40, 45, 48,
        64, 146, 147, 150, 152, 254,
        259, 267, 272

sends opera (Rusticity) to TGW
    188
visits to TGW 69–72, 175, 201,
    253, 267
Wright, Mr Thomas (father)
    advises TGW 45, 47, 48, 56, 57,
        59, 63
    coal machine 112, 122, 243–4,
        244, 249, 250, 256
    communicates with TGW 147,
        150, 185, 187
    death of 32
    health of 150–1
    holidays with TGW 214, 234–6,
        272
    residences of 29, 31, 40, 45, 48,
        64, 146, 147, 150, 152, 254,
        259, 267, 272
    musician and tutor 29, 29n, 32,
        153, 157, 183, 235
    Music Primer and Supplement
        154, 154n, 157
    visits to TGW 69–72, 104, 106,
        175, 188, 253
Wright, Thomas Giordani
    activities, *see also cards, concerts,
        festivals, horse races, theatre,
        dancing*
    holidays/travel 32–3, 48–51,
        71–2, 152–3, 214, 233–6,
        267, 271–2, 281, 319–20,
        321, 322–5
    music 62, 62n, 92, 96, 133,
        142–3, 145, 149, 161, 183,
        185, 208, 224, 232, 252,
        259, 314
    public occasions 144, 187–8,
        196, 201, 227, 237, 252,
        285, 292–3, 296
    reading 132, 132n, 135, 169,
        169n, 170, 170n, 174, 175,
        176, 193, 201, 210, 212–4,
        215, 219–20, 221, 263,
        267–8, 273, 299, 313
    social occasions 42, 42n, 101,
        135, 137, 138, 142, 150,
        151, 153, 154, 161, 166,
        183, 186, 195, 198–9, 208,